Memories of Violence

Simone Remijnse

Memories of Violence

Civil Patrols and the Legacy of Conflict in Joyabaj, Guatemala

ISBN 90 5170 674 X
NUR 740

© Simone Remijnse, 2002

Cover design: Puntspatie, Amsterdam

All rights reserved. Save exceptions stated by the law, no part of this publication may be reproduced, stored in a retrieval system of any nature, or transmitted in any form or by any means, electronic, mechanical, photocopying, recording or otherwise, included a complete or partial transcription, without the prior written permission of the publishers, application for which should be addressed to the publishers: Rozenberg Publishers, Rozengracht 176A, 1016 NK Amsterdam, The Netherlands.
Tel.: + 31 20 625 54 29, Fax: + 31 20 620 33 95 E-mail: info@rozenbergps.com

Contents

List of illustrations	9
Preface	11
Chapter 1 Introduction: concepts and methodology	17
Close encounter	17
Central questions and concepts	18
The armed conflict	18
Reseach aims and questions	20
Dealing with the past	21
Violence and terror	23
Surveillance and control	27
Obedience and dehumanization	28
The concept op memory	30
Constructing memories	32
Coherence and consolidation	34
The influence of context and audience	36
Forgetting and denial	37
Collective memory, social memory or collected memories?	39
Data collection and methodology	41
The municipality of Joyabaj	41
Ethnic tension and racism	43
Fieldwork in three stages	44
My role in the community	49
Safety in a violent society	52
Organization of the book	54
Chapter 2 Conflict and factionalism (1750-1978)	57
Ladinos aquiring indigenous land	58
A divided ladino population	60
Ladino political power: extending government control	62
Political polarization: 1944-1945	68
Local Agrarian Committees	71
Mounting anti-communist feelings	73
MLN and its indigenous allies	74

5

Catholic Action and the indigenous communities	76
Chorraxaj: the cradle of Catholic Action	79
Alliance between Catholic Action and local politics	81
The earthquake: memories of chaos and solidarity	82
Reconstruction efforts of Alianza	85
Political upheaval during the 1978 municipal elections	88
Conclusion	90

**Chapter 3 Random violence:
social and institutional breakdown (1978-1982)** — 91

First guerrilla campaigns in Joyabaj	92
Memories of a nun	94
The killing of the local parish priest	95
Military occupation of Joyabaj	99
The destruction of political leadership	101
Alianza leaves Joyabaj	103
Chorraxaj activism cut short	106
Guerrilla activity increases	108
The death of a pharmacist: conflictive memories	109
Polarizing ethnic relations	113
Scorched earth strategy: the first massacres	115
Home Guards set up in Joyabaj	118
Conclusion	122

Chapter 4 Civil patrols and organized violence (1982-1983) — 125

Structured instead of chaotic violence	126
Joyabaj under military control	128
Military taking over municipal politics	132
Military commissioners: a key component of military counterinsurgency	136
The case of the 164 military commissioners	138
Civil patrols and the military	139
Tasks and figures	142
Joyabaj patrols and local diversity	143
Teachers set up their own patrol	147
Civil patrols in Xecnup	148
Civil patrols in Chorraxaj	150
Diverse accounts and memories of patrol violence	152
Forced participation: the Xeabaj massacre	153

Patrollers abusing their power	158
The Ogáldez clan and local power	159
Positive memories of patrol activity	161
Fearing memory of the past	163
The act of memory in context	164
Conclusion	165

Chapter 5 Authority of civil patrols contested (1984 - 1993) — 169

Democratic elections: start of the peace process	170
Democratic elections in Joyabaj	173
Community life in town re-emerging	176
Initial protest against civil patrols	179
CERJ: organizing rural anti-patrol sentiments	181
Widows feel threatened	183
The Catholic clergy returns to Joyabaj	186
The parish priest gets into trouble	189
Crisis in local politics	191
Verifying memories and opinions	193
Rising conflicts between patrols and municipality	194
The 1993 civil patrol rallies: supporters and opponents	196
The case of Tomás Lares Ciprian	197
Civil patrols inhibiting court procedures	199
Memories of 1993	202
Conclusion	203

Chapter 6 Pacified but not peaceful (1994 – 2001) — 207

Civil patrols: national road to abolition	208
Patrols in trouble at the local level	210
Denouncing abuse: a complicated business	212
Violence continued	214
A failing justice system	215
Patrols finally dismantled	216
Conflicting memories of past performance	219
Lynchings: a legacy of the civil war?	222
Former patrollers stir up trouble	226
Local rumors: patrols reorganizing	228
Political space opening up	230
Water, a source of municipal conflicts	234
1999 elections: former guerrillas campaigning	235

Consulta Popular: visible polarization	239
Changing economic power relations	242
Human rights: a tainted concept	243
Distrust: a legacy of the civil war	245
Conclusion	247

Chapter 7   Dealing with the past (1996-2001) — 251

Discussing Guatemala's violent past	252
Dealing with the past in Joyabaj	256
Creating space: the role of the local priest	257
Remembering through commemoration	260
REMHI in Joyabaj: implementation and results	267
Exhumations: a factual recording of the past	270
The first exhumations in Quiché and Joyabaj	274
Exhumation behind the Joyabaj convent	276
Exhumation triggers reactions	280
Not wanting to remember?	282
A civil patrol memorial	285
Conclusion	286

Chapter 8   Concluding and reflecting — 291

From open terror towards control and surveillance	291
Conflicting memories and narratives	293
Stigmatization and denial	295
Joyabaj: a changing society	297
Dealing with the past	299

Prinicipal abbreviations and acronyms — 301

Glossary — 305

Bibliography — 309

Index — 323

Summary in Dutch / Samenvatting in het Nederlands — 331

Curriculum Vitae — 335

List of illustrations

Maps

1.	Departments of Guatemala	14
2.	Municipality of Joyabaj	15
3.	Central square of Joyabaj (2001)	16

Photographs
Cover photo: Xeabaj at the end of market day (author, 2001).

1. The *Virgen de Tránsito* is carried around the town of Joyabaj during the *Fiesta* in August (author, 1998) — 64
2. The front of the Catholic Church in Joyabaj was one of the few remains left standing after the earthquake of 1976. Behind it a new church was built (author, 1999) — 83
3. Indigenous men attending an Alianza course (Redd Barna, 1977) — 87
4. DCG mayor Felípe Natareno speeches while inaugurating a stretch of road (anonymous, 1978/1979) — 89
5. Shrine remembering Padre Villanueva, located in the church yard (author, 1999) — 99
6. Military guardpost behind the Catholic Church of Joyabaj (anonymous, around 1984) — 120
7. A second military guardpost behind the church (anonymous, around 1984) — 121
8. Military parade on Joyabaj's main street (anonymous, around 1986) — 129
9. Military posing on the village square in Joyabaj (Foto Color, 1983) — 129
10. Former military torture chamber in the convent of Zacualpa, now converted into a place of prayer (author, 2001) — 131
11. Beauty Queen (*señorita* or *reina de patrullero civil*) of the Civil Defense Patrols is driven around town in a cardboard army tank (Foto Color, 1983) — 135
12a. Identification card of a civil patroller, front (1983) — 141
12b. Identification card of a civil patroller, back (1983) — 141
13. Civil patrollers from Las Lomas Chuacorral (Foto Color, mid 1980s) — 144
14. Guerrilla pamphlet. On the right civil patrollers, pretending not to notice guerrillas who are hiding in the bushes on the left (ORPA, *Siembra*, December 1982) — 146
15. The central square in Joyabaj is packed with people protesting against mayor Amado Osmin Quiroa (Foto Color, 1988) — 176

16. Protests against mayor Osmin Quiroa (Foto Color, 1988) 177
17. Ríos Montt, with the white hat in his hand, holding a speech in Joyabaj during a visit of the FRG election campaign (author, 1999) 229
18. Soldiers from the local military base were also present when the *Palo Volador* was put up, not exactly knowing what to do (author, 1998) 233
19. A small shrine inside the Catholic Church of Joyabaj, remembering the death of Padre Villanueva (anonymous, 1993) 261
20. The Catholic Church in Santa Cruz de Quiché: remembering the murder of Bishop Gerardi 40 days earlier. The banner reads: we demand to be witnesses to the truth (author, 1998) 262
21. Altar inside the Catholic Church of Joyabaj, remembering Bishop Gerardi and the victims of the civil war in Joyabaj (author, 1998) 264
22. The small wooden crosses, which were carried during the commemorative procession for the civil war victims in Joyabaj (author, 1998) 265
23. Reburial of Padre Villanueva on 10 July 2000; largely an indigenous affair (anonymous, 2000) 266
24. The mudslide behind the convent, uncovering a massacre site. Concrete foundations are already laid, while family members are looking for human remains further down the slope (author, 1999) 279
25. Memorial for fallen civil defense patrollers, located on the central square of Joyabaj (author, 1999) 287

Preface

This book is the result of nearly six years of intensive study of the legacy of violence in a very small part of the world. Although the region is as small as a single municipality in Guatemala, called Joyabaj, the topic was enormous and only grew while I was exploring it. Armed conflict, and especially the issue of dealing with this violent past in general, appears to be a booming subject, not only in anthropology but also in sociology, political science, law, psychology and every other imaginable field of study. Recent outbursts of violence worldwide, in such diverse countries as former Yugoslavia, Rwanda, Liberia and East Timor, unfortunately made my research very up to date and added to the growing pile of books, articles, human rights reports and Urgent Action Appeals of Amnesty International. Truth commissions, such as the ones set up in South Africa and Guatemala, and international tribunals, such as the ones on Rwanda and Yugoslavia and the recent debate on the International Criminal Court, have directed national and international attention to human rights violations, genocide and other atrocities committed during civil wars or other violent conflicts, and to the way countries and people deal with such situations. However, these efforts to collect and analyse information on war and violence do not automatically imply an increasing interest in the topic among the general public.

    Who, then, will be the readers of this material, so carefully gathered in sometimes difficult circumstances? Will only a small group of interested and involved scientists, NGO workers and individual government officials use this material to learn from past events, to influence policy or to try and change things? If this were the case, this book would probably never have been written. A pressing argument for proceeding to write this book came out of this one small region of the world itself, and the people living in it. From the very beginning, *Joyabatecos*[1] were asking me when my book on their municipality would be finished and when they could see it and read it. Although I always explained that I was writing in English, this never seemed to be a problem for them because they just wanted to keep their history in their hands. It would be their story, and other people would hear about it. It was therefore incomprehensible to most *Joyabatecos* that I did not have a finished product as proof of my research at the beginning of the second fieldwork period. I had just spent six months back in the Netherlands, sufficient time, in their eyes, for me to put their words on paper. This local interest in what I was going to write was what really inspired me to finish the book and continues to inspire me to try

---

[1] The inhabitants of the municipality of Joyabaj are called *Joyabatecos*.

to have the book translated.

This book is my way of dealing with Joyabaj's multi-layered and multi-storied past, which I encountered when walking the streets of Joyabaj, when talking to people and when digging endlessly through the local archives. I had the opportunity to listen to what people were willing to tell me, to compare oral testimonies with archival information, to have access to the files of REMHI, the truth commission report of the Catholic Church, and I had ample time to observe. Observe how *indígenas* and ladinos interacted on a daily basis, how former guerrillas tried to explain their former political position to a hostile audience, how people behaved when visiting an exhumation site, how people reacted furiously to the proposed constitutional changes or their wait-and-see attitude when the right-wing FRG came to Joyabaj during election time and former *Junta* leader Ríos Montt made a compelling speech. The combination of these different sources, which I compared, analysed and commented upon, led to the creation of a new story and a new way of looking at the municipality of Joyabaj. While looking at the way *Joyabatecos* deal with the legacy of the civil war, by giving testimony to truth commissions, by attending commemorative masses, by helping out during the exhumation of a mass grave, by going about their lives as usual or by not getting involved so as to avoid trouble, I found my own way amidst the stories of many.

I would like to thank everyone who has made it possible for me to write this book. First of all Dirk Kruijt and Arij Ouweneel, for being the supervisors they were. They gave me the freedom to make it my research and my book. I would also like to thank my colleagues at the Capacity Group Cultural Anthropology at Utrecht University, especially my room-mates Marja Kusters, Judith de Wolf and Elisabet Rasch, who made the writing process rather agreeable. Special thanks to Marie-Louise Glebbeek, with whom I spent time in Guatemala while she was doing research for her dissertation on police reform. I also want to thank my Ph.D. colleagues from Overleg Latijns Amerika (OLA) for providing comments and, even more important, deadlines.

In Guatemala City I received help from several research institutes that generously opened their archives and libraries to me. These include Flacso, *Fundación* Friedrich Ebert, *Fundación* Myrna Mack, *Fundación* Rigoberta Menchú, Cirma (Antigua), Landivar University and the offices of Noticias de Guatemala and Inforpress Latinoamericana. ODHAG generously gave me permission to view the REMHI archives, and the PDH in Santa Cruz de Quiché let me spend many afternoons going through the files. I especially want to mention the research institute Avancso, where I had many stimulating conversations with Matilde González, who was doing similar research in another community in the Quiché department. At a later stage, Rosa Torras and Maria Victoria García also joined the discussions at Avancso. I also want to thank the people working at the *Heremoteca* of the Central American Archive in Guatemala City, where I spent considerable time going through stacks of old newspaper clippings and dusty old documents. They were very patient with my numerous requests for yet another edition of a newspaper. Support also came from the NGO Redd Barna in Norway, which sent me original documents of its work in Joyabaj from the 1970s, complete with photographs, for me to use as I chose. I also want to thank Paul Kobrak for sharing with me his research and ideas on civil patrols in Aguacatan, and Paul Yamauchi, whose index of human rights violations in the 1980s provided many points of reference.

I want to thank the people of the *Oficina de Paz y Reconciliación* in Santa Cruz de Quiché, especially former coordinator Fernando Suazo, and Lya Vollering for putting me into contact with them. They were my first point of entry into the Quiché department, and generously gave assistance to my research. I also want to thank two Peace Corps volunteers, Sarah Lansdale and Karen Santora, who had been working in Joyabaj for more than a year and eagerly introduced me to everybody. And of course Liz Oglesby and Diana Nelson, who kept me company in Joyabaj for several weeks during my second fieldwork period in 1999. Their enthusiastic discussions and questioning provided me with new angles for my research. Special thanks also to Tom Lent, for his enthusiastic support and insightful comments on my final draft. I also want to thank Brigitte, Raul, Joris and Clara for making me feel one of the family. And of course Vicky and Isabel at *Mujer de Esperanza*, my home in the past. I am also extremely indebted to the people of Joyabaj, who gave me a very warm welcome and patiently answered my many questions. Early morning walks, beans, eggs and tomatoes, loads of sweet coffee, rattling typewriters, numerous masses, patience and friendship. I experienced it all.

Many have commented upon this manuscript, but I want to give special thanks to Marlies Glasius (London School of Economics) who faithfully worked her way through the first drafts of every chapter. Thanks for all your work! I also want to mention Dr. Roy Kessels of the Helmholtz Institute (Utrecht University), who carefully read the section on memory, and Kees Koonings (Utrecht University) for his detailed comments on my final draft. Michael James, who did an outstanding job, edited the English. I also want to thank the Jurriaanse Stichting for their financial support.

Finally, I want to thank my friends and family for their endurance and support, especially my partner Roy Schilderman, who never read a letter I wrote, but never doubted my ability to write this book.

Utrecht, 14 October 2002

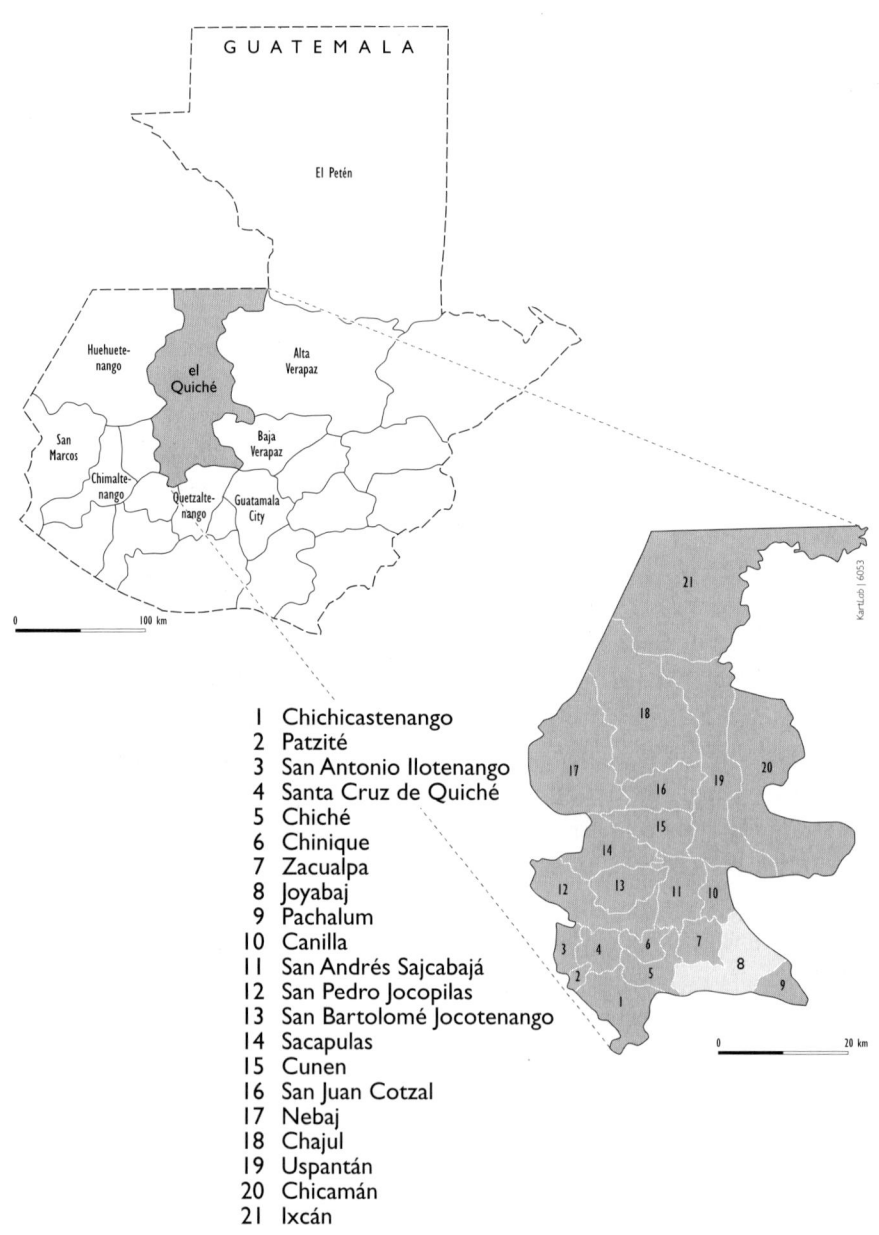

1 Chichicastenango
2 Patzité
3 San Antonio Ilotenango
4 Santa Cruz de Quiché
5 Chiché
6 Chinique
7 Zacualpa
8 Joyabaj
9 Pachalum
10 Canilla
11 San Andrés Sajcabajá
12 San Pedro Jocopilas
13 San Bartolomé Jocotenango
14 Sacapulas
15 Cunen
16 San Juan Cotzal
17 Nebaj
18 Chajul
19 Uspantán
20 Chicamán
21 Ixcán

Map 1. *Departments of Guatemala*

Map 2. *Municipality of Joyabaj*

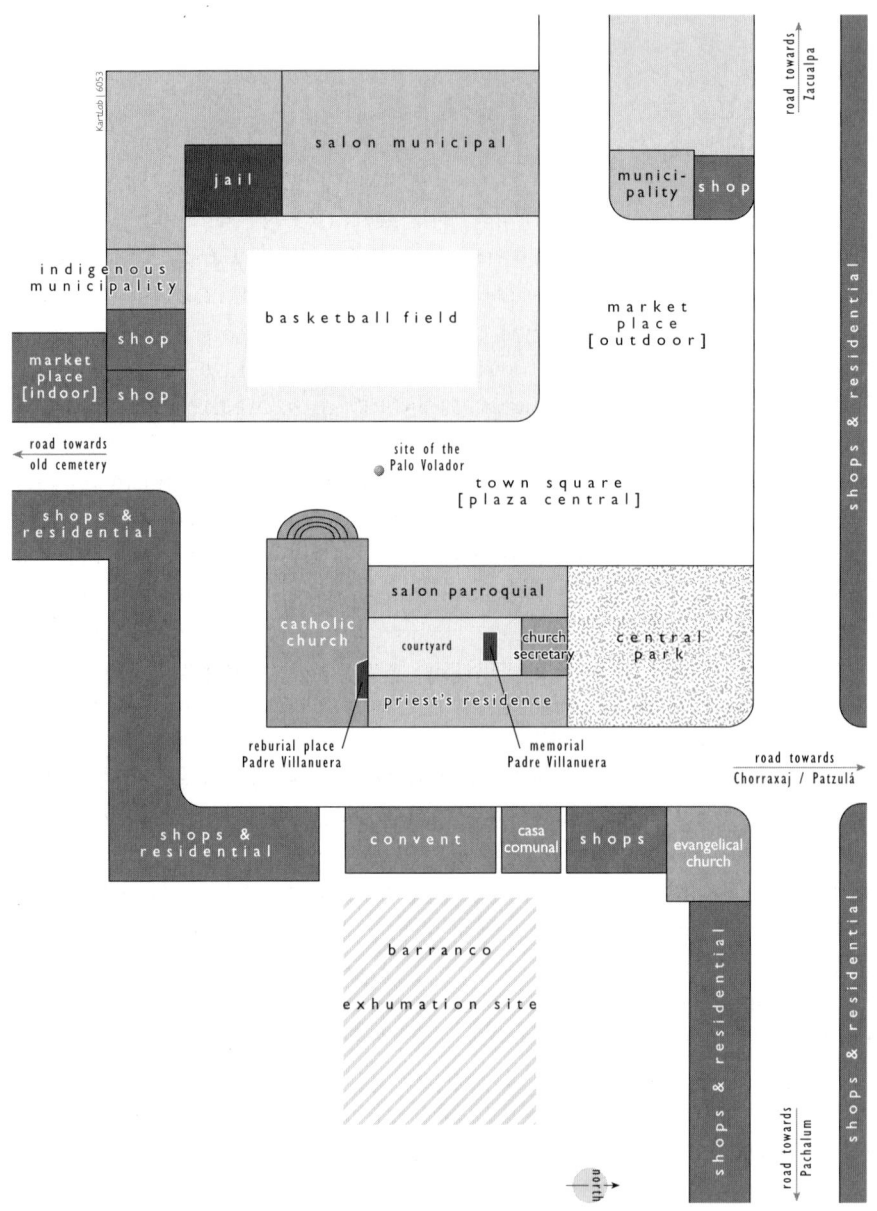

Map 3. *Central square of Joyabaj (2001)*

1

Introduction: concepts and methodology

Close encounter
Working as a human rights observer in Guatemala in 1995, I accompanied Guatemalan refugees who had fled their country during the civil war in the early 1980s, many of whom were now returning to Guatemala. These returning communities were often hours' or days' walk from the nearest roads. During one of these walks I had to stay overnight in another village along the trail, together with my travelling companion, a returning refugee. The community where we had to stop for the night was one whose inhabitants had remained in Guatemala during the civil war and had not sought refuge in nearby Mexico. They had experienced military rule during the civil war and had been taught by the military that the refugees were all guerrillas, who on returning to Guatemala would only make more trouble. My companion was therefore not at all happy about our overnight stop and he became more and more nervous as we approached the community. He explained that we could not stay in the village without permission. Permission from whom, I asked, expecting him to say the mayor or a local priest. But he said that we had to go to the chief of the civil patrols, who seemed to be the one in charge of local affairs.

Although I had heard of these organizations, at that moment I did not realize what their role during the civil war had been. We entered the village, where a number of armed men hung around in the village square, carrying rifles over their shoulders and machetes tied to their waistbands. Although machetes are commonly carried in the Guatemalan countryside, where they are used to fell trees, build houses, and even peel oranges, rifles are not. People looked at us with suspicion and tried to avoid talking with us, although many more of them gathered in the village square to take a look at us. Finally, when it became clear that we wanted to stay the night in the village, a small boy was sent to look for the civil patrol chief. We were told to sit down on the doorstep of a small shop and wait. We waited in silence and had no intention of doing anything else. After an hour or so a man, also armed, came walking slowly out of the fields towards us. He conversed briefly with my companion in *Kekchi* and took us to our sleeping quarters, an abandoned shed which had not been in use for many years. I was glad to be able to put my things down, but I kept feeling uneasy and distinctly out of place. Never before had I experienced such a feeling of dread as when sitting on the doorstep of that store, waiting for the patrol commander to appear while surrounded by armed men. I was relieved to leave the next morning at dawn. After a few hours walking we arrived at the refugee community, where we heard that patrols from the surrounding communities had made direct threats to the refugee communities. The situation was tense because less than a week before more then ten people had been killed by the military in a nearby refugee community. This all happened at the end of 1995, a year before the peace agreement was to be signed between the Guatemalan government and the guerrilla forces, and the civil defence patrols finally dismantled.

Central questions and concepts

The armed conflict

Although I analyse the Guatemalan civil war and its legacy in detail in the succeeding chapters, I wish to present a very short sketch of the general process. For 36 years, until a Peace Accord was signed in 1996, the guerrilla and the counter-insurgency campaigns of the military resulted in a continuous state of low-intensity civil war in Guatemala. Political, economic, and ideological power in Guatemala had always been concentrated in the hands of a small ladino[1] elite, whose position was guarded by an strong army. The indigenous majority (*indígenas*) were politically, economically, and socially excluded and lacked the means and opportunity to participate fully in Guatemalan society. Any attempt to change this situation met with fierce military repression. This increasing resort to force in the 1960s and 1970s to suppress social unrest and to combat popular discontent eventually led to the rise of different guerrilla groups.[2] At the beginning of the 1980s the fighting, and especially the military repression, intensified. The indigenous population in the western highlands, where the guerrillas were most active, was hardest hit by the violence which resulted from clashes between the two parties.[3] Between 1981 and 1983 the military used so-called 'scorched earth' tactics, resulting in more than 400 villages being destroyed, 75,000 people

---

1 There is no clear definition of *ladino* (or *mestizo* as they are called in other Latin American countries), because the term is a socio-cultural construction designed mainly to distinguish between ladinos and the indigenous part of the population. People define themselves as ladino when they consider themselves to be of white (Spanish or European) or mixed (white and indigenous) origin, speak Spanish as their first (and often only) language, dress European and in general adhere to Western norms and values. *Indígenas* are of Indian descent, speak an indigenous language, speak Spanish only as a second language and have separate cultural norms and values.
2 Le Bot (1995).
3 See for example Le Bot (1995), ODHAG, Vol. III (1998: 25-89) and CEH, Vol. I (1999: 123-178) for a detailed account and analysis of the Guatemalan civil war, its background and causes.

being killed and more than 1 million people fleeing their homes.⁴ At the same time the military institutionalized its control over the western highlands by organizing the local population into civil defence patrols (*Patrullas de Autodefensa Civil* – PAC), one of which I encountered when working as a human rights observer. A tight network of repression was in place, encompassing not only the civil defence patrols and military forces (army, air force, navy and special forces), but also police, military police, private security forces, death squads and various intelligence units.⁵ A society of fear was created 'in which a climate of insecurity, anxiety and suspense overshadowed all other feelings'.⁶ People lived under constant surveillance and local society was thoroughly militarized. A change in military strategy, 'to establish a more legitimate presence in the disputed regions, with "positive actions", local development projects and protection of allied peasants',⁷ heralded a slow transition towards civilian government, resulting in democratic presidential elections in 1985. However, a large part of the apparatus of repression was left intact and civilian rule was still under military control.⁸ After a series of complex and prolonged peace negotiations between guerrilla forces, the military and the Guatemalan government during the 1990s, a final peace agreement was signed in December 1996.

The focus of this research is on civil defence patrols because they turned out to be one of the most important mechanisms of military control of the Guatemalan countryside. Their legacy of violence continued even after the civil war had ended.⁹ Civil defence patrols were set up by the military towards the end of 1981, just before civil war violence reached its peak, to defend the villages against guerrilla attacks. Participation in the patrols was obligatory for all males between the ages of 18 and 60, on penalty of severe punishment by patrol commanders or the local military commander. Besides village defence tasks, they acted as an information network for the military, and were forced to take on military tasks such as sweeping areas for guerrillas and attacking so-called subversive villages. Although initially they were set up to help the military to win the war against guerrilla forces, they eventually evolved into a local force in their

---

4   Between 1980 and 1985 more than 150,000 *Guatemaltecos* sought refuge in Mexico, notably in the border state of Chiapas. Only a third, who had arrived at the numerous spontaneously formed refugee camps and settlements that were set up only a few miles inside of Mexico, were officially recognized as refugees by the Mexican government. Another 100,000 non-recognized refugees were scattered over Chiapas, Mexico and other urban areas (Deli Sante, 1996: 96-97).
5   Deli Sante (1996: 273); ODHAG, Vol. II (1998: 65-79).
6   Kruijt and Koonings (1999: 16).
7   Kruijt and Koonings (1999: 50).
8   For an inside view of the military on Guatemala's civil war see Schirmer (1998 and 2002), and Rosada-Granados (1999). On the issue of political ambitions of the military, see Koonings and Kruijt (2002).
9   See Jay (1993), Popkin (1996) and Solomon (1994).

own right. Although the patrols were officially dismantled in 1996, shortly before the signing of the peace agreement, it was clear from newspaper articles, human rights reports and daily conversations that the role of civil patrols in the local power structures in the villages in the western highlands was not over yet. Civil defence patrols have been the most visible, long-lasting and active military presence at the local level in Guatemala during and even after the civil war. Civil patrols influenced economic, political and social relations within and between communities, and their often violent activities and behaviour had a lasting impact on people's memories of the civil war. Civil patrol duty made it impossible for people to refrain from taking part in the civil war, causing outbreaks of violence between and within communities and families.

Research aims and questions
This book presents a historical sociology of civil defence patrols and their violent legacy in the municipality of Joyabaj, which is situated in the south of the Quiché department. This research fits into the scientific debate about countries dealing with the legacy of a civil war or other violent conflicts: a legacy of violence, fear, distrust, and polarization. Numerous articles and books[10] have appeared on the effects of civil war and how countries deal with them, by way of truth commissions, tribunals, trials, reconciliation and revenge, in countries as diverse as South Africa, Northern Ireland, Argentina, Chile, El Salvador, Rwanda, former Yugoslavia, and of course Guatemala. Much of this research is focused on the national level, sketching a general picture of how a government or a people deals with its past. However, this book presents a *local* study of the effects of a civil war, by looking at civil patrols and the way in which people at the local level deal with that past.[11] In what way are day-to-day relationships still shaped by the legacy of civil war, and how is this past represented in individual and collective memory?

The first aim of this book is to reconstruct the different local narratives on civil war violence in Joyabaj. How did the conflict engulf Joyabaj, and in what ways did *Joyabatecos* engage in it? What role did civil defence patrols, which were the most important local actor involved in violent activities, play during this period? How were they set up, organized and trained, and why did people agree to participate in the patrols?

The second aim is to analyse the way in which the establishment and the

---

[10] See for example Hamber (1998 and 1999), Hayner (2001), Kaiser (2000), and Teitel (2000), to name only a few.

[11] Other recent *local level* studies on the legacy of the civil war in Guatemala are Zur (1998), Green (1999) and González (2002). See also Kobrak (1997) who focuses specifically on the role of civil defence patrols at the local level, in Aguacatán, Huehuetenango.

activities of civil defence patrols, in the context of civil war violence, have influenced power relations at the local (municipal) level. In other words, what were the effects of the installation of the civil defence patrols at the local level? To answer this question, I first examine how social relations, in which the focus is on political and economic relations, were organized before the war. We then follow the process of changing power relations during the war, looking at the installation of the patrols, their actual organization, aim and activities. It will become clear that enormous diversity existed among the patrols in different communities, and that civil patrols were not inherently violent. A third and final step is to look at local power relations after the peace agreement was signed in December 1996 and the patrols dismantled. This historical approach enables me to look at the entire process of changing power relations as a result of the civil war, especially patrol violence.

Finally, I want to examine how, at the local level, current memories of the civil war, especially memories of the activities of civil defence patrols, still shape people's perceptions, actions, and social relations in a post-war situation. These relations are marked by fear, prejudice, and distrust, thereby creating important impediments to erasing the legacy of violence and building local democracy. To answer this question we have to investigate how, at the individual level, memory works, how memories are stored, retrieved and distorted during this process. How does the social, economic and political context influence the memory process? How does the actual context and space in which the interview is taking place influence memory? How does the enormous diversity of memories about civil war violence and patrol activity come about? At the personal as well as at the community level, we have to examine how the existence of different memories of the war at the local level relates to attempts to construct a unified and generally accepted past, by way of truth commission reports, tribunals and other means of dealing with the past. How do people, and communities as a whole, deal with this past?

Dealing with the past

Why is it important that Guatemala, or any other country recovering from a civil war, deals with its violent past? Should this past be told, written down and thus reconstructed in truth commission reports, trials and commemorative events? Or should it be forgotten and buried? Both are ways of dealing with the past, although 'many would argue that the impact of large-scale political violence and its resultant silence needs to be seriously dealt with by societies in transition or the divisions of the past will return to poison the present'.[12] The South African

---

12 Hamber (1998: 2)
(http://www.incore.ulst.ac.uk/home/publication/research/dwtp/hamber.pdf) [29/11/01].

psychologist Hamber (1998), who has written extensively on truth commissions, reconciliation and dealing with the past in both South Africa and Northern Ireland, talks about the 'dirty business of remembering, acknowledging responsibility and even finger pointing'.[13] According to him the memory process will reveal that the past is made up of multiple and contradictory truths and that the goal of a single unified narrative, or version of the past, can never be achieved. 'The past will remain a contested debate.'[14] Nevertheless, one of the main reasons for remembering is that it is important to create a historical record, however contested this may be. This record, according to Hamber,[15] could act as a symbolic closure of a violent past, while opening up the future in which the same mistakes are not repeated.[16] The title of the *Recuperación de la Memoria Histórica* (REMHI) report,[17] that is, the truth commission report of the Catholic Church, is *Nunca Más* (Never Again), which clearly symbolizes the hope that it will never happen again.

Others are more critical, stressing that in many countries institutions set up to deal with the past, such as truth commissions, are tightly controlled inquiries 'constrained from the start by government-asserted purposes of reconciliation'.[18] A trade-off is often thought to exist between truth and justice, especially when the 'tolerance for multiple representations of the "truth"' is not very high. According to Teitel, there is often an attempt to constrain other competing historical accounts because they do not fit 'the shared historical account' which is represented in, for example, a truth commission.[19] Symbolic closure of a violent past and truth before reconciliation are not the only reasons to deal with the past. Remembering also creates space for debate between individuals and groups, it can weaken or counteract official memory or the memories of perpetrators, and it can help family members of victims in their process of mourning.[20]

---

13 See for an overview of Hambers' publications: http://www.brandonhamber.com
14 Hamber (1998: 2)
    (http://www.incore.ulst.ac.uk/home/publication/research/dwtp/hamber.pdf) [29/11/01].
15 See Hamber (1998); Hayner (2001) and Minow (1998) on the issue of dealing with the past. See Hamber and Wilson (1999) for a detailed analysis of symbolic closure through memory, reparation and revenge. (www.csvr.org.za/papers/papbh&rw.htm).
16 Initiatives geared towards dealing with the past are of course not without critics. See for example Buur (2000) and Henry (2000) on the South African truth commission. Reparations to victims of apartheid were rejected by the government, while some of the people testifying to the commission felt that their memory had been taken from them after it had come out into the open and was in the public domain.
17 Recuperation of the Historical Memory. The REMHI investigation resulted in 1998 in the publication of *Guatemala: Nunca más* (Guatemala: Never Again), a four-volume report on civil war violence in Guatemala.
18 Teitel (2000: 69).
19 Teitel (2000: 69).
20 On the process of mourning in the case of disappeared family members in Argentina, see Robben (2000: 87-90).

In Guatemala most of the strategies to uncover and deal with the past, including formal truth commissions, exhumations, trials against perpetrators and commemorative ceremonies have been put into practice in one form or another during the last few years, with the two truth reports of REMHI and the *Comisión para el Esclarecimiento Histórico* (CEH)[21] featuring prominently. The Catholic Church in particular stresses the importance of knowing what happened because without this knowledge reconciliation and forgiveness would be impossible.[22] The Guatemalan clergy, who consider reconciliation to be an important mission of the Catholic Church, use these two Christian concepts extensively.[23] In the Pastoral Plan of the Diocese of the Quiché department for 1999-2003, reconciliation was the priority.[24] However, according to the Guatemalan clergy, reconciliation can be accomplished only when the truth is known, on the assumption that only one truth exists—which is debatable, as I try to show in this book. Bishop Juan Gerardi, coordinator of the REMHI project, referred, in a speech given during the presentation ceremony of the REMHI report, to a passage in the Bible: 'to know the truth will set us free (Juan 8:32).'[25] The bishop was killed only two days after the REMHI report had been presented to the public.

The ways in which communities and people in Guatemala have experienced the civil war vary immensely, leading not only to different and sometimes competing memories of this past, but also to different attitudes towards memory initiatives. In many communities memory activities *do* open up yet another political and social space for discussion and activity, and communities are indeed mobilized around exhumations, commemorations or even trials. Other communities, however, are much less open towards memory initiatives and try to keep them at bay. In some cases exhumations or even commemorative events polarize or seriously damage community relations.

Violence and terror
To answer the different questions I have raised in the first section of this chapter, I introduce two important concepts, violence and memory, which, together with the data gathered in the field, have shaped this book. I will explain how and why

---

21 Commission of Historical Clarification. The CEH was set up as a result of the Peace Accords, and operated by MINUGUA *(Misión de las Naciones Unidas para la Verificación de los Derechos Humanos en Guatemala)*, the United Nations verification mission in Guatemala.
22 See Carta Pastoral Colectiva de la Conferencia Episcopal de Guatemala '!Urge la Verdadera Paz!' (CEG, 1997: 720-783), and Discurso de Monseñor Juan Gerardi con ocasión de la presentación del informe REMHI (CEG, 1999: 182-185).
23 Carta Pastoral Colectiva de la Conferencia Episcopal de Guatemala '!Urge la Verdadera Paz!' (CEG, 1997: 764).
24 Diócesis del Quiché (1998: 55-59). For a detailed analysis of the role of the Guatemalan Catholic Church in the peacemaking process at the national level, see Jeffrey (1998).
25 CEG (1999: 183).

I decided to use these concepts and how they served to analyse the data gathered. I will refrain from giving a complete and all-embracing overview of the theoretical debate surrounding each concept, but limit myself to those elements relevant to this research.

While carrying out fieldwork for this book, the topic of violence crept into almost every conversation or interview I conducted with people in Joyabaj. The references were numerous, including everyday criminal violence such as recent bus robberies and the increasing number of lynchings, as well as political violence connected to the civil war past such as in massacres, disappearances, and stories of having to flee aerial bombardment. It was clear that violence played an important role in people's daily lives as well as in their stories and memories of the civil war, especially civil patrol activity. The civil war period is locally referred to as *La Violencia* (The Violence), *'cuando vino la Violencia'* (when the Violence came) or *el problema* (the problem). The use of *La Violencia* to denote the civil war has been noticed and analysed by various researchers working on the Guatemalan civil war.[26] It is interesting to note that in Joyabaj the civil war period is sometimes also referred to as *el tiempo de la subversion* (the times of the subversion), which hints at a more negative attitude towards guerrilla forces, who were also called subversives. It was mainly used by ladinos who blamed the war on the guerrilla forces. When recounting the past, people situated events before, during or after *La Violencia*, which in their eyes changed everything. I therefore give the concept of violence a prominent place in this book, using the terms '*La Violencia*', 'armed conflict' and 'civil war' interchangeably, and incorporating closely related concepts such as terror, control and surveillance. These appeared to have been central elements of the army's strategy of militarizing the Guatemalan countryside, and crucial to the functioning of the civil patrol system.

In this book, I touch upon political as well as criminal violence, past as well as current violence, violence as a national military strategy as well as the implementation of this strategy by individuals at the local level. The boundaries between these different forms and levels of violence are not as clear-cut as I have presented them. Past violence influences, and might in some instances even be the cause of, current violence, while criminal acts may have been carried out during the *La Violencia* disguised as political violence. The focus in this book is, however, on state-sponsored violence and its effects at the local, including community and individual, level. In discussions about violence at the state level, an important distinction has to be made between state and anti-state violence. The function of state violence is 'to maintain the status quo while that of the other [anti-

---

26 See for example Zur (1998), Davis (1988) and Warren (1993).

state violence] is to achieve political change' (Sluka, 2000:1). However, the distinction becomes somewhat blurred when paramilitary groups set up by the state 'go private', as in Colombia for instance. This complexity will be touched upon also in relation to the civil patrols, whose functions and activities changed over time. I concentrate on state violence because the focus of this research is on socalled agents of the state, in this case the civil defence patrols, at the local level and their use of violence. Another reason for focusing on state violence is that according to both of the Guatemalan truth commission reports it was the Guatemalan state that was responsible for most of the atrocities committed during *La Violencia*. However, this study will also pay some attention to guerrilla violence within the context of the conflict.

State violence is used whenever states, or, more precisely, the political, military and economic elites, feel threatened by popular protest or other forms of 'deviant' behaviour. Most people accept that the use of certain forms of violence by the state as a response to certain forms of deviant behaviour by its citizens is, in principle, justified and necessary. Claridge (2000), in his study on state violence in Indonesia and Guatemala, uses the term 'state terrorism' when states overstep the boundary between legitimate force and illegitimate violence. He derives the term from Walter, author of *Terror and Resistance* (1969), the classic work on state terrorism. Walter distinguishes three actors within the terror process: the source of violence, the victim and the target (Walter, 1969: 9). 'In its most simplified form, terrorism is a process by which violence is applied by one group ('the source'), against another group ('the victim'), with the intention of influencing the behavior of a wider group ('the target').'[27] A system of terror suggests violence that is deliberately random so that everybody is a potential victim and has to be afraid for his or her own safety. Violence against part of the population is used to instil fear in the remainder of the population and thus control them. The term 'state terrorism' fits the activities of the Guatemalan state during the civil war well. The initial terror campaign, which killed thousands, burned hundreds of villages and displaced more than a million people, was followed by a pacification programme involving control and indoctrination of the remaining population, which created widespread distrust between communities and community members. The result of this military campaign was the destruction of the social fabric of society, which is still evident today.

It is important to look at the source of terror, which Walter (1969: 9) calls the 'terror staff'. Within a terror staff he distinguishes between 'a directorate—men who can design, initiate, control, define, and justify the terror—and agents of violence—executioners, warriors, and the "king's knives," who carry out orders

---

27 Claridge (1999/2000: 13).

and perform acts of destruction'.[28] In the Guatemalan case the civil patrols can be identified as agents of violence or terror, who carried out orders from those higher up in the military hierarchy (the directorate). Although Walter's model is useful to clarify the Guatemalan situation, according to Claridge there is considerable overlap between directorate and agents of violence. He also argues that the agents of violence have much more room for manoeuvre at the local level than Walter's model allowed for. In this model agents of violence are 'presented simply as conduits for the will of their leaders, as facilitators of their violent intentions'.[29] Claridge goes on to say that 'factors such as local rivalries, or a desire to excel at the lower levels of the terror staff, may be as significant, or more so, than any "rational" command decisions made by the directorate of terror'.[30] It is useful to combine Walter's idea of a directorate of terror with Claridge's notion of room to manoeuvre at the local level. How do tensions between being 'conduits for the will of their leaders' and local room to manoeuvre affect local power relations? How much space for manoeuvre did the civil patrols in Guatemala have at the local level, and what role did the local patrol commanders play? Do *Joyabatecos* remember the civil patrols as following orders or having freedom of action?

What makes it even more complicated is that Guatemala's 'agents of terror' largely overlap with the actual target of violence. Civil patrollers were part of the population that was targeted by the military to change its behaviour, out of fear of acts of violence against the state. The patrollers themselves were, in some cases, even the objects of violence. They were, however, also the ones who had to carry out these acts of violence. The roles of victim, perpetrator and bystander were therefore constantly blurred. Warren (2000: 238) also refers to the difficulty of defining the civil patrols as agents of terror because, although they fit the profile of state agent, they are mostly civilians forced to participate in the civil patrol structure. In the cases of, for example, South Africa and East Timor, the difference between perpetrator and victim appears to be somewhat clearer because in these cases the state, together with the military, clearly targeted a civilian population without actually incorporating it into the terror structure, as was done in Guatemala. It is precisely this forced incorporation and participation in the civil war which still influences daily life in Guatemala. Not only did the local population suffer the direct consequences of a civil war, such as death, disappearances and destruction of livelihood, but they were also forced to participate in the process.

---

28 Walter (1969: 9).
29 Claridge (1999/2000: 13).
30 Claridge (1999/2000: 14).

Surveillance and control

Use of open violence and terror are not the only options open to a state trying to maintain order, protect the privileged position of its elite and stay in power. In his book *Discipline and Punish* (1977), Foucault focuses on the disciplining of minds and bodies through hospitals, prisons, courts and schools, and labels modern society with all its surveillance and control mechanisms the 'carceral society'. The central concepts in his work are surveillance, control and self-discipline or self-censorship, which he derives from Bentham's discussion of the panopticon.[31] Bentham had proposed to construct the ideal prison as a panopticon, a circular building with cells built around the outside edge. In the centre was the inspection tower. Two windows were placed in every cell, one facing the inspection tower and the other facing outside the building. The aim of the design was to make each prisoner visible to the guards at all times, while the prisoner could never see the supervisor or the other inmates. In this case, surveillance meant the open and veiled monitoring of people's activities by way of, for example, policing or administrative supervision. Through the panopticon (surveillance) people are constantly aware of their visibility, which 'ensures the automatic functioning of power. So to arrange things that the surveillance is permanent in its effects, even if it is discontinued in its action; that the perfection of power should render its actual exercise unnecessary'.[32] This mechanism seems to have been at work in Guatemala not only during *La Violencia* but also even after the peace agreement was signed. The fear of being watched continued even after the civil patrols were dismantled and their surveillance functions had officially ended. Surveillance and control were the most important functions of the civil patrol system in Guatemala, apart from the use of brutal violence at the beginning of the civil war. First of all, civil patrols openly carried out surveillance tasks, controlling the movement and activities of people by way of checkpoints, pass control, observation posts, registration of foreigners and nightly patrols. Civil patrols were also actively involved in gathering information about possible subversives, thereby helping to draw up blacklists and maintaining intelligence archives. In the long term, these surveillance functions possibly have had a significant influence on how people relate to each other at the local level. They could account for the mutual distrust that still exists within communities or the fear of getting involved with outsiders or outside organizations because this could lead to trouble.

According to Foucault, the ultimate goal of a panopticon was to ensure a permanent feeling of being watched, even if no actual surveillance was being carried out. People were to regulate their activities themselves, from within, because

---

31 Foucault (1977: 195-228).
32 Foucault (1977: 201).

there was always the possibility that they were being seen and their activities reported. Although people at the local level knew who was active in the civil patrols, who the patrol commanders were, which commanders and patrollers were willing participants in human rights violations and which ones tried to avoid problems, there could always be other military informers or people who held personal grudges against others. Fear of being branded subversive, fear of violence, fear of chaotic terror, fear of surveillance would foster mutual distrust and discipline people's minds and bodies. Eventually people would discipline themselves out of fear of repercussions. In this way terror or the threat of terror (or punishment) is used to 'to sap the potential for disobedience in advance and to break the power to resist'.[33] These long-term effects of such mechanisms of control can still be observed in the current Guatemalan context. In Joyabaj, people refrained from talking about certain sensitive topics, they identified people responsible for human rights violations by a nod in the direction of those persons' houses and painstakingly avoided to mention their names, while others did not want to talk at all about what had happened to them during the war because they were certain that those times could return.

Obedience and dehumanization
Surveillance and control of people are only two ways to influence people's actions and behaviour. A related topic is obedience, which is often mentioned in relation to the actions of agents of the state, whether military or paramilitary groups like the Guatemalan civil patrols. Many researchers have asked themselves why people acted in a certain way during times of war. Why did people look the other way? Why did some people help victims, while others did nothing? Why did people deny what was going on? Bauman touches upon this issue in his book *Modernity and the Holocaust* (1989), in which he explains how people who come under the control of bureaucrats or other experts are socialized into obeying commands from above. Responsibility is fulfilled simply by obeying dutifully, and people do not need to consider the moral implications of their actions beyond that.

To explain how this process works, Bauman refers to Kelman and Hamilton's *Crimes of Obedience* (1989). Kelman and Hamilton explains how individuals who would normally not be able to act in such a way participate in mass violence. Looking at the psychological disposition of the perpetrators or the existence of hatred and rage against the victims is not enough, according to Kelman and Hamilton. Although these factors have to be taken into account, they alone cannot explain people's participation in mass violence. They propose not to look at

---
33 Walter (1996: 19).

the motives for violence 'but at the conditions under which the usual moral inhibitions against violence become weakened'.[34] They identify three processes that can create such conditions and which made the Holocaust possible: *authorization*, *routinization*, and *dehumanization*. The first two transfer moral responsibility to the state. Authorization takes away the responsibility of the individual to make personal moral choices, while routinization organizes the action in such a way that there is no opportunity for raising moral questions. Dehumanization takes place by ideologically defining a group of people as different and subhuman, and therefore unworthy of humane treatment.[35]

While Kelman and Hamilton focus mainly on the process of authorization (their work is on military obedience in times of war), Bauman draws attention to the process of *dehumanization* in his discussion of the Holocaust.[36] In his work he analyses the construction of 'we' and 'the other' out of fear for the unknown or out of a desire to create the perfect society in which certain groups of people do not have a place. Nagengast explains the connection between state violence and the creation of the other as follows: 'the goal of state violence is not to inflict pain; it is the social project of creating punishable categories of people, forging and maintaining boundaries among them, and building the consensus around those categories that specifies and enforces behavioral norms and legitimates and de-legitimates specific groups.'[37] This 'radical otherness' seems to be psychologically necessary in order to be able to inflict pain on another individual. Bauman draws upon the experiments of psychologist Milgram,[38] in which assistants were to administer electric shocks to an individual with a learning problem whenever he gave the wrong answer to a question. The voltage was turned up after every mistake.[39] It turned out that a large part of the assistants were capable of administering very dangerous levels of electric shocks to this person. The percentage of people willing to give higher shocks increased when the relative distance to the individual increased, that is, when they could not hear or see him. Social distance includes physical distance but especially mental distance. The other was not seen as a human being, not as 'one of us' or one that had to be taken into account. Under the circumstances individuals stopped acting as autonomous individuals and adopted an 'agentic state', that is, acting merely as the agent of,

---

34 Kelman and Hamilton (1989: 15-16).
35 See Kelman and Hamilton (1989: 16-20) for a detailed analysis of the three processes, using the 1968 My Lai massacre in Vietnam as its main case.
36 Bauman (1989).
37 Nagengast (1994: 122).
38 See Bauman (1989: 151-168) for a description of Milgram's research and Milgram (1974) for the original publication.
39 In reality the individual with the learning problem was an actor, who did not really receive electric shocks, but acted as though he did.

for example, the state.[40] Responsibility is attributed to the legal authority and no one feels feel morally accountable for what has happened.

Here the term 'agent of the state', which was introduced in the discussion of Walter's analysis of state terror, comes into focus again. How do the Guatemalan civil patrols fit this picture of individuals obediently carrying out orders originating from higher up in the military hierarchy? How does obedience interact with room to manoeuvre for agents of the state, or agents of violence, at the local level, as introduced by Claridge? The patrols consisted of people who also largely belonged to the indigenous part of the population, which had been stigmatized and excluded from mainstream society since colonial times. Therefore, distance, both physical and mental, probably plays a very different role in attempts to explain obedient behaviour among Guatemalan civil patrollers. For example, during World War II the enemy was much more clearly defined and treated accordingly. How did the processes of authorization, routinization and dehumanization emerge during the Guatemalan civil war?

Thus, several processes are at work here. When one looks at the issue of victimization, on the one hand there is the idea that everybody can be targeted as a victim, and thus be the object of deliberate and random violence (Walter), while on the other hand dehumanization (Bauman) takes place, in which only a specific group within society is targeted as the victim. When one looks at the role of perpetrators, there is on the one hand the agent of the state who has no choice (Walter) and on the other hand room for manoeuvre (Claridge). The ambiguity which clearly exists between these different processes and the blurring of lines between the different groups give people a certain space or even freedom to act or to take on a certain role (as victim, bystander, mother) in the memories they present. It is clearly appealing to take on some roles while rejecting others because of the consequences attached to such roles. Presenting oneself as a perpetrator may ultimately result in a jail sentence, while the role of bystander may elicit a less negative response. How did these processes work in the Guatemalan situation, and how did they influence people's perception of the civil war violence? Tensions between the different boundaries and roles could account for the different and sometimes conflicting memories of civil patrol violence.

The concept of memory

How do *Joyabatecos* today remember and represent their own past behaviour in the civil patrols and the civil war period in general? How do they explain what happened, how do they explain their behaviour and that of others? In order to

---

40 See Milgram (1974: 132-134) on the topic of 'the agentic state' and the related loss of responsibility (145-148).

answer those questions it is necessary to look at how the memory process works, especially memory of war and violent events.

As with the concept of violence, I realized the importance of the concept of memory while undertaking research in Joyabaj. It is more correct to say that I encountered the *problem* of memory because I came across an enormous, sometimes conflicting variety of memories people had of civil war violence as well as other topics. People presented very diverse narratives of what happened in their village during the war, of civil patrol activity, of massacres that had been carried out and of people involved. The fieldwork took place almost 17 years after most atrocities in Joyabaj were committed and *Joyatabecos* had come up with a variety of explanations about the past. It was therefore difficult to produce *the* definitive reconstruction of what had happened before, during and after the civil war, because people presented me with their own, constantly changing constructions of the past. These constructed memories were clearly influenced by past and current power relations in the community, as well as by the violence of the civil war itself. People also used their memories to present a specific picture of the past and their own behaviour in that past. Some things were left out, while others seem to have been added at a later stage. People not only created the past and thereby their current selves through their memories; they also seemed to portray a collective feeling of belonging or togetherness among certain groups within the community.

A final factor that led to the incorporation of the concept of memory in this book is the fact that memory as such, for example in the form of commemorative initiatives, was prominent in Joyabaj at the time of the research. At the national as well as at the local level, discussions were taking place on the issue of whether and how to deal with the civil war and its violent legacy. From the mid-1990s onward several groups within Guatemalan society have taken initiatives to document civil war violence. Popular or human rights organizations gathered testimonies of their members about human rights abuses, held protest marches and were involved in trials and exhumations of mass graves. Other important national initiatives include the investigations and subsequent publication of the REMHI report and the CEH report. Memory was fought over at the national level by way of the two reports, in newspaper articles following trials of civil patrol commanders and the opening of military archives about activities during the civil war.[41] As well, at the local level memory was a recurrent theme in the work of the Catholic Church, through celebrations of martyrs who died during the civil war, commemorative processions and the exhumation of mass graves.

---

41 See National Security Archives website for information on military archives in Guatemala. (http:www.gwu.edu/~nsarchiv/latin_america/Guatemala.html).

These activities triggered people's memories about *La Violencia* and influenced their opinions on such topics.

Constructing memories

As a social anthropologist, I found it very useful to look at the research carried out by cognitive psychologists on the topic of memory. 'Psychologists and others interested in the ways individuals understand their own history usually approach memory as a cognitive and emotional process',[42] while anthropological studies of the memory process pay more attention to the larger social and institutional contexts of memory. Although this book presents an anthropological approach to memory, in this section I explore the cognitive process because it explains some of basic underlying processes at work in the brain.

In 1932, Bartlett was among the first to introduce the idea that memory is an active process during which individuals reconstruct rather than remember a story. According to him, 'Remembering is not the re-excitation of innumerable fixed, lifeless and fragmented traces. It is an imaginative reconstruction or construction'.[43] People present a construction of the past in the present to the listener (for instance, to the interviewer) in a specific context (for instance, a post-war period). So which factors influence and distort the coding and storing of memories? It is also important to understand how memory is reconstructed when it is retrieved during the process of remembering (putting the memory into words), and which factors influence the act of remembering.[44]

Before Bartlett it was widely accepted that memory worked like a photocopier, faithfully spitting out the same images that had been engraved on it years or decades earlier: the so-called storehouse metaphor. However, cognition psychologist Neisser, following Bartlett, concluded that only bits and pieces of the incoming information are registered in memory. These stored fragments of experiences are the basis of a reconstruction of the past.[45] According to neuro-psychologist Schacter, '[E]ncoding is the procedure of transforming something a person sees, hears, thinks, or feels into a memory'.[46] The storage of these images or memories is influenced by a number of factors. According to Alba and Hasher (1983) 'what is encoded or stored in memory is heavily determined by a guiding schema[47] or knowledge framework that selects and actively modifies experiences

---

42 White (2000: 494).
43 Bartlett (1932: 213).
44 For a comprehensive analysis of memory distortion see Schacter (1996).
45 Neisser (1967: 284-286).
46 Schacter (1996: 42).
47 Cognitive psychologists define schemas as cognitive structures with which people organize their knowledge about the social world. Schemas contain basic knowledge, codes, and impressions about people, ourselves, social roles and events (Aronson, Wilson and Akert, 1994: 118).

in order to arrive at a coherent, unified, expectation-confirming and knowledge consistent representation of an experience'.[48] Schacter goes on to explain that 'We remember only what we have encoded, and what we encode depends on who we are—our past experiences, knowledge and needs all have a powerful influence on what we retain. This is a reason why two different people can sometimes have radically divergent recollections of the same event'.[49]

How exactly are memories retrieved? According to Schacter (1996), an important aspect of the memory process is the role of cues. People are being given cues to remember a certain event when others tell about it or ask about it, or when they hear a certain song or smell a certain scent. These cues trigger people's memories. However, this is not to say that a memory is waiting to be released when the right cue is given. Memories are not simple activations of packages of information stored in the brain.[50] When we remember we temporarily activate different parts of the brain, in which different memory fragments are encoded and thus stored. Together they form a temporary construction of a past event. During storage, but also during retrieval, of memories a host of factors have been identified that influence memory. Factors such as 'the mood you are in at the time of the recall; uniqueness—you are more likely to recall things that stand out ... and will find it difficult to remember events that were one of many ... ; frequency of recall—if you recalled an event time and again you are more likely to remember it than if you have never thought or spoken of it'.[51]

Apparently, while we remember some information stored during the perception of an event (particularly that which our schema leads us to notice), we also remember information that was not there at the time but that has been added later. One study concluded that 'questions asked subsequent to an event can cause a reconstruction in one's memory of that event'.[52] This external information supplied after the event is, over time, integrated into the memory in 'such a way that we are unable to tell from which source some specific detail is recalled'.[53] According to cognitive psychologists, source amnesia[54] is a recurrent phenomenon in people's memories. When people do not know where informa-

---

48 Alba and Hasher (1983).
49 Schacter (1996: 52). For example Antjie Krog (1999: 82-100) examined the conflicting testimonies of perpetrators of one and the same crime in her book *Country of My Skull*. The book provides a very personal account of the proceedings of the Truth Commission in South Africa. Antjie Krog is a South African poet and essayist of Afrikaans descent, and an outspoken critic of apartheid.
50 Schacter (1996: 71).
51 Engel (1999: 8).
52 Loftus and Palmer (1974: 585).
53 Loftus and Palmer (1974: 588).
54 Source amnesia is also called 'source confusion' or 'misattribution'. See Schacter (1996: 118-121) and Schacter (1999: 188-191) for a detailed analysis.

tion came from, or what or who their source was, they tend to incorporate such information into their memories. People read and talk about an event and they discuss it with others who have different memories and opinions. People think they experienced an event as they memorize it, but sometimes other aspects have been added over time.

An additional factor is that general opinion about a certain national or local event can change, and that may also influence people's memories of it. What is correct to remember and what is not? What was considered correct behaviour in the past, for example during the civil war in Guatemala, and what is considered correct behaviour now? Expectations, just like general knowledge (schemata),[55] influence the encoding and retrieval of memories. Although it can be an intentional act on the part of the narrator to change a story and add other facts, it is also very possible that after a time people are unable to distinguish between their own memory of an event and elements added later. Apparently, they either do not remember the source of the information or have made other mistakes during reconstruction.

Coherence and consolidation
According to Schacter (1996), when people recollect about their own lives (autobiographical memories), they tend to present them as more coherent and consistent than they really were.[56] People 'exaggerate the consistency between their past and present attitudes, beliefs and feelings'.[57] They do so because, when people hold two inconsistent beliefs, it causes an unpleasant state of mind (dissonance). People reduce this dissonance by changing one belief to make it consistent with the other. The theory of cognitive dissonance, which was developed by Festinger (1957), implies that people streamline certain beliefs because they are dissonant with other beliefs people have of themselves or certain events. The past, and memories of the past, have to be in some way consistent with the present. Telling a life story or recalling a memory is a means of finding continuity between past and present.[58]

This does not mean that people live a world of fantasies, because their memories about the general events in their lives tend to be correct. According to Schudson (1995), people have, in general, enough grounds to arrive at a degree of consensus about the past. 'People normally accept some sorts of standards of what counts as true distortion and what counts simply as the inevitable variability of perspectives of people looking at the same phenomenon from different

---

55 See Bartlett (1932) for a discussion of schemata.
56 See Pasupathi (2001) and Schacter (1996) for an analysis of the principle of consistency.
57 Schacter (1999: 193).
58 Engel (1999:82).

values and viewpoints at different points in time.'⁵⁹ In a way people are, through remembering, reconstructing themselves and the image they have of themselves in the past.⁶⁰ According to Schacter (1996: 63), memories form the basis for our beliefs about ourselves. We continuously draw upon memories of the past that support the selves we are presenting to others. People have the tendency to put themselves at the centre of events when recalling memories of the past. Schacter (1996: 21) makes a distinction between remembering as an observer and remembering as a participant (seeing yourself in the memory). People can talk about an event either as observing from the sidelines or as playing a central role in the event. This also results in different memories of the same event. Even people who were not present during the event but heard several accounts of it over time can incorporate them into one memory in which they themselves participate in the event. This seems to have occurred frequently during the fieldwork in Joyabaj, when people who could never have witnessed certain events during the civil war because they were too young nevertheless produced detailed accounts of them.

Another aspect of memories is that they tend to consolidate when we think and talk about our experiences. The older a memory, the more opportunity we have had to recall an event.⁶¹ Time also allows for perspective 'because distance can give people historical perspective on matters that may have been hard to grasp at the time they happened'.⁶² Additional information becomes available and other opinions are heard. But time also appears to influence memory in another way, because memories seem to fade when not recalled frequently and details get blurred. According to Wagenaar and Groeneweg (1988), even the traumatic memories of concentration camp survivors lose some detail after two decades and are mixed with public recollections of that past (such as films, documentaries, and publications). Their research showed that, while the memories of what had happened were generally correct and accurate, they differed on specific events and facts. Some things, like the appearance of a torturer or witnessing a murder, were forgotten while others had been distorted by time or source amnesia. They concluded that 'intensity of experience is not a sufficient safeguard against forgetting'.⁶³ Apparently, memories of traumatic or other distressing events, just like memories of normal events, can be influenced by factors such as source amnesia.⁶⁴

---

59 Schudson (1995: 348).
60 See Engel (1999), Schacter (1996) and Antze and Lambek (1996) for discussions of the construction of the self through memory.
61 Schacter (1996: 87 and 112).
62 Schudson (1995: 349).
63 Wagenaar and Groeneweg (1988: 77).
64 Throughout the 1990s, an intense debate was conducted among psychologists about the validity of recovered memories of long-past events. Did these traumatic events indeed happen, or is it >

The influence of context and audience

The importance of the influence of *context* on memory has already been mentioned. Context can be understood as the general socio-political background of a country and a community, like past and current relations of power. Which group or individuals wielded power in the past and in the present, and in what way do they influence people's memories? Are some *Joyabatecos* afraid to remember past events because they implicate former civil patrol commanders who still play an important role in community affairs? Context can also be understood in the sense of the environment in which a memory is being retrieved and narrated. Who else is present during the retrieval moment, who is absent, does the conversation about past events take place in a public or a private place, and what exactly is the role and influence of, for instance, an interviewer who acts in many cases as a 'memory-trigger'? Pasupathi (2001) goes deeper into the role of audience during recall of memories, explaining that 'people tell events to their listener in ways they hope will engage and interest them, and listeners contribute their own insights and reactions to the retelling. Telling is a joint product of the speaker and the audience and thus influences the way we subsequently remember the told event'.[65]

People have numerous goals when recalling an event, and these goals may determine what they recall. They might want to impress their audience, present a positive self-image by minimizing their responsibility in past negative events,[66] or establish a relation of intimacy with the listener. Some things are left out because they are thought to be insignificant, distressing or socially undesirable. Engel (1999) stresses the importance of the *purpose* of the memory retrieval. For what purpose will the memory be used? Will the memory be used to create testimony of the violence for a truth commission, will it be used during trials of alleged perpetrators, or is the memory narrated during a therapy session?[67] Is the memory retrieved to satisfy the curiosity of a researcher who wants to know about the past,[68] or does the person narrating the memory see a possibility to present a certain picture of the past and thereby of himself or herself? These are

---

> possible for people to remember things they never really experienced, be it through suggestion, source amnesia or other forms of memory distortion? The most prominent proponent of the pliability of memory is the psychologist Elizabeth Loftus, who is often asked to testify as an expert witness in sexual-abuse cases during early childhood. She critiques some of the techniques used by psychoanalysts, such as hypnosis and visualization, which according to Loftus encourage patients to blur the line between imagination and memory. See Loftus and Ketcham (1994) and Pendergrast (1995) for an extensive discussion on the topic of false or repressed memories.

65 Pasupathi (2001: 651).
66 Ross and Buehler (1994: 215).
67 See Engel (1999) for an analysis of recalling memories in courtrooms and therapy rooms.
68 For example, my position as a person, not necessarily a researcher, interested in the civil war triggered and possibly influenced people's memories of that war.

important questions that readers of this book should bear in mind. Clearly, remembering is not an easy and straightforward process but fraught with intentions, expectations and perceptions.

Forgetting and denial

The process of storing and retrieving memories appears to be a complicated process, heavily influenced by context, cues, the role of the listener, the social acceptability of the memory and the process of narrating itself. A discussion of the concept of memory is, however, not complete without a discussion of the issues of forgetting and denial. Remembering implies forgetting. When people remember stories about the past, which are then told to a listener, there are also the memories that are not told, for whatever reason. Sometimes they are truly forgotten because they were not deemed significant enough to be stored, or they were thought insufficiently important to be told. Other memories are withheld because they do not fit the image the rememberer wants to present of himself or herself, or because they touch upon traumatic events which the narrator prefers to forget. In these cases it becomes very difficult to distinguish between genuine forgetting and conscious denial. This holds true especially for people who have been involved in violent incidents in the past, whether as perpetrators or as victims. For some of these people denial is one way of coping with their violent past.

According to Cohen (2001), who in his book *States of Denial* discusses in detail how denial works in case of atrocities and other war-related incidents, 'people, organizations, governments or whole societies are presented with information that is too disturbing, threatening or anomalous to be fully absorbed or openly acknowledged. The information is therefore somehow repressed, disavowed, pushed aside or reinterpreted. Or else the information "registers" well enough, but its implications ... are evaded, neutralized or rationalized'.[69] He touches upon denial at the state level, but also denial at a more personal level by perpetrators, bystanders and even victims. Boundaries between these groups are not as clear as is sometimes presented. The blurring of boundaries can be a *factual* process whereby perpetrators can actually become victims and vice versa. Claridge (1999/2000) notes the absence of clear boundaries between groups when commenting on Walter's model of the terror directorate and the agents of terror. The different roles people played, or were forced into playing, during the civil war and especially the blurring of these roles could account for the different memories people present of the civil war. However, the merging of roles and boundaries can also occur in the people's *perception* of the past. People who were

---

69 Cohen (2001: 1).

victims can feel guilty, while perpetrators can see themselves as victims. Remembering a civil patrol action as active participant, reluctant bystander or victim gives very different perspectives on things, and thus generates very different memories of what happened during such an action.

Cohen identifies three forms of denial used by perpetrators as well as bystanders: literal innocence, not-knowing and forgetting.[70] Literal innocence or literal denial means that the fact or knowledge of the fact is denied 'for whatever reason, in good or bad faith, and whether these claims are true (genuine ignorance), blatantly untrue (deliberate lies) or unconscious defense mechanisms'.[71] Such literal denials by perpetrators of what happened during, for example, genocide are difficult to sustain.[72] But they are, nonetheless, offered. The second, much more interesting, position is that of not-knowing. People who are reasonably expected to have known about some of the things that happened in their country use phrases such as 'I did not know' extensively. It implies denying what was going on at the time, although it is sometimes very difficult to believe such a statement in view of what people 'could have known, must have known, or should have known'.[73] Cohen divides the position of not-knowing by perpetrators into a denial of *responsibility*, denial of *knowledge* and *not having an enquiring mind*. Denying *responsibility* involved people claiming that their instructions had been misunderstood or that they never explicitly ordered anyone to be killed. Others denied any *knowledge* of what happened because they had never received information that people were actually killed. *Not having an enquiring mind* relates to those who claim not to have realized the importance of a certain event or not having had an overview of what was going on. Tasks were compartmentalized, people did not know to what end they were carrying out certain tasks and nobody around them knew what was going on.[74]

Let us now look at the third form of denial, forgetting, whereby Cohen distinguishes between two extremes: at one extreme is memory loss or amnesia, at the other extreme is the full-fledged lie. While people remember very well what their role was, for example, in a massacre, they deny it. 'There are infinite possibilities in between. Without them ... twentieth-century literature would not exist: the weaknesses and failures, the blank and blind spots of memory, but also its powers, conscious and unconscious, to create, invent, image and rearrange the past.'[75] This has been argued in the earlier sections on memory distortion during

---

70 Cohen (2001: 126).
71 Cohen (2001: 7).
72 See Huttenbach (1999) on denial of genocide in the cases of, among others, Armenia and the Holocaust.
73 Cohen (2001: 126). See also Hannah Arendt (1965) on her discussion of Eichmann's trial.
74 Cohen (2001: 126-129).
75 Cohen (2001: 130).

the storage and retrieval process. It will be instructive to see how mechanisms of forgetting and denial work in the Guatemalan context, and how different groups in society (victims, perpetrators, bystanders and possible combinations of all three groups) cope with the legacy of the civil war.

Collective memory, social memory or collected memories?
It may seem that, so far, I have mainly looked at personal or autobiographical memory, and how it is encoded, recalled and distorted. But memory is always a social act and never a purely individual one. Remembering is mostly done in relation to and with others, in a specific context and with a specific purpose.[76] Although 'Individuals remember in the literal, physical sense', it is 'social groups which determine what is "memorable" and also how it will be remembered'.[77] In this section I discuss the topic of collective memory, or social or cultural memory, as some prefer to call it. The concept of collective memory is often used in historical and anthropological research, and contrasted with individual or autobiographical memory, which is perceived as the territory of cognitive psychologists.[78] One of the first people to explore and introduce the concept of collective memory was the French sociologist Halbwachs in the 1920s. He argued that social groups construct memories, and it is these groups that determine what is memorable and how it will be remembered. Through collective memory a group of people maintain a shared identity through their lifetimes. Collective memory, according to Halbwachs, is thus the public representation of the past, in contrast with an individual or autobiographical memory, which is an individual representation of one's past.

However, there appears to be considerable overlap between individual and collective memory because people are simultaneously individuals and members of a community or a country. People do not remember in a social or political vacuum, but do so in a context in which specific knowledge about the past, norms and values play an important and influential role in memory. Fentress and Wickham agree that 'this distinction between personal memory and social memory is, at best, a relative one. Typically, our memories are mixed, possessing both a personal and a social aspect'.[79] When people narrate an individual memory, they also narrate information about common beliefs and memories within a community or even a society. Some memories are specific to a certain

---

76 I refer to remembering in an interview situation or recounting memories to someone else. However, sometimes memories just emerge spontaneously when one is alone.
77 Burke (1989: 98).
78 Fentress and Wickham (1992), Schudson (1995), Eidson (2000), Boyarin (1994), Burke (1989), Antze and Lambek (1996).
79 Fentress and Wickham (1992: 7).

group within a society or a community, while other memories have a more national scope. For example communities or groups within a community have their own historical memory of the past, which in some cases 'transcends the experience—and, hence, the "autobiographical" memory—of the individual members of the community'.[80]

The existence of different memories within one nation, or one community, often leads to a struggle over which memory of the past will be representative. Which one will be the officially sanctioned public memory? This is especially the case in countries emerging from a violent conflict, such as Guatemala, Argentina or South Africa. During a post-conflict period different versions of the past are presented and contested, both by those responsible for much of the violence and by victims and bystanders.[81] In many countries truth commissions are established and different groups in society struggle to get their representation of the past civil war recognized.[82] How does a government or a political elite want its country to be remembered? Which memory of the past will be authorized as the official past? What will be collected for the archives and what will be neglected and forgotten?[83] This, often political or ideological, struggle over memory also exists at the community level, where people played different roles during a civil war and want to remember it or to forget it. In the case of Joyabaj, not everybody was pleased when a forensic team came to exhume a mass grave behind the convent, because it was not a past they wanted to be reminded of. Which past does a community want to remember, and which past does it want to forget? People draw upon the past when defining themselves and thus their identity. This also holds for collective identities that often refer to a distant past.[84] Therefore, local struggles frequently break out over the question 'which past is to be representative', because it touches upon the very identity of the people.

---

80   Eidson (2000: 580).
81   The publication of Stoll's book *Rigoberta Menchú and the Story of All Poor Guatemalans* (1998) in which he questions several statements made in the book *I, Rigoberta Menchú* (1983) from Nobel Prize Laureate, Rigoberta Menchú, initiated an intense debate among social scientists and human rights activists, not only on the accuracy of Menchú's book as such, but also on the use of memory for political aims (Cohen, 2002).
82   See Teitel (2000) for a detailed analysis of the relationship between truth, official accounts of the past, and justice.
83   See Osiel (1997) on the influence of trials on collective memory.
84   See Gillis (1994) for a discussion of the relationship between memory and identity.

Data collection and methodology

The municipality of Joyabaj

The research took place in Joyabaj, a municipality[85] located in the southern part of the Quiché department. Why was the research carried out in this particular area? Initially, the two most important criteria were that the area should have been hit hard by civil war violence and that a large number of civil patrols should have been active. Especially in these more militarized areas, traditional local power structures seemed to have broken down or changed and new ones emerged after the end of the civil war. According to the CEH report, the mainly indigenous departments of Quiché, Huehuetenango and Alta Verapaz all fit these two criteria. According to official figures, Quiché was hardest hit with 344 massacres, followed by Huehuetenango with 89 massacres and Alta Verapaz with 62 massacres.[86]

A second reason to focus the research on Quiché was my contacts with the *Oficina de Paz y Reconciliación*, an organization that is part of the Catholic Church and that was, at the time of the research, actively involved in the exhumation of mass graves and other post-war reconciliatory practices in the Quiché department. The *Oficina de Paz y Reconciliación* was an important point of entry into the local communities in the Quiché department, helping me to locate a community and make first contacts with local Catholic dignitaries, and providing access to their network of contacts and information. But why choose to enter a community by way of the Catholic Church? In many other Latin American countries, the church had played a conservative role during many national conflicts, often siding with government or even military forces. However, the Catholic Church in Guatemala has played a very progressive role in the civil war, having lost many of its priests and catechists during the violence. The Catholic Church was also actively involved in human rights issues and presented its own truth commission report (the REMHI report) about the civil war. The Catholic Church also had an extensive network of local priests, nuns and catechists in the local communities, which could ease my entrance into the communities and help gain people's trust.

These criteria—that is, civil war violence, patrol activity and contacts in the area—were all present in the municipality of Joyabaj, located in the south of the

---

85 A municipality (*municipio*) is the smallest political unit in Guatemala, consisting of one large town called the *cabecera municipal* (municipal capital) and numerous smaller communities. Guatemala is divided into 22 departments (*departamentos*), which each consist of a number of municipalities. The department of Quiché consists of 21 municipalities, one of which is Joyabaj (FUNCEDE, 1995).

86 CEH, Vol. V (1999: 100-101).

Quiché department. I had already decided to focus on one municipality, mainly because of the sensitivity of the research topic. First of all, it would take a considerable time to reconstruct what had actually happened during and before the war, although I have already explained that reconstruction was not so simple and posed problems of its own. Second, an effort would have to be made to gain people's trust so that they would be willing to talk about the civil war, the civil patrols and local power relations. However, I chose not to limit myself to one small community because part of the research aimed to analyse the complexity of power relations in all its facets. A larger research area, such as a municipality, was necessary to observe relations and interaction between different actors like, for example, political parties, religious groups, community organizations, and different communities. I therefore decided on the middle-sized municipality of Joyabaj, consisting of a small municipal capital called Joyabaj surrounded by 60 or so small villages and hamlets scattered north and south of the municipal capital.[87]

Joyabaj is representative of many municipalities in the Guatemala highlands, with a largely indigenous population next to a ladino minority, the influence of evangelical churches next to the dominant Catholic Church, a significant annual migration to the sugar and coffee plantation on the southern coast, extensive commercial relations with other municipalities and a civil war history with a large presence of military, para-military and guerrilla forces in the area. These factors also make it a very complex municipality. The civil war had hit the municipality hard, resulting in numerous massacres and mass graves and heightened civil patrol activity. Some of the civil patrols in the area had been among the most violent in the southern Quiché department. Another important consideration that evoked my interest in Joyabaj was the fact that so little was known about the effects of the war in this area and that people were very reluctant to come forward with their stories about the atrocities that had been committed. Unlike other communities, Joyabaj had not yet requested the exhumation of mass graves, of which 12 were officially documented by the CEH and REMHI.[88] Another interesting feature of the municipality is that it is situated on the border between higher, colder grounds (*tierra fría*) in the north, where the mainly indigenous population produces maize and beans on small subsistence plots, and the warmer areas (*tierra caliente*) in the south, where commercially more profitable crops like sugar cane and vegetables are grown for the market by both ladinos

---

87 When discussing the municipal capital of Joyabaj, I use the terms 'town', 'urban area' or 'municipal capital'. For the settlements in the surrounding rural area I use the terms 'village', '(rural) community' or 'hamlet' (for the smallest unit). The populations of these rural communities differ considerably in size, ranging from 100 to 3,500 (FUNCEDE, 1995: 17-19).
88 CEH, Vol. X (1999) and ODHAG, Vol. II (1998: 43).

and *indígenas*. The municipal capital is situated between these two quite distinct areas, which do not only differ in their agricultural production, but whose inhabitants have experienced the civil war in very different ways. I will further explore and highlight some of these differences in the succeeding chapters, while also contrasting the political and economic centrality of the town of Joyabaj with the rural communities surrounding it.

Ethnic tension and racism

Ethnic relations in Joyabaj are exemplary for many of the rural communities in the Guatemalan highlands. The majority of the population (85 per cent) belongs to the largest indigenous group in Guatemala, the *K'iche'*, and mostly live in the rural communities. The ladinos (a significant minority of 15 per cent) mainly live in the municipal capital.[89] Relations between ladinos and *indígenas* were and still are unequal and strained, with little economic and political space for the indigenous majority to manoeuvre. Ethnicity clearly functions as a mechanism to exclude the indigenous population from full participation in society.[90] Although ladinos in Joyabaj have occupied most of the important political and economic positions in the town of Joyabaj since 1800, they have always felt threatened by the indigenous majority, resulting in sometimes open racism towards *indígenas*, who are often regarded as inferior.[91]

These racist attitudes sometimes complicated my relationship with people in Joyabaj. Although racism is not always open and people are cordial when meeting on the streets or during business negotiations, it surfaces quite innocently in many conversations. When I had my living quarters in the convent, ladinos asked me if I was not afraid to live there on my own. I said 'no', explaining that during the weekends and on market days indigenous people stayed in the building next door to the convent, which was used as sleeping quarters. 'But they are only *indios*', ladinos murmured, meaning that no ladinos lived nearby. Many such remarks cropped up in everyday conversations with ladinos, and it was sometimes difficult not to get entangled in endless arguments. I refrained from engaging too much in these discussions, because I wanted to be able to develop and

---

89 According to the FUNCEDE report (1995) the municipality of Joyabaj has around 53,000 inhabitants, of whom 10,000 live in the municipal capital and the rest in the surrounding rural areas (FUNCEDE, 1995: 16). The official figures of the government census 1994 give a somewhat different picture, with a population of around 34,000 inhabitants, of whom around 4,000 people live in the municipal capital and the rest in the surrounding areas (FUNCEDE, 1995: 16). Although it is impossible to know which figures approach reality more closely, I am inclined to agree with the FUNCEDE numbers, which are closer than the census figures to my own estimate at least of the number of inhabitants in the urban area.
90 Baud (1994: 50-51).
91 See Casaús (1998) and Arenas (1999) for an extensive discussion of racism in Guatemala.

maintain relations with both ladinos and *indígenas*. Ladinos seemed to regard me as a kind of fellow ladino, who was white and European and closer to them than to the indigenous population. Some of the more activist *indígenas* categorized me as just another white left-wing activist interested in the indigenous cause, while a large majority thought I was a North American nun. Often it felt as if these two groups lived in two different worlds, which were separated by language, dress, food, religious interpretation and the feeling of 'otherness' that seemed to exist on both sides. In many ways, however, ladinos and *indígenas* also depend on each other and multiple relations exist between them. Children meet in the schoolyard and become friends, parents do business together on the marketplace, see each other during mass or meet up during their migration adventures to the United States. Relations have improved, also because the indigenous majority has experienced more room to manoeuvre and improve its economic situation. This is not always to the liking of part of the ladino minority, which perceives its territory to be under threat.

Relations and tensions between the two ethnic groups surface in most of the chapters in this book, because the groups experienced and thus remembered the civil war violence in very different ways. However, when discussing relations between the indigenous and the ladino population one has to bear in mind that ethnic identity is not the only organizing principle in *Joyabateco* society. It is too simple to equate ladinos with right-wing politics and being pro-military, and it is also incorrect to associate the indigenous part of the population with left-wing politics or to regard them as pro-guerrilla. The reality was and is much more complex, with ladinos working as social promoters for leftist community organizations and indigenous leaders from right-wing MLN villages backing anti-guerrilla ladinos during the 1980s. Ethnicity (ladino-*indígena*), religion (Catholic, evangelical, *cofradías*), politics (right-wing/left-wing) and the economic situation (ladino elite, seasonal labourer) appear to influence the way in which people have experienced the civil war and currently look back on it.

Fieldwork in three stages
When arriving in Santa Cruz de Quiché (hereafter called Santa Cruz), the departmental capital of Quiché, I immediately contacted the *Oficina de Paz y Reconciliación* and requested help in establishing contacts to get the research going. I presented my research plan and had extensive discussions on what I could do in return for their help. I agreed to write short research papers in which I would present the most important findings. It took more than six weeks before my request for help passed through all stages of Catholic Church bureaucracy, and I received permission to start the research. Entering a community with the

open support of the Catholic Church meant that many doors were opened much more easily. The only bias during the first fieldwork period arose from the fact that I met more Catholics than people from other denominations, and it took a while to make contact with evangelicals and indigenous people connected with the *cofradías*.[92] Permission of the Catholic Church had to be followed by the approval of my project by the local priest in Joyabaj at that time, Padre Rudi Sem, who would be my first contact in the municipality. It was important for me that he should be enthusiastic about the research, and not feel obliged to help me because he had been ordered from higher up the Catholic hierarchy to do so. The priest proved to be crucial during the initial phase of the fieldwork, providing many of my first contacts with both ladinos and *indígenas* and paving my way into the rural communities.

During the first fieldwork period (January–September 1998) I concentrated on obtaining a rough overview of the municipality and its different power players, making an inventory of women's groups, religious groups, indigenous organizations, NGOs and political parties. I visited surrounding villages and hamlets, accompanying the priest when giving mass or a schoolteacher on his or her way to work. I came across enormous differences between the communities in terms of economic and political activity and awareness, but also in people's openness about the recent civil war. Clearly, communities and their inhabitants experienced the war and civil patrol activity very differently, which influenced their willingness and readiness to talk about such topics. As well as the inventory of groups and different communities I focused on reconstructing the events that took place in Joyabaj during and after the civil war. I tried to get information on factual questions such as: when did the military come to Joyabaj, what was the role of the guerrilla movement in the Joyabaj area, in short, what exactly happened in Joyabaj during the civil war? During open interviews, using topic lists, I generally started to ask about the period before the civil war (1950–75). Often, the civil war would automatically enter the picture, because people themselves started talking about it. I left the initiative to them during these first contacts. Once I was talking to an older ladino man, whom I had met only once before. He ushered me into his house, whereas during the former conversation we had sat outside on his cool and shady veranda. It soon became clear why he preferred the stuffy surroundings indoors, because after five minutes of casual talk he embarked on a detailed and sometimes gruelling story of a massacre in which he and most other ladinos from town had been forced to participate while serving in the civil patrols. People were sometimes only too happy to talk about these incidents to someone like me, whom they considered to be an innocent outsider.

---

92 Indigenous brotherhoods.

Apart from open interviews, information was derived from several archival sources, such as the municipal archives,[93] the local church archives[94] and the archives in the *Archivo Centroamericano* in Guatemala City, which included old and more recent newspaper articles and papers about landownership. This last archive also included several boxes containing unsorted documents from the municipality of Joyabaj dating back as early as 1880. Although this era was somewhat beyond the scope of my research topic, it contained a wealth of data on ladino families in the early twentieth century and also on ladino-indigenous relationship during that period. Many files mentioned military activity during that time, giving some insight into local militarization and the role of the state. Other sources of information were the large number of publications on human rights abuses from national and international human rights organizations, in which several cases from Joyabaj were mentioned.[95] This enabled me to verify or disprove some of the information gathered through interviewing, although written documents are not necessarily free from censorship and distortion.

I spend six months back home, organizing and analysing the first data. Because of the multiplicity of sources I started to focus my attention more and more on the enormous diversity of stories about the past. Some stories contradicted one another outright, while others differed only in detail. For example, was a certain newspaper story genuinely observed by a reporter, was it censored by military intelligence, was it a public relations stunt by the military or was it meant to spread misinformation? This also applied to other material, even the interviews I had conducted with numerous people in and outside Joyabaj.

The second fieldwork period (April–November 1999) focused much more on particular groups within the community which had played important roles before, during and possibly after the civil war. Contacts with leftist political groups and former guerrilla combatants were established and the topic of civil patrol violence was now openly discussed during interviews with certain individuals. The interviews were more formal and I took much more initiative in broaching sensitive subjects like civil patrol violence. I had gathered enough information during my first stay to know roughly what had happened in Joyabaj during and after the civil war, although I had also realized the problems of trying to reconstruct such a history. I knew what the sensitive topics were for certain groups and individuals and with whom I could and could not talk to about these topics. Aside from interviews with individuals I also started to conduct

---

93 These included the minutes of the meetings of the different municipal governments from 1923 onwards, and the municipal records on deaths and marriages.
94 These consisted of the archives registering birth and marriages, from which I obtained an overview of when the first ladino families arrived in the municipality and who these families were.
95 See for example Jay (1993), ODHAG (1993), Solomon (1994) and Human Rights Watch (1994).

group interviews, often at the request of the people themselves. *Indígenas* from the rural communities in particular seemed to feel more comfortable in talking with me as a group, especially during the first contacts. Later on during the research they also started visiting my house on their own. Group interviews also had a practical side to them, because it often happened that I interviewed people of political parties or other community organizations after their weekly or monthly meeting. Many of them lived in different communities scattered throughout the municipality, and it would have taken me days to interview them individually in their own community. Of course, interviewing several individuals at the same time did influence the data that was gathered, because several people together tried to reconstruct part of a common past. People filled gaps in the stories of others, asked each other questions and even started discussing conflicting views on certain events among themselves. However, many individual stories were told during such sessions, which were considered private by the other people participating in the group interview.

During this second period I also tried to put what had happened during the civil war in a more historical perspective. Although I had done extensive archival research at the local municipality and in newspaper archives, I had not yet tried to paint an extensive picture of Joyabaj from before the 1970s. A lot of interesting material came out of this approach, enabling me to understand much better why the war had such diverse effects on the different communities, and why it was experienced so differently by different groups in *Joyabateco* society. Other important sources of information were the archives of the *Procuraderia de Derechos Humanos* (PDH)[96] and the REMHI project. Since the opening of the PDH office in Santa Cruz in 1989, people from all over southern Quiché had come to denounce human rights abuses. After a lot of red tape I got permission to analyse the statements denouncing human rights abuses in Joyabaj, thereby gaining much better insight into recent conflicts in the area (since 1989), which persons had been involved and how these conflicts were possibly connected to the civil war. The REMHI files were opened for me after a formal introduction of the *Oficina de Paz y Reconciliación*. These files consisted of very personal testimonies of *Joyabatecos* about the loss of family and friends during the violence of the 1980s. These were some of the many thousands of testimonies gathered by the Catholic Church throughout Guatemala, which formed the basis of the final REMHI report.

In May and June 2001 I went back a third time, after I had finished writing most chapters of the book while back in the Netherlands. I wanted to check details, fill in some gaps in the interview material and look for visual material. It

---

96 Human Rights Ombudsman.

turned out that a number of local photographers had an extensive collection of photographs from the 1980s and 1990s, including of civil patrol rallies, military checkpoints and other interesting events. Although it took a lot of patience and time going through literally thousands of negatives, I gathered quite a number of pictures of Joyabaj's history in the 1980s and 1990s. During these two months I also conducted a large number of interviews with specific persons. I knew exactly whom I wanted to speak to, on which topics, and what I wanted to verify or find out. One group that had been more difficult to reach, probably because of my initial contacts through the Catholic Church, was the evangelical community. I therefore devoted part of my time to interviewing evangelical leaders, some of whom said that they were glad they could also participate in my research, about which they had heard from others. 'Why did you not come sooner?', one ladino leader asked me, 'Now you only have so little time left and we have so much to say'.[97] They had never thought of approaching me.

During these three periods I conducted about 90 in-depth interviews with ladino and indigenous men and women in Joyabaj, aside from numerous informal conversations. Without giving a complete overview of my informants, since I do not want to identify most of them by name for security reasons, I do want to sketch the diversity among the people I interviewed. I talked to former mayors, municipal officials of both the ladino and the indigenous municipality (*alcaldía indígena*), former and current NGO personnel, teachers, former school directors and teachers, people involved in right-wing politics, former guerrilla combatants, housewives, large store-owners, former estate owners, Maya activists, and former civil patrol commanders and rank-and-file patrol members. I also interviewed several priests who had worked in Joyabaj, and numerous *indígenas* and ladinos who were active in the Catholic Church, as well as leaders from evangelical churches.

Although the research focused on male institutions like the municipality, the civil patrols and other male bastions of power, I had a lot of contact with women, several of whom I interviewed about the *La Violencia*. We talked about their experiences with and memories of civil patrol violence and their current life. Conavigua, a national organization of war widows (almost exclusively indigenous), also had a section in Joyabaj and through them I interviewed several of their members. Some of these women were involved in local politics, running for council member for the *Unidad Revolucionaria Nacional Guatemalteca* (URNG),[98] the former guerrillas organization that had turned into an official political party. Another group of women I often talked to were those involved in

---

97 Interview 6-01 (11/5/01).
98 Guatemalan National Revolutionary Unity.

Catholic Church work. This included the weekly Bible study groups of ladino women in the town, called *comunidades*, and also the indigenous women who were involved in Catholic Church activities in their own communities, sometimes acting as vice-president or secretary of their local *Junta Directiva*.[99]

The fact that I did not master the local language, *K'iche'*, somewhat hampered my contacts with indigenous women. Although I took private lessons in Joyabaj, I mastered only some formal greetings, an initial question and a whole range of single words. I never became fluent enough to conduct interviews on my own. To be able to do that, I should have had to devote at least six months solely to learning the language, something that was not possible. My very limited knowledge did help me, however, to catch the general flow of a discussion, so I was able to ask someone to translate specific parts of the conversation. When interviewing indigenous women who spoke only *K'iche'*, I worked with a translator, an indigenous woman who was literate in both Spanish and *K'iche'*. She not only translated but was also considered a trusted person in both the indigenous and the ladino communities. Whether her translation was accurate was another matter altogether, especially because she was not an experienced translator, and translating group interviews during which several people speak at the same time is a difficult task in any language. Unfortunately, my sparse knowledge of *K'iche'* meant that I was never able to really chat with these women when meeting them at the market, in their village or during Sunday market. When we met, we both uttered our few words of Spanish and *K'iche'*, smiling and hugging and trying to explain that it was such a pity we could not communicate with each other. The only way to communicate was by food, which was therefore bestowed upon me in large quantities. Fortunately, most of the indigenous men and a number of indigenous women in Joyabaj did in fact speak Spanish as a second language, so that I could conduct most of the interviews myself.

My role in the community

Initially, people identified me with the Catholic Church, and this could mean only that I was an American nun coming to work in the communities. This image was enhanced by the fact that I lived in the nun's convent during the first few weeks of my stay in Joyabaj, before finding my own place to live. The convent had been empty for some years, and people liked the fact that someone was living there again. Although I had all this space for myself, I did not feel very

---

99 *Junta Directiva* refers to the local leaders (*directiva* – directive) of Catholic Action *(Acion Católica)* who are elected every two years by the people from their community. They are responsible for the upkeep of the church, preparations for when the priest comes to say mass and in general for the smooth running of Catholic Church activities in their community. It is an honorary position, and therefore difficult to refuse.

comfortable, especially after I heard the first tales about military occupation of the convent during the civil war. The military had used it as their military compound, questioning and torturing civilians who were thought to be subversive. The ravine at the back of the convent had served as a mass grave for those who never left the compound after being taken prisoner. At the end of my second fieldwork period a flood did indeed uncover numerous human bones, and an exhumation team was brought in.[100]

To anyone interested, I presented myself as a researcher or an anthropologist working on a history of Joyabaj. Only after I got to know a person well, and knew what his or her background was, was I more open about my research. After discussions with the local priest and others working in southern Quiché, I decided that this was the safest approach. On hearing that I was an anthropologist, people wondered whether I had come to dig up bones, since the only anthropologists they knew were forensic ones working in the exhumation teams. It never got me into trouble, and in some cases such a question was the beginning of an interesting conversation. Because of my contacts with so many different groups in *Joyabateco* society I was constantly changing roles: fitting into what ladino Catholics expected of me (going to church on Sunday), what indigenous left-wing activists expected of me (letting the world know what terrible things happened in Joyabaj during the war), what right-wing politicians thought of me (another one of these human rights activists who only come to write bad things about us), or what people on the streets thought of me (another white nun or NGO worker). The people I interviewed seemed to perceive me as less of a threat because I was a young female researcher. This helped me gain access to the different groups. Even older men who had occupied important posts in several local political or municipal organizations were willing to talk, although they did not always take me very seriously, which was an advantage in terms of access to information. Initially, some men and women were quite protective of me, warning me not to talk to a certain patrol commander or not to wander off alone into the communities to conduct interviews. Although they realized that I listened respectfully to them but did not necessarily obey, they never stopped giving advice as they would to their grown-up daughter. I was generally thought to be a little over 20 or so years old because I wore my hair in pigtails, wore pants and I did not have any children.

For many people it was difficult to talk about the civil war and about their experiences during that war, but only a few people refused to talk to me, although they never said so outright. They maintained that I was very welcome to talk to them and that they had a lot to tell me. However, when I showed up on their

---

100 See Chapters 6 and 7 for a detailed account of this event and peoples' reactions to it.

doorsteps they backed out, ever so gracefully, saying that there was no time, that their son had the flu, or that the rain had flooded their yard. I never pushed people into talking to me, knowing that there would always remain untold stories in Joyabaj, as always when anthropologists do fieldwork. Some people were just not interested, too afraid to tell their story because they were too traumatized, afraid of the consequences of talking to me, or thought I might use the information for other purposes, such as trials or intelligence work. One indigenous man who was also a left-wing activist told me that, when he and his group were first introduced to me, they had joked among themselves that I must be working for the CIA. They agreed to talk to me only because I was introduced by the proper person who could be absolutely trusted.

After the initial barriers came down, most people were quite willing to talk about the past, opening up more and more as the fieldwork progressed. Some of the people I interviewed told me afterwards that they felt relieved about telling their story, although their memories also made them sad. One man said after a two-hour interview, during which he described in detail how he had lost several members of his family, that 'It was good and necessary to get it out of my heart, because it has been there too long. It is a relief, but it also hurts. Thank you'.[101] It was difficult to listen to the sometimes very personal and horrible stories people poured out on me. In such situations one stops being the objective listener who loosely sympathizes with his or her informant. Feelings of unease and helplessness surface, although it is often enough just to listen. The situation became even more complicated when I started interviewing people who had been active in the patrols and directly involved in the atrocities committed. I found it sometimes difficult to listen to their views on the past, in which they often portrayed their own role very differently from what I had read in human rights reports or heard from other villagers. Although I wanted to hear 'their side of the story', I was continuously looking for holes in it to prove them wrong. Although I did not confront people with gaps or discrepancies in their stories during the interviews, since I did not feel safe enough to do so, I always checked these stories more thoroughly than I would normally have done with my interviews. Besides, conducting a group interview in the morning with six indigenous widows who all lost family members during the civil war, then conducting an interview in the afternoon with one of the most notorious patrol commanders in the area, stretched my chameleon capabilities to their limit.

---

101 Interview 20-99 (5/7/99).

Safety in a violent society
Safety, my own as well as that of the people I interviewed, was an important issue throughout the research. Already, during preparations for the first fieldwork period, the questions raised by colleagues when discussing the research were geared towards this topic. Researching the legacy of civil war violence, focusing in Guatemala on the activities of civil defence patrols, is not without risk. Although the civil patrols were dismantled as a structure just before the peace agreement was signed in December 1996, this did not automatically mean that, for example, patrol commanders or patrollers laid down their arms and became quiet citizens. Although most people were glad that they did not have to patrol and carry weapons any more, some people who had occupied important positions within the patrols were not happy to lose their positions of influence. Before my departure for fieldwork in 1998 it was clear from the many newspaper articles and human rights reports on the sometimes violent activities of former patrollers that not everything had quietened down yet. A recent incident, which called close to home, involved threats (by persons probably connected to the government or the military) made against Matilde Gonzalez in October 2001. She is a Guatemalan social scientist working at AVANCSO,[102] a research institute in Guatemala City, who had just finished writing a book on civil war violence in another municipality in the Quiché department. Whenever I was in Guatemala we would discuss our work together, looking for similarities and differences in the municipalities we were working in. She went into hiding for a short time, and her case was picked up by Amnesty International. The harassment was clearly research-related and acted as a reminded to me of the real dangers involved in doing research on such a sensitive topic.[103]

The safety of the people I talked to was an even more important concern of mine because many people perceived the civil war to be a dangerous topic to talk about. I never pushed when people did not want to talk about the war or violent events they had witnessed as patrollers, patrol commanders or victims. During the first fieldwork period I let people themselves come up with the issues of patrols or the civil war and was almost never the one to introduce the topic into a conversation or an interview. Only after people themselves opened up about it did I explore the topic. During the second fieldwork period things were somewhat different, and I took more initiative in talking about violent events and other sensitive topics. This was possible because I had more of an overview of

---

102 *Asociación para el Avance de las Ciencias Sociales en Guatemala*/ Association for the Advancement of Social Sciences in Guatemala.
103 For more information on the case see the following two websites:
htttp://www.cimacnoticias.com/noticias/01oct/01102004.html and
http://www.aprodeh.org.pe/ridhualc/apoyo/ap_58.htm.

whom I was talking to, and which topics to broach and which not. I mostly talked to persons in the privacy of their own homes, their workplaces or my own home.

Most of the interviews were not tape-recorded. Most people did not want to talk with a tape recorder running because of the sensitivity of the topics discussed. They were afraid other people would gain access to the material and use it to their advantage. Some people I interviewed were convinced that military intelligence was still actively gathering material on people considered suspect, writing everything down in the military archives. But I could note everything down on paper, which I did fervently. I typed up my notes as soon as possible. Therefore most of the quotes from conversations with people are short, consisting of only one or two sentences. I was extremely careful about access to my computer. Apart from several passwords, to gain access to several layers of information I stored disks and hard copies in several secure places in Guatemala. I also took precautions while travelling, letting people in Joyabaj know where I was going and when they could expect me back, to create some sort of safety net. I also did this when conducting interviews in the more remote communities north or south of Joyabaj or when I went to interview a local patrol commander or other individuals who were well known for their pro-military attitude.

Apart from civil patrols and their legacy, political and especially criminal violence was and still is an enormous problem in Guatemala.[104] Mechanisms of negotiation hardly exist, which means that in many instances people resort to violent solutions to problems. During the civil war most problems were solved by violence, thereby creating a culture of intolerance, which continued after the peace agreement was signed. This is a common phenomenon in states in a post-war transition process, such as El Salvador and South Africa. Throughout Guatemala conflicts erupt frequently over such diverse but for many people crucial issues as land, natural resources, local politics, labour issues, public services and resettlement of refugees. A clear example of the solving of local problems by violent means is the enormous increase in the number of lynchings in Guatemala since the signing of the peace agreement in 1996. MINUGUA registered 337 lynchings between January 1996 and December 2000, most of which occurred in the western highlands of Guatemala.[105] These were also the departments that were hit hardest during the civil war. In most lynching cases presumed delinquents were caught and subsequently killed by a group of angry locals, using machetes, sticks and gasoline to burn their victims alive. Of course, two decades of state terror, including the forced formation of civil patrols and the

---

104 See for example reports from MINUGUA (2001) and Amnesty International (2002).
105 MINUGUA (2000a).

destruction of community networks, did have disastrous effects on rural communities and their way of dealing with crime, and of course former state agents were involved in several of the lynchings. However, the picture is more complex, according to Snodgras (2000). Lynchings can also be seen as a local answer to the increasing number of violent incidents in the countryside and the incapacity and/or unwillingness of the proper authorities to deal with these situations. The security situation had not improved much after the peace agreement was signed in 1996. Organized crime was on the rise and the number of youth gangs, organized crime groups, and other violent incidents multiplied. Politically motivated crimes dwindled, making way for large-scale bus robberies and the kidnapping and killing of wealthy Guatemalans. This situation was aggravated by the numbers of former military and security personnel, former civil patrol commanders and ex-combatants, who all had to find other ways of making a living after the peace was signed in December 1996. The military was reduced in size, the police reorganized and the guerrillas reintegrated in society. But some of these people had lived off their guns for the last decade or two, and were not always willing to give up their way of life.

Organization of the book

I have chosen to present the material I gathered during this research in chronological order, starting the story in 1750 and finishing in 2002. This appeared to be the most logical way to order the material, in view of the fact that I have studied the influence of civil defence patrols at the local level, looking at the period before, during and after the civil war. I will start each chapter with a short overview of important *national* events during that particular time frame, because national, regional and local events influence each other and do not represent separate topics to be dealt with independently. Chapter 2 deals with the period 1750–1978, and sketches a historical background of Joyabaj. It encompasses several Liberal dictatorships, followed by two democratic presidents and the subsequent takeover of a democratically elected government by anti-communist forces in 1954. This coup heralded a renewed military dictatorship and the beginning of a 36-year civil war between guerrilla forces and the military and government forces. The chapter sketches local power relations in Joyabaj, identifying the different actors, and analysing the different relationships between them. Group boundaries along ethnic (ladino/*indígena*), religious (Catholic, evangelical, *cofradías*), political (right-wing/left-wing) or economic (ladino monopoly) lines, or a combination thereof, will be made explicit. Chapter 3 starts in 1978, when tensions are building between the different groups in society, especially between guerrilla groups on the one hand and the military, aided by paramilitary death squads and other intelligence personnel, on the other hand. The violence reaches its peak during 1980 and 1981, when numerous villages are burnt to the ground, several massacres occur and local NGOs and the progressive Catholic Church has to leave the area. During these years local power relations change radically, due to the violent campaigns of the military and the establishment of the civil patrols. Local politics are in a vacuum and the economic monopoly of the ladino elite collapses. Chapter 4 starts in 1982, when military violence becomes more organized under the rule of General Ríos Montt. It gives a detailed analysis of the civil patrol system in Joyabaj, and its diverse and often violent role in local society. Subsequently, the chapter follows the preparations for the first democratic elections, which were held in 1985. Chapter 5 analyses the effects of the democratic elections in 1985, such as re-emerging community life and a returning Catholic Church. Central to this chapter are growing anti-civil patrol sentiments, fuelled by upcoming popular organizations. Chapter 6 follows the peace process, which starts around 1994 and is finalized in December 1996 with the signing of the final peace agreement. It describes how the patrols have been officially dismantled, although threats to reorganize remain. It also looks at how local economic and political power relations have changed since the end of the civil war. Both areas have opened up considerably in the last five to ten years, although it is not always safe to take advantage of these openings. Chapter 7 focuses on the same period as Chapter 6 (1994–2001), but has a more thematic approach. It looks at the different initiatives, at the national as well as at the local level, that have been taken by the Catholic Church and the Guatemalan government to deal with the violent legacy of the civil war. Dealing with the past at the local level can differ greatly from the way the national government prefers to deal with it. Therefore, several local initiatives, such as commemorations, processions and truth commission reports, and the way local people look at these initiatives, are discussed. Finally, Chapter 8 draws together the most important discussion points raised in the introduction and throughout the various chapters.

2

Conflict and factionalism

(1750-1978)

This chapter provides a historical overview of how power relations evolved in Joyabaj from the late seventeenth century until the outbreak of the civil war and the subsequent installation of civil defence patrols. It not only examines the unequal social relations between ladinos and the indigenous population, but also provides insight into the religious, political and other divisions within both groups. These differences and divisions seemed to influence behaviour and activities of people during the civil war period, which will be the focus of Chapter 3.

The chapter starts with the ladino minority in Joyabaj, explaining how they attained their position of wealth and power amidst an indigenous majority. It follows the initial stages of ladino settlement through the acquisition of land from the middle of the nineteenth century onwards, until they occupied not only most of the important economic but also political positions in town. In 1944 the democratic and populist governments of President Juan José Arévalo (1944–51) and Jacobo Arbenz (1951–54) took over power after several decades of Liberal dictatorship under Presidents Barrios and Ubico. Political conflict and factionalism within the ladino community of Joyabaj became more pronounced; and part of the indigenous population started spreading its wings, becoming increasingly organized through the involvement of the Catholic Church, political parties and other communal organizations. Arbenz was ousted from the presidential palace through a CIA-backed coup in 1954, and the anti-communist Castillo Armas took his place. During this period anti-communist legislation was being prepared, blacklists of communist drawn up and the ultra-right wing and anti-communist political party *Movimiento de Liberación Nacional* (MLN)[1] was set up. The chapter then follows the ladinos into the 1960s and the 1970s, when their control over local politics and economic resources started to diminish.[2]

We then turn our attention to the indigenous majority in Joyabaj, which had been experiencing major changes since the 1950s. Religious divisions started surfacing when the Catholic Church intensified its work in the rural areas by way of its Catholic Action (AC, *Acción Católica*) programme. Initially, this lay catechist

---

1 Movement of National Liberation.
2 Thanks to stimulating conversations with Elizabeth Oglesby and Diane Nelson, I was able to put my fieldwork in a more historical perspective.

movement was a response to the radicalization of national politics under Presidents Arévalo and Arbenz, and initially intended to reestablish orthodox Catholicism in the countryside. This anti-communist vision changed in the late 1960s, when the Catholic Church became much more involved in development projects, and priests were influenced by liberation theology. From that period onwards the Catholic Church became a progressive force in Guatemalan society, and became the object of military violence during the civil war in the 1970s and 1980s.

Apart from religious frictions, political factions were created when part of the indigenous population continued to ally themselves with right-wing ladino politicians belonging to, for example, the MLN, while others opted for more progressive parties, such as the *Demócracia Christiana Guatemalteca* (DCG).[3] The work of the Catholic Church, political parties and development organizations also enhanced the organization and awareness of the political and economic situation in Guatemala among part of the indigenous population. Many of these people got involved in development organizations or in the building of churches or schools, or attained positions on different committees.

The chapter ends with the aftermath of the earthquake of 1976, which destroyed the town of Joyabaj and damaged many surrounding hamlets. The influx of national and international organizations after the earthquake had a profound impact on local power relations, resulting in the emergence of new, often indigenous, leadership. In this hectic period the first rumours surface concerning guerrilla activity in the area, and the first threats are made against so-called *subversivos* (guerrillas), implicating NGO personnel and local activists.

Ladinos acquiring indigenous land
The first ladinos settled down in Joyabaj in the middle of the eighteenth century, although the law forbade ladinos to settle in a *pueblo de indio* (corporate Indian town), such as Joyabaj, in order to protect the indigenous communities from ladino encroachment. The town, Santa María Xoyabah, which had been a *pueblo de indio* since 1549, was attractive to ladinos because of the relative short distance from the capital to Joyabaj and its good cattle lands. According to Cabezas Carcache (1995), the opportunity to rear cattle was an important reason for the appropriation of indigenous lands by ladinos. Ladinos would allow their cattle to roam free, destroying the crops of indigenous owners in the process, after which ladinos would claim that the land was not being used and request the government to sell it to them.[4] Cattle rearing became a major economic enter-

---

3   Christian Democratic Party.
4   Cabezas Carcache (1995: 285).

prise in Quiché between 1770 and 1820, and was originally started by the Dominican order.[5]

Liberal President Barrios, who came to power in 1871, emphasized clear measurements and legally recognized and registered titles. The Liberals clearly preferred private property rights, although they also recognized communal rights to an *ejido* or communal village grounds.[6] The indigenous communities started to seek titles from the state for these common lands, to the extent that they had not already done so in previous decades. The indigenous community (*común indígena*) in Joyabaj had already titled its land around 1750, thereby acquiring one of the largest *composiciones*[7] in the Province of Guatemala at that time (243 *caballerías*).[8] However, as a result of one of several Liberal governmental decrees,[9] between 1892 and 1894 a large part of their communal land (34 of the roughly 60 *caballerías*) was expropriated and divided among individual owners, including a large number of ladinos.[10] The amount of land to be allocated to any one person was limited to 20 *manzanas*.[11] However, ladinos and *indígenas* were able to purchase much more; for example, Juan Rodríguez received a total of 167 *manzanas* in 1893, and acquired more in succeeding years by buying land titles given out to indigenous people.[12] In 1920 he sold most of his land to the Ogáldez family, which arrived in Joyabaj around 1850 as relative newcomers. A member of the Ogáldez family explained these land sales thus: '*Indígenas* are interested in working instead of owning [the land], the ladinos like to own it.'[13] An additional point is that, through the illegal sale of *cusha* (alcohol made from sugar cane) by ladinos to the indigenous population, many *indígenas* became indebted to the ladinos and lost their land.

Thus the ladinos who arrived in Joyabaj in the middle of the eighteenth century, whether as traders or to recruit labour, bought or otherwise acquired large amounts of land in the area in which cattle were reared, marketable crops like

---

5 Remesal (1620) in: Instituto Geográfico Nacional (1978: 436). Especially the Dominican order was a dominant economic force in the western highlands in the seventeenth and eighteenth centuries (Piel, 1989 : 253-256 and McCreery, 1994: 45).
6 McCreery (1994: 238-239).
7 Regularization of land possession with the state.
8 Map of Joyabaj (1750). See also Cabezas Carcache (1995: 282). One *caballería* equals approximately 66 *manzanas* (or 112 acres). One *manzana* is approximately 1.75 acres.
9 *Acuerdo Gubernativo* 28/4/1892 (AGST, paq. 26, exp. 6, Pueblo de Joyabaj: Ejidos).
10 AGST, paq. 26, exp.6, Pueblo de Joyabaj: Ejidos (25 Julio 1912) and *Plano de le medida del ejido de Joyabaj* (1912) and personal archive of an anonymous *Jojabateco*. See McCreery (1994: 182-184) for an overview of the Liberal's Land Laws, including the *desamortización* (nationalization) of all church property, which was ordered by Barrios in 1873.
11 One manzana is approximately 1.75 acres.
12 *Archivo del Municipio de Joyabaj* (*AMJ*), sent to the *Archivo General de Centro América* (*AGCA*). It contains six unsorted parcels (1870–40) and personal archives of an anonymous *Jojabateco*.
13 Interview 43-99 (24/9/99).

sugar cane were grown, and indigenous people lived and worked as *rancheros*.[14] The indigenous population held on to some of the land in the villages north of Joyabaj, where people still owned their small subsistence plots, and to a sizeable part of the communal grounds surrounding the municipal capital.

A divided ladino population

According to a very popular story among ladino elders, the Méndez family was the first ladino family to settle in Joyabaj. Supposedly, Pedro Méndez was an organist who came regularly with the priest to Joyabaj to play during sermon. However, in the church archives of Joyabaj, the first ladino names (Peña and Mota) appear around 1786, several decades before the first Méndez is mentioned.[15] Several ladinos explained that the Méndez were regarded as the first ladinos to settle in Joyabaj because they were considered a literate, educated and musical family; they were '*profesionales*',[16] whereas the Peña's and the Mota's were considered illiterate farmers deriving a meagre living from the countryside alongside their indigenous neighbours. Legend also has it that Pedro Méndez, who knew much about medicinal plants, cured several sick indigenous people in Joyabaj. Presumably out of appreciation for his good deeds, Pedro received large tracts of land surrounding the central square from the indigenous community.[17] Although this story could very well be true, ladinos hardly ever mention the other legal and illegal ways their forefathers acquired land in Joyabaj.

During the more than two centuries of ladino settlement in Joyabaj, different groups within the ladino population used to be separated rigidly from one another. First of all, the ladinos themselves distinguished between *la gente buena*[18] (the good people) and 'bad people, of a lesser category'.[19] *La gente buena* referred to the first ladino families who arrived in Joyabaj and made their fortune through land and hard work. The Méndez, the Alvarado and also the Ogáldez family, who arrived somewhat later, were included in this group. The other group consisted of ladinos who came to Joyabaj in a later period, making money from trade, for example the transportation business. In the 1950s the differences between the two groups were still clearly visible because *la gente buena* lived on the main streets leading to the central town square and on the town square itself (*barrio central*), while the other group lived in more remote neighbourhoods.[20] The

---

14 *Rancheros* is a term used in Joyabaj to refer to people (mostly *indígenas*) who live and work on the land of someone else, in exchange for part of the crop.
15 *Libro de Bautizos* (1792) and *Libro de Confirmaciones* (1786).
16 Interview 43-99 (24/9/99).
17 Interview 42-99 (25/7/99) and interview 19-99 (22/5/99).
18 Diary 9/8/99.
19 Adams (1964: 254).
20 *Barrio La Libertad* and *Barrio La Democrácia*.

town square was the economic and political centre of town, where the ladino and indigenous municipalities were situated, as well as the jail, church, parish house, convent, big stores, and the first school. Living close to the centre enhanced a family's status. Obviously, intermarriage and relationships of mutual dependence through trade or political affiliation created alliances between the two groups. Therefore, nowadays the difference is much less obvious and the words *la gente buena* crop up only in references to ladinos 'from the first hour'.[21] Traces of the initial distinction between the two groups can still be found in the residential pattern today, as the more prominent ladino families still live close to the centre, and newcomers, whether indigenous or ladino, have houses further away. However, the earthquake of 1976, which destroyed the town entirely, and the violence of the 1980s contributed to a more diverse settlement pattern, as a result of which indigenous people nowadays also own houses and stores around the central town square.

A second distinction was made between ladinos who lived in the rural areas surrounding Joyabaj, owning small plots of land sufficient to subsist on, and the urban ladinos. Ladinos in the rural areas were, and sometimes still are, often referred to by ladinos from the town as *los del monte* (the ones from the mountain), a phrase with a negative connotation that is also used for the indigenous population in the rural areas. Like most of the indigenous population, many were illiterate, had never been to school and were not listed as voters. Rural ladinos did not automatically benefit from ladino control of municipal politics. Many ladinos who did not have close relationships with powerful ladino families in the municipal capital were excluded from positions of influence. One of the few advantages of being ladino in the rural areas was that one was free from labour, tax and other obligations to which the indigenous was subject.[22]

From around 1880 onward, economic power in Joyabaj became more and more concentrated in the hands of a small group of wealthy ladino families who had been steadily acquiring land and had monopolized most of the important economic activities. They controlled land, labour, trading facilities and community resources. Apart from owning the most fertile land south of the municipal capital, which was suitable for growing the sugar cane from which *cusha* (alcohol) was made, they owned the local stores, providing the town and the surrounding rural areas with food supplies, household goods, building material and agrarian supplies such as fertilizer and chemicals. They also controlled the transportation of goods and people by owning virtually all the buses and trucks and the only gas-station in the area.

---

21 Diary 9/8/99.
22 Piel (1995: 32).

Many ladinos also worked as labour contractors (*contratista*) and organized the yearly migration of indigenous labourers and their families to the coffee and sugar estates on the south coast.[23] One of the large local contractors was the administrator of the Chuacorral estate south of Joyabaj, which was a so-called *finca de mozos*.[24] Chuacorral was owned by the Herrera family, one of the largest plantation owners in Guatemala. They had several labour plantations, especially in the highlands, which provided the labourers they needed on their coffee and sugar estates in the south. The Chuacorral administrator made good money from labour contracting. According to some sources, he was paid 10 *centavos* per day per labourer. On average about 1,500 to 2000 labourers from the Chuacorral estate went to work on the coast for periods of two months. This meant that the Chuacorral administrator earned an income around 35,000 *Quetzales* a year, an incredible sum in those days.[25]

Together, a few wealthy ladino families formed a powerful group that almost entirely precluded other people, notably indigenous people, from going into business or expanding their economic horizons. Adams already noticed in 1950 that 'Joyabaj offers an example of a community in which the ladinos not only conserve their social supremacy through the control of the commercial and political nerves of the village, but also through the possession and active exploitation of the best lands in the municipality'.[26]

Ladino political power: extending government control

The ladinos' ascent to local power in Joyabaj became also apparent in the political arena. Joyabaj received the status of municipality in 1823/1824,[27] which was quickly becoming the realm of local ladinos. The ladino municipalities took over most of the functions of the indigenous municipalities, whose powers were reduced significantly. They lost their direct relationship with the national state and were no longer in charge of general municipal business. But they still had some functions, such as governing the indigenous community and maintaining its social and ethnic cohesion.[28] In Joyabaj, the indigenous authorities continued to exert influence through the *Alcaldía Indígena* (Indigenous Municipality), albeit with less power and authority. Today it has its own building at the central plaza, opposite the 'ladino municipality', as a 1886 document from the *común de indíge-*

---

23 See Oglesby (2002: 20-35) for an analysis of pre-war and current labour contractors an their changing position in the economic and social arena of Joyabaj.
24 Labour plantations; property held for the use of labour of people living on it.
25 Interview 9-99 (23/5/99).
26 Adams (1964: 253-254).
27 '*Ley del 23/07/1823 sobre municipalidades*' and '*Ley del 10/05/1824 sobre organización de las municipalidades*', both mentioned in: Piel (1995: 33 n. 20).
28 Piel (1995: 32-33).

nas called it. This has not always been the case. In 1950 people working in the indigenous municipality 'sat down at some benches at the bottom of the stairs that went up to the ladino offices';[29] they did not have their own premises and conducted their business outside the doors of the ladino municipality. The indigenous municipality always kept its separate sphere of influence within the indigenous community, dealing mainly with domestic problems and legal disputes concerning communal landholdings, and administering the communal grounds belonging to the *Virgen de Tránsito*, the patron saint of Joyabaj. They are also responsible, together with the seven *cofradías*, for the organization of the *Fiesta Titular de Virgen de Tránsito*, which is held in August every year.[30]

Ladino rule over many of the local municipalities consolidated during the Liberal Republic (1873–1920). From 1870 onwards, 'the [ladino] municipalities become the most important institution of ladino power in the region, without any participation of the indigenous element of the population'.[31] This is also apparent in Joyabaj, where the first ladino mayors start appearing in the municipal books and archives around 1880.[32] At that time only a very small portion of the population participated in the elections because only a fraction of the ladino minority—only literate men above a certain age—and thus none of the indigenous majority was allowed to vote. Because the male ladino population around 1880 numbered only about 200 individuals, ladinos like Felis Ramos could be elected mayor in 1883 with only 20 votes and Sinforiano Alvarado second mayor with also 20 votes.[33] This changed when the indigenous population was allowed to vote. The reaction of the ladinos in Joyabaj was to 'prohibit indigenous participation, including not letting them register to exercise their right to vote, but gave preference to the villages that were under their [ladino] control'.[34] To register for voting, people had to have an identity card. However, only a few of these cards were given out at the ladino municipality every day, so that many indigenous people ended up not voting at all.

Another important feature of the Liberal Period was the centralization and militarization of government control over the rural areas. Two of the most prominent Liberal presidents, Barrios (1873–85) and Cabrera (1989–20), implemented many of the Liberal reforms that were to facilitate increased control. The power of the Church in the rural areas was curtailed by stripping it of its pro-

---

29 Adams (1964: 169-170).
30 The most important day of the *fiesta* is 15 August (*Asunción*), when the Virgen is brought to a new home where she will be cared for by the *Cofradía de la Virgen de Tránsito*.
31 Piel (1995: 31).
32 No municipal documents were found relating to the period 1823/1824 (when Joyabaj received the status of municipality) and 1870.
33 *AMJ*, send to the *AGCA*. It contains six unsorted parcels (1870-1940).
34 Interview 8-01 (9/5/01).

photo 1. *The Virgen de Tránsito is carried around the town of Joyabaj during the Fiesta in August (author, 1998)*

perty, roads and railroads were built and the use of telegraphs was promoted. The telegraph office in Joyabaj was opened in 1895,[35] which accounts for the enormous amount of correspondence between the central government and its local representatives in Joyabaj.[36] A final important change was the creation of the position of *Jefatura Política*, who was to be the most important and direct representative of the central government at the departmental level and who was appointed by the president himself.[37] Apart from being the political and administrative head of the department, he was above all a military leader, both of the local militias (military reserves) and of the local garrisons. The largest garrison, apart from the central military post in the departmental capital of Santa Cruz, was located in Joyabaj, whose militia amounted to more than 300 individuals in 1890.[38] Its function was to preserve order in the municipality, to represent the power of the state and to activate the local ladino militias in case of trouble elsewhere. All male adult ladinos were obliged to serve in the militias, from which the indigenous population was excluded. Ladino prominence in both the local garrison, the militias and the municipality in Joyabaj is apparent from the large amount of correspondence between the *Jefatura Política* and the different garrison commanders in Joyabaj; several ladino names appear again and again.

In spite of, or possibly because of, intensified state control over the rural areas, which resulted in better and shorter communication lines, and the reorganization of the garrisons and militias which were to uphold ladino and state authority[39] and keep order in the countryside, criminal activity did not seem to reduce during this period. According to Piel (1995), a culture of violence evolved during the Liberal Period, which was internalized by local ladino minorities in the rural areas. Excessive violence in this particular period 'seems to be a normal form of relating to others; a frontier culture under military rule, a far west with its garrisons, its indians, its own delinquents, where the "rule of law" seems to be very badly consolidated, both in peoples minds as well as in the institutions'.[40]

In 1931 President Ubico came to power, with ideas about government that were very much those of a nineteenth-century Liberal dictator. 'Ubico's desire to stamp out communism ... generated a rapid increase in state surveillance through formal and also less formal means, such as the dictator's loyal network of spies, and was facilitated through extension of the road and telegraph network.'[41] Ubico's fear of communism was fuelled by a peasant revolt in El Salvador, which

---

35 Diccionario Geográfico de Guatemala, 1978: 438.
36 *AMJ*, send to the *AGCA*. It contains six unsorted parcels (1870-1940).
37 Piel (1995: 20).
38 Piel (1995: 121, 140).
39 McCreery (1994: 179-181).
40 Piel (1995: 118).
41 Sieder (2000: 15).

erupted in 1932 and was quickly suppressed by government forces. A similar revolt in Guatemala was thought possible, although 'the Guatemalan Communist Party was far weaker than its Salvadoran counterpart'.[42] The anti-communist activities of Ubico resulted in the crushing of the labour movement and the tiny Communist Party. He created the post of military commissioner (*comisionado militar*) in every municipality and small village; his tasks concentrated on enforcing military conscription, capturing criminals and act as informants for military intelligence. Military commissioners were regarded as local representatives of the army, but often had close links to local ladino elites. 'The post was valued by ladino settlers because of the relative authority it gave them over the local indigenous population.'[43] The role of military commissioner would change markedly in the years to come, and would become an important element in the military counter-insurgency campaign during the civil war in the 1980s.

Another measure to extend central government control throughout the country was the Municipal Law of 1935, which severely curtailed the autonomy of the municipalities. Mayors were no longer elected, and *intendentes* who were appointed by the president himself took over their functions. The *intendentes* carried out their duties under the supervision of the *Jefatura Política*, and had to submit monthly, weekly or sometimes even daily reports on every imaginable subject, like the number of arrests made and the registration of visitors. The *intendentes* were Ubico's new system for controlling local government. This was not necessarily a bad thing, because it might have served as a means whereby the government could take over power from the local elites. In several areas, however, elites retained their control over local government even during the *intendente* period.[44] After Arévalo was elected president in 1944, the earlier system of chosen mayors and autonomous municipal government was reinstated.[45]

Apparently, the ladinos in Joyabaj were able to reclaim their powerful position in the municipality after Ubico was ousted from office. During the Ubico period the *intendentes* in Joyabaj, as elsewhere in Guatemala, had been ladinos from outside Joyabaj, although some relationships were formed between them and the local ladinos. From 1944 onwards, a dozen ladino families reappear constantly in the minutes of the *Libros de Actas* (Municipal Acts), alternating positions among themselves. Many of these family names also appeared in the earlier *Libros de Actas* before the *intendente* system of Ubico was introduced. Most important were the Ogáldez family with 11 mayors and a total of 18 municipal

---

42 Gleijeses (1991: 9).
43 Sieder (2000: 16).
44 McClintock (1985: 14-25).
45 McClintock (1985: 23).

posts, followed by the Rodriguez family (21 municipal posts, only two mayors), and the Quezada and the Méndez families (16 municipal posts each).[46] From 1946 onward several new ladino names appear in the *Libros de Actas*. Most of them appear only two or three times and were obviously not those of permanent figures in the political arena. This was possibly related to the political upheaval surrounding the election of President Arévalo in 1944, during which new political alliances were forged and new people took their place in the municipality, although for only a short time.

Numbers do not tell the whole story, but they can be an indication of the political prominence of some of the ladino families. Take for example the Ogáldez family, whose members surface throughout *Joyabateco* political history up until the outbreak of the violence in the 1980s. Although they were not among the first ladino families to arrive in Joyabaj, they were considered to be *gente buena* because they made their fortune from land. An important member of the family was Rogelio Ogáldez, who played a central role in Joyabaj in the 1940s and 1950s, as one of the main landowners and labour contractors. He started his political career as council member in 1923; his uncle Eliseo had already become mayor in 1922 and his brother Francisco became mayor in 1927. Between 1946 and 1957 Rogelio occupied the post of mayor five times. He was described as a politically cunning leader, who spoke excellent *K'iche'* and who was on good terms with the indigenous notables whom he needed to help him get re-elected. His position of influence was taken over by his nephew, Próspero Ogáldez, who started his political career as a council member in 1948, becoming mayor in 1970. He occupied the post of mayor during eight years, until the left-wing opposition took over.[47]

Older *Joyabatecos* have quite vivid memories of the Ubico regime, which surfaced in many conversations on current rising crime rates and feelings of insecurity. It is regarded as a kind of golden era, when it was still possible to walk the streets alone, criminals could not bribe their way out of jail and rules were respected. An older ladino women explains that she was sometimes laughed at because she talked in such a positive way about Ubico. 'I know he was a dictator, and he did bad things ... like shooting people on the spot', she said, 'but people feared him and he did a lot of good, like order and security'.[48] Other memories are not so positive. According to a former plantation administrator, 'everybody said that in the times of Ubico there was honesty, but that is not true because there was corruption and black marketeering'.[49] On another occasion he

---

46 *Libros de Actas* 1922-1978.
47 Interview 11-99 (14/7/99).
48 Interview 33-99 (3/10/99).
49 Interview 46-99 (15/7/99).

continued to explain that 'It was a real dictatorship ... in the countryside everybody felt the pressure. In the communities ... you had the local commanders, who were terrible people'.[50] A military reserve was active in Joyabaj at that time, in which all ladino men between 18 and 60 years old had to 'give their service'. They received military training every Sunday, which was supposedly voluntary. However, 'not showing up meant going to jail'.[51]

Political polarization: 1944-1945

Until the Revolution[52] of 1944 Guatemala was reigned by a succession of Liberal autocratic and centralist rulers, of whom President Ubico was the last. The subsequent democratic and populist governments of Presidents Arévalo and Jacobo Arbenz embarked on a series of social and economic reforms which caused anxiety as well as hope in the countryside. Hope was felt by those people in the rural areas who began having access to education, land and new forms of organization. Anxiety was felt by the power elite, especially the ladinos, who saw their position threatened. Both the Arévalo and the Arbenz governments were accused by a threatened elite of working with communists. These accusations were made in an international context of Cold War conflict and strong anti-communist sentiments in the United States. Anti-communist rhetoric was taken over by Guatemalan newspapers and politicians in their criticism of Arévalo's and Arbenz's reforms, and subsequently repeated at the municipal level. Ultimately, the United States became directly involved in Guatemalan politics, when the CIA backed a coup which ousted President Arbenz from office in June 1954.[53] Anti-communist feelings, however, were not only an import from the United States or the international arena but were already apparent in Guatemala during Ubico's presidency when several anti-communist measures were taken.[54]

Especially after 1952 under President Arbenz, when Congress passed the Agrarian Reform Law (*Ley Decreto 900*), tensions mounted in the municipalities. 'The reforms ... fostered a bewildering series of conflicts in rural Guatemala. These struggles took shape around a complex mix of class tensions and ethnic,

---

50 Interview 48-99 (21/9/99).
51 Interview 12-99 (20/8/99).
52 The word 'revolution' was used by Arévalo himself a few days after the revolt of 20 October 1944 which forced Ponce out of the presidential palace. At that moment Arévalo was a candidate in the forthcoming presidential elections. In a radio address he explained that 'What has happened in Guatemala is not a golpe de estado; it is something more profound and more beneficial: it is a revolution . . . It is a revolution that will go to the roots of the political system . . . to purify our political life, to quiet everyone and to honour Guatemala' (Arévalo, *Escritos políticos* no. 126, in Handy, 1994: 23-24).
53 See Gleijeses (1991) and Handy (1994) for a detailed analysis of the period 1944-54, including the role of the CIA in the overthrow of President Arbenz.
54 Gleijeses (1991: 8-11).

geographic, and religious loyalties.'⁵⁵ It was a hectic period for the ladino elite in Joyabaj, especially in the months after Arbenz had resigned as president, as the following article from *El Imparcial* (9 July 1954), one of the leading right-wing newspapers[56] at that time, shows:

> Today, people from the municipality of Joyabaj visited our offices ... to explain that a climate of anxiety exists in their town, because of the constant threats from a small group of opportunists, who have been part at one time or another of all political parties, with the aim to vent personal quarrels towards those who do not follow them like sheep. Figure heads of this group are Rogelio Ogáldez Sánchez, Próspero Ogáldez Sánchez, Alberto Caballeros Pérez y Efraín Elías Roca. [57]

The article continues summing up the shifting political alliances of these four men. Apparently they started out as ardent pro-Arbenz activists, waving red banners with the image of Arbenz at the May Day parade and fulminating against the drawing up of an anti-communist manifesto in which other prominent members of the ladino community of Joyabaj[58] were involved. The article then accused them of being involved in the *Partido de la Revolución Guatemalteca* (PRG),[59] a temporary coalition of revolutionary parties that was founded in 1952 after the introduction of the agrarian reforms.[60] The coalition lasted only a short time, because 'in many communities, the merging of the various parties threw together people representing the two extremes of local political expression, whatever their parties might represent in the national arena'.[61] Finally, after Arbenz was ousted from the presidency in 1954, the four *Joyabatecos* radically changed their political position, and became supporters of President Castillo Armas, who had adopted a clear anti-communist stance.

The article illustrates the complex political situation in the year 1954, highlighting political conflicts between the ladino elite in the village of Joyabaj. It hints at political factionalism and opportunism within and between different

---

55 Handy (1994: 4).
56 Regarding the political colour of *El Imparcial*, Handy (1994: 174) remarks that 'El Imparcial published constant warnings about communism and horror stories concerning the atrocities of communist regimes elsewhere and provided free advertising for meetings of anticommunist leagues throughout the country.'
57 *El Imparcial*, 9/7/54.
58 For example, Francisco Méndez Escobar, writer and editor of *El Imparcial*.
59 Party of the Guatemalan Revolution.
60 See Handy (1994: 41-46) for an extensive overview of the political alliances during these years.
61 Handy (1994: 44).

ladino groups and accuses them of changing political sides from right to left and back again: not an uncommon occurrence in local or national politics. The four accused men tried to defend themselves by way of a letter published in the right-wing newspaper *El Mundo Libre* (30 July 1954) in which they tried to blacken the other side.

> The communist tactic to accuse real anti-communists is obvious. You only have to ask: Who were the ones that denounced in those days the parish priest ... Presbyterian Don Santiago Gil Blanco; who could count on a legion of enlightened *indígenas* to overthrow the *Arbencista* regime? Because of whose denunciation did Francisco Barrios and Efrain Elias Roca go to jail ... because of whose denunciation was citizen Luis Tárano Villatoro persecuted to be brought in alive or dead ... because of whose denunciation did the Department of Agriculture give a fine of 2,000 Quetzales to each of the following gentlemen: the municipal mayor Don Olayo Santos Herrera, Don Rogelio Ogáldez Sánchez and Prospero Ogáldez Sánchez, for being anti-agrarians?[62]

Both articles clearly show the rising anti-communist feelings among many ladinos in Joyabaj. Conflicts arose between those who had greeted the election of President Arévalo in 1944 (*Arevalistas* they called themselves), and those who had regarded the proposed changes and reforms with distrust. After the dictatorship of President Ubico, many *Joyabatecos* had voted for Arévalo and supported the changes he envisaged. Especially the younger generation of ladinos felt attracted to this new man with new ideas, who did not belong to the old political guard. A former *finca* administrator and initial supporter of Arévalo remembers when he first heard the news of Arévalo's victory on the radio.

> Look, I have never again experienced such patriotic emotions. I have felt it then and I have not felt it since and will never feel it again. Because the movement [Arévalo's victory] that was most pure and most popular in the whole of Guatemalan history ... was the one of 20 October. Because the people rose without any *cacique*, there was not one leader ... there was no one who proclaimed himself leader ... no one was thinking like that ... After so many years of dictatorship, a doctor in philosophy came forward, a guy with

---

62 *Mundo Libre*, 30/7/54

much, very much preparation. And politically clean, totally clean. How could we, Guatemalans, not prefer him above the others?[63]

But these initially positive images of clean politics projected by an academically schooled leader changed, especially after a start was made with the implementation of the agrarian reforms.

Local agrarian committees

The agrarian reform and the subsequent setting up of *Comités Agrarios Locales* (CALs)[64] to implement the reforms provoked unrest and protest among the landowning elite in Joyabaj. The CALs had to divide so-called *tierras baldías* or uncultivated lands over two acres. Many ladinos in Joyabaj saw this as a sign of Arévalo's alliance with the communists, who, they feared, would take away their land and houses. Several *Arevalistas* shifted sides, and those who continued to support Arévalo and Arbenz were looked upon with suspicion.

The CALs consisted of five members with one nominated by the governor, one by the municipality and three by the local *unión campesina* (farmers union) or syndicate. '[T]he CALs also became important centers of power and influence. To a great extent, they were able to control the allocation of the most important local resource, land, and enjoyed almost unlimited discretion in determining who would benefit from the law.'[65] According to several ladinos in Joyabaj, people were not against the agrarian reform itself, but they opposed its poor implementation at the local level by the CALs.[66] The only ones benefiting from the CALs were the members of the committees themselves and their close friends. Supposedly, they divided the land among their *cuates* (mates) or enriched themselves. An 88-year-old ladino widow remembered how her husband, an *Arbencista* who worked at the telegraph office, also did some secretarial work for the CALs. She did not like this at all. For a start, her husband did not know a thing about agriculture, so how could he possibly assist in an agrarian reform? As well, the local coordinator of the CALs had promised her husband free land for his help, something she refused to believe. 'Land is bought with one's own money, not given out for free.'[67] She did not trust the land reform proposals from Arbenz and was convinced that the CALs were organized only to steal land from other people.

A document, dated 26 January 1954, drawn up by the villagers of Los Llanos

---

63 Interview 48-99 (21/9/99).
64 Local Agrarian Committees.
65 Handy (1994: 92).
66 Interview 48-99 (21/9/99).
67 Diary 23/9/99.

serves as an illustration of the increasing opposition against the Agrarian committees, especially, although not solely, among the indigenous part of the population.[68] Apparently the people from Los Llanos were not satisfied with the way the agrarian reform was carried out in their village, and complained about the parceling out of their communal land. According to them this was not done according to agrarian reform stipulations and served only the people who were organizing the distribution. Locals were threatened and most of the land was distributed among ladinos who already owned vast estates, while small farmers got only one or two *manzanas*. The names of the ladinos receiving the land were those of powerful ladino families, like Alvarado, Gil, Méndez and Ogáldez.[69] They all received three or four pieces of land, measuring five *manzanas* each. The inhabitants of Los Llanos did not approve of this and 'because of that we protest and we ask that the parceling is done according to the law and that an agrarian inspector from the capital is appointed'.[70] In this case it was the wealthy ladino minority in Joyabaj that seemed to profit from the agrarian reform, a group of people who already owned vast amounts of land. But some non-landowning ladinos too benefited from the reform, because it gave them the opportunity to buy land at cheap prices with money borrowed from the state. When Arbenz fell from the presidency these debts were never repaid but the families held on to the land.[71]

The *común indígena* in Joyabaj also protested against the land reforms and reacted against the proposed division of the communal lands, which provided land to the landless, grazing area for cattle, wood for the *cofrades* and households and incense (*pom*) for religious ceremonies. According to *Joyabatecos*, these lands belonged to the *Virgen de Tránsito*, the patron saint of Joyabaj. Although the Virgen herself could not own land, the *común indígena* administered these lands and the cattle roaming on it in her name. A ladino remembered that his father was involved in this case on behalf of the *común indígena*. He was a respected man within the conservative part of the indigenous community, possibly because he spoke both Spanish and *K'iche'* and was married to an indigenous women. His intervention helped to prevent the communal grounds of the *Virgen de Tránsito* from being divided. Soon after, supporters of President Arbenz threw him in jail because, according to them, he had opposed the agrarian reform activities of the local CALs.[72]

---

68 Personal archive (see n. 10).
69 Among the names mentioned are Arturo Peña Sarmiento, who already owned two *caballerias* in the area, Pablo Gil Quiroa (75 *manzanas*), Ramon Quezada Resinos (36 *manzanas*), Isaias Albarado (one *caballería*) Alfredo Méndez Ogáldez (52 *manzanas*), Enecon Ramos (25 *manzanas*) and Candelario Ramos Porras (22 *manzanas*).
70 Personal archive (see n. 10).
71 Interview 22-99 (30/7/99).
72 Interview 22-99 (30/7/99).

Mounting anti-communist sentiments

After Arbenz was ousted from the presidential palace by a CIA-backed coup in 1954, Castillo Armas became the new president. He had been waging a small war from behind Honduran borders to 'liberate Guatemala from the communists',[73] as a former estate administrator explained. When he came to power anti-communist committees were set up; anti-communist legislation was being prepared, and blacklists of communist drawn up. According to the estate administrator, 'it was a big party here [in Joyabaj] just like everywhere else' when they heard the news of Castillo's victory on the radio.[74] The town square was packed with people, firecrackers were going off and a marimba was playing in front of the church. There was an enormous queue in front of the telegraph office of people waiting to transmit their congratulations to the new government. The widow of a former telegraph operator explained, with a wry smile on her face, that she was scared during these festivities. Her husband was *Arbencista*, and she did not like it one bit that he had to send all these telegrams in favour of Castillo Armas. People were shouting 'Up with Castillo Armas, down with the communists, communists out!' She stayed indoors most of the week, while her husband slept in the telegraph office.[75] Not only did individuals pay their respects to the new government by way of the telegraph lines, but the *Joyabateco* community as a whole drew up a statement that was entered into the minutes of the municipality of 21 October 1954. In the statement *Joyabatecos* expressed their profound thanks to the new president 'who saved our fatherland from the claws of communism'.[76] There followed 13 pages of signatures (ladinos) and thumbprints (mostly *indígenas*), paying their respects to the new government of Castillo Armas, who was called 'our liberator'.

After Castillo Armas became president, the *Castillistas* took control of the municipality in Joyabaj. Actions against *Arevalistas* and *Arbencistas* increased, especially against a number of teachers who were accused of being communist infiltrators and subsequently thrown out of town or transferred to other municipalities.[77] Apart from aggression towards some teachers, several former *Arevalistas* and *Arbencistas* were captured, put into jail for a few days or thrown into the river. However, nobody was killed and, compared with what happened in other municipalities, the situation in Joyabaj never became very heated. As one ladino explains, 'they fought among each other, they did not talk to each other. There was a certain distance between people from different political sides. But it never

---

73 Interview 46-99 (21/9/99).
74 Interview 48-99 (21/9/99).
75 Diary 23/9/99.
76 *Libro de Actas*, 21/10/1954, *acta* 78.
77 *Libro de Actas*, 3/1/1955, *acta* 1.

came to *esquadrones* [death squads]'.[78] In other towns death squads were active, and people did disappear.

Supporters of Castillo Armas and the liberation of Guatemala set up the MLN, an ultra-right wing and fiercely anti-communist political party.[79] The MLN spread quickly throughout the Guatemalan countryside, and fed the rising anti-communist sentiment. Also in Joyabaj the MLN became a strong political force, especially with powerful members like Rogelio and Próspero Ogáldez, Alberto Caballeros and Pablo Gil. The names are familiar from the article in *El Imparcial* in which other *Joyabatecos* accused them of switching political sides from right to left and back again.[80]

MLN and its indigenous allies

The MLN, through leaders like Rogelio Ogáldez, was one of the first political parties that tried to broaden its sphere of influence into the indigenous villages, with some success. Participation of the indigenous majority in the arena of municipal politics remained limited until the late 1960s. Although they had their own sphere of political influence and authority, through the indigenous municipality and the *cofradías*, relations with official political parties participating in national and local elections were not close. Only in a few instances was their presence in politics recognized by ladino political leaders, like Rogelio and Próspero Ogáldez, for example, when they were seeking re-election as mayor and needed the votes of the indigenous majority.

The MLN's growing support among part of the indigenous population led to conflicts and division within indigenous communities. The indigenous communities were already dividing over religious issues, between those embracing Catholic Action (AC), a Catholic renewal organization, and those who wanted to keep their old religious customs (*costumbristas*). The older indigenous generation was losing power and authority fast especially because younger people were joining Catholic Action, which they saw as a way to avoid the religious and communal obligations imposed by *costumbre*. Possibly, the loss of authority among indigenous elders fostered a closer relationship between the right-wing MLN and *costumbristas*, while Catholic Action was more inclined towards political parties of the left. Several ladino informants viewed an alliance between the MLN and *costumbristas* in a negative way and drew a mental picture in which the poor indigenous villagers were being manipulated and exploited by smart caciques like Rogélio and Próspero Ogáldez.[81] A former municipal employee explained

---

78 Interview 11-99 (14/7/99).
79 In 1955 the ultra right-wing *Movimiento Democrático Nacionalista* (MDN) was founded, becoming the MLN in 1960.
80 Interview 11-99 (14/7/99).
81 Interview 11-99 (14/7/99) and 23-99 (1/9/99).

how Próspero manipulated the *sajorines* (priest *de costumbre*): 'He paid the *sajorines* to help him win the elections ... to do their ceremonies so he would win.' This way they probably felt themselves to be as religious advisers to the mayor, which meant 'personal prestige [*elevación*] for the *sajorin*'.[82]

From the late 1950s until the end of the 1960s Joyabaj was the stage of a fierce political struggle between the MLN and *Redención (Partido Democrático de Reconciliación Nacional)*.[83] *Redención*, which was slightly less radically anti-communist, was set up by Miguel Ydígoras Fuentes during the 1957 presidential elections, which were held shortly after the assassination of Castillo Armas. *Redención* became the '*partido oficialista*' or ruling party from 1958 until 1963. At the local level, at least in Joyabaj, *Redención* was considered an opposition party to the MLN. It organized local ladino leaders like Ramiro Paíz, Abraham Alvarado, Jorge Mencos, Pantaleón Quezada and the Méndez brothers. According to an older ladino explaining ladino factionalism in the 1960s, many people backed *Redención*, not because they were in favour of its politics but because it was the only viable local option to oppose the powerful MLN party during municipal elections.[84] Before *Redención* there was hardly any real opposition to the MLN and its spearhead Rogelio Ogáldez Sánchez. Ogáldez had been elected mayor several times but, according to several *Joyabatecos*, never did much for the population as a whole, because he was mainly servicing a small group of friends. In 1958 *Redención* won its first municipal elections in Joyabaj,[85] repeating its victory at the elections of 1960 and 1962. When the opposition won on the first two occasions, Rogelio Ogáldez supposedly said, 'Well, let the boys also win sometime ...'.[86] But when the opposition won for the third time in a row, Ogáldez was so devastated that, according to one *Joyabateco*, 'he died within three months. He was used to win always ... it is just like a disease.'[87] Probably no actual connection existed between the MLN's electoral defeat and the death of Rogelio Ogáldez, but *Joyabatecos* often referred to this incident when stressing how unhealthy politics could be for an individual. In 1964 the MLN regained its central position in the political arena of Joyabaj, supplying mayors until the elections in 1978, when local politics changed radically.

---

82 Interview 23-99 (1/9/99).
83 Democratic Party of National Reconciliation.
84 Interview 11-99 (14/7/99).
85 From 1945 until 1974 mayors were chosen every two years; after that, every four years. The suffrage did not become universal until the Constitution of 1965, when also illiterate women (read: indigenous women) were allowed to vote.
86 Interview 11-99 (14/7/99).
87 Interview 11-99 (14/7/99).

Catholic Action and the indigenous communities

While the MLN was losing the municipal elections three consecutive times and internal divisions among the ladino population were becoming quite pronounced, major changes were taking place in the indigenous communities surrounding Joyabaj. The governments of Arévalo and Arbenz had been the starting point of significant changes in local power relations within the indigenous communities and between the rural areas and the municipal capital of Joyabaj. The indigenous population not only participated in the agrarian committees as members or beneficiaries or in the protests against them, but was also drawn into the municipal political arena. This had already started when alliances were forged between *costumbristas* and the MLN, while from the early 1960s onwards significant indigenous participation of Catholic Action activists in the left-wing *Democrácia Cristiana Guatemalteca* (DCG) became visible.[88] Le Bot describes the overall situation in a nutshell:

> During the sixties and the seventies, a movement of emancipation and modernization in various areas—economic, social, ethnic, political, religious—occurred in the Guatemalan indigenous society. One of the objectives of this movement and one of its most obvious manifestations was the progressive taking over of several positions of power ... in numerous municipalities on the Altiplano ... It was about gaining power at the cost of a ladino minority.[89]

An important factor that contributed to these changes, and which was largely responsible for the mounting political activities of the indigenous population from the 1960s onwards, was the Catholic Church and its Catholic Action (*Acción Católica* - AC) programme. AC originated in the 1930s and was formalized in 1948 by Monsignor Mariano Rossell y Arellano. Initially it was a lay catechist movement, meant to re-establish orthodox Catholicism in the countryside. It was a response to the radicalization of national politics under Presidents Arévalo and Arbenz and the spread of Protestantism in rural areas. Originally the missionaries were anti-communist, and were set upon wiping out the traditional *cofradías*. In its initial period AC was regarded as just another attack on the traditional religious structures, causing a lot of unrest in the rural areas.[90] It created opportunities, especially for young people, within the indigenous communities to move outside the traditional hierarchy of the *cofradías*.[91] Through AC

---

88 Guatemalan Christian Democrats; a political party founded in 1955. Originally it was a party of the petit bourgeoisie, but it gradually moved towards the left of the political spectrum.
89 Le Bot (1992: 23).
90 Handy (1994: 143).
91 In Joyabaj the highest positions in the traditional indigenous hierarchy were first and second *Alcalde Indígena* and first *cofrade* of the *cofradía Virgen de Tránsito*.

they were able to reach positions and accumulate wealth outside the traditional community structure that was dominated by indigenous elders or *principales*.[92] A breach was opening between the older generation who held on to *costumbre* and a younger generation, many of whom became active within AC. A *K'iche'* activist from AC remembers the following:

> In the beginning people didn't like the ones from AC. They were fighting among each other. That was because there was no priest and the people burned incense and candles in the church. And when the priest and AC came, they had to leave the church with their candles. They did not like this and they became angry ... and because AC was in favour of the priest, they [*costumbristas*] thought that meant they [AC] were against them. Against *costumbre*. There was sort of a division and argument ... but afterwards AC became bigger ... AC won.[93]

AC had an enormous influence on the existing power structures within indigenous communities and created both opportunities and division.

From 1952 onwards AC spread over the department of Quiché, promoted by visits from the Bishop. At that time Padre Santiago Gil Herrera, a ladino from the departmental capital of Santa Cruz de Quiché, was the resident priest in Joyabaj. Initially, according to some *Joyabatecos*, Catholic Action mainly converted *ladinos* to Catholicism because they were the ones living in town and could be reached most easily. Accordingly the first AC group in Joyabaj consisted of ladinos. In those years ladinos carried around the image of the *Sagrado Corazón* (Sacred Hart) in processions and they were its *celadores* (guardians).[94] This changed gradually towards the end of the 1950s. Although several indigenous men from the village of Chorraxaj were already active as sacristans in the church, they did not participate in AC until Padre Santiago Gil started 'giving capacity training to them, so that they could go from house to house with the word of God'.[95]

With the arrival of the Spanish Missionaries of the Sacred Heart (MSC - *Misionarios del Sagrado Corazón*) in the Quiché department in 1955, the development activities of Catholic Action spread more quickly to the indigenous villages. Not everybody was happy with the new Spanish priests and the activities they were promoting in the indigenous communities. The MSC priests quickly

---

92 Arias (1990: 233).
93 Interview 30-99 (6/7/99).
94 Interview 33-99 (3/10/99).
95 Interview 29-99 (1/10/99).

took over the reigns in the Catholic community from the older priests, directing themselves more towards the indigenous population. This created ill feeling, especially among the ladinos in town who saw their privileged relationship with the Church endangered.[96] Most ladinos did not want to have any more to do with AC because it had become 'an Indian thing' in their eyes. As a result, the MSC priests started organizing separate Catholic groups for ladinos, like the *Guardianes del Santísimo* (Keepers of the Sacred) and *Hijas de María* (Daughters of Maria). These were women's organizations, because women were more active in the Catholic Church than ladino men, who considered Sunday mass to be sufficient Catholic activity.

After Fernando Carbonell (MSC) replaced Santiago Gil as priest in Joyabaj, AC groups and *Juntas Directivas Locales*[97] were formed in the indigenous communities. From the beginning of the 1960s onward AC became actively engaged in organizing and capacitating the rural communities. Schools were build, roads constructed, housing and drinking water supplies improved, the formation of cooperatives and *Ligas Campesinas* (farmer unions) promoted, and civil and political groups organized.[98] Much of the material necessary to carry out these projects was obtained by applying to the proper authorities, development organizations or church funds, while the labour was in most cases provided by the local population in exchange for food supplies. After a while many of these committees started operating independently of their original founder, Catholic Action. The initial anti-communist attitude of AC had changed markedly during the late 1960s, especially among local priests working in the rural areas. 'They became radicalized and politicized by what they saw. The poverty, malnutrition, the treatment of the ladinos towards the indígenas, the migration ... few with any kind of sensitivity could not help but be transformed.'[99] The breach between *costumbristas* and AC also seemed to widen, because the former started allying themselves more closely with right-wing political parties like the MLN, while AC activists were more inclined towards left-wing parties like the DCG.

---

96 Diocesis del Quiché, 1994: 75.
97 These are local Catholic Action committees in the rural communities, consisting of a president, vice-president, treasurer, secretary and several members. They are elected every two years.
98 Diocesis del Quiché (1994: 65-68).
99 Comments from a former Alianza coordinator (23/9/02). The radicalization of the Catholic Church in Guatemala was not an isolated incident in Latin America. Liberation theology was ascendant, and both the Second Vatican Council (1962-1965) and the Bishops Statement of Medellín (1968) with its pastoral focus and its option for the poor were crucial turning points (CEH, Vol. I, 1999: 139-140).

Chorraxaj: the cradle of Catholic Action

The changes which took place in the indigenous communities, ultimately leading to the partial seizure of local political power from the ladinos during the 1978 municipal elections, was especially visible in Chorraxaj, an indigenous community north of the municipal capital. The first school and church buildings in the rural areas surrounding Joyabaj were built in Chorraxaj, a market place was organized and a *Liga Campesina* set up. Many of the new indigenous political and cooperative leaders and Catholic lay activists came from this community, and it was in Chorraxaj where the DCG found its most active members, especially among AC activists. Chorraxaj was known as 'the cradle of AC activity'.[100]

Why did Chorraxaj seem to be more open towards AC activities than the surrounding communities? Possibly education played an important role, because the first indigenous children that started attending school in the municipal capital around 1956 were from Chorraxaj. At that time no schools existed in the rural areas. According to the first indigenous pupils, their fathers had send them to school to learn Spanish, because trade with towns were nobody spoke *K'iche'* was increasing and because Spanish was becoming more important in contacts between the indigenous population and local and national government. Many of these educated children came back to their villages full of new ideas and the ability to speak, read and write Spanish. They were called upon again and again to help write petitions, to draw up papers for a new committee or documents requesting aid from outside agencies, or to serve on a committee as secretary.

Some of these indigenous youngsters went on to a secondary school in Chichicastenango,[101] which was set up in 1961 especially for indigenous children. Most of them needed the financial and moral support of the local parish priest at that time, Father Fernando Carbonell,[102] because most parents had little money and were not too keen on sending their children to a boarding school, where they would be interns for several years. At that time, the priests in Chichicastenango were involved in setting up committees and cooperatives and encouraged their students to organize similar committees in their own villages. Ever since the downfall of Arbenz, only the Catholic Church was allowed to organize cooperatives. While most students were still attending school in Chichicastenango, some of them came home during weekends applying in practice what they had learned at school: for example, in 1964 a savings and loans cooperative was organized in Chorraxaj. They also started helping the members of the *Junta*

---

100 Interview 8-01 (9/5/01).
101 Chichicastenango is an indigenous municipality, located two hours by bus from Joyabaj. However, in the 1960s the infrastructure was much less developed and it could take up to two days to travel from Joyabaj to Chichicastenango.
102 Interviews 29-99 (1/10/99) and 28-99 (18/9/99).

Parroquial (municipal parish board), most of whom were illiterate men from Chorraxaj, with the paperwork involved in buying land. Others became active in local development organizations, giving Spanish lessons to indigenous men and women. In 1966 a school and a church were built in Chorraxaj, a football club was organized and the first of many *Comités de Pro-mejoramiento* (Improvement Committee) was inaugurated.

Many of the young indigenous students involved in the cooperatives, the committees and Catholic Action were also participating in training courses in Santa Cruz and Guatemala City. The University of Rafael Landívar in Guatemala City was sponsoring *Centro de Adiestramiento de Promotores Sociales* (CAPS),[103] training centres where people from the rural areas received courses on social promotion, community organization, human rights and a host of other topics. 'Campesinos from different linguistic groups received training, and heard of each others' situation ... they jointly analysed the common reality they shared. One Mayan colleague told me [a former Alianza coordinator], "before this course, I used to thank God for rich people, who gave us jobs on the coast. Now I thank God for poor people, who are responsible for creating the wealth of the country".'[104] There were also courses on how to organize a *Liga Campesina*, touching on topics like 'how do farmers live, what do they sow ... and how to help in buying land'.[105] This training resulted in the organization of the first *Liga Campesina* in Chorraxaj, involving almost the same group of people that was active in many of the other organizations. According to former *Liga Campesina* activists, it never worked very well in Chorraxaj, because the need was not that great. Most people in Chorraxaj owned a piece of land, however small, and were not obliged to work several months a year on the coastal plantations. However, in other areas of Joyabaj people lived on labour plantations such as Chuacorral, and had to migrate several times a year to the coffee or sugar cane plantations in the south. In exchange they could live on a small plot of land on the *finca*, big enough to built a house and grow some corn and beans for the family. Eventually the *Liga Campesina* was transferred to the labour plantation of Chichop, whose inhabitants were trying to get individual property titles to the land they tilled.

This influx of educated youngsters full of new ideas led increasingly to conflicts within the Catholic community of Chorraxaj itself. It resulted in a serious break between the educated AC youth and the older AC activists during a conflict about a football field. Many youngsters in Chorraxaj wanted to play football, but the older generation did not think much of it, especially because the

---

103 Training Centre for Social Promotors.
104 Comments of a former Alianza coordinator (23/9/02).
105 Interview 29-99 (1/10/99).

youngsters also played during religious processions and Sunday mass. The local president of AC in Chorraxaj at that time told the youngsters that attending mass was enough 'diversion' for them. The youngsters got angry and looked for an empty field on the outskirts of Chorraxaj to play football. The president became furious and told them they could leave the community once and for all. The youngsters decided to act on his suggestion and started organizing their own community. They bought land with loans from outside organizations, completed all the necessary paperwork, organized their own AC group and build their own church and school. When the older generation began to see where these activities were leading, they tried to stop the youngsters from forming a separate community. But things were already too far advanced, leading to the foundation of *Nuevo Chorraxaj* (New Chorraxaj) in 1973.

Alliance between Catholic Action and local politics

A second important factor that contributed to changing power relations in the countryside was the rise of the Guatemalan Christian Democratic Party (DCG). It was founded in 1955 as a party of the small mainly ladino bourgeoisie, but gradually moved towards the left of the political spectrum. Many of its initial founders came from urban AC groups, and promoted in their political role many of the same activities as AC. A kind of 'non-declared alliance' (*alianza no declarada*) was formed between the Catholic Church and DCG.[106] The Church saw in the DCG the only political party that had established a rapport with the indigenous population, spoke their language, and helped in the formation of indigenous political leaders. The DCG was considered a political alternative and became the legitimate and electoral vehicle through which the indigenous population were gaining political power at the municipal level. Other political parties, such as the MLN, did not allow *indígenas* to become candidates or ascend to important positions within the party, and saw them primarily as potential voters.

A former DCG mayor remembered when the DCG first showed up in Joyabaj. It was around 1956, while he was still in school. After mass on Sunday they would help the DCG people pass out flyers: 'that way it started spreading inside AC.'[107] However, it took until 1965 for the DCG to become popular among the indigenous *Joyabatecos*, especially AC activists. This was partially due to contacts with Julio Hamilton, a ladino from Santa Cruz who was heavily involved in DCG politics. He was a regular guest of the MSC priests in Joyabaj, and became a known face to the catechists whom he helped to set up the first savings and loan cooperative in Joyabaj. He also explained to them what DCG stood for,

---

106 Diocesis del Quiché (1994: 73).
107 Interview 20-99 (5/7/99).

stressing the Christian component of the party.[108] In 1966, some of the educated youngsters from Chorraxaj and Xeabaj decided to organize a DCG affiliate in Joyabaj. Another important relationship was established with Oscar Enríques Guerra, who was rector of the Landivar University and representative in Congress for the DCG. Some of the Chorraxaj students already knew him from the human rights course they had attended at the Landivar University.[109] He helped them with the necessary paperwork involved in setting up the consumer cooperative in 1967.

In 1968 the first DCG candidate for mayor participated in the municipal elections in Joyabaj. He was a *K'iche'* from Xeabaj, but not considered very suitable because of a severe alcohol problem. Apart from that, he had a formidable ladino candidate opposite him: Ramiro Paíz, a local pharmacist who was very well liked in Joyabaj. Against him, the DCG candidate did not stand a chance. The DCG candidates in the 1972 and 1974 elections were also *K'iche'*, respectively from Xeabaj and Chorraxaj. They were both beaten by another section of the old ladino establishment, the right-wing MLN headed by Próspero Ogáldez. It was not until 1978 that a DCG candidate, Felipe Natareno, won the municipal election in Joyabaj and became the first mayor of mixed (ladino and *K'iche'*) descent.

It is clear that a clustering of power took place among the young indigenous students from villages like Chorraxaj and Xeabaj and their Catholic Action friends. They surfaced whenever indigenous people were organizing themselves or were starting up committees and other interest groups. They were active in politics as well as in the Catholic Church. They were the ones who could read and write Spanish and were asked when papers had to be drawn up or petitions had to be signed. They were also the ones who became active in local and national organizations that flocked to Joyabaj after the earthquake in 1976.

The earthquake: memories of chaos and solidarity

On 4 February 1976, at 3.33 a.m., an earthquake (7.5 on the Richter scale) struck Guatemala. In a country of then 8 million people, 25,000 thousand died, 100,000 were injured and 1 million were left homeless. The earthquake struck especially hard in the rural areas surrounding the Motagua river, including the municipality of Joyabaj. The town was almost entirely destroyed; only the church front was left standing. Six hundred people died and more than 5,500 were seriously injured. Over 95 per cent of the buildings were destroyed, leaving nothing but 'rubbish, uncertainty and fear'.[110] The first responses to the earth-

---

108 Interview 29-99 (1/10/99).
109 Interview 29-99 (1/10/99).
110 Muj Miculax and Schramm (1989: 226).

photo 2. *The front of the Catholic Church in Joyabaj was one of the few remains left standing after the earthquake of 1976. Behind it a new church was built (author, 1999)*

quake were unorganized and chaotic. Many people were still buried under the rubble of their houses, others slept on the street, victims were being brought in from the surrounding rural hamlets, and the dead were piling up in the town square. The municipality was wrecked, archives and administration lost, people in central positions unaccounted for and everybody was looking for family members. Some people, however, after having brought their own family to safety and constructing some sort of shelter for them on the remains of the old houses, started organizing things. For example, two ladino teachers went to check the cemetery, reporting to the mayor at that time, Próspero Ogáldez, its complete destruction and the possibility of an epidemic outbreak. However, he was not interested and apparently exclaimed that he could not concern himself with the dead while there were still so many survivors to be cared for.[111] The teachers took matters into their own hands and organized the digging of mass graves in which the bodies were burned.

Soon after the initial chaotic days, daily flights began arriving at the local airstrip, bringing in aid and taking the wounded to nearby hospitals. Transport over land was still impossible. Even the Herrera family, owners of the finca Chuacorral, flew in by helicopter to view the damage and offer financial assistance. It was agreed that the Herrera's financial help would be used to rebuild the municipal capital, focusing on roads, sewage systems and public buildings like the municipality and jail. The rural areas would be covered by other national and international donor organizations. 'The earthquake also created new patterns of association and organization in the rural areas. Nearly every community organized a reconstruction or a betterment committee. They were not just spaces to talk about potable water, school or housing reconstruction. They were spaces to talk about *la realidad nacional* [the national reality].'[112]

Most ladinos in town remember only the Emergency Committee (*Comité de Emergencia*) they themselves had set up a few days after the earthquake. Not much contact or collaboration seems to have existed between the different committees in the indigenous communities and the ladino committee in the municipal capital. In a way this exemplifies the relationship between the indigenous and the ladino communities of Joyabaj at that time. The Emergency Committee set up by the ladinos was largely ineffective because the military, who had arrived in Joyabaj immediately after the earthquake, were monopolizing the distribution of incoming aid and had virtually taken over control of the town because it was considered a disaster emergency zone.[113] Some ladinos accused the military of

---

111 Diary 17/5/99.
112 Comments of a former Alianza coordinator (23/9/02).
113 Interview 13-99 (4/10/99) and interview 16-01 (14/5/01).

keeping the best aid for themselves, and even violating local girls. 'The military caused a lot of damage in these days, a lot of damage. They did not help in any way', a former member of the Emergency Committee complained.[114] Another ladino added that 'the military could have done so much to bond with the people, but they were they ones that stood over all the indians and all the ladinos that were at work, to make sure we worked hard ... they [the military] could easily put down their weapons and dig in, and I don't recall seeing that at all'.[115]

Apart from the destruction, the chaos and the apparent corruption, *Joyabatecos* also remember a feeling of enormous solidarity among the villagers: neighbours helping neighbours and villagers starting to organize and coordinate help. Some older ladinos paint an almost romantic picture when talking about the days immediately after the earthquake. An evangelical pastor remembers the earthquake as a turning point in Joyabaj, 'because for the first time there was one goal in mind and that was basically survival and then rebuilding. The town worked together ... we experienced a major tragedy together and that bonded us. For at least a generation'.[116] His positive memories might have been influenced by the fact that evangelical church attendance in Joyabaj received a boost after the earthquake. The image of the *Virgen de Tránsito*, the patron saint that stood above the altar in the Catholic Church of Joyabaj, had been shattered during the earthquake. According to the pastor, this incident caused several people to back away from Catholicism and embrace the evangelical church.

Reconstruction efforts of Alianza[117]

An important consequence of the earthquake, besides the destruction of the town of Joyabaj and the heightened self-organization of many people, was the influx of national and international assistance into the area. While the Herrera family focused on the reconstruction of the municipal capital, Alianza, an international NGO in which *Save the Children* projects from seven different countries cooperated,[118] worked in the rural areas. According to Alianza, 'This should help to counter-balance the paternalizing effects of the Herrera aid in this area'.[119] It was Alianza and the activities it implemented and local organization it stimulated which would have a significant impact on local power relations in Joyabaj. Alianza could build upon the foundations of community development already

---

114 Interview 16-01 (14/5/01).
115 Interview 10-01 (17/6/01).
116 Interview 10-01 (17/6/01).
117 Alianza was an international NGO working in Joyabaj and other municipalities affected by the earthquake.
118 These countries were Norway, Sweden, Denmark, Austria, Canada, Great Britain and the United States.
119 DeCormier (1976: 4).

laid out for them in the indigenous villages by the Catholic Church, Catholic Action and other initiatives that had been developing since the 1960s. 'The education and formation was already there',[120] a former Alianza activist explained. However, Alianza realized that many communities experienced serious internal divisions as a result of religious and political alliances. For example, Catholic Action groups in most rural hamlets were participating much more in the reconstruction efforts of Alianza than, for example, the *costumbristas*. AC activists sometimes even 'planned meetings when they knew the more traditional "costumbristas" or strict adherents to the Mayan religion and calendar ... would not want to participate'.[121] When Alianza started targeting the *costumbristas* specifically, they were more successful in drawing them into participating in the projects.

Alianza started working in Joyabaj immediately after the earthquake of 1976, concentrating its efforts on relief and reconstruction. The idea was that this initial relief project could be expanded into a more comprehensive development programme. Although an Alianza document from 1978 still has a paragraph on its 'Joyabaj Reconstruction Program', listing the number of houses built and carpenters and builders trained, the other programmes already focused on agriculture, reforestation, health, social promotion, leadership training and education. Eventually more than 75 per cent of the Alianza staff were locals, ladinos as well as people from indigenous communities such as Chorraxaj, Xeabaj and Chichop.[122] These were the villages where Catholic Action was most active and from which many local leaders had emerged since the late 1960s.

Ladinos regarded Alianza as an organization that mainly worked for the benefit of the indigenous population and did not do anything for the ladinos. According to a former Alianza employee, many ladinos did not realize that the NGOs working in Joyabaj had divided up the area, with Alianza working in the rural areas while Caritas, governmental organizations and the Herrera family were to focus their attentions on the municipal capital.[123] Already during the first days after the earthquake, Alianza and local ladinos in the municipal council clashed over the organization of the local reconstruction committee. The mayor wanted to hand out posts on the committee to political friends, while Alianza wanted an open election. After this argument, which Alianza won, relations between Alianza and the municipality remained strained.[124] Joyabaj was regarded by several former Alianza employees as a very difficult community to work in,

---

120 Interview 19-01 (5/6/01).
121 Lent (1996: 5).
122 Also in other NGOs working in Guatemala at that time, like CARE (United States) and Oxfam (Great Britain), indigenous staff were hired and put into important positions in the field.
123 Interview 44-99 (22/4/99).
124 Interview 19-01 (5/6/01).

photo 3. *Indigenous men attending an Alianza course (Redd Barna, 1977)*

because conflicts erupted not only between the indigenous part of the population and the ladinos, but also between Catholic Action and *costumbristas*, between MLN and DCG, and between evangelicals and Catholics. Apparently it took quite some time to gain the trust of the people and some villages did not want Alianza to work in their community. Not surprisingly, distrust of outside agencies and unknown individuals only grew stronger during the civil war period.

Apart from numerous local conflicts and divisions, the community reconstruction work of Alianza and other NGOs was also hampered by the increasing violence. A former Alianza employee explains:

> A terribly unfortunate negative consequence of these improvements in community organization should be noted. During the 'Violence' of the 1980s, individuals who had developed their personal capacities during the post-disaster relief project were seen as troublemakers. Many were killed by the army and others sought exile in neighbouring countries.[125]

Many of the indigenous people actively involved in the reconstruction work of Alianza, many of whom had also been among the first indigenous men to go to school, who had been involved in setting up the first school in Chorraxaj or in the organization of the first *Liga Campesina*, and who had often become local leaders in their communities, were among the first to be targeted by right-wing organizations and the military. The military generally considered many of the activists to be dangerous subversives or communists, who had been organizing indigenous communities and promoting indigenous leadership.

Political upheaval during the 1978 municipal elections
The first signs of unrest leading to wholesale violence between 1980 and 1982 were already visible during the municipal elections of 1978. I have already explained that the elections broke the MLN's domination of local politics. The mayor's candidate for the Christian Democrats (DCG), Felípe Natareno, won the elections, but was opposed by the more wealthy ladinos, most of whom had supported the MLN, both because the DCG had won a first victory, and because Felípe Natareno was part indigenous. The ladinos saw the victory of Natareno as a serious threat to their own position of power. The DCG had won in several indigenous municipalities in the Quiché department. In fact, the victory in Joyabaj had come rather later than in neighbouring towns like Zacualpa and Chiché, where the DCG first won the elections with indigenous candidates for

---
125 Muj Miculax and Schramm (1989: 238).

photo 4. *DCG mayor Felipe Natareno speeches while inaugurating a stretch of road (anonymous, 1978/1979)*

mayor in 1971 and 1968 respectively.

Tensions mounted when Natareno was actually installed as mayor in June 1978 and the indigenous population of Joyabaj organized a large village *fiesta* for him. During his installation they carried him on their backs around town, just as they used to do when the new mayor of the *Alcaldía Indígena* was installed.[126] Many ladinos did not like this display of electoral victory and stayed indoors. Afterwards Natareno heard that some ladinos had threatened to disturb the festivities and that armed indigenous men had been stationed on the street corners to prevent trouble. Of course, not all ladinos were opposed to the new mayor. It was mostly the old right-wing MLN guard that was openly against him. They saw him as a pro-indigenous man who would concern himself only with indigenous problems and not as someone who would care for the ladino community. Many younger ladinos however, some of whom were active in Alianza or other community organizations and were more to the left of the political spectrum, expected change from the new mayor. People hoped for a new focus on community development and more backing for groups like Alianza, which had not had an easy relationship with the former MLN-dominated municipality.[127] Alianza had already experienced conflict with the local ladino elite and were trying to

---

126 Interview 20-99 (5/7/99).
127 Lent (1996: 82).

carve out a niche for their work in *Joyabateco* society. However, they did not get much opportunity to do so because they had to break off their projects in Joyabaj as a result of the violence, which targeted many of their local employees. Felípe Natareno's time as mayor was also curtailed because he had to flee Joyabaj in 1980. The struggle between guerrilla forces and the military had reached town and the mayor was quickly becoming a prominent target of right-wing groups in town who had put his name on a local blacklist.

Conclusion

Towards the end of the 1970s enmity between different groups in Joyabaj had grown, and divisions along ethnic, political, economic and religious lines became more pronounced. The ladino minority had risen to important positions of wealth and political influence during the previous centuries, having received backing from authoritarian governments which had extended their direct control over the rural areas. From the 1950s onward ladinos slowly started losing some of their control over land, labour and municipal affairs. Political factionalism within the ladino community grew more pronounced, especially during the governments of Arévalo and Arbenz, who started to implement various reforms that led to conflicts over land in the rural areas. At the same time, part of the indigenous majority was becoming more and more involved in political and religious affairs inside and outside their own communities. The work of Catholic Action, the political left and NGOs like Alianza were crucial elements in the process of social and political development of part of the indigenous population, especially the young men. Influence within the indigenous communities started clustering itself among these youngsters, who were among the first to attend school.

During the 1978 elections, the DCG and its local indigenous leaders had become a force to be reckoned with, gaining votes and political confidence, and nominating their own candidates. A shift of power was taking place, which threatened to put the ladinos in the position of a permanent political minority. Alliances were forged between indigenous Catholic Action activists and left-wing politicians from the DCG, while the right-wing MLN, which had been the leading ladino party from the 1950s onward, allied itself with indigenous people *de costumbre*. As a result, the already polarized relations between ladinos and *indigenas* were further complicated by conflicts *within* indigenous and ladino communities, creating divisions along religious and political lines within ethnic groups. Clearly, an uncertain and volatile situation had developed in Joyabaj, leading to wholesale violence in the early 1980s.

3

Random violence: social and institutional breakdown

(1978-1982)

By 1980, the Sandinistas had won in Nicaragua, a strong *Frente* existed in El Salvador, strikes were occurring on the Guatemalan south coast, and miners were holding protest marches in Huehuetenango.[1] These national and international events influenced the attitude of Guatemala's ruling elite towards those groups that were proposing change, including political parties such as the DCG, Catholic Action activists, the newly formed local indigenous leadership, community workers and guerrilla organizations. They were all considered potentially dangerous to the existing power structure.

Chapter 2 ended with the installation of Felipe Natareno as first DCG mayor in Joyabaj. During his two years as mayor, the situation in Joyabaj, as elsewhere in Guatemala, deteriorated rapidly as a result of increasing clashes between guerrilla groups and government forces. Since the 1960s, guerrilla activity and the counter-insurgency campaigns of the military government have left Guatemala in a continuous state of low-intensity civil war. At the end of the 1970s the violence, especially military repression, intensified. Guerrillas also stepped up their anti-government activities and were in control of several areas in the western highlands by the early 1980s. The military government regarded them as a threat to national security and stepped up repression. They were afraid of the growing support for the guerrillas, especially among the indigenous population. They changed their tactics from the selective targeting of specific groups and individuals to the mass destruction of more than 400 mainly indigenous villages in the countryside, indiscriminately killing thousands of men, women and children. More than half a million refugees fled to Mexico while another half million were internally displaced. The aim of this military terror campaign was to destroy any base of popular support the guerrilla enjoyed among the indigenous population and to regain control of the Guatemalan countryside. The violence reached its peak around 1982.

This chapter focuses on a period of chaotic violence in Joyabaj during the presidential rule of General Romeo Lucas García (1978–82). It examines the way in which the civil war and its ensuing violence affected economic and poli-

---

1   ODHAG, Vol. III (1998: 125); Anderson and Simon (1987: 22).

tical power relations in Joyabaj, paying special attention to the use of terror by agents of the state (such as the military, military intelligence, police and paramilitary groups). The chapter starts with the first guerrilla activities in the area. It then shifts attention to the killing of the local parish priest and the subsequent military presence in Joyabaj. According to local memory, the murder of the priest signified the start of difficult times in Joyabaj. The church was closed and the Catholic clergy withdrew from the Quiché department for some years. At the same time Alianza left the area because 'there were rumours that Alianza personnel were on the list of targets by the government, communities were being intimidated, and the general situation made it impossible to do any kind of work'.[2] Subsequently, the paralysing effects of the clashes between military and guerilla forces on political and economic life in Joyabaj are examined. Military campaigns wiped several indigenous villages north of Joyabaj off the map and violence seemed random. Guerrilla groups stepped up their actions and were implicated in the murder of a local ladino pharmacist, whose death caused an important shift in attitude of local ladinos towards the guerrillas. The chaotic and random violence created a power vacuum in which the military, aided by its right-wing MLN allies, stepped in to expand its grip on the countryside. This resulted in the organization of so-called home guards, which may be regarded as forerunners of the paramilitary civil patrols that were to be organized on a national scale from the end of 1981 onwards.

The murders of the local priest and the pharmacist are analysed more closely in this chapter because they reappear constantly in conversations with *Joyabatecos* on the civil war. Both cases appear to be central to the way *Joyabatecos* represent the violent civil war years. The different memories and interpretations of these incidents are described in some detail in order to show the complexity at the local level of attempts to give meaning to, and deal with, some of the events that happened during the war. As I explained in Chapter 1, memories of events differ as a result of a variety of factors, such as past and current power relations, what people are willing to say, what they think the researcher would like to hear, and what is the 'normal' thing to say. I will present and discuss the two cases, bearing these factors in mind.

First guerrilla campaigns in Joyabaj
From 1979 onwards Joyabaj started receiving attention from several guerrilla groups, especially the *Ejército Guerrillero de los Pobres* (EGP),[3] which was most active in southern Quiché. These first visits were relatively peaceful and consis-

---
2   Comments of a former Alianza coordinator (23/9/02).
3   Guerrilla Army of the Poor.

ted mainly of distributing propaganda and organizing meetings on the central town square and in front of the *Calvario* (a small church on top of a hill, near the centre of town). In these early days many *Joyabatecos* did not really mind these meetings and young ladinos even cheered the guerrillas on, shouting 'Death to the *Kaibiles*' (an elite unite of the Guatemalan army) and 'Long live the Revolution' during the rallies.[4] One ladino considered the initial ideas of the guerrillas to be quite good. He was a student at that time and received a lot of propaganda material from them. 'But everything changed when the guerrillas started to bring many indigenous people into their ranks, and it changed into a war between *indígenas* and ladinos. That should never have happened.'[5] Not all ladinos were thrilled with the guerrilla visits, especially the financially well-to-do owners of the local stores. They were harassed frequently by guerrillas, who would come heavily armed into their stores, asking for red and black paint and paintbrushes. These were supplied free, out of fear of the repercussions, and used to paint guerrilla slogans on the front of the houses.[6] These incidents were not taken too seriously by *Joyabatecos* at the time, because it had not yet come to direct personal threats or intimidation.

Apart from visits to the municipal capital, a lot of political work was done in the indigenous communities surrounding Joyabaj, especially those north of the municipal capital, like Chorraxaj and Xeabaj. The EGP focused on the formation of *cuadros políticos* (political cadres) and refrained from organizing any military units as they had done in neighbouring Zacualpa, since Joyabaj was much more populated and a guerrilla compound would be too easy to spot.[7] Once, during an interview with a former EGP combatant, I commented on the fact that the military unit in Zacualpa had been very small, amounting to only 25 men. My companion grinned and explained that 'it is no wonder we never won the war'.[8] The *cuadros políticos* educated people on politics, the national situation and the principles and goals of the EGP. Without this type of work 'one doesn't know in which direction one is heading'.[9] The political work started some time before the first open guerrilla visits to the municipal capital were staged. Already in March 1979 20 seminarists from the Catholic Church came to do social work in the indigenous communities north of Joyabaj. María de Jesús Boládo, a Spanish nun who had been working in Joyabaj since 1977, introduced the whole group properly to mayor Felípe Natareno. Only after the mayor had fled to the

---

4   Interview 19-99 (22/5/99) and 42-99 (25/7/99).
5   Interview 6-01 (11/5/01).
6   Interview 3-01 (7/5/01).
7   Interview 36-99 (19/8/99).
8   Interview 36-99 (19/8/99).
9   Interview 36-99 (19/8/99).

capital in 1980 was he told that the seminarists had little to do with the Catholic Church but were guerrillas doing political work in the communities.[10]

Memories of a nun

During her years in Joyabaj (1977–80) the nun María de Jesús Boládo created quite some controversy and her behaviour is commented upon frequently during the interviews, in both a negative and a positive way. Everybody agrees that she was very open about her somewhat revolutionary views on society. She danced around town when the *Sandinistas* came to power in Nicaragua in July 1979 and sang revolutionary songs during the Holy Week church procession in April 1980. 'The sister had revolutionary spirit.'[11]

Several *Joyabatecos* are convinced that María de Jesús did indeed have guerrilla sympathies and even had contact with guerrilla groups. A former student of hers remembers the following incident.[12] During needlework class the nun used to write on the blackboard a list of events during the previous week, after which her students would discuss some of them. One day she included a massacre which had occurred in the village of Panzós, department of Alta Verapaz, the week before. Several hundred indigenous women, men and children were killed by the military during a protest meeting. Because it had received national media coverage, the story had also become public knowledge in Joyabaj. Although this massacre was extensively documented and verified afterwards by national and international human rights organizations, some of the nuns' students maintain to this day that the nun had lied about the Panzós massacre. According to them, the military would never have shot innocent people, and probably started shooting only out of self-defence. Besides, it was impossible that President Lucas García would have ever given orders for such an action, for he had visited Joyabaj several times after the earthquake and donated a huge amount of money to the community. 'He came to visit us three times', one ladino lady kept repeating.[13] Some of the older ladinos recount this story as proof that the nun must have had sympathies for the guerrillas; otherwise she would never have blamed the military for the massacre at Panzós. The people, who condemn the nun for her pro-guerrilla sentiments, also seem to reject her sometimes quite radical feminist views. They accuse María de Jesús of 'not behaving as a nun at all. She did not dress like a nun, and she was very against men in general'.[14] Her annual Mothers' Days talk at the local school in 1979 turned out to be somewhat con-

---

10 Interview 23-99 (1/9/99).
11 Interview 10-99 (5/7/99).
12 Interview 32-99 (27/8/99).
13 Interview 32-99 (27/8/99).
14 Interview 32-99 (27/8/99).

fronting for the locals. She explained to the assembled families that in her opinion women were only being used by men as breeding machines and that they should stand up to them. Angry husbands told her to stop giving 'bad advice to their women' and that in Joyabaj the men ordered women what to do, and not the other way around.[15]

This contrasts with a smaller group of *Joyabatecos* who have a more positive memory of the nun and remember her as a 'broad-minded and brilliant person, full of socialist ideas' and 'a revolutionary feminist far ahead of her time'.[16] According to some younger ladinos, who remember having had catechist lessons from her, she did not talk so much about Church during class but much more about preparing for the coming violence. What to do when the military enter your house? Do you run away to get help or do you stay? What to do when you see someone being picked off the street in front of you by military? Although most children saw these simulations more as a game than reality, some of them remember very vividly that the military, and not the guerrillas, were portrayed as the bad guys. This was in stark contrast with prevailing sentiments at their homes.[17] In this respect the nun was a very important figure in the lives of several ladino youngsters, for whom she was their first contact with a revolutionary train of thought. It remains unclear how far her influence reached and whether youngsters really started behaving differently.

Clearly there are very different versions of the work of María de Jesús and what she and her work meant for Joyabaj. Some of them overlap while others clash. Talking negatively about the nun coincides with an anti-guerrilla attitude without actually admitting it, while the opposite is true for talking in favour of her actions. While the anti-guerrilla viewpoint is widespread and openly voiced among local ladinos, both old and young, the pro-guerrilla attitude is voiced with much more caution.

The killing of the local parish priest

The Catholic Church was one of the first targets of government violence in Guatemala. Their community work in the rural areas, through Catholic Action, was seen as a threat to the power base of the military and its allied elites. Organizing people into cooperatives, sending them to courses in the capital to become peasant leaders and making it possible for people to voice their ideas and complaints were considered 'subversive' activities. Besides, many members of the clergy were considered to belong to the guerrilla movement, or at least to be

---

15 Interview 22-99 (30/7/99).
16 Interview 20-99 (5/7/99) and 22-99 (30/7/99).
17 Interview 8-99 (20/6/99).

sympathetic towards them. At the end of 1979, blacklists containing the names of priests who were to be killed were circulating throughout Guatemala. These were drawn up by right-wing death squads, often helped by local informers such as military commissioners and *orejas*.[18] In a way, the use of blacklists was a formalization of the denunciation process[19] and a terror method that was being used by the Guatemalan military on a large scale. The mere possibility of one's name appearing on such a list as a result of, for example, an anonymous accusation caused enormous uncertainty and anxiety among the population. In this case, church personnel were branded 'subversive' and 'communist' and put on blacklists as such, thus becoming prime targets of the military and right-wing groups.[20] Many priests, nuns and Catholic laymen were killed or disappeared, or had to flee during the early 1980s. The summer of 1980 was an especially tragic one. Threats and bombardments caused the flight of the priest of Uspantán in March 1980; and on 4 June the priest from Chajul, Padre José María Gran, was killed by the military together with his sacristan. The remaining priests in Quiché, however, decided to stay put until on 10 July a second priest was killed by the military. His name was Faustino Villanueva, a Spaniard of the *Misioneros del Sagrado Corazón* (MSC) order, who was parish priest in Joyabaj at that time. He had been working in the municipality since 1968.[21]

The priest was killed at 8.00 p.m. immediately after saying mass. Two unknown men had come to ask for him at the parish house, encountering the priest's cook who went to look for him. After Padre Villanueva welcomed the two men into his office, he was shot in the back and left for dead. The men rode off on their yellow motorcycle towards Zacualpa. An hour and a half later they were seen entering the garrison of the *Guardia de Hacienda* in Santa Cruz de Quiché.[22] The next day, 11 July, the same two men returned on their motorcycle to look for the parish priest in nearby Zacualpa, who had left in time. On 12 July they were spotted looking for two nuns at the Dominican College in Santa Cruz. Finally, they were also implicated in an attempt to kill the bishop of the Quiché Dioceses, Monseñor Gerardi, on 18 July. The next day Monseñor Gerardi convened a meeting of all priests, nuns and other pastoral agents working in Quiché. He announced his decision to close down the Quiché Dioceses for some time 'as a form of protest and accusation, and also as a way to save lives and to be able to continue church work with the communities in other ways'.[23] Eventually,

---

18 *Oreja* means literally 'ear'. They were local spies who were connected with military intelligence, collecting information within their own communities.
19 Claridge (2000: 205).
20 *Frente Guatemala* (November 1980).
21 Diócesis del Quiché (2000).
22 *Frente Guatemala* (November 1980). The *Guardia de Hacienda* was a police unit, under tight military control. It was notorious for its human rights abuses during and after the conflict.
23 Bulletin CUC and other popular organizations, 31/7/80.

Monseñor Gerardi was killed in 1998, three days after the public presentation of the REMHI report,[24] of which he was the chairman. In June 2001, three military officers and a priest were convicted for the murder of Monseñor Gerardi.

The murder of Padre Villanueva shook the *Joyabatecos* and showed they could no longer stay out of the trouble the rest of Guatemala had already been experiencing for some time. His murder, presumably committed by military forces although nobody was ever caught, was incomprehensible to many *Joyabatecos*. They could not imagine any connection between Padre Villanueva and guerrilla organizations. According to a former colleague, 'he was a good priest, very popular, very much a friend of the people, but not a leader in the community, he was not a restless pastoral agent talking about social revolutions. On the contrary, he was a typical traditional priest; humble, simple, loved, good company, but not a man of initiatives or an organizer of people'.[25] Many ladinos and *indígenas* share this version and remember him as a martyr; but they do not accord him the same revolutionary fire that many *Joyabatecos* attribute to the nun María de Jesús.[26] A former Catholic Action activist explains that 'the others [MLN] thought the priest, the nuns, the people from Alianza and the *gringos* were all guides ... guides of the *Ejército de los Pobres*. When the priest gave communion to the people, they [MLN] accused him of telling people to vote for the DC'.[27] Most people are convinced that the priest never did such things, because when he noticed people giving a political message in church he always told them to take their political views elsewhere. It is said that the priest used to say, quite frequently, that 'politics is OK, but outside the church'.[28]

Padre Villanueva had been the only remaining member of the clergy in town, for the three nuns, including María de Jesús, had already left because of the violence. Villanueva's death left Joyabaj bereft and in chaos. People higher up in the Catholic Church hierarchy decided not to bury the priest in Joyabaj but in Chichicastenango, where Padre José María Gran was also laid to rest after he had been killed a month earlier. Around 50 *Joyabatecos* attended the funeral, among them various leaders from Catholic Action and several ladinos. A priest who was present at the funeral thought it remarkable that these people had shown up at all, especially because only a few months earlier the most influential ladinos in the area had been summoned to attend a meeting with the commander of Military Zone 20 in Santa Cruz and were told that they were either

---

24 Report of the truth commission of the Catholic Church, in which several thousand testimonies are collected about the civil war period.
25 Frente Guatemala (November 1980).
26 Lent (1996: 84-85).
27 Interview 13-01 (10/6/01).
28 Interview 13-01 (10/6/01).

with the military or against them.²⁹ Attending Villanueva's funeral clearly deviated from the military directives. But most thought it too dangerous: military commissioners in Joyabaj had already issued warnings that the names of everybody who attended would be put on a blacklist that would be presented to the military. The DCG mayor was explicitly warned by his own people not to go, 'especially if he had decided to talk during the funeral'.³⁰

Joyabatecos did organize some kind of commemoration in Joyabaj in honour of Padre Villanueva. Immediately after his murder they decided to collect the blood that had been spilt on the floor. Manuel Tol, who was sacristan at that time, covered the bloodstains with white sand, swept it all up and put it in a bucket, covering it with an altar cloth. Leaders of Catholic Action organized a procession the next day, during which the blood of Villanueva was carried around town. Between 200 and 300 men and women participated, mostly *indígenas* from the surrounding communities who were active in Catholic Action. It was quite a turnout for such a potentially dangerous activity.³¹ When the procession was already on its way, the military arrived in Joyabaj. They entered town in eight military trucks, machine guns pointed outwards. It was considered by many locals more as a display of power to 'fill people up with fear' than a search for the killers of Padre Villanueva.³² However, they only circled the central square a few times and watched the procession from a distance, without interfering.

Finally, during a symbolic funeral the blood was buried under the church altar and a small memorial tablet was placed over it. In 1992 another, larger memorial was erected for Padre Villanueva in the courtyard between the church and the parish house. This was done by Padre Juan Vasquez, who was the first Catholic priest in Joyabaj to arrive after the violence in 1988. A photograph of Villanueva was placed on the memorial, together with those of two other two priests who were killed in Quiché during the civil war.³³ They were accompanied by the words 'martyr priest', which was quite a statement to make, even in 1992 when the military still had an active presence in Joyabaj. It would be the beginning of a yearly commemoration of Padre Villanueva as a martyr of the Catholic Church on 10 July. The death of Villanueva marked the start of 'difficult times in Joyabaj' not only for many *Joyabatecos* but also for the Catholic Church.³⁴ This feeling was strengthened by the fact that the military had come to Joyabaj for

---

29 Diócesis del Quiché (2000: 90).
30 Interview 23-99 (1/9/99).
31 Interview 8-01 (9/5/01).
32 Interview 23-99 (1/9/99).
33 The other two priests were Padre José María Gran who was killed on 4 June 1980 and Padre Juan Alonso, who was killed on 15 February 1981. Although nobody was ever convicted, military responsibility was presumed.
34 Interview 14-98 (19/6/98).

photo 5. *Shrine remembering Padre Villanueva, located in the church yard (author, 1999)*

their first prolonged stay, immediately after Padre Villanueva's death.

Although civil war violence had claimed other victims in Joyabaj before Padre Villanueva, his death stirred up many more feelings because he was a public figure who was known for his aversion to politics inside the church and who had never voiced pro-guerrilla sentiments. His murder seemed to convey the message to the locals that, if someone like Padre Villanueva could become a target of government violence, everybody could. In this respect, government terror was effective in confirming the uncertainty of the violence.

Military occupation of Joyabaj
Initially the army concentrated its offensives in the department of Quiché, which it considered a guerrilla stronghold. Especially the Ixil area in the north of Quiché and the southern fringe, where Joyabaj is situated, were thought of as a potential threat to the unity of the state.[35] Until the second half of 1981 military and paramilitary forces, such as the right-wing death squad *Ejército Secreto Anticomunista* (ESA, Secret Anticommunist Army),[36] concentrated on selective repression with the aim of removing local leaders, whether church leaders, politicians or community workers. Both indigenous and ladino leaders on the left of the political spectrum were targeted. Military visits to the communities were also

---

35 GNIB, March/April 1982: 3-6.
36 McClintock (1985: 142).

used to gather basic information on the area, such as the location of the different hamlets and the whereabouts of certain individuals. The first military operations in rural areas were organized and carried out by regional and local military authorities (Zone Commanders) of the military zones themselves. Military Zone 20 in Santa Cruz de Quiché (*Zona Militar* or *Brigada Quiché* as it was called before 1983) was responsible for the southern part of the Quiché department, including Joyabaj.[37] Information about these early military activities is scanty and not very detailed, possibly because no central records were kept of actions that were not directly planned and carried out by a central military command.

Until the summer of 1981, the military visited Joyabaj sporadically and for only a few hours at a time, often in hot pursuit of guerrillas who had been spotted in the area or had temporarily occupied the municipal capital. Although the first guerrilla visits were quite harmless, the subsequent army visits were not and the army's behaviour angered many *Joyabatecos*. Women were harassed and people were threatened and killed on the street if they did not have the right identification papers with them. Ladinos commented that they 'were behaving like animals'.[38] One military action is mentioned time and again during interviews with ladinos, who were able to witness the results for themselves because it was carried out in town. It happened on a Sunday morning, a market day, after the guerrillas had organized a meeting in town during which flyers with guerrilla propaganda were distributed. Shortly after the guerrillas had left town, the military entered and gathered people on the town *plaza* asking for identification papers. Many indigenous people, who did not understand Spanish and could not read or write, handed over the papers they had picked up during the guerrilla meeting. The military arrested most of them and locked them up in jail and the *Salón Municipal* (assembly hall for community use) on the town square. The night after the arrests were made nobody was allowed on the streets and screams were heard. Very early the following morning the dead bodies of the people who had been picked up the previous day were thrown out of a truck along the road to the nearby municipality of Zacualpa. This way everybody could see what happened to 'presumed' guerrilla collaborators.[39] The open display of corpses was a clear example of how people were intimidated and terrorized into complying with military orders.[40] Government forces openly used random terror, which could target anybody. Probably most of the people who had been picked up had nothing to do with the guerrillas at all, and the military probably realized this. However, an example had to be set and thus people were to be killed. Violence

---

37 ODHAG, Vol. III (1998: 102).
38 Interview 44-99 (22/4/99).
39 Interview 24-99 (31/5/99).
40 See Claridge (2000: 218) on the terrorizing effects of public executions and display of corpses.

had hit Joyabaj hard.

The military's first prolonged stay occurred after the death of Padre Villanueva in July 1980. They put up their camp north of Joyabaj, just outside town and stayed until a few days after the inauguration of the annual town *fiesta* in August 1980.[41] 'The *fiesta* of August 1980 was very sad. We organized a committee, and we also invited a very good marimba group. But not many people came, because there were soldiers all over the place.'[42] The soldiers had received permission to attend the annual festivities, which resulted in a *Salón Municipal* full of heavily armed men applauding the newly elected *Señorita de Joyabaj*.[43] The military also started roaming around town, checking up on people, asking questions and listening. They visited schools, talked with the headmasters, enquired about the class 'religious morality' which was taught by the nun María de Jesús, and listened carefully to speeches made during an annual school celebration. A former school master explained, 'We refrained from saying anything about Villanueva during the speech, it was just to dangerous because they were all listening'.[44] People remember this first military visit quite well because during this period various locals disappeared. Among them was the mayor's brother, who had been seen talking to some military men on the day of the inauguration of the *fiesta*, after which he disappeared.[45] He was never seen again. 'They [the military] did not respect anybody or anything ... they were only interested in sowing terror ... many persons who had important positions within the Maya religion were killed ... somebody who knew something ... or talked about the guerrilla movement ... they were taken away.'[46] The actual presence of the military and the knowledge that they were prepared to use violence against the local population indiscriminately caused many people to leave town or else keep their mouths shut.

The destruction of political leadership
The Christian Democrats were another prime target, like the Catholic Church, of the military and right-wing organizations. At the national level the DCG had already decided to close down all its offices in the countryside and in the capital, because of the increasing violence directed at DCG members. During the first two weeks of June 1980, just before Padre Villanueva was killed in Joyabaj, six national DCG leaders were killed, among them Julio Hamilton Noriega from

---

41 *Fiesta de la Virgen del Tránsito* (10-15 August).
42 Interview 3-01 (7/5/01).
43 Beauty Queen.
44 Interview 3-01 (7/5/01).
45 Interview 13-99 (4/10/99).
46 Interview 8-01 (9/5/01).

Santa Cruz de Quiché. It was he who had helped to set up the DCG office in Joyabaj and had been involved in the local cooperative. The right-wing death squad ESA claimed responsibility for his murder. In a newspaper add they explained that they would not rest 'until we have eliminated all communist traitors of our fatherland'.[47]

Two weeks after the murder of Padre Villanueva, when the situation became really heated, Felípe Natareno, who had become the first Christian Democratic mayor in 1978, fled Joyabaj. He had already been receiving threats since he was installed as mayor, and these had multiplied gradually. He was accused of being a 'communist' and 'guerrilla leader'. After hearing that his name was definitely on a local blacklist he left with his family for Guatemala City. According to him 'only fools did not leave after such threats'.[48] Former EGP combatants accuse 'groups in society, formed by the MLN' of being responsible for the murder of Padre Villanueva and the flight of Felípe Natareno'.[49] He was not the first one in the municipality to feel threatened. Violence already affected municipal officials as early as August 1979 when DCG council member Manuel Grave Castro disappeared. The minutes of the *Libro de Actas* (municipal acts) at that time were not censored, and the fact of his disappearance was recorded. Victoriano Gil, a ladino and former police officer who was on the list of municipal substitutes (*supplente*), was appointed in his place and moved to the top position in local politics after replacing Felípe Natareno as mayor in September 1980.[50]

Between August 1980 and April 1982 all the DCG council members dropped out of the municipality and left Joyabaj, some of them for good. Only the *Partido Revolucionario/Partido Institucional Democrático* (PR/PID)[51] council members stayed on, while some of the DCG members were replaced by people not directly connected to the DCG. Most of them lacked any political experience or guidance and did not belong to ladino families who were known to be politically active. Clearly the municipality was severely weakened in its operations. Hardly any decisions were taken, especially with DCG and other local activists and leaders leaving and the right-wing *Joyabatecos*, allied with the MLN, feeling stronger. The municipal council convened only sporadically, and little of real

---

47 Inforpress Centroamericana, no. 396 (12/6/80: 6).
48 Interview 20-99 (5/7/99).
49 Interview 36-99 (19/8/99).
50 *Libro de Actas*, 9/9/80.
51 The Revolutionary Party (PR) originated in 1957 as a continuation of the social democratic governments of Arévalo and Arbenz. After 1974 the PR took a turn to the right, especially after forming coalitions with the Institutional Democratic Party (PID) in 1978 and 1982. The PID was founded in 1964 by the military. Its base consisted of the commercial sector, the military and state bureaucrats. It presented itself as a pragmatic and bureaucratic party, but was in fact very close to the right-wing MLN (Sichar Moreno, 1999: 18, 25).

importance is mentioned in the *Libro de Actas* during these years. Barely a word was written down about the mounting violence or military and guerrilla actions, and discussions during municipal council sessions in these months centred on problems with the water supply and the distribution of cemetery plots.[52]

From December 1981 until 13 April 1982, when Victoriano Gil presided over its last meeting, the municipal council convened only four times. No records exist mentioning the formal end of the four-year term of the council, which had begun in 1978 when the Christian Democrats had won the elections, with Felípe Natareno as their candidate for mayor. Moreover, no mention is made of the installation of a new municipal council. In the years before, even at the height of political problems, such events were always noted in detail. The non-existence of these municipal records was of course due to the violence and its devastating effects on local politics. A 1981 article in a right-wing newspaper discussed the upcoming presidential elections in March 1982 the following terms: 'Guerrilla destruction of municipal buildings and documents (including voter registration lists) as well as attacks on mayors and local military representatives has left an absence of military and administrative control in many areas. This disruption of traditional local power structures will make it difficult to organize and control the electoral process.'[53] The devastating effects of military violence on local politics and the electoral process are not mentioned.

Alianza leaves Joyabaj

Another prime target of military repression was Alianza, the international NGO that had been working in Joyabaj since the earthquake of 1976, and which had intensified its presence thereafter. Friction had already emerged as early as 1976 between Alianza and the local ladino elite over the way in which the reconstruction committee should be formed. The mayor at that time, Próspero Ogáldez, started appointing people to the committee, while Alianza wanted an elected committee. Alianza won the argument but, as a former Alianza coordinator stated, 'this "victory", while significant for strengthening unity at the community level, began a history of antagonism between our organization and some of the elite (ladinos) of the municipality'.[54] The relationship was also strained because Alianza started working in the indigenous villages, while other NGOs worked in the municipal capital. Alianza was thus accused of being biased *(partidaria)* towards the indigenous community. As mentioned before, the victory of the DCG in 1978 had upset the local power elite but caused optimism among

---

52 *Libro de Actas* from September 1980 until April 1982.
53 GNIB, March/April 1982: 6.
54 Lent (1996: 81).

Alianza personnel, who hoped that a DCG council would mean more support for rural development projects and fewer problems for Alianza while carrying out their work. However, the national situation deteriorated rapidly and Alianza became a prime target for right-wing extremists.

The relationship between Alianza and the local ladino elite became even more strained when rumours started spreading through town about presumed connections between Alianza and guerrilla groups. Words like "social promotion,' 'community organization,' and 'awareness raising' were branded as subversive activities by many authorities at municipal, departmental, and national levels'.[55] These words were central to Alianza's work. An indigenous woman remembers that 'When the Violence came, they [military] said they [Alianza] were bad people. They said that the help of Alianza was bad help ... and that the houses Alianza had built, were no good ... they said that Alianza had planted the guerrilla'.[56] Although sympathy towards guerrilla activities among Alianza personnel did exist, active involvement was a very different matter. Nevertheless, the nature of their work and projects seemed to be enough to cast doubt on the entire organization. 'These program principles and activities of Alianza, and the actions and beliefs of the Mayan communities, became themselves a source and cause of conflict, misinterpretation, political manipulation, and violence.'[57] According to an older ladino, a former headmaster who was quite positive about Alianza, 'they [Alianza] gave ideas to the *indígenas* ... after which the *indítos* started to say that they had to get everything back, all the land in the village ... that everything was theirs'. He remembered one of the Alianza people telling him, while drunk, that 'from now on things are going to change. We are going to rule (*mandar*). You ladinos are only a few, we are many'.[58] These memories possibly indicate a fear on the part of the ladinos of the indigenous majority, fear that they could and would indeed take over power and fear that the ladinos could indeed lose their land and other possessions. Such feelings of 'we' and 'they', which indicate a further polarization in relations between different ethnic, political and religious groups, were exploited by the Guatemalan government and the military during the civil war years. They were enforced by official anti-communist rhetoric, which was spread throughout the country by extensive media campaigns.[59]

From 1980 onwards several of Alianza's employees started receiving nightly visits from armed, non-uniformed men, warning them not to associate with

---

55 Lent (1996: 85).
56 Interview 26-99 (21/8/99).
57 Lent (1998: 7).
58 Interview 13-99 (4/10/99).
59 Inforpress Centroamericana, no. 396 (12/6/80: 7).

NGOs. The situation became really heated after the killing of Padre Villanueva in August 1980. Immediately after the murder, Alianza called a meeting of all its personnel to discuss the future of its work in Joyabaj. 'Will our continued presence make local staff more or less vulnerable?',[60] they asked themselves. They came to the conclusion that 'the situation appeared to be much too polarized to continue any kind of effective work, and one year "ahead of time", the program decide to suspend activities and close down'.[61] The Alianza Southern Quiché programme (covering nine neighbouring municipalities in the south of Quiché), however, concluded that withdrawing would indicate guilt and would imply abandoning responsibilities within the communities. After ample discussion the Southern Quiché programme agreed to recommit itself and everybody returned to Quiché after the meeting. However, during their absence staff members' families and friends had been tortured and killed by right-wing paramilitary groups (ESA) and the army. The next day, the decision to stay was revoked and the programme closed down. Some staff members stayed in their communities, most of whom survived, while others were killed, sought refuge in neighbouring municipalities and departments, went to the coast or the city or migrated to Mexico. A small number joined the guerrillas. According to some *Joyabatecos*, 'people were not quite ready yet for the work of Alianza, they did not have the right mentality'.[62] Many ladinos became afraid when Alianza started to work actively with indigenous people, especially when organizing them. The same ladinos plundered and subsequently burned down the Alianza buildings as soon as the organization had left town.

A former Alianza coordinator explained that in August 1981, 'after the initial wave of intimidation and violence ... former staff began to come back to us and say that the communities were asking us to come back. They explained that conditions had improved, and that community committees were anxious to carry on with their suspended projects'.[63] According to Alberto Quezada, a ladino from Joyabaj who had been responsible for Alianza's infrastructural projects for some years, it was possible to carry out infrastructural projects because the authorities did not view these with suspicion. After meetings with the military commander in Santa Cruz de Quiché and the governor of Quiché, Alianza restarted a small number of its projects in Joyabaj. On 18 October 1981, only two weeks after the killing of the pharmacist Ramiro Paíz, military from the army base that had just been established in the buildings of the Catholic Church picked up Alberto Quezada, who was taking a stroll in the Sunday market. He was never seen again.

---

60 Lent (1998: 10).
61 Lent (1998: 10).
62 Interview 20-99 (5/7/99).
63 Lent (1998: 11).

This case can serve as an example of an attack on 'leaders and others in an attempt to break the functionality of an organization by selecting victims whose loss will in itself be significant, but whose death will also have profound effects upon the psychology of their colleagues'.[64] This was clearly the case after Alberto Quezada was killed. Although people 'wanted to organize a protest and complain to the authorities [...] they were afraid and certain that they would meet a similar fate. If it could happen to Beto [Alberto Quezada], a well respected ladino, it could happen to anyone'.[65] During a discussion with a former employee of Alianza, it became clear that the decision to leave Joyabaj was a very difficult one and that people felt they were letting down the people in Joyabaj. He also asked himself whether Alianza's presence in the communities had not helped provoke the violence in any way, and whether they had made the right decisions.[66] Maybe they should not have listened to the requests of people like Alberto Quezada to reopen the programme. Maybe they should have done things in another way.[67] But at that time they did not know in which direction the violent events were going and what was still to come. Some of these people, who have not been back to Joyabaj for many years, still carry the burden of these questions asked and decisions made more then 20 years ago.

The murder of Alberto Quezada also influenced Alianza's outlook on the future, and since then the organization started to devote a lot of time to informing authorities on how they worked and what they exactly did and why. Over the next two years meetings with military commanders, diplomats, departmental governors, rotary club members, ministers and even the president were held, during which Alianza's work and programme philosophy were presented. Although it did not bring back Alberto Quezada or other disappeared Alianza staff members, it did open up more space and decrease the tension for Alianza and their work in communities in other parts of the country.

Chorraxaj activism cut short

In the previous chapter the village of Chorraxaj was introduced together with some of its more active inhabitants who were participating in Catholic Action projects, Alianza and local politics. From the end of the 1970s onward 'individuals who had developed their personal capacities during the post-disaster relief project were seen as troublemakers. Many were killed by the army, while others

---

64 Claridge (2000: 222). Possibly the same tactic was used during the killing of Padre Villanueva, which caused the withdrawal of the Catholic Church from Quiché and uncertainty among *Joyabatecos* who could not comprehend the murder of a priest who, according to most people, did not have any connections with the guerrilla.
65 Comments of a former Alianza coordinator (23/9/02).
66 Interview 44-99 (22/4/99).
67 Interview 19-01 (5/6/01).

sought exile in neighboring countries'.[68] This especially applied to villages such as Chorraxaj, which were centres not only of reconstruction efforts but also of the formation of local indigenous leaders who had become active in the cooperative movement, local politics, church groups and other committees. These were the people most heavily persecuted by military violence. In many cases, the same persons were involved in several of these groups and were thus prime targets, like for example Juan,[69] an indigenous man from Chorraxaj who was council member for the DCG in the municipality and had been politically active for quite some time. He was also involved in the organization of the Improvement Committee in Chorraxaj, in the formation and leadership of the local cooperative, the *Ligas Campesinas*, and was part of the *Junta Parroquial* of Catholic Action. He fled to the capital after having been accused of being responsible for the killing of Ramiro Paíz, the pharmacist, in October 1981. Presumably some local ladinos with close ties to the military supplied the military with his name, claiming that a black ski mask he was wearing during the guerrilla attack had fallen off, revealing his face.[70] Leaflets were distributed around town, displaying Juan's photograph together with those of two other men, seeking information on their whereabouts. 'They were not looking for them just to say hello', a ladino man commented.[71]

Whoever was really responsible, the accusations of some prominent local ladinos were enough to drive Juan and his family away from Joyabaj for more than a decade. He returned to Joyabaj for the first time in 1996, albeit without his wife and children.[72] He decided not to return permanently because he still felt threatened and because he had built up his life elsewhere, as many other displaced people had done. His parents, who returned to Chorraxaj after living in the town of Joyabaj during the most violent years, also decided against his permanent return. He visits mainly during town *fiesta* days and during the sugar cane harvest when *panela*[73] is made, as he still grows sugar cane on one of his old plots in Chorraxaj.

Together with Juan, many other indigenous leaders from Chorraxaj and surrounding communities, who had been climbing the social and political ladder, fled Joyabaj, some of them immediately after the killing of Padre Faustino Villanueva. They were told their names were on the blacklists that were circulating around town. The flight of these men had major repercussions for local power relations. Whole segments of indigenous society were killed, left or kept

---

68 Muj Miculax and Schramm (1989: 225-240).
69 The name Juan is an alias.
70 Interview 44-99 (22/4/99).
71 Interview 13-99 (4/10/99).
72 Interview 12-98 (17/5/98).
73 *Panela* is the sugary end-product of sugar cane after it is harvested, cooked and pressed into round moulds.

their heads down. They were hunted down not only by the military, but also by local right-wing death squads who, supposedly, had close ties with political groups in Joyabaj like the right-wing MLN. Some of these *Joyabatecos* also had close relations with military intelligence, through their work as military commissioner or *oreja*.

Guerrilla activity increases

Guerrilla activity in southern Quiché intensified in the beginning of 1981. On Sunday 25 January 100 guerrillas from the EGP, the *Organización Revolucionario del Pueblo en Armas* (ORPA)[74] and the *Partido Guatetemalteco del Trabajo* (PGT)[75] occupied the town of Joyabaj for several hours. They organized meetings, distributed propaganda, captured and disarmed the local police force, freed six people from jail, cut the communication lines and took medicine from the local hospital. Later on that day a shoot-out with a military patrol took place. This action was part of a larger guerrilla offensive in which Zacualpa and San Pedro Jocopilas, two other municipalities in southern Quiché, were also attacked.[76] Another massive guerrilla offensive hit southern Quiché on 19 July 1981, when Joyabaj, together with several other municipalities, was once more occupied. The government building in Santa Cruz was dynamited, large stores were ransacked (the owner belonged to a wealthy ladino family in Joyabaj), buses were burned, roads made impassable and police stations attacked. According to the Guatemalan newspapers, the attack was to celebrate the birthday of the Nicaraguan Revolution (19 July 1979) and the organization of a new EGP front called *Frente Agusto Cesar Sandino* (FACS).[77] Government officials became increasingly alarmed at the guerrilla threat and President Lucas García admitted on 1 August that his regime was facing a 'well-organized rebel army'.[78]

During the second half of 1981 the guerrillas intensified their activities and focused on attacking military, police and government buildings and personnel. They also increased their attacks on the economic and physical infrastructure of the country in an attempt to destabilize the economy and isolate part of the Quiché department from the rest of Guatemala. Electricity plants were bombed,

---

74 Revolutionary Organization of the People in Arms. ORPA was founded in 1976 as a splinter group from the *Fuerzas Armadas Rebeldes* (FAR or Revolutionary Armed Forces). For a detailed analysis of the complicated alliances and secessions between the most important guerrilla organizations (PGT, FAR, ORPA and EGP) see Sichar Moreno (1999: 31-43).
75 Guatemalan Workers Party. The PGT started in 1949 as a communist party (*Partido Comunista de Guatemala* – PCG) and changed its name to PGT in 1952 to facilitate its legalization as a political party (Sichar Moreno, 1999: 59).
76 Inforpress Centroamericana, 29/1/81; Prensa Libre, 26/1/81; La Nación 26/1/81.
77 (IISG, doos 42, doc. 4) El Dia, 21/7/81; Unomásuno 21/7/81; Prensa Libre, 20/7/81.
78 Latin American Regional Reports, 14/8/88.

bridges were dynamited, highways sabotaged and buses ambushed and burned.[79] Joyabaj was hit badly during these attacks; water and electricity supplies were destroyed, and transportation to nearby municipalities became hazardous. The Guatemalan military were convinced the guerrillas were trying to create a 'liberated territory' in the south of Quiché which would be solely in the hands of the guerrilla.[80] However, after a major military offensive in the south of Quiché that started late 1981 and continued until the end of 1982, the guerrillas had to withdraw from the area in 1982, 'admitting that they had lost the battle, but not the war'.[81]

As a result of the increase in guerrilla activity in the area, the initial positive feelings of some of the ladinos in Joyabaj towards the guerrillas had declined somewhat. People felt that guerrilla presence in the area also meant an increased military presence, bringing trouble and violence. In general guerrilla violence or presence provoked strong counter-attacks from the military.[82] Thus indirectly the guerrillas were blamed for much of the military violence because, so the argument goes, if the guerrillas had not started stirring things up, no military actions would have been needed. The ladino population of Joyabaj used this argument extensively, also in connection with Alianza and the Catholic Church. If these organizations had not started educating the indigenous people, they would never have sympathized with the guerrillas and hence no violence would have come to Joyabaj.[83]

The death of a pharmacist: conflictive memories

An important incident which contributed significantly to the growing negative sentiments among local ladinos towards guerrilla forces was the guerrilla visit on 1 October 1981, when a local pharmacist was killed. It was the first visit to Joyabaj during which the guerrillas actually used violence against the ladino population. Before that memorable visit, 'the guerrillas did not harm anyone, they only freed some prisoners, organized a meeting and left again. But afterwards they came back with rancour, especially towards political people'.[84]

The general story of what happened on 1 October goes as follows. In broad daylight a group of guerrillas arrived in a covered truck, rode into the centre of town and went to search the houses of several former mayors, some of whom were MLN activists or were rumoured to belong to right-wing death squads.

---

79 GNIB, Jan/Feb 1982: 9.
80 Inforpress Centroamericana, 3/12/81.
81 Carmack (1988: 59).
82 Interview 19-99 (22/5/99).
83 Interview 13-99 (4/10/99).
84 Interview 12-01 (21/5/01).

Ramiro Paíz Balcárcel, a well-liked pharmacist and former mayor, was the only one unable to escape and was killed by the guerrillas.[85] This incident hit both the ladino and the indigenous communities in Joyabaj hard. It was the first time guerrillas had actually killed somebody. Furthermore, they killed someone who was well known and respected, and had authority in town. People did not understand why he was singled out to be killed. Many ladinos argued that he was not a member of the right-wing MLN, did not belong to a death squad, and was not connected to military intelligence. People readily supplied the names of other possible targets for the guerrillas, who would have been much more likely to be killed because of their known right-wing sympathies at the time. Several stories about the reason for the killing of Ramiro Paíz circled and still circle around Joyabaj. Was he just in the wrong place at the wrong time, did he indeed have contacts with guerrilla forces, or was he silenced by them because he had been a witness to the murder of Padre Villanueva? Or was he indeed a victim of a military operation? The different and sometimes contradictory stories will be described in some detail, because they vividly show the various and sometimes contrasting interpretations by different people of the same events. Being a ladino who has seen his position in town diminishing, or an indigenous activist struggling for political representation, clearly coloured the way people presented memories of certain, possibly politically charged, events.

Some of the more ardent anti-guerrilla ladinos explain the killing of Ramiro Paíz solely in terms of his influential position in town, and ignore any possible connection with the guerrillas. He was a former mayor and owner of the largest pharmacy in town, which left him financially well-off: reason enough for the guerrillas to kill him. They stress the fact that the guerrillas were also looking for other ladino leaders, who were able to escape in time. Some of them make the story even more interesting by adding that Rigoberta Menchú, the Nobel Peace Prize laureate, was present during the guerrilla attack that killed Ramiro Paíz.[86] This embellishment to the story can be seen as a way for locals to give meaning to the death of Ramiro Paíz. However, it is also a way to present a current indigenous Nobel Peace Prize laureate in a negative way. The people who offered this account were mostly ladinos who had been strongly opposed to guerrilla activities. A second group of people, ladinos and *indígenas* with a more positive view on past guerrilla activity, made a connection between Ramiro Paíz and the guerrilla, but did so through his friendship with the Spanish nun María de Jesús Boládo, who was considered pro-guerrilla. The pharmacy of Ramiro Paíz was situated opposite the church buildings and next to the convent and thus he could

---

85 Interview 14-98 (19/6/98).
86 Interview 2-01 (10/5/01).

observe everything going on there. Allegedly he helped the nun by receiving some boxes with church material at the address of his pharmacy, which could otherwise have got the nun into trouble. According to the story, the daughter of Ramiro Paíz opened one of the boxes and found propaganda material for the guerrillas. Although closing the cases afterwards, the guerrilla found out and killed Ramiro Paíz to prevent him from talking.[87] Supposedly the whole guerrilla operation was a cover for the killing of Ramiro Paíz. A third story has it that the killing was done by accident. Ramiro Paíz had a gun in his hand, threatening the guerrillas who were trying to capture him. A weapon went off, and he was killed. He was just in the wrong place at the wrong time.

A fourth and final account, which contrasts markedly with the different local narratives surrounding the death of the pharmacist, forms part of the suit that Nobel prizewinner Rigoberta Menchú presented to the Supreme Court in Spain in 1999. The complaint implicates three former Guatemalan presidents (Lucas García, Ríos Montt and Mejía Víctores) in the murder of Spanish citizens during the civil war years. One of the cases presented is the murder of Padre Villanueva in July 1980. According to the complaint, the killing of Villanueva and of the pharmacist Ramiro Paíz more than a year later were connected. The pharmacist was not killed by the guerrilla, but by military posing as guerrillas because he allegedly witnessed (*testigo presencial*) the killing of Padre Villanueva.[88] The cook of Padre Villanueva, who had seen the two men who murdered the Padre, fled to the pharmacist after it had happened and told him everything. Therefore the pharmacist had become a threat to the military and had to be killed: a 'burning of archives' in military intelligence terms.[89] Some former Alianza employees were stunned but, upon reflection, not in disbelief when I presented them with the explanation given by the *Fundación* Rigoberta Menchú. It had never occurred to them that Ramiro Paíz could have been killed by military forces posing as guerrillas, because they had received information from *Joyabatecos* only about guerrilla involvement. They added, however, that this military strategy had been used in other areas where the military, disguised as guerrillas, had indeed killed locals with the aim of winning them over to their side and set up civil patrols without much protest.[90]

The killing of the pharmacist in Joyabaj also resulted in ladinos adopting a more negative attitude towards guerrilla forces. It is strange, however, that the pharmacist was killed more than a year after Padre Villanueva's death and that

---

87 Interview 14-98 (19/6/98) and CEH, Vol. XI (1999: 1422).
88 Organización Rigoberta Menchú (2000).
89 *Querella de Rigoberta Menchú Tum* (1999: 47). www.pangea.org/impunitat/querella.html [February 2001].
90 Latin America Regional Reports (RM-82-08), 24 September 1982: 7.

local narratives never mention a possible connection between the two deaths. Most ladinos I confronted with the account remained convinced they saw guerrillas entering Joyabaj, and not soldiers dressed up as guerrillas.[91] They are certain they would have spotted the difference because of the boots: even dressed up as guerrillas, soldiers would always wear their own shiny footwear. Some of the younger ladinos, however, who were children at the time the murder took place and not direct witnesses are willing to allow for military involvement in the case. They have heard about such cases in other municipalities, and accept the possibility that the military might have dressed up as guerrillas in order to win over the local ladinos to their side.[92]

These local, and not so local, narratives concerning important events in the community of Joyabaj differ in many aspects. This is due to a complex interplay of different factors such as past and present power relations in the community, age, ethnicity, the political affiliation of the person doing the remembering and other 'outside' influences such as the presence of an interviewer. According to Wilson (1997b), who also came across a variety of local people's views on the murder of an important local figure while doing fieldwork in Alta Verapaz in 1988, 'each murder draws on a heterogeneous field of interpretations and memories, in a social space where meaning is contested, assertions are vague ... and where anyone and everyone could have had a motive. Narratives on murder then serve to crystallize social relations and feed off perceived tensions and discordance'.[93] While some of the narratives might be or might sound truer than others, they all try to give meaning to the death of an individual that shook many *Joyabatecos* to the core. They consider it a traumatic event, and thus worthy of a lot of attention even if it means adding to or spicing up the truth. The story that Rigoberta Menchú was part of the group that day can probably be explained in this way. In 1981 she was yet to become well known, but her current prominence as a Nobel peace prizewinner gives more meaning to the death of the pharmacist. It also makes it clear that nowadays many ladinos in Joyabaj consider the indigenous Nobel prizewinner to belong to the other side, that is, the former guerrilla, and do not see her as representative of the Guatemalan population.

Ramiro Paíz was not the only victim of the guerrilla visit on 1 October 1981. During the same incident 15-year-old Fredy Ogáldez, the youngest of the four Ogáldez brothers, was kidnapped and 100,000 *Quetzales* was demanded for his release.[94] The remaining Ogáldez brothers never paid up, but neither did they succeed in finding their brother. He was never seen again. Allegedly he was taken

---

91 Interview 6-01 (11/5/01).
92 Diary 8/5/01.
93 Wilson (1997b: 138).
94 El Gráfico, 14/10/81.

instead of his father, former mayor Próspero Ogáldez, who was not at home when the guerrilla visited. Other voices add that the Ogáldez family also had strong ties with the military, with two of the older brothers being directly involved in military intelligence work. The kidnapping of their younger brother was thus seen as retaliation against their military connections. Not only the kidnapping caused major unrest among the ladinos in town. When Fredy was taken, his mother was also captured by the guerrilla and put into the truck. As the truck reached the outskirts of town, the mother was released and thrown out of the truck. Many ladinos are still angry about this incident. How could the guerrilla have so treated such an innocent and religious lady, let alone the wife of a former mayor? One ladino man, who has a somewhat ambivalent attitude towards the guerrillas, argues that the kidnapping of Fredy Ogáldez and the treatment of his mother only tightened the relationship between the military and the three remaining Ogáldez brothers and fuelled their anti-guerrilla sentiments. The kidnapping seemed to be presented as a legitimate reason for one of the remaining brothers, Leonel Ogáldez, to become a civil patrol leader and act in the sometimes violent way he did.[95] In Chapter 4 I will discuss his activities as patrol commander in more detail.

Polarizing ethnic relations
The death of Ramiro Paíz significantly changed the attitude of many *Joyabatecos* towards the guerrillas. Violence had come very close to their doorsteps, and many ladinos felt unprotected and open to guerrilla attacks. The death of Ramiro Paíz caused unrest and raised suspicion about the motives behind guerrilla actions and triggered strong anti-guerrilla sentiments in the community.[96] 'The mentality of the people changed ... because the guerrilla started to do bad things, instead of good things.'[97] Relations between ladinos and *indígenas* were already very tense, and only deteriorated more rapidly after the violent incident. Guerrilla visits had ruptured daily life with their surprise visits and meetings on the town square. The conflicting sympathies of the locals towards the guerrillas became more polarized by these weekly incursions, and tensions between different groups in society heightened. The killing of Ramiro Paíz seems to have accelerated this process.

This change of attitude among ladinos was not lost on the military, which were more easily able to find allies in their struggle against guerrilla forces. Furthermore, the ladinos of Joyabaj now openly requested the help of the mili-

---

95 Interview 5-99 (26/5/99); 42-99 (25/7/99) and 6-01 (11/5/01).
96 Interview 6-01 (11/5/01) and 12-01 (21/5/01).
97 Interview 12-01 (21/5/01).

tary in their fight against guerrilla incursions. Immediately after the guerrilla attack of 1 October 1981, a group of ladinos (*comité de vecinos*) went to the capital to hand over a petition to the president, requesting military help to defend them against further guerrilla attacks. This request appeared on 14 October 1981 in *El Gráfico*, a national Guatemalan newspaper. They asked for 'security to be able to continue with their normal activities' and warned that a strategy was planned by the guerrilla to 'eliminate the ladinos whom they have already warned to leave town or be eliminated physically'.[98] Because of this threat, 'we need much more attention from the government to solving this problem'.[99]

This ladino fear of the guerrillas, together with their fear of indigenous people in general, was still quite apparent in many of the interviews, although 15 years had past since the height of the conflict. *Indígenas* accused wealthy ladinos of belonging to death squads, collaborating with military intelligence and drawing up blacklists with the names of indigenous activists. Conversely, ladinos accused *indígenas* of belonging to the guerrilla or at the very least harbouring communist sentiments, and were thus held responsible for the violence. A violent incident such as the death of Ramiro Paíz only antagonized already existing divisions between ladinos and *indígenas* and made it difficult for both ladinos and *indígenas* not to choose sides and remain outside the political polarization. The situation was even further complicated by the fact that some indigenous communities supported right-wing ladinos. This was the case with indigenous villages like Xecnup and Cruz Chich, which were staunch supporters of former MLN mayors like Próspero Ogáldez and Beto Caballeros. There were also ladinos who were known for their leftist sympathies and who were, for example, active in organizations such as Alianza.

Another result of guerrilla activity, apart from the polarizing of ethnic relations, was the exodus of wealthy ladinos from Joyabaj. Guerrilla visits to local stores had become grimmer, and instead of demanding paint and brushes they started looking for the owners whom 'they demanded to talk to, and not only to ask for more paint'.[100] People like Alfredo Méndez and Efraín Elías, who belonged to the top layer of the economic elite, left town for good after selling their houses and other assets.[101] They feared they were next on the guerrillas' list of those who were to be captured and killed because of their accumulated wealth as landowners, large shop owners and labour contractors. And as the few wealthy ladinos departed to safer places, their economic monopolies broke down. The local economy was no longer in the hands of the wealthy few, but

---

98 El Gráfico, 14/10/81.
99 El Gráfico, 14/10/81.
100 Interview 3-01 (7/5/99).
101 Reyes Illescas (1982: 9).

open to other competitors, who started coming forward after the worst of the violence was over. Apart from this wealthy elite, most ladinos left town for only a few months during the height of the military offensive at the end of 1981 and came back after the worst violence was over. During the summer holiday in November and December 1981, many people, especially ladinos working as teachers, left for Guatemala City,[102] unlike in, for example, the nearby municipality of Zacualpa, which remained virtually abandoned for years and to this day has not regained the number of inhabitants it had before the war. At the same time another massive population movement was brought about by military violence, causing mainly indigenous people to flee their homes, leaving their houses, land and animals behind. Many *indígenas* left for the capital or the plantations on the south coast, fled to neighbouring Mexico, or went to live in the town of Joyabaj.

Scorched-earth strategy: the first massacres

In contrast with the early military visits, which were often carried out under the authority of a local or regional military zone commander, from June 1981 onwards offensives were planned and executed centrally and directly by the *Estado Mayor General*, the highest military command.[103] By then military strategy had changed from selectively killing individuals to the indiscriminate destruction of entire villages suspected of collaborating with the guerrillas. The aim was to cut off all indigenous support for the guerrillas. According to Claridge (2000: 232), the massacres were used by the military as a way to *regain* control over the countryside, which they had steadily been losing as a result of guerrilla activities. '[I]f existing surveillance and repressive structures are performing properly there is no need to adopt massacre as a tactic ... the use of massacre was born out of a failure of more selective forms of terror.' These scorched-earth tactics took effect in the second half of 1981,[104] when a major military offensive was launched against the indigenous villages in the western highlands, lasting until the end of 1982.[105] This offensive *was* centrally planned and executed, under the direction of the new minister of defence since August 1981, General Benedicto Lucas García. He was the president's brother and had been trained in the 1950s by the French military forces while fighting in Algeria. Some of his Algerian experiences were used by the Guatemalan military to combat the guerrilla movement.

---

102 Interview 13-99 (4/10/99).
103 ODHAG, Vol. III (1998: 102).
104 ODHAG, Vol. III (1998: 102).
105 The start of this offensive was called Ceniza 81 (Ashes 81), changing its name to Victory 82 in 1982, but continuing its strategy of scorched earth. CEH, Vol. III (1999: 301).

As part of this offensive a total of five 'areas of operation' were established, each with its own target areas. Joyabaj fell under the responsibility of the first military unit to be set up, *Fuerza de Tarea Iximché*, which was also active in the municipalities of Chichicastenango and nearby Zacualpa and the departments of Chimaltenango and Sololá.[106] *Tarea Iximché* coordinated its actions with the air force and the judicial police (*Policía Judicial*). The attacks started in San Martín Jilotepeque, a municipality bordering on Joyabaj, after which they reached Joyabaj and Zacualpa and ended by striking the Panamerican highway and its surrounding villages. Military attacks on Joyabaj intensified during the last two months of 1981,[107] with aerial bombardments throughout the western highlands. According to a newspaper article, the town was evacuated first, and then bombed. 'Television reports tried to pass off the damage as a result of guerrilla action. But this attempt to discredit the guerrillas backfired, as many residents had already arrived in Guatemala City and were able to tell the real story.'[108]

According to the CEH report, the *Fuerza de Tarea Iximché* was responsible for about 26 per cent of the massacres committed in Guatemala in the period between June 1981 and December 1982.[109] This means they were responsible for 110 of the 415 massacres that were recorded for this period, of which most victims were indigenous civilians. REMHI registered eight massacres in Joyabaj between 1981 and 1983, while CEH reports at least six more.[110] Several hundred men, women and children were killed as a result.[111] The reports conclude that the military were responsible for most of the massacres, followed by civil patrollers and military commissioners. After the military had settled down in Joyabaj, many of the indigenous communities in the north were hit hard because they were presumed to be guerrilla strongholds. This was not only a military assumption, but also the way many local ladinos and even indigenous people who lived

---

106 CEH, Vol. III (1999: 305-309).
107 El Gráfico, 21/11/81.
108 Latin American Weekly Report, 11/12/81.
109 CEH, Vol. III (1999: 308).
110 This discrepancy is probably due to the definition of 'massacre' and the evaluation of the information that is received. For example, the REMHI interviewers could not integrate written statements into their database, but were obliged to obtain oral statements from witnesses. Not everybody was willing to cooperate. Sometimes it was general knowledge that a massacre had been committed in a village, but no witnesses could be found who were willing to talk. An additional factor is that the REMHI report was published before the CEH report, so that the CEH was able to build upon the already existing information from the REMHI report.
111 The CEH uses the following definition of 'massacre': 'the arbitrary execution of more than five persons, realized in the same place and as part of the same operation, while the victims were relatively or absolutely defenceless' (CEH, Vol. III, 1999: 251). The CEH recorded a total of 626 massacres during the civil war in Guatemala, for which the military, security forces and paramilitary structures like the PAC or the military commissioners were responsible. CEH, Vol. III (1999: 256).

in town looked at the northern indigenous communities. Tightly organized communities like Chorraxaj (including Patzulá and Nuevo Chorraxaj) and Xeabaj, in which Catholic Action and Alianza had been very active, were the most prominent targets. The first recorded massacre carried out by military forces together with military commissioners occurred in Chorraxaj, on 14 January 1981.[112] Nine of the 14 people killed were children who had fled into the forest when the military arrived. Massacres not only occurred in the indigenous villages north of Joyabaj but also hit several southern, predominantly indigenous, villages.[113]

The number of massacres increased in the second half of 1981 with the killing of eight people in Saljij in October, and the subsequent killing of 40 people in Pericón Chuacorral, seven in Talaxcoc, 20 in Chicotón and ten in Paxtup during November[114] and 18 men in Xecnup in December.[115] A second wave of killings occurred in February and March 1982, concentrating on Chorraxaj, Patzulá and Xebalamguac.[116] Apart from these recorded massacres many individuals were brought to the newly established military base in Joyabaj and tortured, killed or disappeared. From November 1981 onwards many of the massacres were carried out by a combination of military forces and civil patrollers, sometimes with military commissioners present. The terrorizing effects of the massacres were increased by the mutilation or decapitation of the victims, and by military orders prohibiting the burial of the bodies. This was the case in Pericón Chuacorral where 'they [the bodies] were eaten by dogs ... until they got fat'. The military had explicitly forbidden people to bury the bodies, and 'if someone tried to do so, he would die just like the corpses'.[117]

Most of the massacres are still not a topic of conversation and are hardly ever mentioned. Some ladinos do not seem to know what really happened in many of the indigenous villages, or have no wish to know. Some of them had already left Joyabaj when the first massacres were carried out, while others commented that these communities were a long walk from town and information about what happened did not reach town easily. Also, many of the indigenous people who survived the massacres do not feel comfortable enough to talk about them, and only some of the massacres appear in testimonies that were given to both of the truth commissions or in private to the researcher.

Phrases frequently used during interviews, such as 'when violence came to

---

112 CEH, Vol. X (1999: 1027).
113 CEH, Vol. X (1999).
114 ODHAG, Vol. IV (1998) and CEH, Vol. X (1999).
115 CEH, Vol. XI (1999: 1348).
116 CEH, Vol. XI (1999: 1385).
117 REMHI archives [June 1999]. Testimony no. 00945.

Joyabaj', are a clear indication of the way a large group of *Joyabatecos*, mainly ladinos, view the past. They think the war just happened to them, and was clearly not something of their making. Most do not claim any responsibility or a direct involvement, and present themselves as pawns in the hands of bigger entities, like the military or civil patrol commanders. Besides, *Joyabatecos* who agreed with military intervention at that time stated that 'most of the people killed were guerrilla ... and were enemies of the people',[118] possibly implying that the killing of guerrillas was not that bad even if it meant wiping out entire villages.

Home Guards set up in Joyabaj

Despite major military offensives, the war was not going well for the Guatemalan government in 1981. 'Although General Benedicto Lucas García's counter-insurgency campaigns of late 1981 and early 1982 failed to crush the guerrillas in the promised short order ... innovations introduced by the chief of staff largely set the pattern for the coming years.'[119] These innovations included the already mentioned scorched-earth policy in the western highlands, hitting hardest the areas with the greatest guerrilla presence. Another innovation consisted of an expansion of the regular army and its reserve forces through the creation of an auxiliary force within the army's permanent (active) reserve system. 'The new forces, partly raised by calling up former servicemen, were described as local territorial forces which would serve in their home areas under the local army commandant's or military commissioner's orders.'[120] The goal was, first of all, to organize a massive network of military control over the countryside and, second, to involve the local population in the war, not as victims of military or guerrilla activity but as active participants on the side of the military. That would mean that everybody would get their hands dirty and be responsible for the atrocities committed. According to a 1981 document, 'the new units organized as part of the reserves will be assigned militia type tasks—guard duty, local logistics and communication'.[121] These units can be regarded as the forerunners of the civil defence patrols (*Patrullas de Autodefensa Civil* - PAC), which were to be set up by the military throughout the rural areas of Guatemala towards the end of 1981. Matilde González, who conducted research on conflict and power in the municipality of San Bartolomé Jocotenango, situated north of Joyabaj, mentions the existence of a similar organization called *Civiles Provisionales de Emergencia*, which the people from San Bartolomé regarded as the 'seeds of the PAC'.[122] The civil

---

118 Interview 14-98 (19/6/89).
119 McClintock (1985: 221).
120 McClintock (1985: 221).
121 This Week, 30/11/81, in McClintock (1985: 222).
122 Gonzalez (2002: 382-383).

patrols were part of the military counter-insurgency strategy, designed to cut off public support for the guerrilla and extend military control over the countryside. Their organization was fine-tuned under the guidance of President Ríos Montt, who came to power after a coup in March 1982. Their duties were to expand into various areas of military activity, which will be discussed in detail in Chapter 4.

Joyabaj figures prominently in the installation of these new auxiliary troops, or 'home guards', as they are called in one of the first publications on the topic.[123] Different sources mention an anti-communist rally, which took place in Joyabaj in the middle of November 1981, during which Chief of Staff Benedicto Lucas García made a speech.[124] More than 4,000 people were present to 'express their help and collaboration in the struggle against subversion'. According to Lucas García the people from Quiché asked the military for help to fight the guerrillas, and therefore he would be arming and training 800 farmers in Joyabaj and 1,000 in nearby Rabinal (Baja Verapaz).[125] Most of them were described as 'former veterans' and 'ladinos', becoming active in a mainly indigenous environment.

It is interesting to note that this meeting, which was recorded in several newspapers and documents of solidarity groups, does not seem to be part of the 'historic memory' of many ladinos in Joyabaj. It never surfaced in the interviews and, when I asked specifically about it, most people did not know about it. Possibly, many ladinos had already left by then, because the visit of Lucas García occurred shortly after the attack on the pharmacist. The few ladinos who had heard of the meeting pointed out that it was strictly for military commissioners and other people connected to the military, like *orejas*, who were involved in military intelligence. A final reason could be that it was just not considered an important event at the local level. The discussions in the national and international media focused on the fact that the army was willing to give arms to people who allegedly had requested them to protect themselves against guerrilla attacks.[126] At that time, preparations for the coming elections were under way and the presidential candidates were asked their opinion. Every one of them was positive about making use of civilians to combat the guerrilla, but stressed that they should be incorporated officially into the military. They were not to act on their own, but only under military orders. It is not surprising to hear such positive reactions, because there was little scope for protest against or criticism of military activity and initiatives such as the organizing of paramilitary groups.

Ladinos in Joyabaj, however, do remember that they themselves organized

---

123 This Week, 30/11/81, in: McClintock (1985: 222).
124 McClintock (1985: 221-222); Inforpress, 26/11/81; El Gráfico, 18/11/81; El Imparcial, 18/11/81 and 19/11/81.
125 Inforpress Centroamericana, 26/11/81; El Gráfico, 21/11/81.
126 Prensa Libre, 21/11/81; El Impacto, 21/11/81; El Gráfico, 21/11/81.

photo 6. *Military guardpost behind the Catholic Church of Joyabaj (anonymous, around 1984)*

the first patrols, or *rondas* as they were called by the ladinos at that time, as early as November 1981. According to several ladinos, these first groups were organized voluntarily, immediately after the murder of pharmacist Ramiro Paíz. Presumably, some ladinos had gathered in front of Ramiro's house after his murder, debating what they could do to protect their families and their village against guerrilla attacks. The men decided to organize themselves in small groups of five or six men, who would patrol the area. They did not have any leaders and operated independently of the military. 'The initial idea was to defend the community. There was no police, there was no authority here ... but it was never the idea to help the army. But when the army came afterwards and called all the men together to organize them in patrols, everything changed and we became paramilitary groups.'[127] The initially voluntary *rondas* (doing rounds) were quickly moulded by the military into something more coerced and organized. In the end, anyone who refused to patrol was branded a subversive.[128] During the interviews some of them kept repeating that the guerrilla forces had made a grave mistake that day when they killed the pharmacist. With him, they had also killed most of the sympathy for the guerrilla in town.

---

127 Interview 6-01 (11/5/01).
128 Interview 17-01 (10/5/01).

photo 7. *An second military guardpost behind the Catholic Church of Joyabaj (anonymous, around 1984)*

In November 1981, around the time of the 'forgotten' meeting with the Chief of Staff and shortly after the killing of the pharmacist Ramiro Paíz, the military installed themselves permanently in Joyabaj. Two factors probably contributed to the installation. First of all, local ladinos had openly petitioned the military for help against guerrilla forces. The second factor was the military strategy of installing several smaller military garrisons in most municipalities in an attempt to keep a better control over the areas after they had 'liberated' them from the guerrillas. A direct and constant presence of the military, including the proposed creation of local auxiliary forces, was supposed to effect stricter military control over the local situation. The military installed themselves in the Catholic Church buildings, prominently situated on the *plaza* in the centre of town. The buildings had been abandoned since July 1980, when Padre Faustino Villanueva was killed. Settling into Catholic Church buildings in town centres was a common military strategy in Guatemala.[129] Occupying such a symbolic site was meant to affirm military power over the Catholic Church and the local community in general.[130] The whole area surrounding the buildings was sealed off, guardhouses installed, deep pits that served as temporary holding cells were dug in the yard of the convent and part of the convent was converted into a torture chamber. Military control, by way of terror, of the town of Joyabaj was a fact, and control of the surrounding countryside, through the installation of the civil defence patrols, could begin.

Conclusion

The effects of the civil war on local society during the presidency of Lucas García were many. First, the use of selective and massive terror by military and paramilitary forces caused widespread fear and uncertainty among the population. The random and often massive violence could target anybody. Blacklists, arbitrary arrests, individual killings, mutilation and exposure of bodies, disappearances and massacres were used by the military to regain control over the rural population. Second, military violence brought social life to almost a complete standstill. The Catholic Church closed its doors after the parish priest was killed, schools remained empty and indigenous villages were almost completely abandoned. Local leaders were murdered or fled their communities. NGOs like Alianza stopped working in the communities, and everything connected with community work was suspended. Third, economic monopolies broke down, local markets ceased functioning, credit and other cooperatives were closed

---

129 See CEH, Vol. VII (1999: 53-59) for a detailed analysis of the military occupation of the church and convent in San Andrés Sajcabajá, a municipality not far from Joyabaj.
130 See also Le Bot (1993: 18-19).

down, and their leaders killed or disappeared. Guerrilla activity caused the permanent flight of a top echelon of wealthy ladinos, and the temporary flight of other ladinos during the height of the violence. Fourth, civil authority ceased to exist and a virtual power vacuum was created as the majority of the council members were killed, disappeared, or fled. After the re-establishment of a military presence in and control over the municipality, local government was reorganized, aided by military commissioners and right-wing ladinos in town. A new local force appeared on stage in November 1981 in the form of home guards, or civil defence patrols as they were called later on, adding to the militarization of the municipality.

Finally, ethnic relations between ladinos and *indígenas* deteriorated and divisions were sharpened. Selective violence and the subsequent scorched-earth tactics caused unrest and distrust within and between communities and even families. Ladinos' fear of the 'other', that is, the indigenous part of the population, was exacerbated by military propaganda, which labelled them subversives and communist revolutionaries. The difference between 'us' and 'them' became more pronounced. Left-oriented groups and those closely connected with the Catholic Church, Alianza and other community organizations felt threatened by military presence and right-wing activists with ties to the MLN and military intelligence. Likewise, the ladinos, especially the more wealthy and right-wing families, felt threatened by the constant guerrilla activity in the area. Each group accused the other of responsibility for the violence coming to Joyabaj. The ladinos accused the *indígenas* of belonging to the guerrilla and thus being indirectly responsible for military retaliation in the area. The indigenous people for their part accused the ladinos of belonging to right-wing death squads and military intelligence. However, I want to stress that the lines between the two groups, ladinos and *indígenas*, were not that clearly drawn. Left-wing ladinos were actively engaged in community work with indigenous people, while right-wing *indígenas* backed right-wing ladinos.

How then are we to interpret the focal points or main events in this period, such as the death of Padre Villanueva, the actions of the 'radical' nun, the killing of the pharmacist, the work of Alianza? *Joyabatecos*, who kept referring to them during conversations and interviews without prompting, clearly considered them important incidents. These recurrent themes represent different turning points in *Joyabateco* memory. For example, the killing of Padre Villanueva is seen as the moment when 'violence came to Joyabaj', while the killing of Ramiro Paíz triggered an anti-guerrilla stance among the *Joyabateco* ladinos. They also give insight into the very diverse ways in which different groups in society look back to and experienced the war. While one group presented the activities of the nun as motivated by sympathy for the guerrilla and thus holds her partially responsible for the violence in Joyabaj, others remember her as a very liberal and open person, far ahead of her time. The same goes for the NGO Alianza. While one group looks upon it with suspicion and even hatred, because it 'put bad ideas in the heads of the Indians', others still regret the fact that Alianza had to leave Joyabaj and are certain that the development of the town suffered as a result.

Apart from these central events, which are talked about quite openly and often, there also appear to be some gaps in local memory of the war. Some events are not talked about although they have been extensively covered by the media and human rights organizations: for example, the ladinos in Joyabaj petitioning the president for help in their fight against the guerrillas late 1981, or the visit of Benedicto Lucas García in November 1981, which heralded the creation of the first civil patrols. These events have been checked and cross-checked, but are not acknowledged in the memory of ladinos, possibly because some ladinos had already left during that period and really did not know, while others do not want these events to be remembered. In the course of time it has become clear that the international community, human rights organizations and the Catholic Church did not look favourably upon the existence of close relations between ladinos and the military. The aforementioned 'forgotten events' focused almost exclusively on these relationships, and clearly indicate an active participation in the war on the part of a group of *Joyabatecos:* something most people do not wish to be reminded of.

4

Civil patrols and organized violence (1982-1983)

Chapter 3 ended with a rather bleak description of Joyabaj at the end of 1981. A virtual power vacuum had been created, caused by both guerrilla activity and various military offensives during the presidency of Lucas García. Selective violence and numerous massacres caused the death or flight of a large part of the indigenous population in Joyabaj. Villages were deserted due to continuous military attacks, and wealthy ladinos left town.

This chapter starts in 1982, when General Ríos Montt took over presidential power after participating in a coup which ousted President Lucas García from his position. The presidency of Ríos Montt lasted until August 1983 and is regarded as one of the most violent periods in Guatemalan history. This chapter focuses on the way in which *Joyabateco* society was militarized by the joint forces of the local military base, military commissioners and the civil patrols. Special attention is given to the impact of civil defence patrols, because their installation and subsequent involvement in many of the atrocities committed during the civil war had long-lasting effects on society.[1] As a key component of the counter-insurgency strategy of the military, the patrols were put in charge of the control and surveillance of the local population. In a way, military control over the countryside was being decentralized into the hands of the civil patrols, which were allotted a certain amount of freedom to act as they saw fit.

After a short introduction on the change from chaotic to structured violence under Ríos Montt at the national level, I focus on the situation in Joyabaj. The situation quietened down somewhat after the military occupation of Joyabaj and the subsequent installation of the civil defence patrols. The military took control of municipal affairs aided by their traditional allies, the local military commissioners and the recently organized civil defence patrol. To understand the enormous impact of civil patrols on local society and local power relations in particular, it is necessary to take into account the diversity that existed between civil patrols in different municipalities and villages, and look at the factors which contributed to these differences. Diversity is a central aspect of civil patrols: diversi-

---

[1] See Starn (1999) and Fumerton (2002) on *rondas campesinas* in Peru. These organizations share many characteristics with Guatemalan civil defence patrols, although their historical roots, their role in society and subsequent development at the local level differed markedly.

ty in organization, hierarchy, activities, level of violence, and their relationship with the military. The civil patrol is very often portrayed as an inherently violent institution, while little attention is given to its enormous diversity and changes through time. Initially civil patrols were set up as a military instrument to help win the war, but over time they evolved into a local force in their own right. Three patrols are described to portray their differences. The chapter ends with an overview of the different memories of patrol violence by people trying to give meaning to what happened.

Structured not chaotic violence

On 7 March 1982 presidential elections were organized during a violent civil war. A right-wing coalition with the Minister of Defence as presidential candidate won, as a result of widespread fraud, with 35 per cent of the votes.[2] Two weeks later the military staged a coup and a military *Junta* was organized, comprising three high-ranking military officials of whom General Ríos Montt was one. The other political parties participating in the elections supported the coup, which was officially staged to 'reinstall a democratic-representative regime'.[3] On 31 May the Constitution was revoked and an amnesty for political crimes was announced. The guerrilla organizations,[4] which started cooperating in the *Unidad Revolucionaria Nacional Guatemalteca* (URNG)[5] in February 1982 shortly before the elections, commented that 'the faces change, but the regime is the same'.[6] On 9 June the military Junta was dissolved and general Ríos Montt was appointed president by the military. A state of siege was decreed on 1 July, lasting until the end of October 1982.

The seizure of presidential power by Ríos Montt resulted in a radical change in military operations. First of all, most paramilitary death squad activities in the cities were halted, to pacify both the urban population and the international community which had become more and more concerned with Lucas García's chaotic counter-insurgency actions. Ríos Montt promised to replace the anonymous terror of urban death squads with the formal procedures of army firing squads. A system of special secret courts was empowered to impose the death penalty, and secret trials were held without defence or appeal procedures.[7] The biggest

---

2   This was a PR/PID/FUN coalition. See Chapter 3 for a description of the PR and the PID. The *Frente de Unidad Nacional* (FUN - Front of National Unity) was an ultra-right political party, founded in 1972. It always took part in right-wing coalitions (Sichar Moreno, 1999: 19).
3   Sichar Moreno (1998: 65).
4   The four guerrilla organizations that reorganized themselves into the URNG were PGT, FAR, ORPA and EGP.
5   Guatemalan National Revolutionary Unity.
6   Inforpress, 1/4/82.
7   McClintock (1985: 230).

change occurred in the rural areas, where violence also continued, though in a less chaotic way than before.[8] The counter-insurgency strategy was streamlined and structured, combining attacks on peasant villages suspected of sympathy for the guerrilla with a civic-action programme in which the military assisted villages in local construction projects. The campaign was started in July 1982 and was dubbed *fusiles y frijoles* (guns and beans, or *Victory 82*). The first phase of the campaign consisted of military sweeps of the highlands and the destruction of highland villages, killing most of their inhabitants, creating streams of refugees and resettling the rest of the population in army-controlled towns. The sweeps consisted of a few brief but fierce campaigns, beginning around May 1982 and concluding sometime in October 1982. The second phase, *techos, tortillas y trabajo* (roof, tortilla and work or *Firmness 83*), concentrated on reconstructing village life in accordance with military plans and under military orders. Their goal was to 'win the hearts and minds' of the population.[9] The counter-insurgency operations, even in isolated rural areas, were tightly controlled. The actions on the ground were coordinated directly from the top and 'field commanders ... received their orders through a chain of command which places only three steps – the minister of defence, the army chief of staff, and a colonel in the provincial capital – between themselves and Ríos Montt'.[10]

Ríos Montt's old allies who had backed him during the coup in March 1982 were not always very taken by his actions as president. Although there was no major disagreement on the way the counter-insurgency war was run, a power struggle developed between Ríos Montt and senior army officers and civilian elites from the far right. A factor that intensified opposition to Ríos Montt, was the influence of his evangelical background on the government. He brought many evangelical advisers and officials into the government, with the result that the conservative and Catholic elite felt threatened by his populism and charismatic Protestant message. In August 1983, only 16 months after Ríos Montt became head of state, he was asked to leave his post by the military. His successor was the second in the army's hierarchy after Ríos Montt, Minister of Defence General Oscar Humberto Mejía Víctores. He was regarded 'a throwback to the Lucas García days in his inability to disguise his contempt for human rights and human rights advocates'.[11] However, during his presidency, which lasted until 1986, Guatemala was prepared for a controlled return to democracy under military supervision. I will now turn my attention to the situation in the municipality of Joyabaj in order to examine the effects of structured terror under Ríos Montt at the local level.

---

8   Nairn (1983: 17).
9   Deli Sante (1996: 8).
10 McClintock (1985: 242).
11 McClintock (1985: 238).

Joyabaj under military control

After the permanent installation and occupation by the military in November 1981, 'difficult times began for Joyabaj', according to many *Joyabatecos*.[12] What was still left of municipal politics stopped functioning, all men between the ages of 15 and 60 were forcibly organized into civil patrols, and military actions in the surrounding countryside intensified noticeably. In the early days of the occupation the military base, which was situated in the former convent and parish buildings, became the focal point of local power and authority. It served as a detention and torture centre for guerrilla suspects; military commissioners and patrol commanders came in regularly to report to the military; military orders were issued from the convent and civil patrols were obliged to participate in weekly Sunday training sessions. Commenting on this last aspect a former patroller remembers the training 'as a campaign of penetration ... until it was engraved in their heads'. They were bombarded with anti-guerrilla and anti-communist rhetoric, having to recite slogans like 'A guerrilla seen is a guerrilla dead' and 'For the guerrilla neither bread nor tortilla'.[13] According to Claridge, the 'dehumanising effect of referring to local populations as communists, subversives, snakes, should not be underestimated as a motivating factor in the sustained use of terror violence'.[14] The Guatemala military clearly used anti-communist and anti-subversive rhetoric to create a rift between 'us' and 'the other', that is, between those favouring the military and those opposing it. The enemy was thus clearly separated from the rest of the population, and could therefore be targeted more easily. The irony of the situation was that many of these so-called enemies were also forced to participate in the civil patrols.

Initially the military seems to have kept strict control over the patrols and ordered civil patrol commanders to hand over a fixed number of guerillas to the army base every week or month. Often prisoners were brought into the military compound alive, but in some instances patrol commanders took evidence only of their killings to the army base. One notorious patrol commander from an indigenous village north of Joyabaj used to decapitate his victims and present their heads to the army commander,[15] while the patrol commander of Las Lomas robbed his dead victims of their identification cards (*carnet*). The more he brought in, the more weapons he received in return from the military.[16] He had excellent contacts with the local military base, and was eager to please. Allegedly his eagerness reflected the fact that he had been a former guerrilla, and was very

---

12 Interview 14-98 (19/6/98).
13 Interview 13-98 (13/5/98).
14 Claridge (2000: 239).
15 Interview 24-99 (31/5/99).
16 Interview 2-99 (14/7/99).

photo 8. *Military parade on Joyabaj's main street (anonymous, around 1986)*

photo 9. *Military posing on the village square of Joyabaj (Foto Color, 1983)*

anxious to prove that he was now entirely reliable.[17]

In addition, *orejas* (ears) and *judiciales* (informers), local people working for military intelligence, provided the army base with information about other *Joyabatecos*. They regularly drew up lists of people thought to be subversives, and handed them to the military commander. Some people saw the work of informer as a step up the social ladder, and quite a few former military men pursued this line of work. A ladino told me that 'the problem was that many people liked the activities of a *judicial* ... so many collaborated with the army or with the G2, the military intelligence section. They received a special identification card and the people felt themselves powerful (*con el mando del poder*)'.[18] Contacts with the military and the G2 were thus used as a way to attain local status and authority. Denouncing people as subversives, in person or by putting their names on blacklists, was enough to get people killed. Many people who entered the compound as suspects never left. Most of them were tortured, killed and afterwards buried in communal graves in the canyon behind the convent or thrown into a nearby river. The military either carried out the killing and torturing themselves or turned the suspects over to the civil patrol commanders of their respective villages with orders to kill. A common method of torturing people consisted of putting them in pits (*pozo*) in the convent garden. A person could just stand in the pit, which was covered with a lid and sometimes partially filled with water.[19] The prisoners were left there without food or water for days, until someone remembered to take them out. The former church grounds became dreaded as a place of torture 'where they did with people whatever they wanted'.[20] In the nearby municipality of Zacualpa, where the military also installed themselves in the church buildings at the beginning of the conflict, one of the torture chambers was left intact, and is open to the public for viewing, praying and reflection. Iron handcuffs can still be seen hanging from the ceiling, the bloodstained fingerprints have not been removed, while a small drainpipe still runs through the floor to carry off any evidence of the torture.

Heavy government censorship prevented this grim evidence of local military activity in Joyabaj from being reported in the local or national media. For example, in a 1982 newspaper article titled 'Little by little normality returns in Quiché', a reporter visiting Southern Quiché and Joyabaj described the devastating effects of the war while driving through the area. The first thing he noted, after arriving in Joyabaj, was that 'a military base has given protection to the inhabitants of Joyabaj, a municipality that had been hit hard by the guerrillas

---

17 Interview 2-99 (14/7/99).
18 Interview 38-99 (19/8/99).
19 Diary 1998 (8/4/98).
20 Interview 18-99 (20/5/99).

photo 10. *Former military torture chamber in the convent of Zacualpa, now converted into a place of prayer. The image of Christ was damaged together with many other religious statues, when the military first occupied the Zacualpa convent (author, 2001)*

during previous months. Today it is a quiet place, where the people have started to trust (*tomar confianza*) the authorities'.[21] This example of military propaganda contrasts sharply with local accounts from *Joyabatecos* of the violent activities on the military compound and the massacres that were being carried out around the same time the article was published.

The military takes over municipal politics

Apart from its activities as a military force, the army took over effective political power from the town hall. Local municipal authority was suspended and the military appointed its own trusted people as mayor and municipal secretary. After Ríos Montt came to power in March 1982, he decreed that mayors were no longer to be elected but were to be appointed by the new government. In many cases the mayors were supposedly 'elected' by the civil patrollers, although the candidates were put forward by the local military. Appointed mayors ran a puppet municipality which was installed and controlled by the military. On 21 June 1982, shortly after Ríos Montt decreed that all municipal authorities were to be appointed by the government, the military installed Beto Caballeros, a former right-wing MLN mayor (1972–74) in the municipality. Although the *Libro de Acuerdo*[22] has no entry regarding his appointment, his signature can be recognized under some of the entries in the book. Caballeros himself is not very anxious to talk about this period but does mention that his position as mayor 'gave one a headache ... mayors were candidates for death'.[23]

Caballeros was replaced in August 1983, when José Angel López was appointed mayor and Pascual Pérez vice-mayor by the local military. The two men were called to the *Salón Municipal* where the military had assembled all civil patrol commanders. After the two men arrived, the local military commander (lieutenant or *teniente*) announced to the audience that 'from this moment onward you accept the post of mayor and vice-mayor'.[24] The newly appointed mayor tried to explain to the *teniente* that he was really unable to accept the post of mayor, to which the *teniente* responded, 'look, times are militarized. In the army we do not discuss decisions, we only obey'.[25] This ended the argument and the two men were installed in the municipality, where they remained until January 1986, when the first democratic elections since 1978 were held. As well

---

21 Prensa Libre, 30/4/82.
22 Book of Decrees. Before Ríos Montt came to power, these were called *Libros de Actos* (Books of Minutes). Ríos Montt ruled by decree and not by discussion or consent. Until March 1985 municipal activity was recorded in the Book of Decrees. Only after the 1985 elections were the Books of Minutes reinstated, together with the actual power of the municipal council.
23 Interview 5-98 (20/7/98).
24 Interview 13-99 (4/10/99).
25 Interview 13-99 (4/10/99).

as a mayor and vice-mayor, a municipal secretary was appointed. There were no council members at that time and no sessions of the municipal council were convened. The actual power of the three appointed municipal officials was severely limited, since everything went through the hands of the local military. Every decision had to be signed by the highest-ranking military chief in Joyabaj at that moment. Even if the municipal officials wanted to organize a town *fiesta* or some other social occasion, they had to get military approval. The only visible reminder of municipal activity at that time was the remodelling of the stairs to the Calvario (a little church on a hilltop in the centre of town), which was carried out with the help of the civil patrollers.[26] In several cases, patrollers were forced to participate in construction projects, sometimes in exchange for food.[27] Some *Joyabatecos*, however, are quick to comment that the patrols never undertook any constructive projects because 'killing people ... that was their project'.[28] Thus, municipal authority was almost non-existent and the appointed officials appeared to have been not much more than puppets of the military.

Military violence and control also had repercussions on the functioning of traditional indigenous authorities, such as the *Alcaldía Indígena* (indigenous municipality) and the *cofradías* (religious brotherhoods). One of the main functions of the *Alcaldía Indígena*, besides mediating between conflicting parties over small thefts, adultery and the shifting of boundary markers, was the control and maintenance of the municipal lands belonging to the *Comunidad Indígena de Santa María Joyabaj*. This *comunidad* organizes a large part of the indigenous population of Joyabaj, entitling them to a considerable amount of communal land surrounding the town of Joyabaj. They lend land to landless indigenous people, let people use the communal land to graze their animals and gather firewood, and collect the taxes that users of the land have to pay every year. The power of the *Alcaldía Indígena* diminished because the military and civil patrol leaders were taking over most of the powerful positions in town. The attitude of the people regarding their obligations towards de *Alcaldía Indígena* therefore began to change too. People stopped paying taxes or started selling the land lent to them by the *Alcaldía*.[29]

As well, the *cofradías* (indigenous brotherhoods organized around a Catholic saint) were restricted in their religious activities and authority. First, several *cofrades* were killed, while others had left, were too busy patrolling, or did not want assume positions of leadership. This meant that it was impossible to fill all *cofradía* positions. Second, as gatherings of all kinds were suspect in the eyes of the mili-

---

26 Interview 15-01 (15/5/01).
27 ODHAG, Vol. II (1998: 139-140).
28 Interview 40-99 (23/7/99).
29 Interview 7-98 (19/6/98).

tary, and in view of the physical danger involved in visiting ceremonial sites to perform religious rituals, the movements of the *cofrades* were severely restrained. Besides, it was difficult to obtain the goods necessary to carry out the ceremonies. An important function of the *cofradías* in Joyabaj, besides taking care of their respective patrons and their participation in the annual elections of the *Alcaldía Indígena*, is the organization of several festivities, including dances, in honour of the various saints.[30] The *cofradías* were severely restricted in carrying out these tasks during the initial stage of the violence. Often the celebrations became a simple affair, without the traditional communal meals and fireworks.[31] According to a former mayor, the little money that was still earned at that time had to be spent on civil patrol trinkets, such as badges and T-shirts. Little money remained to pay for the 'costumes and the man who plays the marimba'.[32] No sponsors could be found for defraying the costs of the dancing costumes and no volunteers could be found to dance. This was not unexpected because 'men who organized the dances'[33] and several *cofrades* had disappeared during the *Fiesta* in August 1980, when the military had temporarily remained in Joyabaj after Padre Villanueva was murdered. The situation seemed to change somewhat after the military from the local base became interested in the dances and other indigenous ceremonies. This interest surfaced after the guerrillas had supposedly forbidden villagers to participate in the dances. When the local military commander heard of this, he ordered the dances to be organized anyway. People who refused to participate were ordered to appear at the military base, after which they were only too eager to comply.[34] The military also started to promote traditional marimba music, to be played on the central square on market days, supposedly to instil a feeling that 'life goes on as normal'. Normally this kind of music was reserved for special and festive occasions. On another occasion, the Joyabaj patrollers were ordered to appear at a civil patrol rally dressed up in indigenous masks and costumes normally reserved for feast days.[35] The military used indigenous customs and traditions for their own purposes, sometimes making a mockery of them along the way. Also traditional civic parades and beauty queen contests were promoted by the military, resulting in the election of a *Señorita* or *Reina de Patrullero Civil* in 1983. She was paraded around town on a car which was converted into an army tank with the help of some cardboard and green paint.

---

30 Dances like the *Baile de Venados* (Dance of the Deer), *Baile de la Culebra* (Dance of the Snake), *Baile de los Toritos* (Dance of the Bulls) and the *Baile de los Moros* (Dance of the Moors). See García Escóbar (1998: 1) (www.usac.edu.gt:8080/cefol/jul98/cefoljul98.htm).
31 Interview 25-99 (30/5/99).
32 Interview 21-99 (22/7/99).
33 Interview 9-01 (9/5/01).
34 Interview 40-99 (23/7/99).
35 Americas Watch Committee (1984: 82).

photo 11. *Beauty Queen (señorita or reina del patrullero civil) of the civil defense patrols is driven around town in a cardboard army tank (Foto Color, 1983)*

Military commissioners: a key component of military counter-insurgency

It was impossible for the military to carry out their tasks efficiently without accurate information about the situation in Joyabaj. They had to know who was connected to a certain political party, how power relations were structured and where sympathies lay. Joyabaj was a huge municipality with more than 50 villages and smaller hamlets scattered around the countryside, sometimes several hours' walk from the town itself. As elsewhere in the Guatemalan countryside, an extensive network of military commissioners and their auxiliaries was active in Joyabaj, covering the whole municipality. They were the ones who provided the military with the required information.

Military commissioners can be regarded as the traditional allies of military establishment ever since President Ubico organized them in the 1930s. The original task of military commissioners was to enforce military conscription in the countryside. They were generally army veterans who did not bear arms, did not get paid, and had to be residents of the municipalities in which they worked.[36] The position of military commissioner was regarded as an honourable and possibly powerful one, because commissioners were usually closely linked to the local ladino elite. Until the 1960s, their role was the largely passive one of reporting major local problems to their military superiors. After March 1963, when the anti-communist President Peralta Azúrdia came to power, they became an active counter-insurgency instrument. Their numbers expanded, and their status was enhanced by the new army law of 1965, 'placing them on an active status equivalent to that of the standing army, allowing for payment as a normal condition of service'.[37] Their role in the communities changed drastically. They were allowed to bear arms, had to observe and report the presence of insurgents, political organizers and strangers, accompany military patrols, and carry out questioning and detention. They acted as informants of the army and sometimes worked as *consejales* (secret agents) for army intelligence.[38]

In Joyabaj this extensive network of military control comprised several ladino commissioners who were stationed in the town itself, as well as a large number of indigenous and some ladino auxiliary commissioners which were stationed in the surrounding villages. Informing was not the only task carried out by the commissioners, who became more and more involved in direct military actions. The REMHI report implicates several of them in various individual killings and massacres that took place in Joyabaj between 1980 and 1983.[39] Most

---

36 McClintock (1985: 65).
37 McClintock (1985: 66).
38 Paul and Demarest (1988: 150).
39 Yamauchi (1998), ODHAG, Vol. XI (1998: 1332-1345) and testimonies collected by the REMHI project (cases no. 03736, 03752, 03753, 03756, 03763, 03776, 03777, 03788, 03808).

of the names mentioned in these testimonies are of indigenous military commissioners from the rural areas, partly because most testimonies were given by people from indigenous villages like Xeabaj, Xecnup, Cruz Chich and Chorraxaj.

Before the civil war, many ladinos in Joyabaj regarded the position of military commissioner as a way to earn people's respect since it was treated as a position of authority. This changed drastically after the commissioners became more and more involved in military activities. Respect turned into fear and a shift seems to have taken place from authority based on respect to authority based on fear.[40] Some *Joyabatecos* make a clear distinction between the traditional military commissioners, who were mainly concerned with rounding up sufficient military conscripts, and the new commissioners who came into the job towards the end of the 1970s. The traditional commissioners were seen as 'type Ubico ... they did not get involved in these things [violence]'.[41] The new commissioners were considered to have been much more involved in the military terror campaigns. They became 'trusted persons' (*personas de confianza*) of the military and had unrestricted access to the military base in Santa Cruz. Together with the military they organized the patrols and appointed their commanders. In many of the villages surrounding Joyabaj, as elsewhere in Guatemala, commissioners themselves became the heads of civil defence patrols.

As a result of the commissioners' past as an instrument of state terror, the topic is a difficult one to discuss and not something people tend to expand on in Joyabaj. Ladinos were especially reluctant to talk about the ladino commissioners who had been active in the town itself and still lived there. Sometimes during an interview I spelt out the names of these men, and asked people to comment on them. People who normally volunteered information about the violence during the 1980s said they did not know or did not remember the name, or changed the subject altogether. Although they wanted me to know what had happened, they were unwilling to implicate any of the military commissioners still alive. In the rare cases when people would comment on one of the names, they referred to the military commissioner as 'him' or 'that person', or they would nod in the direction of the individual's house or workplace without ever mentioning his name. Many of the commissioners deliberately kept a low profile, although they collaborated extensively with the local military base. They worked 'below the water' (*bajo el agua*), as they say in Joyabaj, and 'only ordered others, they did not involve themselves directly (*no se daban color*)'.[42] According to one ladino, the

---

40   Interview 25-99 (30/5/99).
41   Interview 19-99 (5/6/99).
42   Interview 18-99 (20/5/99).

commissioners in town were intelligent enough not to get openly involved with military activities because they realized that problems could arise with the rest of the population once the military left Joyabaj after things had calmed down.[43]

The case of the 164 military commissioners

Given the outright refusal of many people to talk openly about military commissioners, and the fear many people had and still have of them, an interesting case involving military commissioners in Joyabaj is found in the *Prensa Libre* of 23 April 1982. According to this newspaper article, people from several villages in the municipalities of Joyabaj and San Andrés Sajcabaja, situated north of Joyabaj, jointly denounced a group of 164 military commissioners from the 'former regime'.[44] They were accused of killings, raping women, robbery and setting fire to houses and livestock. Consequently people fled and left everything behind. They did not ask for punishment of the military commissioners but for economic help to return to their villages and their former lives. By 'former regime' is meant the presidency of Lucas García, indicating that people had hopes that the *Junta Militar*, which was still functioning at that time, would do a better job. An official reaction of the *Ministro de Gobernación* (Minister of the Interior) followed the next day, stating that 'laws punish generals and commissioners equally'.[45] The denunciation failed to prompt any other response from the 'new regime'.

On 28 April a reaction followed, written by *Joyabatecos* who ardently defended the same group of commissioners.[46] Apparently, more than 300 *Joyabatecos* drew up a statement in which they challenged the people who had been denouncing the commissioners in the first place. According to them, the people responsible for the *subversión* in Joyabaj were the same as those trying to blacken the commissioners. They were the real guerrillas in Quiché and had formed 'an organization called CUC[47] who hides in the valleys of this municipality'.[48] They specifically attacked the Catholic Church by accusing the catechists and the nun María Jesús Bolado of being subversive and belonging to the guerrilla. The article accused them of being 'like wolves in sheep's clothing. They are the cause of the massive emigration of the people from Joyabaj'.[49] The story continued in the newspaper a few days later, after a few journalists travelled to Joyabaj to find out

---

43 Interview 5-99 (26/5/99).
44 Prensa Libre, 23/4/82.
45 Prensa Libre, 24/4/82.
46 Prensa Libre, 28/4/82.
47 CUC (*Comité de Unidad Campesino* - Committee for Campesino Unity) is a peasant organization set up in 1978. During the military offensives in 1980-83 CUC members were a prime target of government forces, partly because some of the CUC members allied themselves with the guerrillas.
48 Prensa Libre, 28/4/82.
49 Prensa Libre, 28/4/82.

what was going on. Allegedly they spoke to several military commissioners in Joyabaj, who claimed that they had never been threatened by anybody and that they had no idea where the newspaper story came from. In their eyes it was just an accusation written by people who wanted to 'abuse the good faith of the journalists'[50] and who had signed the accusation with names of non-existent persons.

What does this incident mean? Which groups or individuals in Joyabaj felt strong enough to make such a denunciation against military commissioners at that moment? Or were only fractions of the population represented and did it not represent a general feeling? Was the denunciation really presented by the villagers, or was the guerrilla or even the military involved in drafting it, to create a rationale for the violence committed in the area? These questions remain without answers, even after 18 months of fieldwork, because nobody talked about the denunciation or could or wanted to remember anything about it. When asked directly about the incident, some people explained that it was impossible at that time to undertake such an action, because it would almost certainly have meant punishment or worse. They could not imagine that anyone would have done such a thing. It was therefore impossible to verify what had really happened, because the only sources are newspaper articles, which were often under heavy censorship. In Chapter 3 I commented on the fact that people did not remember a meeting with Lucas García, possibly because it did not fit the image people currently want to project of Joyabaj and its population. The same could hold true for the case of the 164 military commissioners.

Civil patrols and the military

The newly organized civil defence patrols were a central element to military counter-insurgency. They were created by the military towards the end of 1981 and set up in conflict zones in the Guatemalan countryside. The first patrols were organized in the last months of the Lucas García administration, under the command of his brother, the Army Chief of Staff Benedícto Lucas García.[51] In the spring of 1982, after dissatisfied young officers disposed of the Lucas García regime, the head of the new junta, Ríos Montt, formalized and expanded the patrol system throughout the western highlands.

The introduction of civil patrols in an area was conditioned for the most part by the intensity of the conflict between the army and the guerrilla and the assumed local sympathy for the guerrilla. The more conflict existed in the area, the more civil patrols were set up and the stricter the military control over the patrols. The military made a distinction between red, pink, yellow and green

---

50   Prensa Libre, 30/4/82.
51   CEH, Vol. II (1999: 182).

zones of conflict. Green zones were thought to be free of guerrillas, and were watched but generally left alone. Pink and yellow zones were visited with more military violence, because of possible ties with guerrillas. Red zones were supposedly in enemy hands from the point of view of the military. In these zones the military made no distinction between villagers and guerrillas and in many of these areas whole villages were wiped off the map. While almost 25 per cent of all civil patrols were located in Huehuetenango, another red zone and thus stronghold of the patrols was the Quiché department, followed by the departments of Petén and San Marcos.[52] It is estimated that a total of 25,000 men were incorporated in the patrol system in Guatemala by September 1982. A year later this number had expanded to some 700,000. At the height of the civil patrol system, in 1984, about 900,000, predominantly indigenous, men were active in the patrols.[53]

It was not until months after the first patrols had been organized that they were formally recognized by way of Governmental Accord 222-83, which created a 'National Office for the Coordination and Control of the Civil Defence Patrols'.[54] Subsequently, at the end of 1983 a 'Fund for Military Protection of the Civil Defence' was created, which was meant to provide economic assistance to the families of patrollers who were killed during combat.[55] The civil patrols were clearly an official part of military strategy. This was also apparent from their military-style chain of command. The patrols were headed by a civil patrol commander, who was often appointed by and under the control of both the local military commander and the military commissioner. Often, military commissioners themselves were appointed to act as heads of the patrols. In the towns, the patrol structure was somewhat more complicated, consisting of battalions, platoons, squadrons and rank-and-file members.[56] Officials from D-5 (*Dirección de Asuntos Civiles* or Directorate of Civil Affairs),[57] who were responsible for the political and psychological aspects of the military operations including relations with the local civil defence patrol, organized weekly meetings at military bases for patrol commanders. Orders involving patrol duty were generated through the military chain of command.

Almost every community in the Guatemalan highlands, however small, had its civil defence patrol. Depending on the size of the communities and the num-

---

52 Popkin (1996: 18).
53 Americas Watch (1986: 26).
54 *Jefatura Nacional de Coordinación y Control de la Autodefensa Civil* (PDH, 1994: 33).
55 Decree 160-83 (PDH, 1994: 33).
56 Americas Watch (1986: 42).
57 D-5 is one of five divisions which together form the *Estado Mayor de la Defensa Nacional* (EMDN or National Defence Staff). The other divisions are D-1 (personnel), D-2 (intelligence operations), D-3 (military operations and training) and D-4 (logistics) (ODHAG, Vol. II, 1998: 81-87).

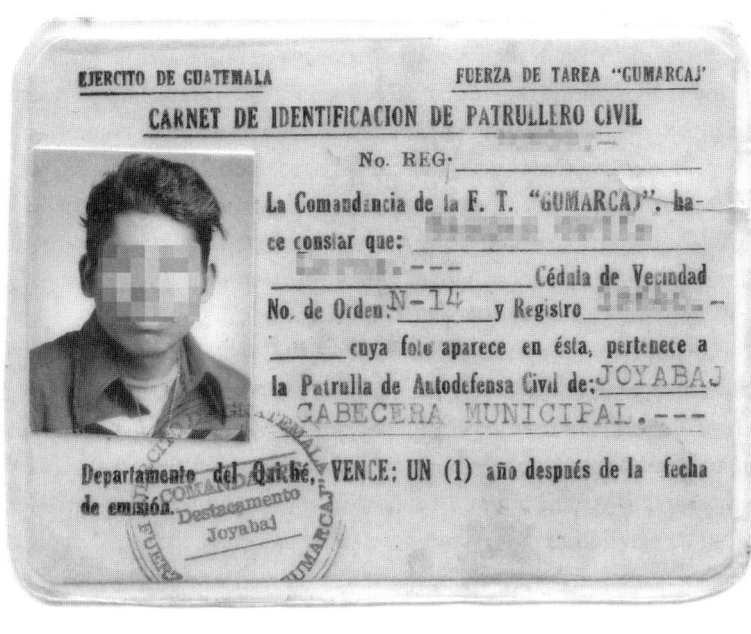

photo 12a. *Identification card of a civil patroller, front (1983).*
photo 12b. *Back of an identification card, saying: The civil patroller is a man, who concerns himself with the peace and tranquility of his land, and participates in achieving this. Constant vigilance is the price of freedom and progress of Guatemala (1983)*

ber of men available for patrolling, people had to patrol at least one day a week, which led to a loss of income for many people. It is estimated that only 5–10 per cent of the patrol members were armed, that is, carrying a gun of some sort.[58] However, they all carried their machetes or wooden sticks when going on a sweep together with the military, weapons that were just as deadly. Some patrols wore makeshift uniforms or T-shirts identifying them as patrollers from a certain village, while all patrollers had to carry an identity card. Failure to produce his civil patrol identity card could land a person in prison for a few days.

Tasks and figures

Officially the patrols were set up to defend and 'protect the villages against guerrilla attacks'[59] and participation in the patrols was supposedly voluntary. Unofficially, participation was obligatory for all males between the ages of 18 and 60, on penalty of severe punishment or even death. Sometimes even youngsters,[60] the elderly or women had to participate, for example, to take the place of a deceased husband.[61] The patrols were used as an extension of the military's control of the Guatemalan countryside. They organized checkpoints at the village entrance, checked identity papers, set up roadblocks, searched buses and patrolled the village at night. They acted as an information network for the military, as well as taking over military tasks such as sweeping areas for guerrillas and attacking so-called subversive villages. According to the CEH report, the civil defence patrols were responsible for 30 per cent of the 626 massacres n Guatemala, mostly accompanied by military forces.[62] As for human rights violations in general, the civil patrols in Quiché were responsible for the 59 per cent of the violations committed in that department between 1981 and 1994.[63] These included massacres, arbitrary execution, disappearances, torture, sexual abuse and deprivation of freedom.

Surveillance and control, two pillars of Foucault's panopticon, were two other important functions of the civil patrols. Communities and their inhabitants were under continuous surveillance and control. People were constantly aware of their own visibility and that of their actions. For example, a man from an indigenous community in Joyabaj was temporarily working on a *finca* on the south coast. One day he received a letter from the patrol commander from his native

---

58 Americas Watch (1986: 28).
59 Interview former General Balconi (18/10/99).
60 Americas Watch (1986: 27) mentions the formation of school patrols (*patrullas escolares*) in larger towns near Guatemala City.
61 Americas Watch (1986: 28).
62 CEH, Vol. III (1999: 256).
63 CEH, Vol. II (1999: 230).

village, enquiring why he had not yet returned and accusing him of being a guerrilla because he was not doing his patrol duty. Together with the *finca* foreman, he went to the local military base near the *finca* to obtain a letter confirming that he was actually working and also patrolling. On returning to his community in the municipality of Joyabaj, he was ordered straight away to the house of the local patrol commander, who did not believe his story and took him to the military, where his letter was read and approved. Surveillance of seasonal labourers, who also had to perform patrol duty, clearly did not stop at the village borders.[64] Surveillance and control extended also towards the behaviour of the people who actually carried out the surveillance, that is, those participating in the patrols. Participation in the patrols forced people to control and supervise their own behaviour and that of their families. Not behaving according to the standards of the patrol commander, the military commander, or the other patrollers could mean punishment or death. Sometimes patrollers were killed by other patrollers, for example when they let a prisoner escape or because they refused to continue patrolling.[65] Patrols incorporated more and more civilians into the terror apparatus, thereby also incorporating part of the target population into that same apparatus. In some instances, the agents of terror (members of the patrols) and the targets of terror became one and the same. This ambiguity made it difficult to distinguish between enemy and friend, between 'us' and 'them'. The boundaries between these groups were not always very clear.

Joyabaj patrols and local diversity

A central aspect of civil patrols was their diversity between and within municipalities, and consequently their varied and often unpredictable impact on local society. Although set up by the military as part of a wider counter-insurgency strategy and having basically the same organizational structure, the differences between civil patrols across and even within municipalities were significant. Civil patrols were not static entities, but differed in background, the type of functions they performed, and their level of military activity. Civil patrol commanders and members also had widely different views on civil patrols and what they stood for. In one area a civil patrol could be highly hierarchically organized, heavily armed and in constant close contact with the military. In another area civil patrol members might be hardly armed at all, might do only some shifts on night watch, might have little contact with the local military commander and might regard civil patrol duty as a minor obligation. Between these extremes there was ample room for variation, depending on such factors as the level and history of violence

---

64 Diary 17/5/01.
65 CEH, Vol. XI (1999: 1372, 1366, 1348, and 1362).

photo 13. *Civil patrollers from Las Lomas Chuacorral (Foto Color, mid 1980s)*

and/or military presence and guerrilla activity in the area. A Guatemalan testified in 1984 for the Russell Tribunal that 'between the patrols that kill and the patrols that die at the hands of the same military (or other civil patrols) there exist a whole range of types of patrols'.[66]

This diversity of patrol activity was partially the result of introducing civil patrols in widely different settings (municipalities) with different histories: of land disputes, of ladino rule, or of rule by *indígenas*. Joyabaj, consisting of around 60 communities and approximately the same number of civil patrols, has always had a ladino minority that controlled most of the political and economic positions in town. Although the indigenous population was and still is in the majority, until 1978 they had not been part of the political elite that normally occupied all positions in the municipality. The only group of *indígena* leaders that came close to local party politics was the one backing the right-wing political parties of the ladinos, especially the anti-communist MLN. Some of these indigenous pro-MLN villages, like Xecnup and Cruz Chich, were among the first to set up civil patrols and were remembered as the most aggressive.

A second factor influencing the diversity of the civil patrols was the degree of military influence in an area. Was it a conflict area, was there a local military base, and how were the communication lines between the military, civil patrols

---

66 Russel Tribunal (1984: 165).

and military commissioners organized? This variety had a major impact on the way civil patrols acted and carried out their surveillance tasks. The ladino population of Joyabaj had a long military tradition with several ladinos on active duty in the national, regional and local military command structure. Ties between ladinos and the military were already close before the civil war broke out and several ladinos had close connections with military intelligence. When the fighting started in the Joyabaj area around 1980, the ladinos felt threatened and used their already existing ties with the military to request a military presence in the area.

A third important factor was the role played by the individual patrol commander. He was the one in direct contact with the military and his views on how patrol duties were to be carried out were important, although not decisive because of the military hierarchy. According to former Defence Minister Balconi, the civil patrols in the department of Quiché were organized locally. Every patrol had its own form and pattern of working, which is why the role of the individual patrol commander was of such importance in Quiché. This is in sharp contrast with the civil patrols in, for example, the department of Huehuetenango, which were much more centrally organized. Central command of the patrols was based in Chiantla, from where it controlled the activities of all patrols in Huehuetenango.[67] In Joyabaj, however, the civil patrols were much more locally organized and local patrol leaders were under less strict control, which accounts for the diversity among the patrols. Some patrol commanders in Joyabaj, like the one from Las Lomas who tried to hand over a certain number of identification cards to the military each month, were quite fanatical and often very anti-guerrilla and anti-communist. Other patrol commanders tried to steer their patrols clear of trouble, and looked the other way when encountering presumed subversives on their patrol rounds. This attitude of looking the other way was being encouraged at the time by guerrilla leaflets distributed in the villages. After the first civil patrols were installed and it was becoming clear what their functions would be, guerrilla organizations tried to influence people's attitude towards civil patrols by distributing pamphlets.[68] They consisted of short picture stories, portraying civil patrollers as the army's vanguard and mechanism of control. One of the drawings depicts a group of patrollers walking through the forest, while a few guerrillas are hidden in the bushes. The patrollers are aware of the guerrillas presence but tell each other 'there are our pals, let's continue as if we haven't seen them', while the speech bubble of the guerrillas says 'hold your fire, it's the civil patrol'.

---

67 Interview former General and Minister of Defence Balconi, 18/10/99.
68 ORPA bulletin *Siembra*, December 1982.

picture 14. *Guerrilla pamphlet. On the right civil patrollers, pretending not to notice guerrillas who are hiding in the bushes on the left (ORPA, Siembra, December 1982)*

Closely related to the role of patrol commander was the post of local military commander, who was the direct superior of the patrol commander. Although the military commander allotted a certain amount of freedom to the patrol commanders, he was the one giving orders and directions to the patrol commanders. Several ladinos commented on the differences between the various military commanders that served in Joyabaj in the early 1980s. While one of the first *tenientes* in Joyabaj was nicknamed 'the assassin'[69] and was remembered as cruel and without any feelings, others were not considered that bad, while some even became drinking buddies. One ladino explained that he was glad that the assassin left when Ríos Montt took over the presidency, because he always ran into trouble with him. His replacement seemed to have come with new orders on how to deal with troublesome ladinos in town, because his attitude was markedly different from his predecessor's. The presidency of Ríos Montt was therefore considered by several *Joyabatecos* to be more relaxed, at least for part of the ladino population in town. When Ríos Montt took over power, 'the tension eased a little bit in town'.[70] This was not strange, because the military had the town firmly under its

---

69 Interview 6-01 (11/5/01).
70 Interview 7-01 (23/5/01).

control at that time, and therefore focused most of their attention and violent activities on the surrounding countryside, where the military still lacked total control. A former ladino patroller commented that the situation in town had quietened down 'because people had learned a lot in the meantime, they had learned to shut up and not to protest, they had learned not to talk, they had learned to show up for patrol duty ... people had learned to survive'. He cynically added that 'it quietened down because there was nobody left to kill'.[71] This patroller belonged to the initial group of ladinos who started patrolling the town of Joyabaj voluntarily, immediately after the pharmacist Ramiro Paiz had been killed; at that time they felt they had to defend their village and their families against attacks from outside. But his attitude towards patrolling changed markedly when the military arrived in Joyabaj and took over control and organization of these vigilante groups, organizing them forcibly into civil defence patrols. He then became one of the few who dared oppose patrol duty and ran into frequent trouble with the local patrol commanders.

I will illustrate the striking diversity among the different patrols by looking at three civil patrols in particular, a ladino patrol in the town of Joyabaj, an indigenous patrol in the village of Xecnup and another indigenous patrol in the neighbouring village of Chorraxaj. While the ladino patrol is a clear example of looking the other way, the other two patrols are remembered because of their violent reputation during the civil war. The differences between the two villages are, nevertheless, enormous. The majority of the people from Xecnup were conservative and sympathetic towards the military presence and patrol duty. They are remembered as carrying out their patrol tasks like 'fanatics'. The village of Chorraxaj was considered more open-minded, with many of its people active in the Christian Democratic Party and the Catholic Church. It was therefore also more divided than Xecnup, along political as well as religious lines. This resulted in a violent patrol leader who forced the majority of unwilling patrollers in Chorraxaj to carry out patrol duty.

Teachers set up their own patrol

Some *Joyabatecos* still remember their own involvement in the organization of a kind of paramilitary group immediately after the murder of Ramiro Paíz. They wanted to defend their families and their town, and decided to start patrolling the streets. After the military settled themselves permanently in the Joyabaj convent, they took over the organization of the patrols. A voluntary organization was changed into a compulsory one for all men in Joyabaj. In general *Joyabatecos* stress that they were ordered into the patrols by the military. Shortly after the

---

71 Interview 7-01 (23/5/01).

military installed themselves in Joyabaj, soldiers paraded through town using a megaphone ordering everybody to attend a meeting during which the town patrols were to be set up. The military divided the town in two neighbourhoods (*barrio*), which were subdivided in blocks (*cuadra*). Each block was organized into a civil patrol, which had to do its rounds during the night. The first shift started at 6.00 p.m. and ended at midnight, while the second shift started at midnight and lasted until 6.00 a.m. Twelve men patrolled together during each shift.

One of the patrols in town consisted entirely of ladino teachers. After they had heard patrols were to be set up, they organized themselves into one patrol and petitioned to patrol on Friday nights. That way their teaching would not suffer too much from the rounds. The military accepted their petition. According to a former patrol commander, the patrol quickly 'turned into a gang of drunks' (*chupaderos*). On Friday night they would take food and especially alcohol with them and hide out during most of the night in an empty house just outside town, until it was almost time for the other shift to start. Then they would take a quick walk through town, trying to avoid any trouble. 'They only patrolled because they had to ... not because they wanted to.'[72] Whenever encountering trouble or guerrillas, they tried to look the other way, although their vision was sometimes already clouded by the consumption of a considerable amount of alcohol. According to this former commander, not all patrols were like that. Some took their tasks very seriously and 'walked in one line behind their leader, like servants'.[73] Before the patrol shift started they had to report to the military base, where they were assigned weapons. They received three or four shotguns (*escopetas*) to be divided among twelve men. Some of the men took their task so seriously that they fought among each other to get hold of one of the shotguns. One ladino still became angry when remembering that only the military and their close friends with whom they went drinking had real weapons, while the majority of the patrols had to go patrolling with sticks and machetes. In his opinion, the military let the *Joyabatecos* do the dirty work at night while they were sleeping sweetly in the convent.[74]

Civil patrols in Xecnup

The civil patrols from Xecnup are mentioned frequently in testimonies of violent incidents in Joyabaj. In twelve of the 37 testimonies gathered in Joyabaj by the REMHI project, the civil patrols from Xecnup are implicated in massacres and the selective killing and torturing of people inside and outside their own com-

---

72 Interview 24-99 (31/5/99).
73 Interview 24-99 (31/5/99).
74 Interview 6-01 (11/5/01).

munity. Targets of patrol abuse were the nearby indigenous villages of Xeabaj, Chorraxaj and Patzulá,[75] whose inhabitants were active in community projects organized by the Catholic Church, Alianza and their own committees. Many *Joyabatecos* nowadays describe Xecnup as an indigenous village where 'the situation (*la cosa*) was very grave, they killed many people'.[76] In the eyes of many *Joyabatecos* the civil patrols in Xecnup are an example of 'patrols that kill'. Possibly the history of Xecnup backing ladino MLN politicians and their own anti-communist stance accounts for part of the violent behaviour of the Xecnup patrols. Because of this attitude they were considered not too averse to setting up civil patrols to combat guerrilla forces and protect their own interests. This seems, however, an inadequate answer to the question why the indigenous patrols of Xecnup were particularly violent towards neighbouring communities. We therefore have to take a look at power struggles within the community of Xecnup. Apart from a conservative majority, which was more inclined towards traditional *costumbre*,[77] a small group was open towards left-wing ideas, especially the catechists of Catholic Action. Some sources mention active support in Xecnup for the guerrillas, albeit amongst a minority of the population.[78] This created a conflict between the two groups, during which the more conservative group accused the other of belonging to the guerrilla. Apparently, this culminated in the flight in early 1982 of the more open-minded people from Xecnup, who sought refuge in the neighbouring villages of Chorraxaj and Patzulá. At that moment no civil patrols existed in Chorraxaj and locals were known to harbour and help fugitives from neighbouring villages. Despite their flight, the refugees from Xecnup were tracked down by the civil patrols of Xecnup and killed together with many of the people who had given them shelter in Chorraxaj.

Another incident that possibly sparked anti-guerrilla sentiments in Xecnup was the killing of some men from Xecnup by the guerrilla at the beginning of the violent conflict because they had refused to cooperate with them. Allegedly their sons wanted to take revenge and called in army assistance. Subsequently the civil patrols were set up in the village of Xecnup at the request of its pro-military inhabitants.[79] The incident reminds one of the anti-guerrilla sentiments in the town of Joyabaj itself, which flared up after the guerrilla had killed the local pharmacist Ramiro Paíz in October 1981. A former member of the Catholic Church, who was telling this story, added that he had the feeling it was told by

---

75 Testimonies collected by the REMHI project (cases no. 03743, 03748, 03755, 03767, 03766, 03791, 03826, 03827, 03828).
76 Interview 30-99 (6/7/99).
77 Interview 30-99 (6/7/99).
78 Interview 17-99 (14/8/99).
79 Interview 20-98 (18/8/98).

the people from Xecnup as a kind of apology or explanation for the violent behaviour of some of its inhabitants when they were in the civil patrols. In a way this incident seemed to be used to justify the violent activities of the Xecnup patrols.[80]

To complete the picture, one has to take into account the role of the civil patrol leaders in Xecnup. Some of the leaders were known to be very '*prepotente*' (powerful in a violent way) and 'pursuing personal interests'. Many people to whom they owed money or with whom they had long-standing personal conflicts were killed. 'Why repay someone if you could also kill him?'[81] Religion is also an important factor in the local understanding of individual patrol violence. According to indigenous Catholic activists, the civil patrol leaders from Xecnup were not Catholics and that is why 'they did so many massacres'. One former indigenous leader explained that 'the ones from Xecnup did not like the Catholic religion and held on to *costumbre* and therefore caused much of the violence'.[82] Old frictions between Catholic Action on the one hand and *costumbre* on the other are implicitly embedded in the story: frictions that had existed not only before and during the violence but also afterwards, when attempts were made to explain the atrocities that had been committed. Some Catholics tried to make sense of the atrocities by explaining they were committed by people who were not Catholics. However, several patrol commanders who were Catholics did participate.

Civil patrols in Chorraxaj

According to local memory, Chorraxaj patrols were set up towards the middle of 1982, somewhat later than the ones in Xecnup and other neighbouring villages. This was done after continuous harassment from the military and surrounding patrols. According to an older *indígena* from Chorraxaj, who had been involved in the Catholic Church, Chorraxaj resisted organizing the village into patrols for a long time. 'We did not want to be part of the civil patrols. We did not want to hurt the other villages.'[83] Chorraxaj was known in the area as a community that opened its doors (*dar posada*) to refugees from other indigenous villages, like Xecnup, Chicotón and nearby Xeabaj. It was also known as a 'sanctuary for the guerrilla ... when someone was in any way involved in the guerrilla, they went there. Here they received help'.[84] The people of Chorraxaj had been actively involved in community development projects from the Catholic Church and

---

80 Interview 20-98 (18/8/98).
81 Interviews 21-99 (22/7/99) and 24-99 (31/5/99).
82 Interview 28-99 (18/9/99).
83 Interview 14-99 (16/8/99).
84 Interview 8-01 (9/5/01).

Alianza, which were responsible for the formation of a number of local indigenous leaders. Many of them had been active in the Christian Democratic party whose leaders were heavily prosecuted by the military during the 1980s.

The military, aided by civil patrols from Xecnup and Cruz Chich, retaliated heavily against what they considered to be 'subversive' behaviour, especially the harbouring of refugees and guerrillas. One of the first violent incidents involved helping refugees from Xecnup, who had arrived in Chorraxaj in January 1981. The army and civil patrols from Xecnup followed them to Chorraxaj, killing both the refugees and their hosts in Chorraxaj. More than 50 people died that day.[85] A man from Chorraxaj, who was 14 years old at the time of the massacre, remembers that some of them had time to flee before the military and the patrols arrived from Xecnup. They climbed a hill from where they could see what was happening in the village. 'It was a pity', the man continues, 'that the refugees did not know the best places to hide. They decided to hide near the river, where they were easily found by the military.'[86] In March 1982 another attack from the civil patrols in Xecnup, together with the military and military commissioners, caused the deaths of another 50 men, women and children.[87]

Finally, after rumours went around that the military planned to bomb Chorraxaj, the villagers decided to talk with the military commander. According to an indigenous woman in Chorraxaj, the women of Chorraxaj convened during the night and decided to march directly to the military base in Joyabaj. 'The men came with us', she continued. When they arrived at the military base they formed a semicircle with the women in front and the men behind them. If problems arose, they thought the military would not shoot women that readily. 'The *teniente* came out and asked us why we kept fleeing from our villages, and why we did not stay put. He told us that we would not have any problems any more, if we would organize civil patrols. So to avoid further problems we elected Santos Chich Us as patrol commander.'[88] Although the amount of freedom people had in the election of a patrol commander is questionable, problems in Chorraxaj lessened somewhat after this initiative.

Santos Chich Us turned out to be a very violent patrol commander and became a close ally of Leonel Ogáldez, who was general commander of the patrols in Joyabaj and member of the Ogáldez family, which had occupied important political and economic positions for decades. According to some

---

[85] CEH, Vol. X (1999: 1023) and NDG no. 93, 1983. The information from interviews with people from Chorraxaj concerning the actual day and year of the massacres differs sometimes from the CEH and the REMHI reports. Exactly when the massacres took place seemed to be of less importance than the fact that they happened.
[86] Morin (1996).
[87] CEH, Vol. X (1999: 1083); Morin (1996).
[88] Interview 26-99 (21/8/99).

members of Conavigua (widows organization), Santos Chich Us was chosen because he was intelligent and spoke Spanish. Somewhat later in the interview, they explain that he was chosen because 'he was a very angry (*enojado*) man, who did not forgive others'.[89] Not everybody was happy with the choice, 'but what could one do?', one of the women explained. When patrollers turned up too late for their patrol shifts they were beaten or thrown in the pit. 'Sometimes', the woman continued, 'my husband came home very sad from patrol duty. He was not hungry ... sometimes he even cried.'[90] Santos Chich, together with his second and third in command, was responsible for many murders committed by the Chorraxaj patrol.

The situation in Chorraxaj remained troubled and not everybody agreed to participate in the newly organized civil patrols. This culminated on 15 April 1983 in a third massacre, which cost the lives of at least a 100 people.[91] During the night more than 500 patrollers from the surrounding villages had been ordered by the military commander to attack the villagers with sticks and machetes. The military followed swiftly, taking prisoners with them to the village square in the town of Joyabaj, where some of them were hacked to pieces (*hicieron picadito*) in broad daylight, for everybody to see. Others were held prisoner on the military compound. Every night two of the prisoners were taken out and handed over to a civil patrol with the order to kill the prisoners. The military told the patrollers that 'only the toughest [patroller] would be daring enough to kill them and that this person was to be congratulated by the military commander, because he had the courage to kill a man'.[92] A common military strategy to implicate everybody in the killing and so get everybody's hands dirty.

Diverse accounts and memories of patrol violence

By presenting the three cases of the patrol of the ladino teachers, the patrol from Xecnup, and the patrol from Chorraxaj, I have tried to show the diversity that existed among them: diversity in the way they were set up, the way they organized their activities, and the way they related to the local military. A range of very diverse factors thus influenced civil patrol activity, thereby complicating the sometimes one-sided picture that exists of civil patrols in general. It is too easy to portray villages that were fierce supporters of ladino MLN politicians, and did not have close ties with the Catholic Church and Alianza, as having the most violent patrols. Although it is correct to say the patrols from Xecnup turned out to be very violent, and they did indeed support the MLN, the situation is more com-

---

89 Interview 26-99 (21/8/99).
90 Interview 26-99 (21/8/99).
91 NDG, no. 93, 1983.
92 NDG, no. 93, 1983.

plex. For example, although Chorraxaj was a Catholic Action village, open to development efforts and to left-wing ideas, the civil patrols in Chorraxaj were also notorious for their human rights abuses. This was caused largely by the behaviour of the local civil patrol commander and his allies, who wielded enormous personal power. Many villages were internally divided, and conflicts over power, land or religion were being played out during the civil war by way of the civil patrols. The patrols were used by the military not only to control but also to divide and rule the villagers.

Another aspect of diversity I wish to discuss in relation to the civil patrols is the different memories—even conflicting memories, in some cases—people have of civil patrols and civil patrol violence. The fieldwork took place almost 17 years after most atrocities in Joyabaj were committed, and both ladinos and *indígenas* had come up with a variety of explanations. People have very diverse memories of what patrols were about and whether or not they were doing a good job. This diversity is caused by, among other things, the way memory is influenced by factors such as time, place and persons present. People remembered things differently at different moments in time, depending on, for example, the times of conversations, how many times a story had been told already, who was present and in which context the story was told. Will the memory be used to create testimony of the violence, or will it be used to accuse and try perpetrators? Another factor is a person's involvement in the events which are remembered. People remember something as a bystander, as a participant, or as having read about it.

I have grouped some of the different memories *Joyabatecos* have of civil patrol violence together, in light of the aforementioned factors. The following groups are identified: the forced nature of patrols, the abuse of power of patrols and especially patrol commanders, patrols as keepers of order and security, patrols fighting communist forces, and people who do not remember or want to remember. While the people in the first two groups have a fairly negative memory of civil patrols, the third and fourth have more positive memories. Of course, the different groups are not mutually exclusive, because people use a variety of reasons to try to make sense of patrol violence.

Forced participation: the Xeabaj massacre

The largest group of *Joyabatecos*, ladinos as well as *indígenas*, stressed the *forced* nature of the civil patrols. According the them it was impossible not to participate, not to get involved. People had to obey orders from the military and civil patrol commander and, whatever they did when patrolling, it was not of their choosing. If you did not participate, you could get punished, killed, or disappear. Many patrollers just did their job, patrolling the area and checking on people, but avoided killing people or assisting in massacres. They tried not to confront people or just waited until things cooled down, like the men participating in the teacher patrol.

When the patrols were initially organized in the town of Joyabaj, a few ladinos apparently protested. One of the men involved in the organization of their own voluntary patrols, immediately after the murder of Ramiro Paíz, refused to participate in the patrols after the military had taken over its organization and participation became obligatory. According to his wife, this attitude of being 'brave, rebel and a perpetual protester'[93] got him into constant trouble with the patrol commanders and the military, who imprisoned him several times. But even a short stay in prison could not persuade him to start patrolling.[94] His attitude changed, however, after he, together with every other ladino patroller in town, was forced by the military to participate in the massacre in Xeabaj in April 1982, during which between 80 and 100 men, women and children were killed. He explained that getting people to appear for patrol duty and getting them to obey military orders became much less difficult after their forced march on Xeabaj. The massacre of Xeabaj served as a turning point for many ladinos, opening their eyes to what the military were capable of doing, implicating the ladinos along the way. 'Everything changed after the massacre of Xeabaj', a ladino who formerly refused to participate in the patrols explained. He had always thought that the words 'river of blood' were the words of a poem, 'but they were only too real in Xeabaj'.[95]

One of several eyewitness accounts that circulate in Joyabaj about the Xeabaj massacre tells the following story. A week before the massacre in Xeabaj took place, a military officer ordered several of the town patrols to be ready at 3.00 a.m. the following Sunday morning because they were going to march to Semabaj, an indigenous village north of Joyabaj. When they arrived at the site in the early hours of the morning there was food and alcohol waiting for them. People were relieved that nothing happened and were encouraged to eat and drink as much as they could. They returned the next morning to Joyabaj with fierce hangovers. Almost a week later once again they were ordered to be ready at 3.00 a.m. the following morning, because they were going to march to Xeabaj. More than 500 patrollers from all over Joyabaj were ordered to approach Xeabaj from different directions. Many of the patrollers thought it would be another

---

93 Interview 6-01 (11/5/01).
94 Interview 6-01 (11/5/01). It is interesting to note that in many cases ladinos who protested against patrol duty were either warned, harassed or imprisoned, but hardly ever killed by the military or patrol commanders. Indigenous people in the surrounding hamlets protesting against patrols duty, however, were killed on several occasions. See for example CEH, Vol. XI (1999: 1348, 1366, and 1372).
95 Interview 6-01 (11/5/01).

drinking party and looked forward to it. It turned out to be a very different experience for every one of them.[96] The preliminary visit to Semabaj turned out to be an example of military manipulation of the patrols, drawing them tightly into their violent actions.

When the patrollers from town arrived in Xeabaj, patrols from other communities had already arrived and were ordering everyone out of their house. About 50 men were sitting on their knees, with their hands tied behind their backs. The women were sitting silently on a nearby hillside. The patroller who told me this story had been standing behind the military commander, who was going through a notebook that belonged to one of the kneeling men in front of him. Apparently the notebook was empty, but the *teniente* (military sergeant) read things aloud, as if something had been written down. 'Lists of names, subversive language', the *teniente* mumbled. The owner of the notebook denied the accusations and said he needed the notebook because he recruited people working on the south coast. After a while the *teniente* took up a machete and asked whose machete it was. A patroller stepped forwards. He was ordered to take the machete and start chopping off heads, but the man refused. The *teniente* became angry and shouted 'Are you really men?' He ordered the patrol commander of the man refusing to carry out his order to come forward. Nobody moved. The *teniente* started threatening the patrollers themselves if they refused to do their job. A patroller from the nearby village of Caquil came forward and beheaded the first man sitting on the ground. After some seconds everybody was using their machetes on the villagers. 'A river of blood ran down the mountain.'[97]

Between 80 and 100 people were killed that day. Afterwards the civil patrollers from town were eager to leave and, when they received orders to do so from the military, 'they left running, like deer down the mountain'.[98] After the worst of the massacre was over, the military took some of the survivors prisoner, marching them down to the military base in town, and locking them up in deep pits. A few days after the massacre, the prisoners were taken out and brought to the central square in front of the church. In front of everybody, including visitors coming to town to celebrate Holy Week, the men were branded subversives, beaten, tortured and eventually killed. Some *Joyabatecos* saw this second action as a signal from the local military commander to his superiors, to let them know he was not afraid of the consequences of the massacre he had ordered.[99] It is possible that the local commander had overstepped his freedom to act at the local level, because afterwards the *teniente* was ordered to appear at the military base in

---

96 Interview 24-99 (31/5/99).
97 Interview 13-98 (13/5/98).
98 Interview 14-98 (19/6/98).
99 Interview 13-98 (13/5/98).

Santa Cruz to explain what had happened to government officials who had come in from the capital. Allegedly, the military denied it ever happened.

According to another ladino eyewitness things happened somewhat differently during the massacre, although the outcome remained the same. In his version of events, the patrols from Chorraxaj and Xeabaj both played a central role in the Xeabaj massacre.[100] After the people in Chorraxaj had been driven from their houses into the central square, the *teniente* started asking the patrollers from Chorraxaj which men from Xeabaj belonged to the guerrilla. Several men were pointed out and taken from the group, sometimes together with their wives and children. Then the men from Xeabaj were ordered to point out the guerrilla sympathizers in the Chorraxaj group. The two groups were put together, while the remaining villagers were ordered to start killing them with their machetes. After initial refusal some men from Caquil and Xecnup volunteered. Allegedly the people from Chorraxaj and Xeabaj were always denouncing each other at the local military base. The military had exacerbated existing problems between the two villages some weeks before the massacre occurred. They had ordered the Xeabaj patrollers, after they had come to the military base again to complain about guerrilla sympathizers in Chorraxaj, to capture them and bring them to the base. After the Xeabaj patrollers returned with their prisoners they were ordered to take them to the central square, again in broad daylight, and kill them with sticks.[101]

The Xeabaj massacre was described in almost every conversation with people, especially ladinos, and apparently left lasting, although sometimes different, imprints on people's minds. It is the first and often the only massacre ladinos mention when they talk about the violence. They described to me their forced participation in it in terms of merely being present but not actively participating. In their stories, it is almost always the others that were doing the burning or the killing. They themselves were only present. People did not deny that the massacre happened, nor denied their presence at it, but they did deny having actively participated in it. This fits the more general attitude of avoiding involvement in anything so as not to get into trouble. Evading trouble is an attitude that is still apparent in many communities in Joyabaj. Engel[102] describes this as looking at an event as an outsider, a bystander or an observer. Family members of those who died during the massacre, human rights organizations and the law were all groups to be reckoned with. This contrasts with the normal behaviour of putting oneself at the centre of a memory that is narrated.[103]

---

100 Interview 24-99 (31/5/99).
101 Interview 24-99 (31/5/99).
102 Engel (1999: 151).
103 Schacter (1996: 21).

Not only people who were actually in Xeabaj at the time of the massacre, like patrollers, bystanders and surviving victims, have their story ready, but also a whole range of people who could not have been present at the time: young people who had not yet been born or were still in kindergarten when it happened, women who never hiked up in the hills north of Joyabaj, or people who had temporarily left Joyabaj. Several of these people tell the story as if they lived through it, as if they were present, using words and intonations copied from other people. The massacre of Xeabaj seems to be common knowledge, like a collective memory that is based not only on what individuals have seen but also on what people have heard others tell or read about in the truth commission reports and the newspaper. As such, the massacre has been incorporated in the collective memory of many ladinos in town.

The memories of what exactly happened in Xeabaj, how many people were killed, who carried out the killing and who ordered it are multiple. I have presented only two versions, but many more versions exist in Joyabaj. Stories alter over time. Names and dates change and several massacres seemed to blend into one. What is important to note is that, while telling the story of the massacre of Xeabaj, ladinos keep stressing that they were *forced* to march to Xeabaj during the night, that they were *forced* to watch everybody get killed, that others were *ordered* to kill. They themselves, however, *did not* kill anybody. Possibly, two of Kelman and Hamilton's conditions for obedience, that is, authority and dehumanization, both played a role in the behaviour of patrollers during the Xeabaj massacre. First of all, military presence and orders during the massacre in a way legitimized the massacre. Kelman and Hamilton note that people do not seem to feel personally responsible for the consequences of the actions, because they see themselves as having had no choice. 'They were not personal agents, but merely extensions of authority.'[104] Dehumanization possibly played a role, because the subjects of the massacre were indigenous people who had been identified time and again by the military, justly or unjustly, as subversives and guerrillas. They had been placed outside the world (or 'moral universe', to use Cohen's words)[105] of the people who were participating in the civil patrols. Kelman and Hamilton use the words 'stripped of their human status' in this respect.[106] A third important motive to obey was fear of what could happen if one refused, fear of also becoming a victim.[107] This is not mentioned in much detail by Kelman and Hamilton, possibly because they deal with obedience within the military chain of command. In their study, disobedience possibly meant punishment for the

---

104 Kelman and Hamilton (1989: 16).
105 Cohen (2001: 90).
106 Kelman and Hamilton (1989: 19).
107 Cohen (2001: 143).

soldiers, but did not lead to the actual killing of the disobedient person. Civil patrollers not carrying out their orders, however, did face death.

Patrollers abusing their power

The memories of a another large group, consisting of both ladinos and *indígenas*, also focus on a negative aspect of the civil patrols, but from a different perspective. The patrol's *abuse of power* and sometimes excessive violence is remembered as its most important feature. Examples are multiple. Some civil patrollers stole land and other goods from refugees, like the patrollers from the ladino village of Caquil. Two ladino families who had always lived in the indigenous village of Chicotón moved to the nearby ladino village of Caquil shortly after the violence started. They accused the people of Chicotón of belonging to the guerrilla, which possibly sparked patrol violence against Chicotón, resulting in the killing of more than 50 of its inhabitants. A week after the massacre in Chicotón, the Caquil patrollers returned to the village to burn down the houses and shoot large livestock. They took the *laminas* (corrugated iron sheets used on roofs) and the *molino de nixtamal*, the village mill that had been recently bought on development credits, back with them to Caquil.[108]

Other patrols went around as roaming bands stealing livestock, like the civil patrol in El Infiernito, a village south of Joyabaj. They had specialized in stealing cattle from farmers in the nearby department of San Martín Jilotepeque. After several raids they made the mistake of stealing cattle from one of the big estates. Shortly afterwards a military contingent from San Martín came to pay the patrols in Infiernito a visit, saying they had come to exchange the old weapons the patrols were using for new ones. The military used the weapons to shoot the patrollers.

Long-standing disputes between villages, hamlets and families, or even within single families, were also fought out within the civil patrols.[109] People were blackmailed into handing over their land titles or their cows when walking them to the market to be sold. It was common to settle old scores by way of the civil patrols.[110] The mechanism was simple: either you gave in to the requests of the patrollers, or you were branded a subversive and taken to the local military base. A former Christian Democrat politician states that 'the patrol leaders were like *caciques*, who could dispose over the lives of others. They enjoyed their power immensely ... for example if they liked a girl they went to harass her parents until they ... [silence] and when they liked a piece of land, they chased off the people

---

108 Interview 37-99 (4/6/99).
109 See files at the PDH office in Santa Cruz del Quiché (1989-98).
110 See Zur (1998) for a detailed study of *envidia* among Quiché war widows.

or denounced them'.[111]

Sometimes people mention a few individuals in particular who revelled in their personal power and took advantage of it—such as the patrol leader in Las Lomas, who was responsible for many killings in neighbouring villages, including the massacre in the ladino village of Boqueron in February 1981.[112] A group of 20 civil patrollers from Boqueron were killed during a local *fiesta* by the civil patrol from the neighbouring ladino village of Las Lomas. The patrol leader of Las Lomas felt threatened by the patrollers of Boqueron, for two reasons. First, he was responsible for much of the civil patrol violence in the area, and so resented by quite a few people including the villagers from Boqueron. Second, he possibly saw them as a threat to his own position of power, and was afraid of losing part of his territory to them. A ladino man who worked in Boqueron at the time of the massacre told me that 'While the marimba was playing on the hill, at the bottom they were killing the PAC of Boqueron'.[113]

These examples of patrol commanders abusing their positions of power were partly the result of what Claridge (1999/2000) calls the directorate of terror (military) giving local agents of terror (civil patrol commanders) some room to manoeuvre in selecting targets, using violence and appropriating property. That way several commanders enriched themselves, although when they overstepped the boundaries set by the military, for example in the case of the patrollers from El Infiernito, they too could become victims of military violence. The role of the local military commander was also important, because some clearly encouraged patrol commanders to take initiatives and make their own decisions, while others expected the patrollers strictly to follow military orders.

The Ogáldez clan and local power

Apart from new, often indigenous local power players, like the patrol commander from Chorraxaj who never played a significant role in the political or economic arena but ascended the social ladder by way of the civil patrols, another group gained from the patrols. Some of the more prominent ladino families regained some of their former authority, although in a less legitimate way than before. The most important example in Joyabaj is the Ogáldez family, which had played a key role in local political and economic life since the second half of the nineteenth century. Their position of power and relative wealth was based on their control over land and people's labour. A close relationship existed between several members of the Ogáldez clan and the military establishment, on both a

---
111 Interview 21-99 (22/7/99).
112 CEH, Vol. X (1999: 1027).
113 Interview 2-99 (14/7/99).

local and a national level. Several members of the Ogáldez family occupied different posts in the municipality, as mayor, member of the town council, or military delegate. Rogelio Ogáldez was an important political figure in the 1940s and 1950s, while his nephew Próspero Ogáldez took over the reigns of political power in the 1970s as mayor for the right-wing MLN. At the end of the 1970s the position of the Ogáldez seemed to decline somewhat and rival political parties won several municipal elections. The political defeat was felt hardest when Felípe Natareno, the Christian Democrat candidate, won the municipal elections in 1978.

Local politics fell apart as violence reached Joyabaj in 1980 and many Christian Democratic leaders left town. The political situation deteriorated even further after the military installed themselves in Joyabaj and started appointing mayors. Despite this, some former right-wing politicians detected and ascended new avenues to local power by way of the civil patrols that had just been set up. Leonel Ogáldez, son of Próspero Ogáldez and nephew of Rogelio Ogáldez, both of whom had had influential positions in local politics, quickly filled the position of general commander of the patrols in Joyabaj.[114]

Several opinions exist in Joyabaj on how and why Leonel Ogáldez obtained this position. A former Alianza employee saw it as a continuation of the position his father had occupied before him. For Leonel, the civil patrols would be just another opportunity to wield power and 'boss people around'.[115] According to him, both Leonel and his two brothers would seize such a chance with both hands, because by becoming general commander of the civil patrols a member of the Ogáldez family would be reinstalled at the centre of the local power arena. 'He really liked this sort of problem', an indigenous left-wing activist explained in a very hushed voice. The activist was a known figure in the indigenous community and everybody knew his face, 'most of all the Ogáldez family ... with whom everything started'. On the fingers of his hands the activist recounted the different organizations he was involved in before having to leave town: the cooperative movement, Alianza, and the Catholic Church. 'In the eyes of the Ogáldez family that was my biggest crime.'[116] During an interview with Leonel Ogáldez himself, I asked him why he had accepted the job of general commander of the civil patrols. He answered that 'we [his family] have felt the whip (*azote*) of the guerrilla on our own flesh ... I was young and full of rancour for what they did to me brother and my mother ... I was a teacher, and never thought of arming

---

114 In Chapters 5 and 6 I will go deeper into the career of Leonel Ogáldez as a patrol commander.
  He has retired and lives with his family in Joyabaj. He has never been convicted for any crime.
115 Interview 44-99 (22/4/99).
116 Interview 29-99 (1/10/99).

myself, but one has to defend oneself'.[117] His younger brother Fredy was kidnapped by the guerrilla during the early days of the conflict, together with his mother, who was released at the outskirts of town. It seems he felt he had no other choice at that time.

Not everybody referred to Leonel Ogáldez in a negative way as a collaborator. According to some older ladinos the military talked Leonel into accepting the job, which was a job he could not refuse.[118] Others argue that, although he was a tough commander (*jefe duro*), he also used his position of power in a positive way and rescued many people.[119] For example, the military commander in Joyabaj often consulted with Leonel Ogáldez when a blacklist containing the names of local subversives came his way. Ogáldez had the power to decide to brand people as subversives and thus ensure their capture and probable death, or he could cross names off the list, informing the military commander these were included on the list only because of some personal dispute. Several ladinos explained that, in a way, they could understand Leonel's behaviour as a patrol commander. The Ogáldez family had been hit hard during the civil war and was a prime target of guerrilla activity, not least because of the close involvement in military intelligence and other military activities by some of its members. They could understand that people like Leonel would accept the job of patrol commander out of revenge. Conversely, they could not understand why some of the other patrol commanders had accepted their respective jobs. They had lost no family members to the guerrillas, 'were educated quite well and should have known better'.[120]

Positive memories of patrol activity

Thus civil patrols and their commanders are seen not only as having had a negative impact. A very practical positive aspect that people mention is that the patrols provided some men with a steady income, because people could pay someone else to take over their shift.[121] Some members of the wealthier ladino families in town never walked a patrol shift but paid ten *Quetzales* for someone to take over the first shift and double that for the second (late) shift. This kind of money was a welcome addition to the meagre household budget of many *Joyabateco* families.

Another group focused on the role of civil patrols as the *keeper of order and security* in the village. In the eyes of some people there was hardly any crime, not

---

117 Interview 12-01 (21/5/01).
118 Interview 13-99 (4/10/99).
119 Interview 24-99 (31/5/99).
120 Interview 6-01 (11/5/01).
121 Interview 24-99 (31/5/99).

counting the human rights violations committed by patrollers and the military. When crimes were committed people were arrested, tried and sentenced by special tribunals set up by the Ríos Montt government. This is told within the current context of a justice system that, according to most villagers, is not doing a proper job. Criminals, including former civil patrollers, buy their own freedom, bribe judges or blackmail them into letting them walk. In this way many older ladinos, but also *indígenas* from pro-civil patrol villages, talk in a very nostalgic way about 'the good old days' when law and order, although by decree and special tribunals, were enforced. The order and security issue looms large nowadays, especially in the light of the many lynchings during the last few years.[122]

People do not use the word 'order' only when talking about the prevention of crimes or law enforcement, but also in relation to control and discipline. 'There used to be order' is common refrain in Joyabaj. People use it to describe the way the military kept the park perfectly in order while they occupied the church buildings, and the way in which the civil patrols helped build the steps to the church in a very orderly way.[123] They contrast this with the current mess in the park and the fact that nobody cleans the street in front of their houses nowadays. In their eyes the patrols were a good way to enforce a kind of moral order and discipline. This view was substantiated by the local military commander stationed in Joyabaj in 1998. According to him, it had been very easy for the army to use the manpower from both the commissioners and the patrols for construction and maintenance tasks in the 1980s. He continued to say that 'unfortunately, nowadays the army can't get anybody to do work like that any more',[124] while the army's budget and manpower also decreased every year.

A last group, consisting mainly of older ladinos who seemed to yearn for a past when ladinos still controlled local affairs, also looks favourably on the past activities of civil patrols. They believed that their way of life was really threatened by either communists or *indígenas*, or both. They saw military action, including the patrols, as the only solution and protection against a communist guerrilla threat. They believed civil patrol violence was necessary. 'The people that were killed were only communists and naturales',[125] an older ladino women told me. It is not uncommon in Joyabaj to hear ladinos voice these feelings of fear of 'the other'. It is fear based on a lack of knowledge of who exactly 'the other' is and a solid conviction of one's own supremacy. Some ladinos express fear of an Indian majority literally pouring down from the mountains, demanding their rights and intent on killing every ladino in sight. The process of dehu-

---

122 See MINUGUA, *Decimo Informe* (2000) and MINUGUA, *Informe de Verificación* (2000a).
123 Diary 15/4/98.
124 Diary 4/4/98.
125 *Naturales* (naturals) is a derogatory term used by some ladinos for the indigenous population.

manizing part of the indigenous population, originating in colonial times, was continued and expanded by way of military indoctrination during the war, and still leaves traces in many of the stories currently told by ladinos. They are still grateful for the military intervention in the 1980s that prevented the thing they their feared from coming true. 'From the beginning', an older ladino man told me, 'they [ladinos] thought that the guerrilla were communists and that they were bad people. That they would rob them [the ladinos] of their houses, their wives ... the people were scared because of this ... especially the ladinos. And when they entered the patrols [civil patrols] they thought they were going to defend their houses, their families.'[126]

Fearing memory of the past

Not all *Joyabatecos* talk easily or willingly about the civil patrols or patrol violence. A large group does not want to remember the violent past and cannot or does not want to express their views on the patrols. It seems to be a case of collective forgetting,[127] or a conscious denial of what really happened.[128] In several cases people were not present at the time or were children or youngsters, and never heard the stories because their parents never told them what happened. In many other cases, especially adults who were present as victims or perpetrators at the time of the violations did not always welcome memories of the past. This is partly due to a lingering fear of the past and fear of talking about the past, fear of people who wielded power as patrol commanders and are still around, and fear of being blamed for what happened

People seemed to prefer to put most of the blame on a small number of individuals, most of whom had conveniently died or emigrated or were already in prison. When the people who committed these acts are still around town, most voices stay mute. During conversations with *Joyabatecos*, only a few individuals still living in Joyabaj were mentioned in relation to the violence. They were familiar names which appeared every now and then in reports of human rights organizations, reports from the Catholic Church and in testimonies to the truth commissions. Locals preferred to stick to these names, which had already been publicized in the media. However, the names of others involved, in massacres for example, were never mentioned or were brushed aside, with the excuse that these people were only acting under orders. Another possible reason for people's reluctance to talk about certain violent events was shame: shame of what they did

---

126 Interview 38-99 (19/8/99).
127 On the topic of forgetting, see for example Schachter (1996), Burke (1989), Fentress and Wickham (1992) and Cohen (2001).
128 In Chapter 7, I will discuss the issues of denial and forgetting in the case of Joyabaj in more detail.

and, perhaps even more so, shame of what they did not do, such as keeping their mouths shuts when people were accused and taken away by the military, not warning neighbours that patrollers were coming to search their house, or standing idly by when someone was killed or raped.

The act of memory in context

At the time this research was being conducted, *Joyabatecos* were still worried about the consequences of talking. Who else is listening, what will be done with the information, and who else will have access to it once it is written down? Is the information used to prepare a court case or is it a testimony to identify killed family members? The context in which the stories about the massacres were told greatly shaped the content of the stories themselves. The situation in which many conversations about this violent past took place was one of 'superficial tranquillity', as a local priest told me. The atmosphere was tense, especially during the second fieldwork period in 1999 because a forensic team had just arrived in Joyabaj to open up a clandestine cemetery that had been located behind the convent, where the military had been stationed during the war. When the forensic team arrived, family members of disappeared people started to come forward, and the town was buzzing with memories.

People started forming opinions about a possible exhumation, and unconsciously the town became divided into different and sometimes opposing groups. Some, such as the indigenous relatives of those who had disappeared, thought an exhumation was necessary to deal with the past, and were not afraid to come forward and sign the necessary papers to initiate the exhumation. They were people who had spoken out before, giving testimonies to the truth commission and denouncing human rights abuses to the office of the *Procuraderia de los Derechos Humanos* (PDH)[129] in Santa Cruz. However, the majority wanted to leave the past alone and did not want to stir up fresh trouble. Talking about the past would not bring back their dead relatives, so why bother? They were especially afraid of the possibility of court cases following the exhumation because this would, so they believed, only create further problems. Discussions within the Catholic Church (on whose land the dig was to take place) and between the Catholic Church and the forensic team were heated.

Most people had agreed to talk with the forensic team about a possible exhumation only because the mass graves had literally been opened during heavy rains, which had caused an avalanche to lay bare several skeletons. One was still wearing a football uniform, while another one had his hands bound together behind his back. The parish priest and other dignitaries within the Catholic

---

129 Human Rights Ombudsman.

Church had understood the avalanche to be an act of God, who was in a way forcing them to deal with the violent past. Although everybody in the community had always known about this particular cemetery, the land had been planted over again after the violence had subsided. Now and then small bone fragments had been found, but until then nobody had felt the need or the strength to present the case to a human rights organization. Another factor influencing the way people talked about the past violence and the massacres in particular was that during the research period civil patrollers in different parts of Guatemala were being brought to trial and sometimes convicted. In the nearby municipality of Chiché, a local ladino patrol commander was being tried for the third time on charges of multiple murders and massacres. At the first two trials he was acquitted, but at the third trial he was sentenced to 220 years in prison. Many of the ladinos in Joyabaj knew this man quite well, and did not really know what to think of his sentence. They explained that they did not really believe he committed these crimes, and blamed them on another patrol commander from Chiché who had conveniently fled to the United States.

Conclusion
During the presidency of Ríos Montt, violence became more structured and organized, and military control over the town of Joyabaj was consolidated by way of the installation of civil patrols. Together with the military, the civil patrols took over effective power in the community. On the one hand they sharpened and polarized an already unequal power structure. The powerful positions of some ladino families were reinforced and their control over part of the indigenous population confirmed. On the other hand civil patrols also opened up new avenues to personal power for individuals who had never been in influential positions before. Patrols were used both to improve economic positions and to attain political goals, often at the expense of others. I will explore this topic in more detail in Chapter 5.

The situation in the town of Joyabaj calmed down somewhat while military violence in the surrounding countryside increased. Civil patrols were forced to accompany the military in their hunt for guerrillas, thereby becoming actively involved in several of the massacres committed in the indigenous communities. Apart from patrolling the surrounding countryside, the civil patrols were used to control the local population and keep everybody under close surveillance. Roadblocks and checkpoints were established, an evening curfew was declared and everybody had to carry identity papers at all times. Apart from open and direct surveillance by way of the patrols, people also became aware of the violence of which military and civil patrols were capable, especially after the massacre of Xeabaj. This seems to have hampered local protest against patrol duty and intimidated the majority of the people in town into obeying military orders without much question. Military tactics such as the dehumanization of the indigenous people of certain communities, by stigmatizing them as subversive, communist or guerrilla, possibly helped persuade several patrollers and their commanders to obey military orders. The 'other' was presented as a guerrilla who was after your land and your family, in which case it was your duty to defend yourself. Only a small group of people actually supported the civil patrol structure and their involvement in massacres or other violent activities, while the majority was just doing their jobs while trying not to get too involved by avoiding contact with guerrillas. Another small minority openly opposed the patrol system. I have brought this diversity to light by presenting the cases of the teacher patrol and the patrols from Xecnup and Chorraxaj. In most cases, the patrol commander played an important role because it was up to him to carry out military orders to the letter or display initiative of his own. This personal initiative, or room to manoeuvre, could result in even more violent behaviour on the part of the patrol commander or in an inclination to avoid trouble.

By presenting the different memories that exist in Joyabaj of patrol violence, I have tried to portray the distinct ways people today look back on the civil war and try to give meaning to it. While a majority stress the negative aspects of patrol duty, such as its forced nature, the abuse of power by its commanders and the use of excessive violence, others, such as older ladinos with close relations to the right-wing MLN and the military, yearn for the order and discipline that existed then. Despite the reluctance of some people to talk about the past, it has become clear from this chapter that several events relating to patrol violence stand out in *Joyabateco* memory. One of them is the massacre of Xeabaj, which has become *the* representative bloodbath in local memory, especially in the memory of ladinos. When they talk about this period, they frequently refer to this massacre, whether they were present or not. Stories of the massacre can be seen as a metaphor for the violence during this period. The different memories people have of it could be an indication of their memories of this period as a whole. While one remembers most vividly that a 'river of blood was running down the mountain', another accuses neighbouring indigenous villagers, while a third stresses the crucial role of the military officer present during the massacre. These images reveal something about the way people look back at this violent period and how they try to understand what happened. Over time people have told and retold the story of the massacre of Xeabaj, all the while incorporating new knowledge, thoughts and experiences into the story. The knowledge that someone was interested in the massacre of Xeabaj, with the intention of using it in a book about Joyabaj, also influenced they way people talked about it and presented it. While the massacre was talked about with much detail, nobody I interviewed on the subject admitted to having played an active part in it. Everybody presented themselves as bystanders, looking at others doing the killing. Putting it down on paper and thus making it part of the 'official history' of Joyabaj was quite a step from the continuous retelling of the story.

5

Authority of civil patrols contested (1984-1993)

The years 1981 and 1982 have been labelled the most violent years of the armed conflict between guerrilla and government forces in Guatemala. Massacres and selective violence were accompanied by a thorough militarization of the rural areas. Almost an entire country was brought under the control and surveillance of a tight network of military commissioners and civil defence patrols, which acted as the eyes and the ears of the military.

Towards the end of 1984, preparations were being made for a transfer of political power from the military to a democratically elected government. This chapter follows the process of democratization from 1985 onwards, starting with the rise of Christian Democrat Vinício Cerezo to the presidency and ending with the attempted self-coup (*autogolpe*) of his conservative presidential successor Jorge Serrano Elías in May 1993. The chapter starts with a short overview of the national situation, thus concentrating on the transfer of power from the military to a civilian government and the initial phase of the peace process, which started in 1987 and culminated in direct negotiations under President Serrano.

At the local level, many rural communities found themselves in a chaotic situation as political activism and community life slowly re-emerged, carefully navigating the available local space to manoeuvre so as not to collide with patrol commanders, military commissioners, and the military. It was a period during which struggles over local power became more pronounced and violent. Civil patrol commanders and others who had been building and expanding their position of power during the armed conflict saw the democratic opening as a danger to their positions of influence and authority, which were based on violence rather than legitimacy. Their authority was being contested by other emerging power holders, and patrol commanders continued to resort to violence in order to hold on to their positions of influence.

An analysis of the local situation in Joyabaj first focuses on the political situation during the municipal elections in 1985. Aside from heightened political activity, which was hampered by inexperience, harassment by civil patrollers and accusations of corruption, community life started slowly reviving. Ladinos in town were the first to voice their protest against the newly elected municipality. They were also the first to oppose patrol duty, which led to its abolition in the town of Joyabaj as early as 1986. In the rural areas, however, where the majority of the *Joyabatecos* lived, people were forced to continue patrolling. Several popular groups such as Conavigua[1] and CERJ[2] were organizing protests against civil patrol duty in the rural communities. Roughly two waves of anti-patrol protest can be observed in Joyabaj, which coincided with protests at the national level. The first wave became visible in 1988, when community organizations, local politicians, the Catholic Church, and other activists were started resuming their respective places in the local community. The first denunciations were made to the office of PDH,[3] the first human rights abuses were made public, clandestine war graves were being disclosed and investigated, and several human rights activists were being harassed by the military and civil patrol commanders. This first wave of protest against civil patrols resulted in heavy countermeasures by the military. They appeared to have had the desired effect and anti-patrol protests died down until 1993, when a second wave of protests emerged. Discussions at the local and the national levels on forced patrol duty intensified, and hopes among anti-patrol activists for a swift abolition were once again on the rise towards the end of the Serrano government. The chapter ends with an analysis of the murder on Tomás Lares Ciprian, a human rights activist from Joyabaj, by civil patrollers. The case was covered extensively by the national media and used by human rights organizations as an example of a dysfunctional legal system.

Democratic elections: start of the peace process
During the presidency of Mejía Víctores (1983–86), the military started preparing for a return to democracy. This was partly due to a worsening of the economic situation and a growing image problem for the military government in the international arena, which could cause the loss of international support and aid. The military felt that a democratic government would provide legitimacy and 'a means for opening the doors to foreign aid, military as well as economic'.[4] Handy (1986) adds that by 1984 the direct threat of a guerrilla takeover had been eradicated, so that 'the main reason for its [the military's] direct intervention in the political process had been removed'.[5] The civil defence patrols had taken over an important part of the military's job of controlling the countryside. After the first democratic elections in November 1985, the continuation of the patrols became the object of much protest and discussion.

---

1 *Coordinación Nacional de las Viudas Guatemaltecas* - National Co-ordination of Guatemalan Widows.
2 *Consejo de Comunidades Etnicas 'Runujel Junam'* - Council of Ethnic Communities 'Runujel Junam'. A farmers' organization, which focused its activities in the south of the Quiché department. Its members were predominantly indigenous.
3 *Procuradería de los Derechos Humanos* – Human Rights Ombudsman.
4 Anderson and Simon (1987: 17).
5 Handy, 1986: 408.

The Christian Democrats won the elections in 1985 in the second round, with 69 per cent of the votes, and their candidate Vinício Cerezo Arévalo was installed as president early 1986.⁶ The elections were accompanied by a new constitution mandating the creation of institutions guaranteeing human rights, such as the Human Rights Ombudsman and the Supreme Electoral Council (*Tribunal Supremo Electoral*, TSE). The 1985 constitution also legalized most institutions that had been set up during the counter-insurgency years, including the civil patrols whose position was strengthened by incorporating them into the military reserve structure.⁷ Instead of being dismantled they were renamed Voluntary Civil Defence Committees (CVDC)⁸ in 1986 in an effort to improve the image of the civil patrols. They continued, however, to be popularly knows as PACs, or, more simply, civil patrols.⁹

The new president had only limited political power and space to manoeuvre and he was held on a tight leash by the military, which defined the parameters for civilian political activity.¹⁰ He was, to use Handy's words, 'on probation'.¹¹ He did not touch fundamental topics like economic issues, the division of land, or the question of civil patrol duty, so that there was little reason for the military to complain. Nevertheless, 'within the army, an intense debate developed regarding its role in the return to constitutional rule', and 'two currents emerged in open dispute: constitutionalists in favour of negotiations with the URNG, and hardliners against it'.¹²

The 1985 elections opened up public space for discussion, and popular organizations like Conavigua, CERJ, and CUC¹³ started to address issues related to the armed conflict such as human rights abuses by and forced participation in the civil patrols. At the same time the army and the guerrilla were still not on negotiating terms. 'Initiatives from each side still aimed at the defeat of the other. Incapable of winning militarily, each side tried to gain maximum advantage for itself from the international context favouring peace and democratization.'¹⁴ In the end, a combination of international pressure and the idea that military control over the countryside had been established resulted in the start of political

---

6   Political Database of the Americas, 1999.
7   Decree 19-86, which legalized civil patrols, was published in El Diario Oficial on 10 January 1986. See Jay, 1993: 33.
8   *Comités Voluntarios de Defensa Civil.*
9   Popkin (1996: 7–8).
10 See Schirmer (2002: 68-70) on the concerted collaboration, or co-governance, between the military and civilian presidents since 1986.
11 Handy (1989: 134), see also Handy (1986: 408).
12 Palencia Prado (1996b: 11).
13 *Comité de Unidad Campesina* – Committee for Campesino Unity. An organization of labourers and small farmers.
14 Palencia Prado (1996b: 8).

negotiations between the two parties. During the second meeting of Central American presidents in 1987 (Esquipulas II), the first regional framework for the promotion of peace and reconciliation was created. This Accord (Central American Peace Accords) prescribed negotiations in Guatemala, El Salvador and Nicaragua, the three countries involved in armed conflicts at that time. Among the obligations were amnesties for subversive groups, a ceasefire, and the organization of a national reconciliation commission.[15]

Guatemala started in October 1987 with the creation of such a National Reconciliation Commission (*Comisión Nacional de Reconciliación*, CNR), which resulted in the first low-level meeting between the URNG, military observers and representatives of the Guatemalan government. In 1990 President Cerezo announced that the government was willing to enter into a direct dialogue with the guerrillas without demanding disarmament as a prior condition. This condition had held up negotiations until then. This resulted in the Oslo Agreement of March 1990, which stipulated the conditions for a direct dialogue between government and guerrilla. In January 1991 presidential elections were held, which were won by the conservative MAS (*Movimiento Acción Solidaria* – Solidarity Action Movement) with Jorge Serrano Elías as its presidential candidate. As a conservative with a past as a youth member of the MLN (the right-wing political party) and a consultant with CACIF (an organization of the business elite), he had sufficient backing from the economically and politically powerful sectors in society to initiate official talks with the guerrillas.[16]

The first meeting took place in April 1991, during which the agenda for the forthcoming official negotiations was drafted and the role of the United Nations (UN) as an observer of the peace process was confirmed (Mexico Agreement). An important theme on the agenda was the strengthening of civilian power and the role of the army in a democratic society. The fact that the army approved of this theme indicated that 'within the army, conditions were being created which allowed for more flexibility and tolerance regarding changes in the state'.[17] Unfortunately, negotiations broke down on the first topic on the agenda, democracy and human rights—one of the issues being the continuation of the civil patrols. Although 'the army agreed not to promote the formation of these groups as long as no insurgent actions took place',[18] the guerrilla insisted on their abolition, while the government refused to discuss patrols until the guerrilla disarmed. Tensions around Serrano's presidency were rising towards the end of 1992 and the beginning of 1993. His political alliance broke up, there was a growing lack

---

15 Palencia Prado (1996b: 9–10).
16 CEG (1993: 21).
17 Palencia Prado (1996b: 14).
18 Palencia Prado (1996b: 14).

of confidence in the government, and charges of corruption grew louder. This situation motivated the president to carry out a self-coup (*autogolpe*) to recover his political power. He dissolved Congress and suspended parts of the constitution.[19] His actions did not, however, receive sufficient support from the powerful sectors in society, causing the coup to fail and the president to step down from office. Former director of the PDH, Ramiro de León Carpio, took over as president in June 1993, with the prime objective of improving the image of the government in the international arena and reactivating the peace negotiations. He was aided in his efforts by the fact that constitutionalist tendencies within the army had gained more power, which had the effect that 'the negotiations were no longer a smokescreen behind which each side attempted to annihilate its opponent'.[20]

Democratic elections in Joyabaj

The struggle over democracy was fought not only at the national level, but especially so at the municipal level. Municipalities in Guatemala have always been relatively autonomous from national politics. The local and national agendas and struggles of political parties often differed considerably from each other. At the time of the democratic opening in 1985, municipal authority was less representative and less autonomous than at any time in recent history.[21] The terror campaigns of the military, with its model villages and civil patrols, had virtually destroyed any basis for municipal government in Guatemala. 'If we see these municipalities as the true building blocks of effective democracy in the country, then it is clear that the prospects of democratic decision-making on issues that concern the bulk of the population were never bleaker.'[22]

Municipal politics in Joyabaj, as elsewhere in Guatemala, focused largely on the individual candidates for mayor and their respective positions in local society. Many indigenous people from the rural areas were not content with the way municipal funds were mainly used for projects in the town itself, and saw little benefit for the surrounding communities.[23] Personal enrichment of some of the ladinos who had obtained positions in the municipality was not uncommon. Discontent about how local politics were run by only a few ladino families who had connections to a limited number of political parties had already led to profound changes during the municipal elections in 1978, when the Christian Democrats (DCG) won.[24] After two years most of the DCG council members,

---

19 Jonas (2000: 41).
20 Palencia Prado (1996b: 18).
21 Handy (1989: 135).
22 Handy (1986: 408).
23 Interview 14-99 (16/8/99).
24 Interview 23-99 (1/9/99).

including the mayor, had been forced to leave town because of the violence. Between their departure and the democratic elections in 1985, the municipality of Joyabaj had been without any real power and was under the direct control of the local military base and civil patrol commanders.

The big winner during the 1985 municipal elections in Joyabaj was the CAN,[25] a right-wing political party with strong ties to the military. It provided a ladino mayor, Amado Osmin Quiroa, and three council members. Presumably the CAN candidate had the backing of the military during these elections because he was a former military commissioner.[26] The DCG did not participate in the elections in Joyabaj 'out of fear ... they were still scared', a former DCG activist explained.[27] At that time, 'the DCG was still seen as guerrillas ... and there were still civil patrols, and the military were still here'.[28] Besides, it had been only five years earlier that the former DCG mayor had been forced to flee Joyabaj because he had been personally threatened and his name had appeared on local blacklists. The elections for president at the national level were a very different matter, with the CAN reaching only fifth place with 6 per cent of the votes and the DCG winning the presidency. Had the DCG decided to participate in Joyabaj,[29] it would have had a good chance of winning, because during the 1984 elections for a national assembly[30] the DCG received the majority of the votes in Joyabaj, with the right-wing MLN/CAN coalition a close second.[31] The DCG won the municipal elections in nine out of ten of the municipalities in which it did participate.

Many locals saw the fact that the DCG did not participate in Joyabaj as a sign that the situation had not yet calmed down. Obviously, this did not encourage many people to take the trouble to vote. Abstention was a big problem. According to a former member of the TSE committee[32] in Joyabaj 'people are indifferent to politics'.[33] According to him 12,500 people were *empadronado* (registered and thus eligible to vote) but only around 5,000 actually voted in 1985. This was probably because people had very little faith in politics in general, especially during these first democratic elections. The low turnout also pointed to a pessimistic attitude towards the return to democracy, of which these elections were to be a first step.

25 *Central Auténtica Nacionalista* – National Authentic Central.
26 Interview 7-01 (23/5/01).
27 Interview 8-01 (9/5/01).
28 Interview 8-01 (9/5/01).
29 Joyabaj was one of nine municipalities in the Quiché department without a DCG candidate.
30 The General Assembly was the first step towards the 1985 elections.
31 Source: Statistical data from the TSE office in Joyabaj (5/5/01). The DCG received 1,285 votes in Joyabaj, and the MLN/CAN coalition 1091.
32 TSE committees supervised the municipal elections.
33 Interview 10-99 (5/7/99).

However, in many instances the reasons for not voting were of a more practical nature. People had to come down to the municipal capital to cast their votes at the assigned table, and they had to register as voters beforehand. This could cost a whole day's work, and thus income. Apart from that, registration was possible only when people possessed the proper identification documents. Many indigenous people lacked these documents because their parents had not always bothered to inscribe them. For example, during the armed conflict, numerous people had not registered their newborns because they were displaced or killed, or because parents thought their children did not stand much chance of surviving, so why bother to register. Others did not want to be registered at all.

Before the new mayor was even installed in the municipality, some TSE members were convinced that he would not survive for very long. To prove their point, one of them sketched the following situation to me during one of several interviews I conducted with former TSE officials. The day before his inauguration on 16 January 1986 the future mayor had send a letter to the TSE committee explaining that he preferred to hold the inauguration in a private meeting at the municipality rather than turning it into a public event. TSE rules did not allow this and the inauguration took place in public. One of the TSE members asked the new mayor afterwards why he had insisted on keeping the inauguration private. Supposedly in all honesty, the mayor answered that two of his municipal officers did not own a tie to wear at the event. The TSE member could not imagine that something as trivial as the lack of a tie was the cause of all the consternation and concluded that 'this man could never be a good mayor'.[34] The new mayor quickly became involved in local scandals; and although people did not think of him as a corrupt mayor, they did find him ignorant and inexperienced.[35] An example was his refusal to participate any further in a donor project, the so-called *Plan Tripartito* (Three Participants Plan), which was carried out jointly by the municipality, the NGO Alianza, and the rural communities. Alianza had resumed work in Joyabaj in 1982, although it had toned down its activities considerably and refrained from doing any political work. It had concentrated on infrastructure projects like water, sanitation, and housing instead. To get as many parties as possible involved in its projects, Alianza had set up the *Plan Tripartito* in which all three parties would contribute to a particular project, in money or in kind. The new mayor, however, decided that the municipality would end this partnership, after which Alianza decided it was time to move on and close its project in Joyabaj. Possibly, the municipality wanted no outside interference in its municipal projects and wanted to do things its own way.

---

34 Interview 13-99 (4/10/99).
35 Interview 13-99 (4/10/99).

photo 15. *The central square in Joyabaj is packed with people protesting against mayor Amado Osmin Quiroa (Foto Color, 1988)*

Apparently, the first democratically elected mayor of Joyabaj was not seen as a strong man or, for that matter, a very competent one. Finally, in September 1988 Amado Osmin was forced to step down after several protest demonstrations were held against him. The local newspaper *Espíritu Xoj* (The Spirit of Xoj) printed some photographs of his resignation, showing the town square packed with people holding banners saying 'The ones responsible for the bad water supply and the bad handling of funds must step down!!'[36]

Community life in town re-emerging

The town of Joyabaj, and especially some of its ladino inhabitants, seemed to come back to life again after a dormant period during the worst of the violence. In May 1987 a *Comité de Pro-mejoramiento* (improvement committee) was formed in the town of Joyabaj by some of its more prominent ladino residents, notably teachers. It was set up because 'the town did not agree with the way the municipality was administering things ... people wanted that its activities would be much more open to the public and that there would be communication between the municipality and the people'.[37] Legalization of the improvement committee turned out to be impossible, and can be seen as an example of the rising tensions

---

36 Espíritu Xoj, no. 6, September 1988.
37 Interview 16-01 (14/5/01).

photo 16. *Protest against mayor Osmin Quiroa (Foto Color, 1988)*

between a non-functional municipality and the local community at that time. According to a former member of the committee, the municipality was opposed to the organization of a *Comité de Pro-mejoramiento* because it wanted to be the only player on the political stage in Joyabaj. It did not want any other group interfering with the lucrative municipal business of development projects and it did not want anyone checking its finances. Recognizing a *Comité de Pro-mejoramiento* would also have meant splitting government funds with it. The municipality therefore vetoed its legalization, and the improvement committee never came into existence. This anti-democratic attitude was already apparent when the municipality decided to end cooperation with Alianza and the local communities in the *Plan Tripartito*.

In the rural communities, several improvement committees had been in the process of organizing just before the violence reached Joyabaj in the early 1980s. Some of them originated in the Reconstruction Committees, which had been set up after the earthquake, while others had their roots in the work of Alianza and the Catholic Church. After the worst of the violence had passed, several villages restarted the process of legalizing these committees. In contrast to the situation in town, the rural improvement committees did not seem to encounter much opposition from the municipality—possibly because they were not considered a direct threat to them, since they were small rural organizations concerned primarily with technical issues like electricity and schools.[38]

---

38 Interview 9-99 (23/5/99).

The anger many ladinos felt after the mayor's negative decision regarding their committee was voiced in the *Joyabateco* newspaper *Espíritu Xoj*, another example of re-emerging community life among the urban ladinos of Joyabaj. A small group of ladino youngsters in Joyabaj had set up the magazine in November 1987. It was quite a progressive group, including teachers and university students who were quite critical of local politics. 'It was a way to express ourselves, and to fight corruption in the municipality.'[39] The refusal of the mayor to recognize the *Comité de Pro-mejoramiento* was an important topic picked up by the magazine. General discontent with the actions of the municipality was further voiced in an additional article from 'the youth from Joyabaj'. They even approached President Cerezo during a visit to the nearby departmental capital of Santa Cruz, explaining to him that they felt that their constitutional rights were being violated, and demanded an investigation of the case.[40] A final announcement in the magazine shows that not only the members of the committee and the youngsters in Joyabaj were dissatisfied, but a large part of the population. Apparently more than 400 people had asked for the resignation of the mayor and his officials on 22 November. The mayor never reacted to this petition, until he finally resigned in 1988.

It is interesting to read such open criticism of the municipality, especially because protest against civil patrol duty had been dealt with quite violently by the military. Apparently both the local military and the patrol commanders tolerated the criticism because it was not directed at them or the institutions they represented. Although the magazine did contain quite a progressive section called 'Let's get to know our Constitution', explaining peoples rights and obligations, topics like violence, the military or the civil patrols were never touched upon. Instead, people's disapproval focused on democratically elected officials and their actions, thus fostering discontent and distrust among *Joyabatecos*. The same happened at the national level where, during the democratic opening, the military were only too happy to leave political activity to the civilian government and other political parties, who were talking, fighting and negotiating mainly amongst each other. Civilian politicians were trying to cancel each other out, while nobody was directly confronting the military.[41] This also seems to have been the attitude among the ladinos in Joyabaj during the second half of the 1980s. *Espíritu Xoj* ceased to exist around 1990, when Juan Toj became mayor, and open criticism of the local municipality was no longer tolerated, according to a former *Espíritu Xoj* reader.[42]

---

39 Interview 14-01 (24/5/01).
40 Espíritu Xoj, December 1987: 2.
41 Anderson and Simon (1987: 42).
42 Interview 14-01 (24/5/01).

Initial protest against civil patrols

After a period of strict military control of the civil patrols during 1982–84, depending on the local military commander, the activity of guerrilla forces in the area and the behaviour of civil patrols and their commanders, the situation changed somewhat around 1985. Violent actions continued, but were no longer initiated mainly by the military to combat subversives, but used more and more by individual patrol commanders for their own purposes. For example, they tried to improve their own economic position in the village by confiscating land and cattle from disappeared or fleeing neighbours. 'That way much land changed owner. They saw where the good land was ... and they stole it.'[43] Even former Minister of Defence Balconi admitted that sometimes the civil patrols 'operated outside the margins of the law'.[44] It seemed that, after tight military control in the beginning, patrol commanders were gradually given and also taking more freedom, for example to select their own targets. According to Claridge, 'a decentralisation of the procedures ... brings advantages' because it allows local operatives (patrol commanders in this case) 'to adapt to local conditions and prevent the policy of terror ... becoming stale'.[45]

The 1985 elections had opened up space not only to criticize local politics but also to oppose participation in the civil patrols. Not long after the elections, ladinos in town started voicing their opposition to civil patrol duty. Many ladinos did not think patrolling was any longer necessary and found it a useless exercise and a waste of time. In their eyes, they ended up protecting the military instead of the other way around. The ladinos had picked a good time to discuss the topic, shortly after the first democratic elections had been held, and Guatemala was supposedly on the road to a more democratic society. National and international attention on Guatemala started influencing the situation at the local level. Journalists ventured into the rural areas again, and information about forced patrolling was slowly coming out into the open. *Joyabatecos* in town also became aware that in the departmental capital, Santa Cruz, the patrols had stopped already, which prompted them to demand, however timidly, an end to the patrols in the town of Joyabaj as well.[46] 'In the end, they just stopped', an indigenous *cofrade* said.[47] There seems to have been hardly any struggle between the ladinos and the local military and patrol commanders over the issue. Officially, the civil patrols were a voluntary organization at that time, as a former patrol commander was quick to point out during an interview. According to him 'at that time

---

43 Interview 15-98 (13/7/98).
44 Interview Balconi (18/10/99).
45 Claridge (2000: 260).
46 Interview 17-01 (10/5/01).
47 Interview 30-99 (6/7/99).

[1986] you could not force people any more into participating in the patrols'.[48] Around 1986 the civil patrols in town had been largely dismantled, random violence had lessened somewhat, and massacres had made way for more selective violence.

In the rural areas, however, civil patrol commanders still wielded a considerable amount of influence and power, and were responsible for many acts of harassment, torture and murder. Their new targets were emerging community leaders, returning refugees, people protesting against patrol duty, local members of human rights organizations and anyone who confronted the local power of the patrol commanders.[49] This is also clear from the large number of denunciations to the PDH office in Santa Cruz made by indigenous activists from rural communities surrounding Joyabaj.[50] Most civil patrollers in the *rural* communities surrounding the town of Joyabaj were forced to continue patrolling, some even until their formal and nationwide abolition just before the peace agreement in December 1996. A former mayor explained that several patrol commanders in the rural communities had built up quite a 'little kingdom', and were anxious not to lose it.[51] Therefore, termination of the patrols was out of the question and patrollers were forced to continue. An indigenous Catholic Action activist added that some of the more violent local commanders held on to the civil patrols not only because it was their only source of power and authority, but because they had been responsible for so many killings within their own and neighbouring communities.[52] They were afraid of possible acts of revenge once the patrols had dissolved. A former patrol commander did not agree with these accounts, and suggested that the rural patrols had refused to stop patrolling because they still felt 'the presence of subversion'.[53] Several ladinos looked at the continuation of the rural patrols from quite a different perspective, stating that 'people from the rural areas had much respect for the government';[54] thus, when the military ordered you to do something, like continue to patrol, you obeyed. Many, mainly older and right-wing, ladinos still regarded the indigenous population as obedient servants carrying out tasks assigned to them by the government or the military. This explanation, however, clashes with the view some of these same ladinos expressed about an indigenous population as dangerous subversives and

---

48 Interview 12-01 (21/5/01).
49 See REMHI report (ODHAG, 1998), CEH report (1999), and bulletins from ODHAG, GAM and other national and international human rights organizations for examples of human rights abuses by civil patrollers.
50 PDH office in Santa Cruz del Quiché, files 1989-98.
51 Interview 21-99 (22/7/99).
52 Interview 30-99 (6/7/99).
53 Interview 12-01 (21/5/01).
54 Interview 13-98 (13/5/98).

revolutionaries, who filled the guerrilla ranks, threatening to take over ladino power in town. It also ignores the movement and activity that was going on within some of the indigenous communities of Joyabaj. Clearly, an ambivalent attitude exists towards the indigenous population.

Several organizations started opposing patrol duty in the rural areas. The first hints of discontent were clear as early as 1986, when a Guatemalan news programme broadcasted an item concerning a written document sent in by a group of *Joyabatecos* to the newly appointed President Cerezo. Apparently, they requested the immediate dissolution of the patrols in Joyabaj because they 'do not result in any benefits for our miserable lives'. The document continued, '[T]he patrols only bring more misery, more malnutrition, more injustice, more threats, more abuses and more exploitation'; therefore they should be stopped, especially now that Guatemala had become a 'pluralist democracy'.[55]

CERJ: organizing rural anti-patrol sentiments

Protests against patrol duty in Joyabaj were not an isolated incident but reflected growing discontent with patrolling throughout rural Guatemala. In many areas, especially in southern Quiché, people cautiously started opposing forced participation in the patrols individually, or were gradually winding down patrol duties as ladinos had done in the town of Joyabaj.[56] This growing opposition was stimulated by popular organizations like CERJ, Conavigua and CUC, culminating in 1988 in the first wave of anti-patrol protests. CERJ became by far the most actively involved in the anti-patrol protests. It was a peasant-based organization that originated in southern Quiché and whose members were mainly indigenous. In July 1988 it came officially out into the open, although its activities had started some years earlier.[57] It based its anti-patrol activities on Article 34 of Guatemala's 1985 constitution, which stated that 'no one is obliged to join nor to belong to self-defence groups or associations or other similar groups'.[58]

CERJ organized marches and demonstrations against patrol duty and helped and advised individuals and communities who wanted to stop patrolling. It provided them with information on Article 34 and its consequences for local patrols and explained how communities could petition for its abolition. It even printed small manuals on how to draft a proper denunciation that could be presented at the various PDH offices. CERJ also started issuing press statements about anti-patrol activities and human rights abuses against CERJ members and other

---

55 Teleprensa, 28/2/86.
56 See for example Prensa Libre (14/6/88) and Diario El Gráfico (22/7/88).
57 For a detailed study of the activities of CERJ see: Americas Watch (1988) and Bastos and Camus (1993).
58 Jay (1993: 22).

activists. In its first bulletin concerning the human rights situation in southern Quiché, published in November 1988, CERJ presented an overview of the villages that wanted to stop civil patrol duty in their communities.[59] Seventy-four communities were on the list, and only one of them was a community in the municipality of Joyabaj. This contrasts with the nearby municipalities of Zacualpa and Chiché, which featured on the list with ten and twelve communities respectively. It remains unclear why Joyabaj was so badly represented at that time. It might have been out of fear of the local patrol commanders, or because CERJ did not yet have a firm basis in Joyabaj and was unable to organize people into signing the petition against patrol duty. According to a former municipal DCG official, CERJ was not that strong in Joyabaj. 'They were quite *parco* [moderate] ... that is to say very cold ... because they were scared that the situation would get worse, and those of the left would be the first to suffer. So they did not do much ... they existed, but not much more.'[60]

The military reacted quite strongly against the growing anti-patrol lobby of CERJ and other organizations. A campaign of harassment, threat and selective murder was directed at CERJ activists and other individuals who started opposing patrol duty.[61] One of the victims was Pedro Pablo Ramos, a CERJ activist from Joyabaj, who was killed in June 1988, one month before CERJ came officially out into the open. Military commissioners from the village of Chuaqenum, Pedro's home town, were held responsible for his murder. No investigation into the murder was ever carried out.[62] According to Jay, who carried out a short study of civil patrol duty in Guatemala in 1992, 'The routine attacks on human rights organizations and activists, such as the leaders and members of CERJ, illustrate the military's violent intolerance of independent community organizations'.[63]

The military also tried to counter the anti-patrol sentiments by organizing meetings with local patrols and their commanders. During these meetings, the military explicitly stated that patrol duty was obligatory and threatened those who refused or had already slackened patrol duty somewhat. They sometimes even threatened to 'send in men from Joyabaj' if they did not patrol.[64] Some patrols from Joyabaj had already been actively involved in human rights abuses

---

59 *'Casos de renuncias al servicio impuesto en las patrullas de autodefensa civil ... , presentados a la procuraderia de los derechos humanos.'* CERJ, November 1988.
60 Interview 8-01 (9/5/01).
61 See CERJ document: *'Informe de denuncias de violaciones de los derechos humanos'* (14/10/88); Amnesty International (1989: 24–6); Jay (1993: 27–9).
62 CERJ, *'Informe de denuncias de violaciones de los derechos humanos'* (14/10/88: 1) and Amnesty International (1989: 26).
63 Jay (1993: 38).
64 Americas Watch (1988: 79).

outside their own municipality, and their reputation was used to frighten others into obeying military orders.[65] The meetings were also used to indoctrinate the patrollers with nationalistic and anti-communist messages. The military constantly linked CERJ with the insurgents and actively portrayed the organization as opponents to peace. CERJ was placed in the enemy camp, together with guerrilla organizations and everyone opposing the civil patrols. Although it is difficult to assess the long-term effects of such forms of stigmatization, some people are nowadays still considered to be former guerrillas to whom some ladinos are careful not to speak.

Despite harassment from the military and the civil patrols, the anti-patrol movement was growing and more and more communities announced that they wanted to stop patrolling. In the PDH archives in Santa Cruz, the first denunciations against patrol duty are documented at the beginning of 1989, a few months after CERJ became official. In February 1989 a group of people from the nearby municipality of Chiché were 'notifying withdrawal from the civil defence patrols', while in July 1989 a 'notification of the decision not to patrol' was made by a group of people from the municipality of Zacualpa.[66] Protests against patrol duty in Joyabaj started appearing somewhat later, in 1993, when a second wave of anti-patrol activities swept through the Guatemalan countryside. Possibly this was caused by the fact that CERJ seems to have been not that strong in Joyabaj during the early years of its existence.

Widows feel threatened

Conavigua was another popular organization, apart from CERJ, through which *Joyabatecos* could channel their complaints about human rights abuses. It was an organization of mainly indigenous widows who had lost their husbands or other family members during the armed conflict. Initially, the widows started meeting at village level, but it soon turned into a nationwide organization. According to some *Joyabatecos*, Conavigua had been much more present in Joyabaj than, for example, CERJ. 'They mobilized a large group of people to protest against forced military service, against the civil patrols, and against military presence here in town.'[67]

Within days of its becoming official in September 1988, a military-led harassment campaign was initiated accusing Conavigua of belonging to the guerrilla. One of the first targets was the Conavigua section in Joyabaj. Widows in Joyabaj had been meeting for some time before Conavigua came out into the open at the

---

65 Joyabaj patrollers were involved in human rights abuses in the communities of Chuchucá and Tunajá (Zacualpa). See CEH, Vol. XI (1999: 1373, 1374, 1363, 1364 and 1401).
66 PDH office Santa Cruz de Quiché, files 1989.
67 Interview 8-01 (9/5/01).

national level. A Conavigua leader in Joyabaj explained that initially they had received help in organizing themselves from guerrillas who were based in nearby municipalities. The women secretly met in each other's houses during the night 'without even lighting a candle for fear of waking up the children'.[68] The Conavigua section in Joyabaj, as in most other parts of the country, was made up entirely of indigenous widows. Initially two ladino widows had participated, but became scared when the other women started talking openly about the violence during the meetings. They pulled out. According to a former Conavigua leader, the *ladinas* left because '[T]he indigenous women suffered the violence in their own flesh, and because of that they were not afraid to demand their rights and talk about the violence. It was different for the ladinas.'[69]

A two-page document written in October 1988 by Conavigua described in great detail the harassment campaign that was carried out by patrol commanders and military officers in Joyabaj.[70] Especially patrol commanders from Chorraxaj, Xeabaj and Pajopop, indigenous villages north of Joyabaj, were involved in the harassment campaign. During the months of September and October 1988, a number of meetings were organized by the local military commander to instruct patrol commanders on how to deal with Conavigua. The women were to be watched and their movements controlled. The widows were accused of 'causing problems and being responsible if something happens in the *canton*'.[71] Although the threats were veiled, its meaning was clear to the widows. The fact that they were organizing themselves was the most important issue against which the patrols agitated. Organizing and having meetings of more than a few people were seen as suspect and thus subversive. Other criticism centred on the fact that 'they do not have any housework to do, and walk around the place'.[72] The patrol commander told them not to move around so much and to stay put in their houses. This freedom of movement, uncontrolled by a husband or other family member, was seen as inherently a bad thing because it did not fit existing gender roles. Indigenous women who were not involved in Conavigua used the same argument. The work and the freedom with which many widows walked around were 'looked upon badly (*mal vista*)'.[73] The way in which the military attacked Conavigua differed somewhat from the campaign against CERJ. Apart from attempts to blacken the reputation of both organizations by labelling them subversive, Conavigua women were also depicted by the military as indecent and

---

68 Interview 15-99 (31/7/99).
69 Interview 15-99 (31/7/99).
70 Conavigua document, 9/11/88.
71 Conavigua document, 9/11/88.
72 Interview 15-99 (31/7/99).
73 Interview 15-99 (31/7/99).

improper women who were involved in activities outside their house, such as attending meetings and demonstrations. According to military propaganda, this was not the behaviour of proper housewives.

The Conavigua document also described several meetings between the military and the patrols during which the military were not only fulminating against Conavigua and other popular organizations, but were increasingly pressuring patrol commanders in Joyabaj to maintain the patrols in their communities. The military had already lost the town patrols and apparently did not want this to happen to patrols in the rural areas. This coincided with the wishes of some of the rural civil patrol commanders, who were afraid to lose their position of power. Patrol commanders from Cruz Chich and El Temal were summoned by the military because people in these communities had become very slack in patrolling. During a mass meeting on 23 October, more than 600 patrollers from all over Joyabaj were instructed by a colonel of the military base in Quiché '[T]hat the patrols will never stop in the *cantones*. Therefore everybody is ordered to continue in the patrols and control their *cantones*, because if they stop patrolling, they will die together with their families, because there will be no one to protect them'.[74] The military clearly did not see protection of civilians as one of their own tasks, but delegated this to the civil patrols.

The commander also explained the patrollers that there were several ways in which to force people back into patrolling. In one village, which had refused to continue patrolling, the military had stolen all the livestock during one night. When the confused villagers went to the military base the next morning to report the theft, the commander told them that such things happened to villages that refused to protect themselves. The animals were returned to the villagers after they had resumed their patrol duty. Several times a week Joyabaj patrollers and patrol commanders were forced to participate in such meetings with the military, hearing stories of how villages fared after they had abandoned patrolling. They were told that all human rights organizations were bad, and that they were all communists, guerrillas and subversives who could not be trusted.

After President Cerezo came to power in 1985, more space for opposition to the government appeared. Several popular organizations were set up only a few years after the installation of Cerezo, and cases of human rights violations like harassment, threats, murder, illegal detention, forced civil patrol duty and the existence of clandestine cemeteries were published in occasional pamphlets and weekly or monthly publications. Also, the information became more detailed and names of both the alleged killers and the victims were written down as more people stepped forward. For example, a publication from the CERJ office in

---

74 Conavigua document, 9/11/88.

Santa Cruz contained eight pages of human rights abuses in southern Quiché between May and October 1988, listing more than 85 violations ranging from harassment to murder. Five cases involved people from Joyabaj, mainly widows and other human rights activists.[75]

Organizations like CERJ and Conavigua were mainly indigenous organizations, and did not have strong ties with ladinos. There seems to have been little or no connection between the ladino protests against patrol duty in the town of Joyabaj and the activities of CERJ and Conavigua in the rural areas; and no anti-patrol alliances were formed between the groups. CERJ and Conavigua also each had their own people supporting them, and local and national networks to get access to and distribute the information. Although the two organizations cooperated when organizing demonstrations or distributing pamphlets, each occupied a different niche in Guatemalan society. CERJ was predominantly a male indigenous organization that was active in the rural areas (especially southern Quiché), while Conavigua was clearly a rural women's organization. In a way, groups like CERJ and Conavigua were testing the limits of military control. CERJ tried to use the constitution to get the civil patrols dismantled, while Conavigua sought national and international attention to get its case out into the open. Although there was more space to voice opposition, and organizations made use of this space, it was often dangerous to occupy it. Many activists lost their lives doing so.[76]

The Catholic clergy returns to Joyabaj

Another opening for community organization was created when the Catholic Church returned permanently to Joyabaj in January 1988, and Padre Vásquez became the first resident priest since Padre Villanueva was killed in July 1980. Shortly before his arrival, the military left the church buildings and moved to another location, after extended negotiations between the Catholic Church and the military at the national level. Such negotiations had also been carried out in other municipalities that had to confront the problem of military occupation of church buildings. Although the buildings remained intact in Joyabaj, the priest found their interior in ruins. The military had robbed the place of every piece of furniture and other removables and destroyed what was left. The church itself had not been used by the military, as had happened for example in San Andrés Sajcabajá, where a massacre site was found inside the church. The church in Joyabaj was kept open and *vigilada* (watched over), even during the height of the

---

75 CERJ document, 14/10/88.
76 See Jay (1993: 27–9) for several cases of assassination and disappearance of CERJ members by civil patrollers. See also files PDH office Santa Cruz de Quiché, 1989–98.

violence, by a few catechists who would say the rosary on Sundays. They would first ask permission at the local military base, which would send some soldiers to the church once in a while to check whether 'we really only talked about religious things, and didn't start preaching other things'.[77] Military control was still tight during the early 1980s.

One of the first things Padre Juan Vásquez did when he arrived in 1988 was to make 'an immediate visit to the communities and stay there overnight ... one night in each village'.[78] This way the priest tried to regain the confidence (*confianza*) of the villagers, letting them feel that he would stay and be with them and that he would not abandon them. He also wanted people to know that celebrations and masses were taking place again, and that people could come to marry and baptize their children. He went from village to village for days on end, celebrating masses and revitalizing local Catholic Action groups. He always avoided imposing a rhythm of visits on the villages but let them invite him when they were ready to do so. He also refrained from asking people about the past and what had happened to them during the war. 'I choose not to take the initiative so as not to create a distance' and thought it inappropriate at that time to take on the role of investigator. 'I did not ask and they did not talk', he continued. According to him, 'the community has other ways of saying what it wants'. For example, people asked him to be with them in their village to celebrate mass on a certain date but without explaining why that particular date. 'Although they did not say it with their lips, I could sense that this was not to lose the memory and respect for what had happened ... the memory of their family members who were martyred.'[79] In these cases, people used masses to commemorate the family members they had lost during *La Violencia*. Although it was impossible to remember victims in a very open way at that time, names of deceased family members were read aloud during the mass: an indirect but apparently safe way of commemorating war victims.

Another important aspect of his approach to getting people involved in the Catholic Church again and to restore their faith not only in religion but in the future in general was music and singing. According to the priest, 'a community could reweave its fabric (*rehacer sus tejidos*) by way of its celebrations'.[80] He wanted people to regain their confidence so that they would be able to resume their prayers in the community church buildings, resume their fiestas and thus resume their lives. Shortly after his arrival he started organizing music ensembles and choir groups, especially involving indigenous youngsters. When he arrived in

---

77 Interview 13-01 (10/6/01).
78 Interview 25-99 (30/5/99).
79 Interview 25-99 (30/5/99).
80 Interview 25-99 (30/5/99).

1988 only five bands existed in the more than 60 villages and hamlets of Joyabaj. In 1994 most villages had their own band, which would play and sing during religious celebrations like the Sunday mass and processions, but also during village fiestas and, for example, the opening of a stretch of road or a new school building.

The priest was not only active in the indigenous community in town and surrounding villages, but also started reorganizing the ladinos in town around Catholic activities. Several women's groups were set up in different parts of town, attracting mainly older ladino women. They started coming together once a week doing Bible study, prepared food for religious celebrations and helped decorate the church for mass. Apart from the women, the priest also tried to get ladino men involved in church activities again. Therefore he initiated a musical group called *San Francisco*, which consisted mainly of ladino men in their early forties. For some of its members, the group also seems to have functioned as a kind of unofficial Alcoholics Anonymous (AA) group. One of its members explained that because of the group meetings he was sober at least two days a week: when they rehearsed and when they performed in church. Alcoholism was, and still is, a severe problem in Joyabaj, as elsewhere in Guatemala. The consumption of large quantities of alcohol in order to sink into oblivion, with the intention of forgetting what happened back then or what one's role was in it all, is a clear legacy of the armed conflict. Apparently, the musical groups served different purposes for different people.

The majority of these initiatives, aimed to drawing people not only into the Catholic Church but also into community work in general, started very slowly, first of all because the military, the military commissioners and civil patrols were still a presence to be reckoned with. They kept a sharp eye on the movements of the priest and his activities. When he was going out into the villages, people refused to let him walk or sleep alone out of fear something would happen to him. A second aspect was the initial hesitation of people to get involved in church and other projects again, even ones as harmless as a choir or music group. For years it had been impossible for groups of people to gather for mass or any other celebration or community activity. The only group meetings allowed were those of the civil patrols. People involved in the Catholic Church had also been prosecuted heavily during the early 1980s because of their involvement in community and development activities. Initially, the Catholic Church started reorganizing people around religious activities rather than, for example, community development, which had been an important aspect of the work of the Catholic Church before the violence. Nevertheless, the parish priest saw these new Catholic groups, like the choirs, the music ensembles, the Catholic Action groups in the villages and the ladino gatherings in town as important emerging *spaces* for people to gather self-confidence and rebuild relations of mutual trust between community members. He saw it as part of his task to 'start opening up these spaces' (*empezar abriendo espacios*).[81] True to his Catholic heritage, he added the thought that they were also spaces where the word of God could help console people for what had happened.

The parish priest gets into trouble

Many people in Joyabaj, both indigenous and ladino, remember Padre Vásquez as a very intense and active person. Civil patrol commanders and the military were less charmed by the priest's performance and community development activities. They criticized the fact that the priest organized large-scale processions, during which he commemorated the death of Padre Villanueva, the parish priest who was killed in July 1980. Villanueva was killed on the day of the yearly celebration of the Sacred Heart (*Sagrado Corazón*), and Padre Vásquez took the initiative of combining the two events. Although he started out on a modest scale, in 1990 more then 50 music groups from the surrounding villages accompanied the celebration of the Sacred Heart. The town centre was packed with people, filling between ten and 15 blocks (*cuadras*). Not unexpectedly, this gathering of people caught the attention of the military and patrol commanders. The Sacred Heart procession turned more and more into the celebration of the martyr Padre Villanueva, culminating in 1992 when the procession was headed by a large photograph of Villanueva. That same year, Vásquez also built a small shrine dedicated to Villanueva. His portrait was flanked by the photos of two other martyred priests.[82]

A ladino man, who belonged to an evangelical church, commented that 'he came to resuscitate the Catholic Church, and of course the patrol commanders thought that he would also resuscitate the people, or the guerrilla. A priest who is so active, they knew such priests from before'.[83] According to the priest, 'they [the patrol commanders] were just suspicious, they felt attacked ... that the people of God, the communities, dared to be open in their expressions during an act in broad daylight'.[84] The processions were mainly an indigenous affair, with *indígenas* actively participating while most ladinos only watched the proceedings from their doors.[85] It was considered to be an activity of the rural communities, which did not really concern them.

---

81 Interview 25-99 (30/5/99).
82 See: Diócesis del Quiché (2000).
83 Interview 7-01 (23/5/01).
84 Interview 25-99 (30/5/99).
85 Interview 4-01 (11/5/01).

In December 1992 the communal hall *(salon parroquial)* belonging to the parish was torched and burnt to the ground. Nobody was hurt but all the musical instruments of the Catholic music groups were destroyed, including a very costly marimba. Although it was never proven, everybody was convinced the military were responsible for the act. It was seen as a warning to Padre Vásquez not to wander too far beyond the boundaries of the Catholic Church set indirectly by the military and the patrol commanders. The involvement of Padre Vásquez in community projects, his sympathy towards organizations like Conavigua, and his activities surrounding Padre Villanueva's commemoration were in themselves considered enough reason for harassment by the patrols and the military. The issue that really angered local patrol commanders and which led to the temporary exile of Padre Vasquez in 1993 was his choice of topics to preach about in church. During one of his sermons he talked about equality between *indígenas* and non-*indígenas* and the need to work together to reconcile the community. Supposedly, patrol commander Leonel Ogáldez classified this sermon as subversive talk and reported to the military base in Santa Cruz that the priest was organizing guerrilla groups in Joyabaj. The priest explained to me that he refrained from openly criticizing the civil patrols in his talks and sermons. He considered this to be much too confrontational at the time.[86] Although surveillance and control by the military and civil patrols was somewhat less strict and open, with the town patrols coming to an end and the military vacating the convent buildings, many people were still convinced that they and their activities were being observed and noted down. The terror campaign of the military seemed to instil a measure of self-censorship into the people, who were very careful about what they said and did.

Padre Juan Vásquez had manoeuvred himself into in a difficult position in Joyabaj. First of all, his activities to 'wake up the people', such as the organization of musical groups, Catholic Action groups and the celebrations of Padre Villanueva, did not sit well with the local military and their allies. Apart from that, Catholic ladinos and several indigenous leaders of Catholic Action looked with suspicion upon his close relationship with *cofrades* and Mayan priests and his initiatives to introduce indigenous elements into the Catholic Church service. A final issue was his mediating role when people wanted to throw the mayor out of office, and a lynching seemed at hand. His involvement, however small, in local politics was not considered proper behaviour for a priest by conservative Catholic *Joyabatecos*.[87]

---

86 Interview 11-01 (20/5/01).
87 Interview 11-01 (20/5/01).

Crisis in local politics

While Padre Vásquez ran into trouble with the local patrol commanders and military commissioners because of his growing activities inside and outside the Catholic Church, another conflict was slowly developing in the local municipality. Amado Osmin, the first democratically elected mayor, had already been forced to resign in September 1988. The political situation quietened down somewhat after another member of the town council took over as interim mayor until new elections were held in November 1990. The outcome of these municipal elections came as a shock to some ladinos, because the indigenous candidate of the DCG, Juan Toj, won with 1,385 votes. He was the first *indígena* to become mayor of Joyabaj. The conservative MAS came in second, followed by the liberal UCN and the right-wing MLN.[88]

The fact that the DCG became the biggest party in Joyabaj was possibly connected to its absence during the 1985 elections. It was therefore able to start the 1990 election campaign in Joyabaj with a clean slate. The fact that the DCG mayor was indigenous also contributed to its victory, because the majority of the voters in Joyabaj were indigenous. Apparently, the indigenous organizations backed the candidacy of Juan Toj and urged the indigenous community to vote for him. He had also included the indigenous mayors in his entourage when touring the indigenous communities to canvass for the coming elections.[89] A former UCN candidate for council member commented that the votes were widely split among the different parties, because 'we were seven candidates [for mayor]'. Apart from that, 'the type of propaganda he [Juan Toj] made, that was only possible because he was candidate for the official party'.[90] This last remark refers to the fact that candidates for mayor whose political party controlled the government at that time appeared to receive much more government resources for propaganda purposes than the other candidates. This is a common complaint during election campaigns in Guatemala.

The majority of *Joyabatecos* remembered Juan Toj mainly as a corrupt mayor. Many people thought his corruption was partially caused by the gradual transfer of financial and decision-making power from the national government to the municipalities. This decentralization process allocated increasing amounts of government funds to the municipalities. The process started in 1987, when the municipalities received control over 8 per cent of the national budget that was allocated to them.[91] According to many *Joyabatecos*, this increased access to and

---

88 MAS: 806 votes, UCN: 574 votes, MLN: 207 votes. Source: statistical data from the TSE office in Joyabaj (5/5/01).
89 Interview 1-98 (26/6/98).
90 Interview 16-01 (14/5/01).
91 Macleod (1997: 70).

control over municipal money corrupted quite a few mayors. In their opinion, people were not ready for this and they changed overnight. A former indigenous DCG activist remembered that 'when Juan became mayor, he really believed himself to be someone important, and he did not want to talk to people any more, although we knew each other very well ... his attitude changed'.[92]

Apart from what is locally labelled as 'normal' corruption, Juan Toj committed a much more serious offence in the eyes of the indigenous majority in Joyabaj. He had been illegally selling large parcels of communal land that belonged to the *común indígena*.[93] Communal land normally would be let to people who had no land of their own. Besides, it was open for people to gather firewood and herd their cattle. During the last 20 years the attitude of people towards communal land had been gradually changing. This was caused largely by the armed conflict, which reshaped many such traditional arrangements. According to a former secretary of the *Alcaldía Indígena*, people stopped paying their rent to the *Comité de la comunidad indígena* (Committee of the Indigenous Community), which was in charge of supervising the communal property. Others stopped asking permission from the Committee if they wanted to use part of the land to farm or build a house on.[94] The minutes of the Committee meetings mentioned the fact that trees were being cut down without permission, large quantities of firewood were taken illegally from the communal woods, and *cofradías* were not allowed to enter previously communal land to collect firewood.[95] This changed attitude to communal land reached its peak with the illegal land sales by mayor Juan Toj. Thus, apart from the loss of land, Juan Toj's actions also seem to have caused a severe authority problem for the *Alcaldía Indígena*.[96] Nothing much was done against the illegal settlement of people or the illegal felling of trees. Some people were convinced that the *Alcaldía Indígena* did not feel strong at the time and tried to avoid conflicts with the people because threats were made and guns waved.[97]

In February 1992 Juan Toj had to step down as mayor after repeated accusations of corruption. He was subsequently tried for his role in the illegal sale of communal land, which was definitely lost to the indigenous community, and spent a year in prison in Santa Cruz. For many ladinos, this sentence confirmed their low opinion of him as a mayor. Several of them said, 'indigenous people are not fit to be mayor',[98] although they seemed to forget that several corrupt *ladino* mayors preceded Juan Toj in his office.

---

92 Interview 28-99 (18/9/99).
93 The *común indígena* consists of the Indigenous Municipality, the seven *cofradías* and the indigenous community in general.
94 Interview 7-98 (19/6/98).
95 *Libros de Actas, del Comité de la Comunidad Indígena* (31/12/91).
96 Interview 2-98 (21/6/98).
97 Interview 1-98 (26/6/98).
98 Interview 1-98 (26/6/98).

Verifying memories and opinions

Although it has become clear from the reminiscences and opinions retailed that local politics were in chaos while Juan Toj was mayor, it remained unclear what exactly happened, aside from his role in the illegal sale of communal land for which he was subsequently convicted. Although many people offered their opinion of Juan Toj when talking to me in private, few had actually witnessed the events they talked about in such detail and with such liveliness. Opinion and memory of Juan Toj's period as mayor seem to be closely intertwined. Few people who were actually working in the municipality at that time, or had had any dealings with Juan Toj, were willing to talk about this period, especially about his last year as mayor in 1992. This was because, first of all, it was a chaotic period during which local conflicts flared up again: conflicts between groups who wanted to stop patrolling and commanders who wanted to force them to continue, conflicts between different political parties within the municipality, and conflicts between the indigenous community and the ladino municipality over the illegal sale of indigenous communal land. Some of these conflicts continue at the time of writing (October 2002).

A second factor was that Juan Toj returned to Joyabaj after spending a year in jail and opened an office for legal services in town. His physical presence possibly influenced the way people talked about him and his past. When interviewed about the time when Juan Toj was mayor, people often said they preferred to forget those days and did not want to be reminded of them.[99] The phrase 'I do not want any problems' kept coming up during the interviews. People avoided problems by keeping their mouths shut and not talking about certain events. People kept to themselves and tried not to get mixed up in things like political or religious struggles. This corresponds with what Cohen calls 'a moral climate in which indifference—dismissal of everything that went beyond routine everyday concern—became an 'active social force'.[100]

A final incident, which made it difficult to get a clear picture of this period and to verify what actually happened, was the absence of the *Libro de Actas*. In these minutes all proceedings of council meetings and the decisions made during them are noted down in detail by the municipal secretary. All through the violence of the 1980s the *Libros de Actas* had been kept safe in the municipality, although little was written down in them during that period. They were never allowed off the premises, even after the military had taken over control of the municipality. In June 1992, the month when Juan Toj was accused of corruption, the *Libro de Actas* that was in daily use disappeared.[101] According to former

---

99 Diary, 4/10/99.
100 Cohen (2001: 156).
101 *Libro de Actas, acta* 01-92 (6/92).

municipal officials, the missing *Libro de Actas* contained evidence of the illegal sales of indigenous communal lands. They were convinced Juan Toj himself let the book disappear because the information it contained could be compromising for him.

Clearly, memory and opinion are closely intertwined and not that easy to separate. Many people who were interviewed about events that happened during this period offered elaborate and detailed accounts. Several of these people, however, had not personally witnessed the situation because they were not present, or out of town, or possibly too young at the time. Nevertheless, they did have clear opinions on certain topics because they had heard about them later on, or they had read about them in the newspapers, or they had been openly and heatedly debated among friends.

Rising conflicts between patrols and municipality

The resignation of Juan Toj seems only to have worsened the chaos in which the municipality found itself. Trust in local politicians had never been very great in Joyabaj and many *Joyabatecos* were convinced that those actively involved in local politics were there only for personal gain. The authority of the municipality was also contested by some of the more dedicated civil patrol commanders, headed by Leonel Ogáldez. According to the 1993 annual report of the ODHAG (the human rights office of the Catholic Church), '[S]ince more than ten years, different mayors and members of the municipal corporation in Joyabaj, who were elected, have been forced to step down because of the PAC'.[102] They especially targeted and criticized Leonel Ogáldez who, in their opinion, had used his position of power to create a circle of impunity around him, which rendered him immune from state prosecution.

After Juan Toj resigned as mayor in February 1992, council member Pedro Miranda (DCG) took over as interim mayor. He was an indigenous man from the village of Chorraxaj, which was hit hard during the violence. Already before the violence he had been active in Catholic Action and the DCG, which had strong roots among the villagers of Chorraxaj. Soon after Pedro Miranda took up the post of interim mayor in 1992 he came into conflict with Leonel Ogáldez. The patrol commander forced Pedro Miranda to step down from office by threatening him and his family and organizing disturbances and riots targeting the interim mayor. A former ladino teacher explained that 'Leonel considered Pedro to be a guerrilla', which seemed sufficient reason for the disturbances.[103] The actions of Ogáldez were effective and in August 1992 Pedro Miranda stepped down,

---

102 ODHAG (1993: 338, 339).
103 Interview 4-01 (11/5/01).

only a few months after he had assumed office. According to the *official* minutes of his last council meeting as mayor, he resigned because he was unable to combine the function of mayor with his obligations in his home village of Chorraxaj. After he left, Fermín Perez, a MAS council member took over as interim mayor, although it was the DCG that was supposed to fill that post. He stayed in office until 1 April 1993. During his time as interim mayor, things quieted down considerably in Joyabaj. The municipal officials were left in peace by the civil patrollers, and relations seemed to improve. People refrained from talking much about this period, which makes it difficult to ascertain the exact relationships that existed between Fermín Perez and the civil patrollers.

After being given the legal protection of the court, Pedro Miranda resumed his duties as interim mayor on 1 April 1993.[104] Shortly afterwards, civil patrols started harassing the municipal officers again, which culminated in the temporary takeover of the municipal building, the detonation of a hand grenade, wounding two persons, and the shooting of a council member.[105] Miranda resigned for the second time, together with all but one council member, after only two months.[106] His second departure from the municipal office was probably also influenced by the murder of an important local human rights activist, Tomás Lares Ciprian, and the ensuing problems surrounding the investigation of this case, which received national media coverage.[107] Although Miranda was quickly replaced as interim mayor by another member of the DCG, it turned out to be very difficult for the TSE members to find replacements for the other departing municipal officials. Four out of six proposed replacements turned out to have left for the United States:[108] conveniently so, because few people were interested in getting into trouble with local patrol leaders. They did not want to get mixed up in things and decided it was healthier to leave Joyabaj for a while. It took until October 1993 to find people who were willing to take over municipal responsibilities.[109]

According to human rights organizations, many of the municipal conflicts in Joyabaj during 1992 and 1993 were the result of a struggle for control over the municipality and its resources.[110] The goal of the disturbances caused by Ogáldez was to force the municipality to resign and locate power in the hands of himself and other patrol commanders.[111] The civil patrol commanders had seen their

---

104 *Libro de Actas, acta* 33-93 (1/4/93).
105 ODHAG (1993: 341).
106 *Libro de Actas, acta* 41-93 (3/6/93).
107 This case will be analysed in the coming sections of this chapter.
108 *Libros de Actas, actas* 42-93 (10/6/93), 44-93 (15/7/93) and 55-93 (15/10/93).
109 *Libro de Actas, acta* 57-93 (28/10/93).
110 ODHAG (1993: 338, 339).
111 Human Rights Watch (1994: 23-28).

power base diminishing as the patrols in town had stopped functioning and rural protest against the patrols were getting stronger. Control over the municipality could possibly compensate for this loss of power. The fight over municipal power and resources went hand in hand with an intimidation campaign by patrol commanders towards anyone participating in community organizations or in the anti-patrol movement, as had been the case during the first anti-patrol wave in 1988.

The 1993 civil patrol rallies: supporters and opponents

As in 1988, the second wave of anti-patrol protest was backed up and encouraged by several human rights organizations, which had been actively campaigning against civil defence patrols. In October 1992 the CUC published a pamphlet titled 'Outcry for the dissolution of the civil defence patrols', initiating renewed action against the patrols.[112] This was done in response to repeated military attempts during the months of August and September 1992 to reactivate rural civil patrols in areas where they had become somewhat slack, including Joyabaj. Anti-patrol actions intensified, for example in Joyabaj, were a large protest march was being organized by the CUC on 25 February 1993. The weekly national newspaper *Siglo XXI* announced that 3,000 patrollers, mainly from indigenous villages north of the municipality, were going to lay down their arms and stop patrolling.[113] A few days before the march was due to take place, a letter signed by more than 500 people was send to several government officials, in which the villagers explained why they wanted to stop. 'We have put up with it for many years, out of fear for the threats and intimidation, that is to save our lives, we have been participating in the PAC ... but we are so exhausted now *(ya nos tiene tan cansado)*, that we have taken the decision to renounce the PAC.'[114] The military were not happy with the protest and the Minister of Defence stated that the march was 'nothing other than a manipulation on the part of organizations which are connected with insurgents'. He added that 'the patrols in Joyabaj are very united and the supposed resignation is ... a sham *(engaño)*'.[115] But the military were worried over nothing. Only about 400 patrollers showed up for the march, possibly because the patrol commanders had succeeded in intimidating the others into staying away. Although the organizers had invited several government officials, such as the departmental governor and the *Procurador General* of the PDH, almost none of the invitees showed up.

---

112 CUC leaflet, 30/10/92.
113 *Siglo XXI*, 25/2/93. The following communities were mentioned: Chorraxaj, Xeabaj, Quiacoj, Talaxcoc and Pasaguay.
114 Copied letter (19/2/93) belonging to the case file of Tomás Lares Ciprian (ODHAG: area legal).
115 Siglo XXI, 25/2/93.

On 29 March 1993, a month after the anti-patrol demonstration, Leonel Ogáldez, together with the military, organized a counter-demonstration in favour of the patrols. Apparently, door-to-door visits were made to pressure everybody into participating. If people did not attend, their names would be put on a list, which would be send to the military base: an old but still familiar and effective threat.[116] Aside from Leonel Ogáldez, Colonel Echeverría, commander of the Military Zone 20 in Santa Cruz, was also present during the demonstration. In a speech the colonel promised that, as long as the conflict continued, the army would provide the patrollers with weapons if requested and within the capabilities of the army. He also stressed that the army controlled the patrols' use of their weapons to prevent abuse and protect the image of patrollers as a counter-insurgency institution. While the colonel's speech was geared towards the patrols and even touched upon possible problems of abuse by patrols, the speech by Leonel Ogáldez was a passionate and direct attack on local organizations and their activities. According to him, '[T]he aid and popular organizations only come to confuse and to divide us', referring to the work of Conavigua, CERJ and GAM.[117] In his eyes, these organizations let themselves 'be used in the political game of the commanders of the URNG'.[118] He was quoted as ending the demonstration with the following words: 'The people will never exchange the blue and white of the national flag for the red of communism.'[119] Anti-communist sentiment had always been strong among *Joyabatecos*, notably ladinos and *indígenas* connected with right-wing politics, finding its roots in the anti-communist policies during the Armas government in the 1960s, long before guerrilla forces first appeared in the area. This sentiment only grew during the height of the armed conflict, when they were fuelled by the military and several civil patrol commanders who constantly labelled guerrillas, but also civilians, as subversive and communist.

The case of Tomás Lares Ciprian

One of the principal organizers of the anti-patrol march in February 1993 was Tomás Lares Ciprian, a 57-year-old indigenous farmer from the village of Chorraxaj.[120] He was active in both CERJ and CUC and had organized several protest meetings in Joyabaj against patrol duty. His name had already been mentioned in connection with anti-patrol activism as early as July 1990 when the

---

116 Interview 1-99 (26/4/99).
117 Prensa Libre, 29/3/93.
118 El Gráfico, 29/3/93.
119 Siglo XXI, 29/3/93.
120 Based on: Human Rights Watch (1994: 23-28), ODHAG (1993: 338-343), and case file on Tomás Lares Ciprian at the ODHAG office (area legal).

Secretary of Internal Affairs (*Secretário de Gobernación*) in San
death threats from patrol leaders from Chorraxaj. The secretar
patrollers to take action against Tomás Lares Ciprian, who at th
refusing to participate in the Chorraxaj patrols.[121]

Tomás Lares continued his protest, and the demonstration
ize on 25 February 1993 received extensive media coverage, including a reaction
from the then Minister of Defence. Several CUC leaders were alarmed by this
national attention and travelled to the capital, together with Tomás Lares, to
explain to government officials why they were organizing the demonstrations
and to ask for protection. According to the CUC, local patrol commanders and
military commissioners in Joyabaj had already been visiting the villages that had
participated in the rally, saying that dismantling the patrols would mean a return
of the violence of the early 1980s.[122] Lares himself had also received several
threats from Chorraxaj patrol commanders and had presented an official denunciation at the PDH office in Santa Cruz on 16 March. According to Tomás
Lares, he was 'accused of being a bad person and this was due to the fact that the
presenter [Tomás Lares] was member of the Water Committee'. In that capacity
he had had several meetings with other members of the committee, trying to
solve some problems. According to the patrol commander 'these meetings are of
the guerrilla'.[123] An order was issued by the PDH to the local police in Joyabaj to
the effect that Lares was to be protected. The order was never carried out. Also,
Leonel Ogáldez, in his capacity as general commander of the Joyabaj patrols,
received a telegram from the PDH, asking him to explain the harassment against
Lares and other activists. His only reaction was to say that he did not know anything and that it sometimes happened that personal problems between people
were the cause of such denunciations.[124]

On 26 March ODHAG also initiated court action on behalf of Lares, asking
for a habeas corpus *(recurso de exhibición personal)* and demanding immediate protection for Lares and other CERJ activists. Although this judicial mechanism is
used especially in cases where protection is urgently needed, ODHAG did not
receive an answer from the courts until 19 May, more than one and a half month
after the demand was made. The answer was negative. In any case, the protection was no longer needed because Tomás Lares was already dead. Three weeks
before, on 30 April, he had been walking back from the weekly market in Cruz
Chich to his house in Chorraxaj when several civil patroller commanders from

---

121 Comité Justicia y Paz, 1990.
122 Comunicado de Prensa CUC, 4/5/93.
123 PDH office Santa Cruz, files 022/93 and 040/93 (16/3/93) and case file Tomás Lares Ciprian (ODHAG – area legal).
124 Letter of Leonel Ogáldez (2/4/93); in case file Tomás Lares Ciprian (ODHAG – area legal).

Chorraxaj attacked and killed him.[125]

The murder of Tomás Lares seemed to signify a brutal end to the hopes of many local activists in Joyabaj. Looking back at the killing of Lares, an indigenous man who had been actively involved in Catholic Action concluded that Lares was too direct and too confrontational. He said what he thought of the army and the patrol commanders 'right in their faces ... and that way does not work'.[126] He continued to explain that, if Lares had not got himself in so much trouble, he probably would still be alive. This attitude of placing a victim of state terror apart from the rest of society seems to have been deeply ingrained in the people living in the rural communities by years of civil patrol indoctrination and military propaganda, which had told them over and over again that, if you behaved well, went about your work and did nothing wrong, you had nothing to fear. If you actually became a military target and got killed, you must have been doing something wrong, like belonging to the guerrilla. Getting killed proved someone's guilt.[127] In a way, persons were even stigmatized after death. Possibly, most people realized that this was military propaganda, but it somehow stayed in their minds and came up again when they discussed topics like the murder of Lares Ciprian.

Civil patrols inhibiting court proceedings

Although nobody was convicted for the murder, an elaborate court case emerged around the Tomás Lares case, which was used by human rights organizations at the national level as an example of a failing justice system unable to operate independently of military orders and civil patrol harassment.[128] The exhumation of Tomás Lares was carried out two months after he was killed, under difficult circumstances. It revealed that he was shot five times, while his throat was slit and his right ear cut off. It was a difficult exhumation because it took some persuasion to get the forensic surgeon and the prosecutor *(fiscal)* to come to the site and examine the body on the spot. It was impossible to take the body to the hospital in Santa Cruz for a thorough examination because the patrollers in the area would not let them. The prosecutor also refused to solicit arrest warrants for the suspected patrollers and got himself transferred from Santa Cruz as soon as possible because of continuous harassment by Joyabaj patrollers. Apart from that, it was impossible to carry out a reconstruction of events at the scene, because the Justice of Peace (*Juez de Paz*) from Joyabaj refused to attend. The exhumation and the reconstruction were organized to gather evidence for the court case

---

125 Human Rights Watch (1994: 26).
126 Interview 29-99 (1/10/99).
127 Cohen (2001: 154-155).
128 See for example Human Rights Watch (1994), ODHAG (1993), and Solomon (1994).

which ODHAG was preparing against three civil patrol commanders from Chorraxaj, who had been seen near the murder site at the time Lares was killed. They also issued a warrant for the arrest of Leonel Ogáldez, who was thought to have masterminded the murder. Although they were never convicted, Santos Chich Us, the patrol leader from Chorraxaj, was sentenced for another crime at a later date. He was found guilty of murdering two men from Chorraxaj in the early 1980s because they refused to participate in the civil patrols.

According to the prosecuting party, several factors contributed to the fact that the Tomás Lares case was never successfully concluded.[129] First of all, the witnesses who were summoned to testify against the patrollers were almost all *indígenas* from Joyabaj, who spoke only *K'iche'* and very little Spanish. The court in Santa Cruz did not have any official court translators, so that many important details were never translated and thus went unnoticed. Second, some of the patrollers were never arrested because the police in Joyabaj said they did not have the equipment to go out into the villages and arrest people. That is to say, they did not have a car. Besides, the police had no idea what the suspects looked like. These and many more reasons were given for not participating in the arrest of the civil patrollers. Finally, the patrollers that were arrested all produced perfect alibis that absolved them of all blame. Leonel Ogáldez did not even have to be arrested because he came to the hearing of his own free will, bringing witnesses with him who could vouch for his claim that he had been somewhere else on the day of the murder. A former lawyer who worked on the case thought it was strange that the witnesses of Leonel Ogáldez were all heard that same day and that the prosecution was not allowed to ask the accused party any questions. At the end of the day Leonel walked out of the courthouse a free man.[130] Normally in Guatemalan courts the witnesses were heard on different days, over an extended period of time, and at the end of the trial the persons were either acquitted or found guilty. The court case against the presumed killers of Tomás Lares, however, proceeded very differently. During an interview with Leonel Ogáldez, he himself broached the subject of Tomás Lares Ciprian, explaining that he had been falsely accused and maintaining that he did not have any power in the communities at that time because he was only general commander of the patrols in town.[131]

An additional problem was that during the court case Leonel Ogáldez denied that he was in fact general commander of the civil patrols, and the military backed him up. Only a few months before, when the PDH had asked Leonel

---

129 Interview 1-99 (26/4/99).
130 Interview 1-99 (26/4/99).
131 Interview 12-01 (21/5/01).

Ogáldez to provide information on an earlier denunciation of Tomás Lares Ciprian, he had signed the telegram, dated 2 April 1993, as 'General commander of the Voluntary Committees of Civil Defence of the Municipality of Joyabaj, Leonel Ogáldez'.[132] In the office of the PDH in Santa Cruz I found several notes from Leonel Ogáldez addressed to the PDH explaining that, if they needed information on the patrols, they should not ask him because he was no longer general commander. They were kindly requested not to ask him for any more information. ODHAG wanted to verify Leonel's statement and asked to see the *Libros de PAC*, which contained the names of all commanders.[133] These were in the possession of the Military Zone in Santa Cruz, and access to them was refused. The only ones who were allowed to enter the base and take a look at the books were the *Juez de Paz* and his secretary. When the people of ODHAG were allowed into the base an hour later, after accusing the military of obstruction of justice, they could hear the *Juez de Paz* being scolded by the commander. Both men were sitting with a cup of coffee next to them, hands between their legs and with their heads bowed. The military explained to ODHAG that they had shown the books to the *Juez de Paz* and that they were not obliged to do so to ODHAG. The *Juez* never said a word about what had happened at the base and never mentioned the books. He felt even more threatened after a black cloth had been hung one day above the door of his house. Normally, such a cloth appears only when someone in the house has died.

The case dragged on until January 1994, when a new judge was appointed to the Santa Cruz court (*Juzgado Segundo de Primera Instancia de Quiché*) after the old one had been accused of corruption. Only days after the new judge arrived, the archives of the court were burned to the ground. The judge openly accused[134] the Joyabaj patrollers who had visited him some days before and bullied him into freeing a Joyabaj patroller who was on trial for multiple murder. Destroying the archives was a setback not only for the Tomás Lares case but also for another important case against the civil patrollers from San Pedro Jocopilas, a municipality in the south of Quiché. A few days later the military reacted fiercely to the accusations made by the judge, pointing out that the burning of the archives had clearly been carried out by subversive groups like the EGP. They stressed that the EGP happened to commemorate its foundation 22 years before on the precise

---

132 Letter of Leonel Ogáldez (2/4/93); in case file Tomás Lares Ciprian (ODHAG – area legal).
133 It was the first time I had read about the existence of such *Libros de PAC*, and I have not yet found any additional information. It is possible, and not unthinkable, that most of these records were destroyed by the military in the late 1990s, to prevent such information being made public. However, in view of the most recent developments (July 2002) regarding the demands of former patrollers for financial compensation from the government, such a list of names would have been quite helpful in identifying patrol members.
134 *Siglo XXI*, 20/4/94.

day of the attack on the archives. According to the military commander the judge himself should be investigated for his irresponsible and biased (tendentious) behaviour.[135]

Memories of 1993

The murder of Tomás Lares and the ensuing court proceedings were among the cases that were picked up nationwide as an example of continuing violence and patrol abuse in Guatemala and of the incapacity of the Guatemalan government to provide security for its citizens. According to the prosecuting party, the whole case was a clear example of 'state impunity' and 'the military zone in Quiché clearly controlled all the instruments of justice'.[136] The case was presented as an example of the incapacity and corruption of the justice system, which prevented many cases from ever coming to court. Not only did the courts not function properly, but the lower echelons of the justice apparatus, such as police officials or a *Juez de Paz*, were often considered corrupt or as acting under military orders. The case was also taken up by human rights organizations as an example of the local power that civil patrols in Joyabaj seemed to wield and the impunity surrounding human rights abuses carried out under the responsibility of some of the patrol commanders. In the mid-1990s the civil patrols of Joyabaj were often used as a case study presented at national and international fora.[137]

This national attention seems to contrasts quite sharply with local recognition and memory of the Tomás Lares case as well as of the civil patrol rallies. Most ladinos seemed to have hardly any memories of either incident. One ladino explained their apparent lack of interest by reference to a sense of self-preservation. Many ladinos preferred to wait and see how the political winds blew, and did not to let others know how they really felt about things: a combination of indifference and self-censorship in not openly talking about what one felt.[138] People were very careful not to get into trouble. Therefore, they did not seem to have a clear memory or opinion of the situation.[139] It was also too much of an 'indigenous thing',[140] just like the processions in commemoration of Padre Villanueva which were organized by Padre Vásquez. People in town also considered it to be something that concerned the people in the communities, and had nothing to do with them. Although the rallies were organized in the central town square, this did not mean that it had any bearing on the urban population. 'They

---

135 *Siglo XXI*, 21/4/94.
136 Interview 1-99 (26/4/99).
137 See Solomon (1994: 25-41). Other cases of patrol violence that were often cited were the patrols from San Pedro Jocopilas, Xémal and Colotenango.
138 Cohen (2001: 154-156).
139 Interview 38-99 (19/8/99).
140 Interview 4-01 (11/5/01).

just didn't pay attention, that is why most people don't know anything about it. As long as it was quiet in town, it didn't really matter what happened in the communities ... where everybody was assumed to belong to the guerrillas anyway.'[141] It is therefore not strange that many people did not have a clue who Tomás Lares was, why he had been killed or that it had become a national example of civil patrol violence. Local memory of the case, especially among the ladinos, was quite different from the official national memory.

One of the few ladinos who clearly remembered the troubles in 1993 was former parish priest Padre Juan Vásquez. He sympathized with groups like Conavigua, but he could not involve himself in their work, he could not organize people or ask them to come to a protest meeting. He could only listen and provide some sort of space for them to continue their activities.[142] Former civil patrol commander Leonel Ogáldez also remembered the rallies, especially the one protesting against the patrols, although from a very different perspective. 'There were groups ... how would you call them ... pro-human rights ... like Conavigua. They protested against the patrols and the military. But they were not all that innocent. Some of them also participated in the guerrilla, they were known around here.'[143] He chose his words very carefully, not blaming anyone in particular and admitting that both sides had made mistakes in those days. 'In a non-declared war there will always be dead people on both sides. They were difficult times ... difficult.'[144]

Conclusion

Although terror carried out by state forces seems to have lessened considerably in the mid-1980s compared with the massacres of 1981 and 1982, the situation did not calm down automatically after the first democratic elections in 1985. First of all, many people had fled the area as a result of the violence, many had been killed, villages were left abandoned and the town itself had grown considerably because of the influx of refugees from the rural communities. Violence still continued, although in a more selective and less open way. In town, open surveillance by civil patrols and the military slowly made way for more veiled forms of control. Indirect control, by which people controlled their own behaviour and words, seemed to evolve as one of the long-term results of state terror. Self-censorship was considered necessary to survive.

The practice of stigmatizing part of the population as different remained a recurrent military tactic. Between 1980 and 1983 individuals and whole com-

---

141 Interview 7-01 (23/5/01).
142 Interview 11-01 (20/5/01).
143 Interview 12-01 (21/5/01).
144 Interview 12-01 (21/5/01).

munities had been branded subversive and communists, which had resulted in massacres and selective violence. During the transition years, when protest against forced patrol duty increased, stigmatization continued and was directed towards human rights groups such as CERJ and Conavigua, people who wanted to stop patrolling, people who had left during the war, people who had stayed, returning refugees, former DCG politicians and people like Padre Juan Vasquez and Pedro Miranda.[145] The list seemed endless, which meant that it was almost impossible for people not to get involved. Everybody was included.

Aside from, and possibly as a result of, a continuation of the violence, albeit in a different form, the newly elected municipal councils did not function very well, and had to step down before the end of their appointed periods in office. This was partially due to a lack of experience, incompetence and corruption scandals. But even more important was the harassment from groups in *Joyabateco* society that were opposed to the changes the new democratic government was proposing. The result was a continuing struggle between the elected officials and the civil patrol commanders for control over the municipality and its resources. At the same time, community initiatives started developing again after several years of virtual absence. Ladinos in town started to organize themselves into an Improvement Committee, although it never came into existence, while a group of young teachers started a local magazine titled *Espíritu Xoj*, in which they criticized the municipal government. During 1980–83 such initiatives would have been unthinkable. Also, the Catholic Church started functioning again, with an active parish priest acting as catalyst. He slowly tried to regain confidence of the people, reorganizing Catholic Action groups and setting up musical groups in the rural communities. He also initiated the first commemorative events in Joyabaj, in honour of Padre Villanueva, who was killed in the early days of the armed conflict. It was an act which got him into trouble with the local military and patrollers.

Ladinos in town also started opposing patrol duty, which was abolished around 1986. In the rural, mostly indigenous, communities surrounding Joyabaj, however, the patrols were not allowed to dismantle and violent activities continued. In some rural communities patrol commanders had created their own personal kingdoms, quite independent of military hierarchy and control, which had been stricter in the initial years of the civil patrol system. They were anxious not to lose their positions of power. This led to a growing opposition among the rural patrollers, culminating in two waves of fierce anti-civil patrol protest in the years 1988 and 1993.

These local initiatives were backed up, and partially initiated, by national

---

145 Personal conversation with Mathilde Gonzalez (19/4/99).

organizations such as CERJ and Conavigua. National and local protest did, however, not result in the dismantling of the civil patrols. It sometimes only hardened the attitude of the military and local patrol commanders against certain individuals and groups who were actively involved in these protests. An example is the murder of Tomás Lares Ciprian, whose court case has been used at the national level as an illustration in human rights circles of continuing state impunity and civil patrol violence. In Joyabaj, ladinos, especially those who regarded the violent incident as something that affected only the indigenous population, paid less attention to this case.

6

Pacified, but not peaceful[1]

(1994-2000)

As I showed in Chapter 5, the power of local civil patrol commanders became heavily contested from 1988 onwards, culminating in a second wave of anti-patrol activity in 1993. The present chapter follows this critical trend from 1994 onwards, reaching a peak with the final dismantling of the patrols in November 1996, only weeks before the final peace agreement between guerrillas and the Guatemalan government was signed. In this chapter I first discuss the national debate surrounding the abolition, transformation or continuation of civil defence patrols. I then describe the process of the dismantling of *rural* civil patrols in Joyabaj.[2] I show that official dismantling did not mean the actual end of the power of patrols or local patrol commanders. Partially because of the chaotic and not very transparent way the dismantling took place, it was unclear who wielded actual power at the local level. Although in some communities patrol commanders were indeed put on trial and in rare cases convicted, in other areas patrol commanders held on to their power, albeit under a different name. Within this process of dismantling special attention is given to the changing position of an important patrol commander in Joyabaj. The differences between his current portrayal of his work as a patrol commander and the way *Joyabatecos* remember his past activities is discussed in the broader framework of memory and denial.

In spite of international verification of human rights abuses and the signing of the Peace Accords in 1996, the security situation in post-war Guatemala did not much improve. Although political violence had decreased, everyday violence was increasing. This is a common phenomenon in states in a post-war transition process.[3] Many individuals who had been active in security forces had to find new ways of earning a living. Undertaking violent activities was one possibility. The war also changed the way people related to each other and the way they solved conflicts. One violent phenomenon—lynchings—receives special attention because several occurred in Joyabaj and surrounding areas. Lynchings were both responses to increased violence (in which people took justice into their own hands) and contributions to a climate of violence. Another local response to

---

1 The title is derived from the novel *Que me maten si...*, from the Guatemalan writer Rey Rosa (1997).
2 As explained in Chapter 5, the town patrols had already been dismantled in 1986.
3 Similar security problems existed for example in post-war South Africa and El Salvador.

increased violence was the threatened and actual reorganization of civil patrols within months after they were formally dismantled. At the same time, human rights organizations such as the PDH[4] and MINUGUA[5] started playing a more prominent role in Joyabaj, because of the increasing number of denunciations concerning civil patrol commanders and other local authorities. As a result, *human rights* became the topic of a heated debate.

The chapter ends by looking at the two power arenas, local politics and economics, which had been severely affected by civil war violence and patrol activity. Although trust (*confianza*) in local politics was still very low, the space to manoeuvre within the two arenas expanded, and both became once again focal points in the quest for power and authority. The participation of civic committees and former guerrillas diversified local politics, while the local economy received an enormous boost due to remittances from large-scale migration to the United States. Throughout this period, polarization between and within different political, religious and especially ethnic groups (ladinos and *indígenas*) became more pronounced. Local divisions between groups at the local level seemed to resurface after the national threat of state terror by way of civil patrols, military activity and military commissioners had diminished.

Civil patrols: national road to abolition

As has been explained in the previous chapter, civil patrols were an important issue during the peace negotiations, over which many conflicts arose between the negotiating parties. After the failed coup by President Serrano in May 1993, former director of the PDH Ramiro de León Carpio took over the presidency. As human rights ombudsman he had condemned human rights abuses[6] by civil patrols, but as president his attitude towards the patrols was more guarded and less critical. During the peace negotiations, which received new impetus under President León Carpio, the patrol issue boiled down to one question: was participation in the civil patrols voluntary or was it not? According to many human rights and other popular organizations, this was an impossible question in a country that had been in a civil war for decades. How was it possible to gather information on such a volatile topic? Despite the criticism, several studies were undertaken on the subject, one of which was financed by the Spanish govern-

---

4 *Procuraduría de los Derechos Humanos* – Human Rights Ombudsman.
5 *Misión de las Naciones Unidas para la Verificación de los Derechos Humanos en Guatemala* - UN human rights verification mission.
6 MINUGUA verifies the following human rights: right to life (extra-judicial executions and deaths), right to security and integrity of a person (torture), right to individual liberty (arbitrary detention, enforced disappearances, illegal or forced recruitment), right to due process, political rights, freedom of expression, freedom of association, freedom of movement (MINUGUA, *Primer Informe*, March 1995).

ment[7], under the supervision of the PDH. The report was highly critical of the civil patrols, but failed to determine conclusively how voluntary the patrols were. The researchers suggested that the people 'speak fearfully, ... they don't express themselves with sincerity ... they say things that won't compromise them'.[8] Keeping in mind that today, in 2001, many people still do not talk freely about this period, imagine what an impact a research team on such a highly sensitive topic as the civil patrols would have had in 1993. The critical stance of this report was corroborated by several international human rights organizations.[9]

In January 1994 the new director of PDH, García Laguardia, recommended that decree No. 19-86, the one which ratified the civil patrols as part of the military reserves and thus in a sense provided legal cover for their existence,[10] be revoked. This recommendation was based primarily on the large number of human rights violations committed by patrols, which were brought to the attention of his office.[11] It was not until 28 November 1996 that the decree was indeed revoked by Congress, thus officially ending all civil patrols. In January 1994, demobilization was still a long way ahead and the Guatemalan government and the guerillas where still in the midst of the negotiating process. On 29 March 1994 the Comprehensive Human Rights Agreement was signed: the first substantive agreement between the negotiating parties. First of all, the agreement specified that the United Nations would establish a human rights verification mission (MINUGUA) in Guatemala. Further topics that were covered by the agreement were impunity, clandestine cemeteries, military conscription and refugees. 'It did not attempt to solve the military or political problems posed by the PACs',[12] but the government committed itself not to encourage the formation of or to arm new civil patrols 'unless the situation calls for them'.[13] The Agreement further stipulated that '[T]he parties agree that other aspects of the Voluntary Civil Defence Committees will be dealt with later'.[14] It was not until September 1996 that the issue of civil patrols was back on the negotiating table, as part of *The Agreement on the Strengthening of Civilian Power and the Role of the Armed Forces in a Democratic Society*. The agreement contained a comprehensive package of measures to strengthen democratic government and reduce the secu-

---

7   The study was carried out by ASADI (a Guatemalan NGO) and AECI (a Spanish NGO).
8   PDH (1994: 45) and Popkin (1996: 15).
9   See publications of the Robert F. Kennedy Memorial Center for Human Rights, which published three studies on civil patrols: Jay (1993), Solomon (1994), and Popkin (1996). See also publications from Human Rights Watch/Americas, the Inter-American Commission on Human Rights of the Organization of American States and the United Nations.
10 Solomon (1994: 54).
11 See Solomon (1994) and Jay (1993).
12 Solomon (1994: 48, 49).
13 Popkin (1996: 11).
14 Quoted in: Solomon (1994: 49).

rity functions of the state. Among other things, the army would be reduced in size, a new civilian police was to be created,[15] and civil patrol legislation would be revoked.[16]

In Chapter 5 it was argued that anti-civil patrol feelings had grown steadily in the Guatemalan countryside, culminating in a first wave of criticism in 1988 and a subsequent wave in 1993. From 1994 onwards, the critical stance was not, as before, limited to human rights organizations and locals actually performing duty in the patrols, but had expanded into other spheres of Guatemalan society as well. The future of the patrols was widely debated in the national as well as the international arena. One of the issues on which the debate focused was their possible transformation into development committees. This conversion was proposed by President León Carpio, who explained that 'as a demonstration of political will, our policy in 1994 will be to review and ascertain the need for civilian self-defence patrols'. He continued, 'they must be organized to serve as a basis for the operation of development committees'.[17] The idea was heavily criticized, for example by the CUC, which declared that, if the idea was to create instruments for development, they could think of many other organizations which would be 'much more legitimate, accepted and not so *rechazada* [rejected]'.[18] Although, according to military sources, some patrols were indeed turned into development committees, there existed little information on exact numbers or on what conversion entailed in practice.

Patrols in trouble at the local level

When León Carpio was elected president after Serrano's failed self-coup (*autogolpe*) in May 1993, patrol commanders feared that, as former human rights Ombudsman, León Carpio would automatically attempt to abolish the patrols. In Joyabaj, this sense of threat resulted in a chaotic and violent period of demonstrations and counterdemonstrations on the issue of civil defence patrols, which I described in detail in Chapter 5. After the first few turbulent months of 1993, the situation in Joyabaj calmed down somewhat. Arrest warrants were issued for some of the patrol commanders who were connected to the murder of Tomás Lares Ciprian, causing some of the more notorious patrol commanders to lie low for a while. They mostly stayed in their communities and did not venture out into the open. Additionally, the police were not to keen to venture out into the rural

---

15 See for a detailed analysis of the creation of the *Policía Nacional Civil* (PNC) and subsequent implementation: Glebbeek 2003 (forthcoming).
16 Armon, Sieder and Wilson (1997: 85).
17 Pinto (1994: 19).
18 Siglo XXI, 20/8/93. For more information about León Carpio's plan to convert civil patrols into development committees, see Solomon (1994: 58-65); Popkin (1996: 35-38).

areas, and preferred to stay in town. They also lacked proper equipment: for example, vehicles for transportation to the rural communities.

In addition, patrol commander Leonel Ogáldez toned down his activities somewhat, stepping down as general commander of the civil patrols in May 1993.[19] In view of the growing negative publicity surrounding civil patrols, it was a logical move to officially step down from such a controversial position. As patrol commander, Ogáldez featured frequently in the PDH files.[20] When investigating a denunciation, the PDH would interview the accused party and ask for additional information from the proper authorities. In practice this meant that requests for information were always sent to the commander of the military base in Santa Cruz de Quiché (departmental capital of Quiché, hereafter Santa Cruz), to the local military commander, to the local police station and to the local civil patrol commander. In this last capacity Ogáldez was frequently asked to act as a witness in local cases of human rights abuses. In the cases I have been able to review, he denied any knowledge of abuses committed by other patrollers and their commanders.[21] He generally replied that he was not at the site when the alleged abuse happened and would play down the seriousness of the case by explaining that 'sometimes there are problems of a personal nature between some people, who then start accusing each other'.[22]

The rapidly deteriorating image of the patrols, accelerated by discussions during the peace negotiations and the various investigations and international fact-finding missions, affected relations between the military and the civil patrols. Initially the military commander in Santa Cruz backed up Joyabaj patrollers and military commissioners when they denied any involvement in human rights abuses in their statements at the PDH office. When asked for additional information about a certain case, the military mostly denied that the person in question had in fact been patrol commander or military commissioners.[23] Or they cited the fact that the *town* patrols had already been abolished some years before, stating that the individuals in question 'do not hold the position of Military Commissioner nor do they belong to the patrol, because the CVDV [*Comité Voluntario de Defensa Civil*][24] in the municipality of Joyabaj was discontinued eight

---

19 PDH case P 054/93.
20 See PDH archives in Santa Cruz (case files on Joyabaj: 1989–98).
21 I have revised most of the case files on Joyabaj. A few could not be found in the archives, although an entry of the case had been made in the PDH logbooks. Some of these cases were still being processed by the judicial system and were not available to the general public.
22 ODHAG case Tomás Lares Ciprian, document 4, PDH case DI 071/94.
23 PDH case P 074/93.
24 In an effort to improve the image of the civil patrols, they were renamed CVDC (Voluntary Committees of Civil Defence) in 1986. They continued, however, to be popularly knows as PACs, or more simply, civil patrols (Popkin, 1996: 7-8).

years ago'.²⁵ In the rural hamlets surrounding Joyabaj, however, the patrols continued their activities and the above-mentioned individuals carried on as patrol commanders as usual.

It seemed that the military was trying to distance itself in several ways from civil patrol commanders and the violent incidents they were identified with now that the peace process was advancing and patrollers were being found guilty by the courts.²⁶ Already in the early 1980s, shortly after most of the massacres were committed, the military sometimes intervened when local civil patrol commanders became too much of an embarrassment due to excessively violent behaviour. Behaviour that had been tolerated and even encouraged only a few years earlier, when the counter-insurgency war was at its peak, could no longer be tolerated. In some cases the military ended up killing patrol commanders whom it could no longer control and who became too much of an embarrassment. This seems to have been the case when a patrol commander from the indigenous community of Xecnup was found tortured and killed near the local swimming pool in Joyabaj in 1994. It was rumoured he had been skinned alive. His murder was often mentioned by many *Joyabatecos* as an example of what could happen to violent patrol commanders. The stories were full of horrible details that tended to change from time to time, depending on the mood of the narrator and the number of listeners. One young indigenous girl explained that 'they let him suffer, like he had done with so many other people'.²⁷ People agreed, however, that this commander was killed by the military themselves.²⁸ Some interpreted his murder as a warning to other patrol commanders to keep their heads down and refrain from openly violent activities.

Denouncing abuse: a complicated business
Increasing criticism of civil patrols, fuelled by the many demonstrations and activities of organizations like CERJ and Conavigua, resulted in an increasing number of denunciations made to human rights organizations. Most denunciations pointed to civil patrol commanders as the principal culprits involved in human rights abuses in Joyabaj. *Joyabatecos* who wanted to denounce human rights abuses could go either the PDH office, which opened its doors in 1988, or to MINUGUA which set up shop in 1994. Both organizations had their offices in Santa Cruz.

The number of denunciations from *Joyabatecos* on civil patrol violence in the PDH archives started increasing from 1993, somewhat later than in other com-

---

25 PDH case DI 044/94.
26 Schirmer (1998: 98-101).
27 Interview 6-99 (27/5/99).
28 Interview 20-98 (18/8/98).

munities. This could be related to the fact that CERJ, the organization supporting and promoting many of the denunciations, did have less of a power base in Joyabaj. Out of a total of 15 cases from Joyabaj in 1993, twelve implicated civil patrol leaders. In the years following, up until 1996, seven cases against civil patrol leaders in Joyabaj were filed at the PDH office.[29] Although the numbers showed that patrols and patrol commanders were still active in Joyabaj, they also pointed to a growing willingness, compared with the late 1980s, to actually go to the PDH office and file a complaint. The PDH office had opened its doors in Santa Cruz as early as 1989, but in the first few years only a few denunciations from Joyabaj were received. It took until 1993 for a significant number of *Joyabatecos* to find their way to the PDH office. The filed complaints revealed that the civil patrols were in conflict with local organizations, like the *Comité de Amas de Casa* (committee of housewives)[30] and the widows' organization GAM,[31] and with several individuals, who accused them of harassment or outright violence.

An interesting case from October 1995 concerned civil patrol duty in Estanzuela, a rural community south of Joyabaj. It looked like a straightforward complaint concerning a group of 13 men who were forced to continue patrolling against their will. They had to pay a fine if they did not show up and they were forced to provide manual labour at the military base. The case became more complex when another group from the same community stepped forward accusing the first group of misinforming the PDH. According to this group, the civil patrol still existed but was no longer actively patrolling. The patrol collaborated in development projects 'to contribute to and look for peaceful solutions for the problems and necessities that are present in our *cantón*, for example defending ourselves against thieves'.[32] It looked as if President León Carpio's propaganda to convert civil patrols into development committees had been understood and used by civil patrollers at the local level to their advantage. In this particular case it was difficult to establish exactly what the real issue between the opposing parties was. Although most of the cases presented to human rights offices were genuine denunciations concerning human rights violations by civil patrol leaders or military commissioners, some did look somewhat questionable in the sense that in some cases conflicts between patrollers and non-patrollers seem to have been used as a thin veneer to hide genuine personal conflicts between family or community members over land issues and other resources.[33]

An additional factor complicated the situation at the PDH office in Santa

---

29 PDH archives in Santa Cruz (case files on Joyabaj: 1989–98).
30 PDH case 039/94.
31 PDH case 075/94.
32 PDH case DI 066/95.
33 PDH case P 100/93.

Cruz. The representative of the PDH in the Quiché department had very close personal and professional ties with the military and possibly military intelligence. He had been in the military himself before starting law school. During his ten years as PDH representative in Santa Cruz (1985–95), some cases involving human rights violations carried out by military or patrollers were not thoroughly investigated and sometimes swept aside as domestic matters between husbands and wives, brothers or neighbours. In the PDH files several examples can be found of patrollers, patrol commanders, police officers and other local authorities who were accused of human rights violations. When summoned to the PDH office to give their versions of the events, 99 per cent denied all charges. In some cases the testimonies of patrol commanders and military or police officials seem to have been given more weight than the testimony of the denouncing party. Further research was deemed unnecessary and the cases were closed.[34] After the PDH representative resigned from his job in 1995, he returned openly to his military roots and went to work in the military zone in Santa Cruz as a legal adviser to the army.

Starting its work as UN human rights verification mission in 1994, MINUGUA became the second largest avenue for Guatemalans to present cases of human rights abuse, after PDH. One of the regional offices was situated in Santa Cruz to provide assistance to people in southern part of the Quiché department. Many of the denunciations made to the PDH office could also be found in MINUGUA's files. People presented their cases to as many organizations as possible. In some of the more violent cases, MINUGUA staff went in person to verify the facts for themselves at the scene of the crime. The local population did not always welcome these visits, which were considered acts of outside interference. I will come back to this issue when discussing *Joyabatecos*' perception of human rights in general.

Violence continued

Despite increased criticism of civil patrol activity, which eventually led to their nationwide abolition in late 1996, violent acts involving civil patrollers continued in the period from 1994 until 1996. Patrol leaders were desperate to hold on to their positions of power and in some cases used all means necessary to ensure that they did. This was also the case in Joyabaj, when in August 1995 a young ladino by the name of Erwin Alvarado was killed. Supposedly, his testimony was instrumental in providing evidence in the Tomás Lares case.[35] The story started in June 1993, when a local patrol commander attacked Alvarado and another

---

34 PDH archives in Santa Cruz del Quiché (case files on Joyabaj: 1989–98).
35 Interview 1-99 (26/4/99).

man. He emptied both his gun and his rifle shooting at the house of one of the two men. They were lucky to escape. Alvarado agreed to drop all charges against the patrol commander after attending a meeting convened by the commander of the military base in Santa Cruz, during which the ladino patrol commander was also present. In return the patrol commander agreed to stop harassing them and to pay all damages.[36] Only a few weeks later Alvarado was attacked again and wounded severely. He was in hospital for two weeks, while the military commissioner who had assaulted him was taken to prison and charged. Things seemed to calm down somewhat after that until August 1995, when Alvarado was once again the victim of a shooting, which proved to be fatal this time. According to a former lawyer connected to this case, Alvarado was silenced so he could not give evidence in the Tomás Lares case, or any other case for that matter.[37] Although many people witnessed the murder, because during the attack a grenade also wounded 16 bystanders, nobody wanted to accuse the military commissioners out of fear of the repercussions. At the time I carried out my research, the murder was hardly mentioned spontaneously by *Joyabatecos*, who did not like to dwell on the topic when asked directly about it. This was in stark contrast to the national and international attention the case received from national and international human rights organizations. This complicated murder case is a test case of the determination that military commissioners and civil patrol commanders showed in trying to hold on to their positions of authority and immunity. Witnesses were harassed and killed and one death led to another.

A failing justice system

The justice system was a recurrent topic in the verification reports that were issued by MINUGUA, because a reformed and functioning justice system was seen as a prerequisite to establishing a proper rule of law. Unfortunately, Guatemala's justice system had not yet recovered from the civil war years, when it had been virtually non-existent. The justice system was also confronted with continuing harassment from the military and civil patrol groups when trying cases involving, for example, civil patrollers. There were multiple examples of trials against former patrollers that failed because of lack of evidence, because police, judges and procurators were not doing a proper job. The justice system was judged corrupt, inefficient and burdened by the legacy of decades of military rule. The lawyers working on the Tomás Lares case had also labelled the Guatemalan justice system corrupt. This case was not the only one in Joyabaj that received national attention and was used as an example of the worsening cri-

---

36   Human Rights Watch (1994: 27).
37   Interview 1-99 (26/4/99).

sis in the Guatemalan justice system. Another illustration is a murder case in the indigenous community of Xecnup, also involving local civil patrol leaders.[38]

In September 1995 an indigenous man from Xecnup reported to MINUGUA an attempted murder attack and several years of abuse and harassment against him, which had started in 1993. The perpetrators were civil patrollers and patrol leaders from the same community. In December 1995 the same individual reported the murder of his father and a close friend by the same group of patrollers. In January 1996 the *Ministerio Público* (Ministry of the Interior) issued a warrant for their arrest, which was sent to the local police station in Joyabaj. The auxiliary mayor of Xecnup was unable to comply with the police orders for their arrest, because the patrollers were armed and threatened the auxiliary mayor. The police were also unable to arrest anyone due to lack of funds and personnel, according to the case file. When they attempted to reach the community in a borrowed pick-up, the commanding police official concluded that the community might react aggressively to their arrival and cancelled the trip halfway through.

MINUGUA then visited Xecnup, where they received warnings from local civil patrols that, if any attempt was made to capture one of the implicated patrollers, the patrols would kill the denouncing party and even MINUGUA if they ever came back to the community. Such threats were not uncommon. MINUGUA alerted the military base in Santa Cruz, which replied that it was unable to help because 'Military Zone 20 does not have jurisdiction or the competence to start an investigation into these allegations, because in Guatemala we have a perfect separation of power'.[39] There could not have been a more ironic answer. An investigation by the military zone was carried out eventually, which concluded that the denunciations made by the individual from Xecnup against the local patrol commanders were completely false and designed only to compromise the civil patrols. The case was never resolved. Not only is this an example of the incompetence of a local police force in carrying out its job, it also portrays the powerful position of many patrol leaders at that time. Threats were made and guns were waved, causing people to retract earlier statements or to clam up altogether.

Patrols finally dismantled

On 24 June 1996, a few months before the final Peace Accord was signed, Defence Minister Julio Balconi announced a plan to disarm and dismantle the civil patrols before the middle of November 1996. It was to be carried out in

---

38 See MINUGUA, *Suplemento al Quinto Informe* (September 1996), caso 38, and PDH case 011/95.
39 MINUGUA, *Suplemento al Quinto Informe* (September 1996) caso 38.

three phases. Phase one would reorient the patrollers, explaining what was being done and why, followed by phase two: disarming the patrols. The third phase consisted of the possibility of civil patrols maintaining their organization, albeit using them for development purposes instead of military goals.[40] This third phase was remarkably similar to the proposals of former president León de Carpio who had already in 1994 proposed to convert civil patrols into development committees. It was heavily criticized by national and international organizations, resulting in the implementation of only the first two phases of the plan in most areas. In August 1996 the first patrols were officially disarmed by the military, although in the preceding months some patrols had already handed over their weapons voluntarily.

There were severe criticisms of the way in which the disarmament and the subsequent demobilization of the civil patrols were carried out by the military.[41] First of all, national and international organizations were not given the opportunity to officially verify the process. Second, nobody knew how many weapons the army had distributed to the civil patrols during the last decades, and how many weapons patrollers had bought themselves. Lastly, the army had also neglected to provide lists of the names of people who served as civil patrol commanders, so that their demobilization could be verified at a later date. There was little overall transparency. WCC/GRICAR, a church-based NGO which participated in the peace negotiations, stated that such a process 'does not ensure that it will be a process that truly leads to demobilization, much less to a lessening of the repressive hold the civil patrols have had over much of the rural community'.[42] The process was also carried out without much thought for the future. For example, what was to be done about former patrol leaders who had abused their power, and about land claims of returning refugees who found their land occupied by patrol leaders? A Catholic priest from Santa Cruz considered the disarmament to be 'only a symbolic act, although it has been widely praised in the international press. There is a big gap between what the army says and what it practises'.[43] Many Guatemalans considered the political will of the Guatemalan government and the military to end the patrol system and actually disarm them to be very small. Others added that the whole process was more 'fanciful than factual', and did not believe that the army would give up such an investment so easily.[44] The military and the Guatemalan government were accused of making a public relations show out of the dismantling process. The actual handing in of

---

40 Latin American Weekly Report, 11/7/96, no. 26.
41 WCC/GRICAR (27 September 1996), #42: 5 and 6 .
42 WCC/GRICAR (27 September1996), #42: 5 and 6.
43 United Methodist Daily News, 15/4/97.
44 GHRC/USA update, December 1996, #25 and 26.

weapons was sometimes done during elaborate ceremonies, during which several military dignitaries resorted to patriotic rhetoric, thanking the communities for having defended their country and their flag. Some communities therefore insisted on handing over their weapons to MINUGUA instead of the army to avoid getting caught up in some army public relations stunt.[45]

Apparently, this was not the case in Joyabaj. According to a small newspaper article, the patrols in Joyabaj were dismantled in October 1996, at the same time as the patrols in the neighbouring municipalities of Chinique, San Andrés Sajcabajá and Pachalum.[46] People in Joyabaj did not really seem to remember exactly how and when the patrols were dismantled. Obviously the event left no lasting imprint in the memories of most *Joyabatecos*, ladinos and *indígenas* alike. Ladinos in particular did not remember much because the patrols in town, in which most of the ladinos participated, had already stopped patrolling around 1986. Different stories were told about the actual demobilization of the rural patrols in 1996, but there was agreement that it was a small and not very elaborate ceremony. It was done during a 'public act where they explained why there was no need any more to patrol ... that there would be no patrollers any more, nor guerrillas'.[47] Some of the patrollers, for example those from Xecnup who had a violent reputation, at first refused to hand over their weapons because they were convinced the war would resume. When forced to hand them over, some of them burst into tears.[48] Many patrollers, who opposed the dismantling, said they would not hand over their weapons until the guerrillas did so first. This argument was used extensively by civil patrols trying to avoid disarmament. In their eyes, the guerrillas were the bad guys and the criminals and human rights organizations were only helping and protecting those criminals. Some patrols were more creative in their refusal to be disarmed. Three patrols in a remote northern part of the Quiché department said they would only trade their guns 'for titles to land, a road to their community and payment for their years of service to the military'.[49] Although their wishes were not granted and they were disarmed just in time for the signing of the final peace agreement, they continued to make demands on the government and even organized themselves in a committee of 'former civil patrollers'.[50] I return to this issue at a later stage in this chapter.

For many patrollers it was difficult to adapt to the enormous changes and occasional contradictions in discourse. Instead of being the saviours of their

---

45 Cerigua Weekly Briefs, 1/8/96, no. 30.
46 Siglo XXI, 5/10/96.
47 Interview 12-01 (21/5/01).
48 Interview 26-99 (21/8/99).
49 Cerigua Weekly Briefs, 12/12/96, no. 48.
50 Cerigua Weekly Briefs, 12/12/96, no. 48.

communities, as the army had told them they were for more than two decades, they were now seen as the bad guys. National and international media pictured them as criminal groups, guilty of committing human rights abuses. This contrasted with army statements made during ceremonies of patrol dismantling, in which the patrollers were told that 'the President wants to thank you for your participation in the struggle to safeguard national sovereignty, and in this case the physical integrity of the townspeople and their property'.[51]

The actual disarming of the patrols did not bring an immediate end to the powerful positions several civil patrol leaders had occupied in the communities for more than a decade. Until several years after their disbanding, some of the former leaders continued to occupy important positions in their communities, whether as coordinators of development or water committees or as evangelical pastors. This was not so strange because many of these men were perceived by others as community leaders and were in some cases among the few literate people in their communities. It was a different situation altogether if such people continued to back up their positions of power by means of threats and violence. A villager from an indigenous community north of Joyabaj, who fled the violence and returned in 1998, told the following story about a former patrol commander in his community. 'He has a galil in his house, a gun (rifle) and several small revolvers ... He said he only handed over two old weapons to the army.'[52] Things were no different in Joyabaj, where patrollers from some of the more violent patrols had bought their own weapons during the two decades they were active. Most of these weapons were never confiscated by the military. It was feared that they would add to an already heightened feeling of insecurity.

Conflicting memories of past performance
Civil defence patrols had been a difficult topic at the negotiating table, trials against patrol commanders had started, and evidence of the abuses was gathered by truth commissions and through the exhumation of clandestine mass graves.[53] Some patrol commanders in Joyabaj had already been taking precautions before the patrols were actually dismantled, trying to limit their responsibility for local human rights abuses. A good example was Leonel Ogáldez, one of the most important ladino patrol commanders in Joyabaj. As I explained in Chapter 5, he had stepped down as *Comandante General de PAC* in May 1993, and, according to him, he had nothing to do with violent incidents occurring after that date. He repeated his claim in a final letter to the PDH in September 1993, when he was

---

51 Cerigua Weekly Briefs, 17/10/96, no. 41.
52 Interview 28-99 (18/9/99).
53 In Chapter 7 a detailed analysis is provided of the exhumation work of various organizations in Guatemala, including the exhumation of a mass grave in Joyabaj in January 2000.

asked to provide information on the murder of a teacher, Professor Alfonso Rámos García.⁵⁴ 'I want to inform you that this will be the last time that I am going to answer your messages, because in this community nobody is in charge of the civil patrols any more. I suggest you send future messages to the Commander of the Military Commissioners.'⁵⁵ The letter was signed '*Atentamente Prof. Próspero Ogáldez S. Ex-Comandante CVDC*'. He was already trying to distance himself from his previous position as civil patrol commander.

Why draw so much attention to these pieces of evidence that confirm that Ogáldez was indeed a former patrol commander? In a direct interview in 2001, a little more than four years after the civil patrols had been dismantled, he denied having been patrol commander of *all* civil patrols in the municipality of Joyabaj, and explained that he had been commander only of the *urban* patrols. He was elected 'president of the committee of the civil patrols' in the urban area and thus had nothing to do with the patrols in the *rural* hamlets surrounding Joyabaj.⁵⁶ He did not deny having been patrol commander in Joyabaj, but played down his own role in and responsibility for the whole situation. It was much more convenient for Ogáldez to paint such a picture, because most human rights abuses in Joyabaj were committed by rural patrols in the communities surrounding the town of Joyabaj. According to Ogáldez, every community had its own patrol leader, who was under direct orders of the military.

Although not denying all responsibility outright, during the entire interview he systematically played down his own responsibility for many of the atrocities committed by the civil patrols in Joyabaj. His account differed considerably from local memories of his activities as a civil patrol commander. First of all, he maintained that he was in charge only of the town patrols, which stopped patrolling anyway in 1986 and were much less active than the rural patrols. A related issue was the year he became a patrol commander. According to several local testimonies, from both indigenous people and ladinos, he was involved in the civil patrols as general commander right from the start, after the military came in and started organizing the patrols at the end of 1981. Ogáldez, however, stated that he was elected commander only in 1983, conveniently after most of the massacres and other human rights abuses were carried out. A final issue around which local memory and the memory of Leonel Ogáldez differed was the frequency of his contacts with local military commanders and officers. According

---

54 The murder of this ladino teacher and president of a teachers' association in Joyabaj is often mentioned by ladinos in Joyabaj when giving examples of the violence during 1993 and 1994. Although ladinos remember his death clearly, it was not picked up by the national media. This case contrasts with the death of Tómas Lares, the indigenous activist killed in early 1993: although it received a lot of national attention, it was not considered an important event by many ladinos.
55 ODHAG case Tomás Lares Ciprian, document 13.
56 Interview 12-01 (21/5/01).

to one informant, he 'was constantly in and out of the military barracks',[57] which were then situated in the convent, while others explained that he was very close to many of the military commanders and went on regular drinking bouts with them.[58] Local memories put Leonel Ogáldez right in the centre of activities surrounding the military base and implicate him in several violent incidents. Ogáldez stated that he was very rarely invited into the military compound, although he acknowledged having had contact with the military in his capacity as patrol commander in the urban area. 'There [in the convent], the military ruled ... they did not invite one just like that, only sometimes I went in to drink a soda ... I did not know that people were buried there, but maybe they were guerrillas.'[59] Most ladinos and *indígenas* interviewed about this topic told a very different story. They remembered him walking in and out of the compound on a very regular basis and were convinced that he knew exactly what was going on inside the military barracks.

The reason why it is interesting to contrast this interview with Leonel Ogáldez with interviews that have been conducted with many other locals from Joyabaj on this topic is not to find out who is telling the truth and who not. The aim is not to point a guilty finger at one person or provide material for a lawsuit. The interview is presented as an example of how people ingeniously reconstruct the past to match the requirements of the present: not by denying certain events or facts ('denial of knowledge', to use Cohen's words), because this is quite difficult in the face of hard evidence, but by diminishing or denying their own responsibility in the situation and by playing down their own importance.[60] It is also important to look at what Cohen calls 'not having an enquiring mind', which he explains as 'a claim either not to have grasped the significance of the event or not to have known the big picture. Information was transmitted on a "need to know" basis; tasks were compartmentalized; everyone deceived us'.[61] It is as if Leonel Ogáldez was apologizing for what happened in the 1980s when he said that 'one was very ignorant back then ... it was not until later that one understood what was going on'.[62]

It is important to bear in mind that the interviews were conducted several years after the peace was signed in 1996. In the meantime, general opinion of civil patrols and their activities during the civil war grew less favourable, to say the least, due to the enormous amount of evidence which pointed at their par-

---

57 Interview 7-01 (23/5/01) and 14-01 (24/5/01).
58 Interview 5-01 (18/5/01) and 34-99 (12/5/99).
59 Interview 12-01 (21/5/01).
60 Cohen (2001: 127).
61 Cohen (2001: 128).
62 Interview 12-01 (21/5/01).

ticipation in many of the atrocities committed.[63] The term 'civil patrols' was uttered more and more with a negative connotation and people at the local level, especially former civil patrol commanders, were very aware of this fact. It is therefore not strange that their stories were polished and adapted to fit present requirements. Although denunciations and other evidence against Leonel Ogáldez seemed to be quite overwhelming, he still managed to tell a coherent and plausible story about his part in the recent violent history of Joyabaj. Becoming patrol commander in 1983 instead of 1981, being commander of the less violent urban patrols instead of all patrols, and not being allowed into the military compound instead of being treated as one of the boys are all examples of attempts to reduce responsibility.

Lynchings: a legacy of the civil war?
Although the number of politically motivated crimes had lessened considerably from the mid-1990s on, 'normal' organized crime expanded rapidly, concentrating on large-scale bus robberies and kidnappings. The proper authorities seemed unable or unwilling to deal with these situations, to judge from the number of criminals who could bribe their way out of custody or intimidate the police into letting them go. Apart from that, mechanisms of negotiation hardly existed, which meant that people resorted to violent solutions instead of non-violent ones. These mechanisms had broken down during the civil war, when problems were solved by violence, notably by the military and civil patrols. The installation of the patrol structure also militarized local society, creating a culture of intolerance, which continued after the peace agreement was signed. A combination of these factors led to the enormous increase in the number of lynchings in Guatemala since the signing of the peace agreement in 1996.

Joyabaj was one of the first municipalities to experience lynchings, starting with the killing of three young men on 9 August 1996. The lynching started as a bar fight between local ladino bus drivers and some ladino visitors who had come to Joyabaj to buy cattle at the annual cattle fair. During the fight one of the bus drivers was shot and killed by the visitors, who subsequently fled town but were quickly taken into custody by the local police. Several hundred bus drivers and their *ayudantes*, most of which were ladinos, had gathered in front of the police station, forcing them to surrender the three captives. Some onlookers said that the police did not need very much convincing and handed the men over without much ado. Subsequently, they were taken to the basketball court in front of the Catholic Church, where they were beaten with sticks, bricks and machetes.

---

63 See ODHAG (1998), CEH (1999), and bulletins from ODHAG, GAM, and other national and international human rights organizations.

Finally gasoline was poured over them while they were still alive, and they were burnt to death.[64]

MINUGUA verified that former patrol commanders or other former agents of the state were possible instigators of several of the lynchings.[65] However, they do not appear to have been so in the case of this particular lynching in Joyabaj, at least not in their former capacity as state agents. It was a spontaneous action, carried out mainly by friends and fellow-workers of the man killed in the bar fight.[66] Many of them had never even participated in the civil patrols, because they had been too young at the time the patrols in town were still active. Others had not been in Joyabaj during the height of the violence and had lived in the capital or worked as migrants in the United States.

Although *Joyabatecos* talked about the lynching with horror in their voices, many approved of it.[67] In their perception it was the only way to deal with criminals and stop the crime wave. Fear of everyday violence was strengthened by the often one-sided portrayal of crime by many tabloids, which filled their pages with full-colour photos of murdered people and violent street gangs. *Joyabatecos* were afraid to go to the capital and conceived of it as 'a dangerous place'[68] that they had no control over. But they felt they could have or regain some control over local events, albeit in a violent manner such as lynchings. According to them it was quieter and more peaceful in Joyabaj than in surrounding areas because of this particular lynching. They had showed the criminals what they were capable of and were convinced that it was the lynching that kept crime at bay. The lynching was also seen as a signal to the justice apparatus that it had to clean up its act and stop protecting criminals.

According to some of the older ladinos, a corrupt justice system was nothing new, and already existed before the civil war. A notable exception was the dictatorships of Ubico (1931–44), when criminals were punished swiftly and harshly (*mano dura*). Some older ladinos yearn for these times because, in their memory at least, there was no crime then and good people could walk the streets without fear. Nowadays 'people have no respect any more, they are not afraid any more', a former MLN[69] leader remarked. This was very different when Ubico was head of state. 'You noted the change ... there was respect then':[70] respect out of fear of harsh punishment or other authoritarian measures, but respect nevertheless. Several *Joyabatecos* are equally nostalgic about the past when talking about for-

---

64 Diary 26/7/98.
65 MINUGUA (2000a: 2).
66 Interview 24-99 (31/5/99).
67 Diary 13/5/99 and interview 24-99 (31/5/99).
68 Diary 16/9/99.
69 *Movimiento de Liberación Nacional* – Movement of National Liberation.
70 Diary 6/7/99.

mer dictator Ríos Montt, who was president at the height of the violence in 1982–83. A heated conversation with a young ladino man concentrated on the participation of Ríos Montt in the forthcoming elections in November 1999.[71] He was thinking of voting for Ríos Montt because in his time there were no delinquents. 'Only murderers, rapists and robbers are afraid that Ríos Montt will win the elections, not the humble (*humilde*) people.'[72] This statement reflects the idea that people who were killed during the war only had themselves to blame. If someone was punished or killed by the military or civil patrols, that person must have done something wrong. Otherwise their deaths would have been inconceivable. Cohen draws on what Lerner (quoted in Cohen, 2001: 96) calls 'just world thinking'. 'In a just world, suffering is not random; innocent people do not get punished arbitrarily.' That is why 'they deserve to suffer because of what they did, must have done, support doing, or will do one day (if we don't act now)'.[73] This denial of injustice and thus of the victim seems to have been a strong mechanism in *Joyabateco* society, not only during but also after the civil war violence.

In 1998 five more people were burnt alive during three other lynchings in the Joyabaj area. While these lynchings, like the one in 1996, could be categorized as spontaneous reactions of locals to (supposed) criminal acts, the Tunajá[74] lynching in August 1999 was different. Villagers from Tunajá I (Zacualpa) and Tunajá II (Joyabaj) killed five people, two women and three men, who supposedly belonged to a criminal organization called *El Especialista* (The Specialist). *El Especialista* had been responsible for several murders, sexual assaults and robberies in the area of Joyabaj and Zacualpa from 1994 on. Despite various complaints and denunciations by the villagers, the authorities never investigated any of the charges. This attitude was one of the underlying causes of the lynching. What was different about the Tunajá lynching was that it was not a 'spur of the moment' kind of situation, but had been carefully planned and organized.[75] In 1999, MINUGUA recorded 90 lynchings (21 in the Quiché department), of which only 28 were the result of a spontaneous reaction.[76]

It started when villagers captured three men on the evening of 22 August 1999. Police officers managed to persuade the population to go to the local *Juez de Paz* and hand over their evidence and their prisoners. The *Juez de Paz* could not to be found and his secretary incited the assembled crowd to lynch their prisoners. According to MINUGUA, this caused the situation to get out of hand so

---

71 Diary 19/9/99.
72 Diary 19/9/99.
73 Cohen (2001: 96).
74 Community bordering with the municipality of Zacualpa.
75 MINUGUA, *Decimo Informe* (January 2000: 20).
76 MINUGUA, *Decimo Informe* (January 2000: 19-20).

that the following morning two of the three men were killed by strangulation and gunshots, while one was able to escape.[77] After this initial lynching, several groups of armed villagers spread out over the area looking for the remaining members of the gang. Seven men were taken prisoner and brought together in the school in Tunajá. In the meantime a large crowd had gathered in front of the school. The police were unable to control the crowd and that same night three of the prisoners were killed by having their throats slit after machetes were used on them. All five victims had been tortured before being killed, probably to get them to reveal the names of the other gang members.[78] On 1 September 1999, a week after the lynching, local leaders from most of the *cantones* in Zacualpa drew up a statement announcing that the authorities had 15 days to capture the remaining members of *El Especialista*. 'Zacualpa demands justice and a warrant for the arrest of these criminals; and when the *Ministério Público* or the departmental judge do not do their jobs, the people will continue to enforce justice.'[79] According to the statement, the villagers had denounced *El Especialista* activities numerous times to the authorities, who had never bothered to listen. The villagers also decided to set up their own security committees (*Comité* or *Junta de Seguridad*) to protect themselves and their families, if the authorities refused to listen.[80]

Several *Joyabatecos* perceived the Tunajá lynching as an example of an active community taking matters into its own hands after several years of deferring to the proper authorities. You had to do something if the justice system did not work properly.[81] Several indigenous activists were convinced that former patrol members had been involved in the Tunajá lynching, because they had been the ones who went out to search for the remaining gang members. 'Not the auxiliary mayors, but the PAC, the former PAC, because the mayors didn't feel like catching them ... they have no weapons ... It all has its roots in the past.'[82] A connection between lynching and the violent past was also made by several ladinos in town, although they looked at it from a very different perspective. During a Saturday brunch on the patio of ladino friends, the Tunajá lynching was the topic of debate. Someone stated that 'they are all guerrillas over there', referring to the *indígenas* in Zacualpa and a former foreign priest who worked in Zacualpa in the early 1980s, who was rumoured to have crossed over to the side of the guerrillas. In his eyes it was not strange that such 'a savage thing as lynchings'

---

77 MINUGUA, *Suplemento al Undécimo Informe* (September 2000: 29-30).
78 Nuestro Diario, 24/8/99.
79 Prensa Libre, 1/9/99.
80 Prensa Libre, 6/9/99 and 14/9/99.
81 Diary 27/8/99.
82 Interview 28-99 (18/9/99).

happened in that area.[83] He was clearly making a distinction between 'them' and 'us', distancing himself and his fellow ladinos from guerrillas and lynching mobs. Immediately after the man had said this, everybody's eyes went in my direction, trying to assess my reaction to this statement. Some nervous laughs escaped and the matter was laid to a rest, as it was obvious I was not going to react. These kinds of incident occurred frequently when people ventilated 'politically incorrect' opinions about sensitive topics in front of me, while others were listening.

Only a minority condemned lynchings outright. A critical note came from the local Catholic priest, who devoted an entire sermon to the Tunajá lynching. The crux of his message was that 'God had not been able to penetrate into the hearts of people ... they only outwardly believed in God';[84] otherwise people could never have committed such atrocities in Tunajá. The largely female ladino audience, who had come together for mass to celebrate the anniversary of their *comunidad*,[85] sat silently in their chairs during these words, staring with downcast eyes at their folded hands. Some of these same women had openly voiced their approval of the Tunajá lynching.

Former patrollers stir up trouble

Apart from the violent atmosphere created by the increasing number of lynchings and violent actions in general, the continuous rumours and actual threats of former civil patrol leaders to reorganize the patrols also fed growing feelings of insecurity in Guatemala. The first national wave of unrest among former civil patrols in the Guatemalan countryside occurred in early 1997, only months after they had been actually dismantled. A group of former patrol members from Quiché and Huehuetenango met with the Minister of Defence Balconi and FRG Congress members.[86] They complained that they had not received the same economic benefits as the recently demobilized guerrillas of the URNG—'those who destroyed Guatemala'. 'We were victims of the subversive violence, we defended our families, the department and the state, and now they do not compensate us for anything, but to the former insurgents they give money, land, water, electricity, and if possible up to two wives or husbands', former patrollers stated.[87] Such perceptions of former patrollers about ex-guerillas receiving preferential treatment from the state were not uncommon and not perceived as an exaggeration

---

83 Diary 29/8/99.
84 Diary 26/8/99.
85 *Comunidades* are Catholic discussion groups in town, set up by the Catholic priest to involve ladinos in Church activities. They are organized by neighbourhoods and largely cater to older ladino women who are more active in the Catholic Church than young women and men in general.
86 Inforpress, 16 May 1997: 4.
87 Siglo XXI, 9/5/97.

of the situation. Even statements like 'up to two wives or husbands' fitted quite well with the views ladinos had of guerillas. At the beginning of the civil war, ladinos connected to right-wing political groups like the MLN had been afraid of losing their houses, land and even wives to the guerillas. Former patrollers used this same rhetoric after the end of the civil war when accusing the former guerrillas.

Most FRG politicians were sympathetic to the demands of former patrollers and gave them the opportunity to vent their problems. One FRG Congress member stated in a newspaper article that 'It is necessary that the Guatemala state does something for these Guatemalans who were active in the patrols, because they did not sell themselves nor gave themselves away to the enemy, but kept their loyalty'.[88] Others added that 'They [former civil patrollers] were also victims of the violence but now nobody takes them into account'.[89] However, words of support were not considered sufficient, and to underline their demands former patrollers occupied the installations of Basic Resources Petroleum near Chiséc (Alta Verapaz) and La Libertad (Petén) in July and again in August 1997. They repeated their claims for financial compensation for their years of service in the patrols. The government refused to negotiate because, it claimed, participation in the patrols had always been voluntary and no labour contract involving compensation had ever existed.[90]

Every move or mention of the activities of former patrollers was enough to stir up emotions and fuel a lively debate about their possible reorganization. The unrest increased when the 1999 elections drew near. Contacts between FRG politicians and former patrol leaders were viewed with renewed suspicion, and the FRG was accused of instructing former patrol leaders to vote in their favour.[91] Although hard evidence of such activity was absent, the discussions about the mere possibility hinted at the importance that was attributed to former patrol structures. A few months before the elections, the FRG announced that it was planning to form local civilian security committees throughout the country to monitor criminal activity. Many human rights organizations reacted fiercely to this proposal, seeing it as a reactivation of the former patrol structure.[92] The FRG denied such intentions during its campaign visits throughout the country.

Demands for financial compensation have resurfaced in recent months (June–September 2002), when former civil patrols started reorganizing themselves all over Guatemala, following the example of former patrollers in the

---

88 Siglo XXI, 8/5/97.
89 El Periódico, 6/10/98.
90 Cerigua Weekly Briefs, 3 July 1997, no. 26.
91 El Periódico, 6/10/98.
92 GNIB (Guatemalan News and Information Bureau), 18 November 1999.

Petén.[93] A huge debate started to enfold, with the FRG government willing to agree to the demands made by the former patrollers, while human rights organizations accused the government of exploiting the situation in view of the coming elections. Human rights organizations also criticized possible financial compensation for patrollers because of their prominent role in many of the atrocities committed. According to the Guatemalan human rights organization CALDH,[94] 'Intimidation, torture, disappearances and massacres cannot be considered a dignified and remunerative job'.[95]

Local rumours: patrols reorganizing

The political circus also descended upon Joyabaj when the FRG arrived to campaign in September 1999. A stage was built on the basketball field in the centre of town, on which sat the candidates for president and vice-president and other FRG dignitaries. The *plaza* in front of the stage was crowded, especially with indigenous people. The atmosphere was one of 'wait and see', with people standing quietly around with their arms crossed. There was little *ánimo* (energy), as people in Joyabaj would say. The first to give a speech was former General Ríos Montt, a very passionate speaker. Although dressed casually in civilian clothes, he spoke like a retired general, spitting out his words. After only a few sentences of introduction he directly confronted the issue of civil patrols. He said some people were afraid that the FRG was going to win the elections, because that would mean a return of the civil patrols. According to Ríos Montt that was 'an outright lie'.[96] But at the end of his speech he returned to the topic, explaining that the FRG was going to combat delinquency by organizing *Juntas Locales* in the communities. They were to act like neighbourhood watches. These contradictory statements did little to calm local feelings of insecurity and only added fuel to the rumours going around about patrols reorganizing.

These rumours had already become reality in Joyabaj a few weeks before the visit of the FRG campaigners. In early September the local priest of the Catholic Church was visited by a group of people from the indigenous community of La Cruz.[97] They complained that in their community former patrol commanders were reorganizing the patrols and had called on them to participate. When they refused to do so, the former commanders threatened to put their names on a blacklist, which would be turned over to ... nobody knew to whom. But it was an

---

93 Prensa Libre, 10/7/02; 11/7/02; 22/7/02; 6/8/02; 12/8/02 (almost daily coverage during the months of July and August 2002).
94 CALDH - *Centro de Acción Legal para los Derechos Humanos* (Centre for Human Rights Legal Action).
95 Prensa Libre, 13/7/02. See also Prensa Libre, 9/8/02; 18/8/02.
96 Diary 25/9/99.
97 This is a fictional name, to protect its inhabitants and the people providing the information.

photo 17. *Ríos Montt, with a white hat in his hand, holding a speech in Joyabaj during a visit of the FRG election campaign (author, 1999)*

old and familiar way to intimidate people into obedience. The group who visited the local priest, however, was determined not to participate. They said they had read the REMHI report,[98] and they were convinced that those times should never return.[99]

While this denunciation was being made, the patrols were already on active duty in the indigenous community of La Cruz, situated in the rural area north of Joyabaj. Apparently auxiliary mayors and several people from Catholic Action participated in these reactivated patrols and, in some cases, had accepted leading positions. The priest decided not to pass the information on to the *Ministério Público*, because he was afraid that police interference would lead to repercussions within the community. He decided to address the issue indirectly during the weekly meeting of all *Directivos* of Catholic Action in Joyabaj. He held a general meeting in which he mentioned that an unidentified group of Catholic Action *Directivos* was participating in the reorganization of civil patrols in their communities. The priest explained that this was not the proper way to solve problems in the communities, thereby also giving credence to the rumours of attempted lynchings in the area. He got no response from the La Cruz *Directivos*, who

---

98 A summary of the REMHI report, in the local languages, had been distributed among Catholic Action groups throughout the countryside.
99 Diary 16/9/99.

kept their eyes glued to the floor during the entire speech.[100] Several indigenous activists living in communities north of Joyabaj corroborated the story and added that increased violence in the area of La Cruz was one of the main reasons for the patrols to be reorganized. Some of them were really scared when they heard about the revitalized patrols. 'Who knows if they will start committing massacres ... because they have guns ... what will happen next if something like Tunajá happens?'[101]

Another wave of unrest hit Joyabaj early 2000, when it was announced that *Comités Junta de Seguridad Local* were to be set up to combat local crime. Auxiliary mayors and *Comités Pro-mejoramiento* were to give form to these new organizations. The complaint of many *Joyabatecos* was that they did not really know what the objectives of this initiative were and where it originated. They were afraid they would be forced to participate, just as they had been forced into the civil patrols.[102] According to government officials and the UN, the formation of *Juntas Locales* had nothing to do with a revitalization of civil patrols. It was the result of cooperation between the United Nations Development Program (UNDP) and the *Ministério de Gobernación*. Representatives of different sectors of local society were to participate in the *Junta Local*, together with the mayor, the auxiliary mayors and the chief of police. The aim was to improve communication between the National Police and civil society, thereby implementing part of the peace agreements.[103] Many human rights organizations and local communities, however, initially saw this initiative as an attempt to remilitarize the rural areas and agitated fiercely against it.[104] After this initial outburst criticism died down, giving room for local *Juntas* to be set up without much media attention, but also without much enthusiasm. A *Junta* was installed also in Joyabaj, although nobody really knew what it was about and what it was supposed to do. There was no indication that former civil patrollers tried to re-establish their lost authority by way of participation in *Juntas Locales*.

Political space opening up

The preceding sections paint a rather gloomy picture of Joyabaj after the dismantling of the civil defence patrols. The number of violent incidents increased, and lynchings became a recurring phenomenon, hardly dealt with by the proper authorities such as the local national police or the *Juez de Paz*. Although civil patrols were dismantled, this did not mean that their positions of power were

---

100 Diary 16/9/99.
101 Interview 28-99 (18/9/99).
102 Cerigua, March 2000 (http://.eecs.umich.edu/~parv/harbury/archive/2000/20000308.html).
103 PNUD (1999: 1).
104 See Prensa Libre 16/5/00; Prensa Libre 29/5/00; Cerigua Weekly Briefs, May 2000.

automatically weakened. Some leaders were still perceived as individuals to be reckoned with. At the same time information on human rights abuses by local patrollers and military commissioners was being brought to the fore by truth commissions, and evidence was gathered against some of the patrol leaders by way of testimonies and the exhumation of mass graves. During this volatile post-conflict period, several spaces opened up at the local level where people could vent their opinions or criticism, providing an outlet for the local tensions that had been building up. This did not happen overnight, but was the result of gradual changes since 1985, when the first democratic elections were held. In addition, people were looking for alternative ways to rebuild their lives or attain local power and prestige. Local politics and economic opportunities through migration were two important arenas in which substantial changes were taking place.

The political arena had opened up considerably, especially since the elections of 1995. In that year a large number of local Civic Committees (*Comités Cívicos*)[105] participated in the municipal elections, as well as the traditional political parties of the right, centre and moderate left. Civic Committees were political groups operating at the municipal level, organized mostly around local themes, with no connection whatsoever to national political parties. The first Civic Committees were formed during the 1985 elections as a result of changes in the *Ley Electoral y de Partidos Políticos* (Decree 1-85).[106] Not only did these Civic Committees offer an alternative to traditional party politics, they also gave people from different walks of life the possibility to enter local politics.

The political arena in Joyabaj had already been undergoing profound change since the late 1970s, when the left-wing DCG participated in the elections and challenged the rule of right-wing parties like the MLN. The ensuing civil war ended the ascent of the DCG, when government forces targeted many of its leaders and other left-wing political activists. Civic Committees did not participate in municipal elections in Joyabaj until 1995, when the Civic Committee *Palo Volador* won convincingly. It was primarily a ladino party, with ladino candidates on their list, some of whom had been active in right-wing political parties in the 1960s and 1970s.[107] Most Civic Committees, however, were placed in the centre or even the centre-left of the political spectrum. Of course, radical changes in political preference are nothing new in Guatemalan politics and obviously do not confine themselves to the national level.

---

105 The first Civic Committees in Guatemala were set up during the 1985 elections, when 48 presented candidates for local mayor. In 1991 this number had risen to 85, while in the 1995 elections a total of 159 Civic Committees participated in the municipal elections (Ochoa García, Sánchez and Pacay Cú, 1995: 41).
106 Ochoa García, Sánchez and Pacay Cú (1995: 23).
107 The candidate for major had been *concejal* in 1964 and mayor in 1966, both times for the right-wing MLN. *Libro de Actas*, acta 158 (6/8/64) and acta 224 (15/6/66).

The Civic Committee Palo Volador was named after an indigenous dance carrying the same name (meaning 'Flying Pole'), which is performed during on August 15, the yearly celebration of the patron saint of Joyabaj, the *Virgen del Tránsito* (Day of Assumption). A tree 35 meters high is placed on the market square, after which indigenous men dressed as monkeys (*micos*) and archangels fly down while attached to ropes. Marimba music accompanies the dance, which goes on for hours.[108] Originally this dance and the elaborate ceremonies surrounding it were a completely indigenous affair carried out by *cofrades*[109] and the *Alcaldía Indígena*.[110] In 1998, however, for the first time the ladino municipality offered to help, and supplied a municipal truck to transport the tree from the mountain to the market place, where it was also used to lift it. Normally, hundreds of indigenous men were involved in the process, but in 1998 'mechanization made its entry',[111] a young ladino man explained while we were watching the spectacle from a safe distance. Ladino municipal officers were hovering around the pole, trying to run the show. He said, in a neutral voice, 'it is a sign that indigenous *costumbres* are disappearing. Young indigenous men nowadays do not want to walk around in white trousers, *moral* and straw hat, but prefer sneakers, baseball cap and rucksack'.[112] Others perceived ladino interference as an example not so much of disappearing indigenous costumes but of the waning authority of the *Alcaldía Indígena* and the *cofrades*. In this view, indigenous authority was being co-opted by a ladino municipality. This was, of course, nothing new. During the 1960s and 1970s, local ladino politicians also used indigenous authorities and symbols to get re-elected and appease their indigenous constituencies. This practice did not seem to have changed much as a result of the civil war violence. Apart from ladino officials, soldiers from the local military base were also present during the erecting of the *Palo Volador*, not exactly knowing what to do.

Placed in this context, the use of the name '*Palo Volador*' for a political party that is almost exclusively ladino can be seen as a modern way of ladinos co-opting indigenous culture. The use of such a symbolic name would possibly appeal to the indigenous majority of *Joyabatecos*, many of whom normally stayed away from the ballot boxes. This double standard among ladinos is often complex and puzzling. On the one hand many ladinos in Joyabaj still see indigenous people as second-class citizens, as possible guerrillas and subversives or left-wing activists, while on the other hand indigenous symbols and names are used by these same ladinos to express the cultural identity and uniqueness of Joyabaj.

---

108 See García Escobar (1989) for a detailed description of the dance of the *Palo Volador* in Joyabaj.
109 Indigenous brotherhoods.
110 Office of the indigenous mayors.
111 Diary 21/6/98.
112 Interview 2-98 (21/6/98).

photo 18. *Soldiers from the local military base were also present when the Palo Volador was put up, not exactly knowing what to do (author, 1998)*

Water, a source of municipal conflicts

Expectations were high after the Civic Committee *Palo Volador* won the municipal elections. As always, the various parties had made many promises during the election campaign. One of the items high on the campaign agenda of *Palo Volador* had been the improvement of the drinking-water system (*agua potable*) in the town of Joyabaj. Although a water project[113] was initiated almost two years after *Palo Volador*'s victory, discontent about the water issue among *Joyabatecos* was widespread and became the focal point of local discord with the municipality. The ladino population in particular protested actively against the water project of the municipality and had set up a water committee to monitor the mayor's activities in that area. Just before the water project was finished, the municipality wanted to install water meters in all houses with running water, and people were to pay for their water. The people protested against this municipal decision because, according to them, it was not clean water from a closed mountain source. The water came from an open river that was polluted, which they tried to prove with video recordings of the water source. The video was shown publicly and featured a dead pig, empty plastic bags of pesticides and other waste at the entrance of the water pipelines.[114]

Many people were furious after seeing the video, while a minority was convinced that the video footage had been staged. Some refrained from commenting at all. They did not see the video, nor wanted to see it. They did not even want to hear about it. An older ladino teacher who had returned to Joyabaj only recently after having fled the violence said 'I do not want to get mixed up in all these problems ... like this video about the water. I do not want problems ... I have to live with these people'.[115] The words 'I do not want any problems' recurred during many of the interviews, during discussions on a variety of topics. It was as if people believed that they could prevent problems, like the violent civil war, by not getting mixed up in things and not offering an opinion on topics. When people did offer their point of view they were often very careful with their words and often lowered their voices.

Authorities at the departmental level noticed the local water conflict and were quick to calm a potentially explosive situation. Since 1995, the number of municipal conflicts had increased in the Guatemalan countryside, some of which had already escalated into violence.[116] The departmental *Gobernador* wanted to prevent this from happening in Joyabaj and organized a meeting during

---

113 This project was named *Cumbre Tzajmá,* after the area in which the water sources originated (Lansdale and Santora, 1998).
114 Diary 4/7/99 and 5/7/99.
115 Diary 5/7/99.
116 See Flores Alvarado (1996) and FUNCEDE (1997).

which the water committee, regional authorities and municipal officials were present.[117] After the meeting the air was cleared somewhat, and the mayor eventually dropped all charges of harassment by the water committee. The conflict did not escalate any further.

It is interesting to look at a second conflict over water that broke out only weeks after the first one, this time involving indigenous authorities. It concerned a water-source near the old swimming pool, which belonged to the indigenous community but had presumably been sold by the ladino municipality without permission. The mayor was the culprit in this version, which was mainly told by indigenous people. A second version of the story was told by ladinos, who explained that the mayor only wanted to restore the municipal swimming pool. Ladinos continued their story to say that it was obvious that the *indígenas* did not want any development and progress, and that they blocked every initiative of the municipality. A small ladino minority, however, had another view on the matter and interpreted the problems surrounding the water-source as a clear example of a ladino population that was afraid of losing the little power it still had.[118]

The Joyabaj ladinos had attacked the same ladino mayor only weeks before on the first water issue. This second water dispute, however, involved indigenous authorities, causing a 'closing of ladino ranks', according to a former priest.[119] In such a situation, it did not matter whether the ladino mayor did a good job or not. He was, after all, a ladino and that was reason enough for the ladino minority in Joyabaj to back him against the indigenous authorities. 'God beware if we would have another indigenous mayor', as one young ladino said.[120] Divisions due to a conflict *within* a group (be it an ethnic, political or religious group) change when a third, outside party is brought in. In general, inter-group conflicts override intra-group conflicts. When the conflict over water between *indígenas* and ladinos surfaced, already existing conflicts over water among ladinos themselves were set aside and the ladino ranks closed in the face of the indigenous complaints.

1999 elections: former guerrillas campaigning

The 1999 elections also brought a broadening of political space for political parties and individuals. Former guerrillas were able to organize themselves into legitimate political parties, and individuals with connections to the left occupied positions as candidates for mayor. Shortly after the Peace Accords were signed in 1996, the former guerrillas of the URNG transformed their organization into a

---

117 Diary 13/7/99.
118 Diary 17/5/99.
119 Diary 17/5/99.
120 Diary 17/5/99.

legitimate political party. They formed a coalition (ANN - *Alianza Nueva Nación*)[121] to participate in the 1999 elections.[122] In July 1999, only four months before the elections, one political party left the ANN coalition after one of many disputes over candidacies and continued to participate in the elections as an independent party.[123] The remaining parties continued as a coalition, but could no longer use the ANN name and symbols. They campaigned under the name URNG/DIA, which in some cases caused problems for local political activists. URNG, being the former guerrilla organization, was not a very neutral name for many people in Joyabaj.

The URNG/DIA coalition participated in Joyabaj during the 1999 elections, presenting Felipe Natareno as its local candidate for mayor. He was the same man who had been elected DCG mayor in 1978 and who had to flee Joyabaj in 1981 because his life was threatened.[124] This was another example of presenting older candidates with political experience, as the Civic Committee *Palo Volador* had done during the 1995 elections. The candidacy of Felipe Natareno was not uncontested among ladinos, some of whom were convinced that the guerrillas had been the cause of all trouble in the past: a view shared by former MLN activists as well as other right-wing groups. One morning at the breakfast table a former ladino teacher and liberal political activist confided to me that he sincerely hoped that Felipe Natareno would not become mayor, because he had been responsible for much of the violence in the 1980s. His wife agreed with his opinion, adding that 'Felipe reminds me of the dark days ... when he was a *guerrillero*'.[125] They considered him to be someone who mainly concerned himself with the indigenous part of the population, going out into the communities to campaign and making promises he would not be able to keep. Others were not very happy with the fact that the majority of the proposed council members of Felipe Natareno were indigenous. It made matters worse that one of them was an indigenous woman who could not read or write and spoke only *K'iche'*. She was also the local coordinator of the widow's organization, and in the eyes of many ladinos thus connected with the guerrillas and 'human rights'.

---

121 Alliance of the New Nation.
122 The URNG formed a coalition together with DIA, UNID and FDNG. DIA (*Desarrollo Integral Auténtico* – Integral Authentic Develpment) was organized in 1993 by several NGOs working on human rights issues. UNID (*Unidad de Izquierda Democrática* – Unity of the Democratic Left) was not a political party, but consisted of left-wing intellectuals and people formerly belonging to the URNG. FDNG (*Frente Democrático Nueva Guatemala*) was founded in 1995 by several popular and syndicalist organizations. Conservative groups within Guatemalan society accused the FDNG of being just an extension of former guerrilla groups.
123 The FDNG left and continued to participate in the elections as an independent party (Bornschein, 2000: 18-23).
124 See Chapter 3.
125 Diary 19/9/99.

The URNG/DIA coalition did not have an easy task campaigning under the URNG banner in Joyabaj. Before the coalition started to disintegrate, campaigners were glad they could use the ANN banner and symbol and refrain from mentioning the URNG openly. But now they were forced to campaign as the URNG, a name that triggered so many different emotions. In some communities, campaigners had to clarify what the URNG was all about, because for years locals had been hearing horror stories from the military. They had also been told that guerrilla organizers were outsiders, who had come to the indigenous communities to recruit people. Campaigners were therefore frequently asked if they themselves were from Joyabaj and 'who their parents and grandparents were'. They had to make clear that they were 'people who could be trusted' *(gente de confianza)*, and not outside left-wing political activists.[126] Although political space had indeed opened up, and former guerrillas were actually campaigning for the coming elections, in most communities people kept very quiet during campaign speeches, especially after the URNG name was mentioned. For example, in an indigenous community south of Joyabaj 'everybody was dead quiet'.[127] After the speech nobody had any questions and, when Felipe Natareno thanked the people for coming, only one man stood up and said 'thanks'. The others only murmured 'affirmative' and left quietly. Three days later some of these same people came to the house of Felipe Natareno and asked if they could have a private conference with him. During this meeting they explained that they had liked his speech very much and that they would definitely support him. They had not been able to speak freely during the open meeting in their community because 'other people could have made trouble for us afterwards'.[128] In many communities, people were still afraid to openly voice their opinion on certain matters, an action that would have had fierce repercussions during *La Violencia*.

Natareno and the URNG were quite popular among indigenous political activists. The Conavigua widows in particular were actively campaigning for the DIA/URNG coalition, because their coordinator was one of the proposed council members. About the work of Conavigua the coordinator explained that '[W]e are very much involved in politics now, because if you don't, nothing will change and nothing will happen ... we are struggling to get into the *muni*, so that someone will be there who will work for the *indígenas* and who will keep his promises'.[129] A former member of Catholic Action told the following story. 'Look, in the first place I am helping [the ANN] with a little money. And I would like it if they would win, because I more or less like their ideology ... the other thing is that

---

126 Interview 17-99 (14/8/99).
127 Interview 23-99 (1/9/99).
128 Interview 23-99 (1/9/99).
129 Interview 15-99 (31/7/99).

Don Felipe is a very good friend of mine, and that is why I am helping, and because the leader of this party is also a friend ... and he is kind of a family member ... also the candidate for *diputado* is related to me.'[130] Family ties and friendship obviously played an important role in this man's opinion of the URNG, besides the fact that he was sympathetic to its ideas and activities. Elections in Guatemala are, on the whole, very person-oriented rather than party-oriented, especially at the local level. This also influenced voting behaviour in Joyabaj, because several ladinos told Felipe Natareno that they ' ... did not like his party, but they liked him as a person'. They said they 'would leave politics out of it' and vote for him as a person.[131]

In the 1999 elections for mayor, the DIA/URNG coalition in Joyabaj came second, with 21 per cent of the votes, after the PAN (*Partido de Avanzada Nacional*)[132] candidate (46 per cent), relegating the FRG candidate to third place (18 per cent).[133] Coming second was in itself a remarkable achievement, if we bear in mind the fact that only a few years earlier the accusation of belonging to the URNG could cost a person his or her life. Many *Joyabatecos* commented on the fact that Felipe Natareno, as URNG candidate, was able to participate in a local election conference together with the other local candidates for mayor. There was 'more space for these kinds of things'.[134] The opening up of such a space was only a first step and had to be filled by people willing to take certain risks.

In general, *Joyabatecos* painted a very gloomy picture of recent political leadership. The last two mayors were considered to have brought them nothing but trouble, and there was no one around able to clean up the mess. Some ladinos complained that, although *Joyabatecos* were disappointed with local politics, they hesitated to take any initiative themselves against a badly functioning municipality.[135] For example, the protests against municipal officials in the mid-1990s were organized by people who worked and lived in Joyabaj but had been born and raised elsewhere.[136] A former priest in Joyabaj considered Guatemala to be 'a decapitated country, which will take a long time to recuperate'.[137] For example, many indigenous leaders had been killed in the 1980s by military or paramilitary violence. People from Chorraxaj, Patzulá and Xeabaj, who had been

---

130 Interview 28-99 (18/9/99).
131 Interview 22-99 (30/7/99).
132 Party of National Advancement, a neo-liberal party with strong ties to the evangelicals.
133 Election results available at: www.tse.org.gt/elecciones 99/Primera Vuelta Elecciones 99/Archivos Acrobat/Corporaciones [2/7/02].
134 Interview 28-99 (18/9/99).
135 Interview 14-98 (19/6/98).
136 Interview 17-98 (9/8/98).
137 Interview 25-99 (30/5/99).

trained by Catholic Action and Alianza (a Guatemalan NGO) as local *animadores* or social workers, had had their names featuring prominently on the blacklist and were the first to be killed during the war.[138] According to many *Joyabatecos*, new leaders are needed, and spaces should be created for people to develop as leaders. However, young people nowadays have little '*formación* [training] and experience', according to a former EGP combatant.[139] They have had only limited opportunity to learn from elders, many of whom were killed or had fled. Those who stayed behind watched the growing activities from human rights activists and left-wing politicians from the sidelines, without actually participating. People did not want to become too involved, because it was considered too risky. This attitude still prevailed when I was carried out this research.

Consulta Popular: visible polarization

Not only the candidacy of Felipe Natareno for the URNG caused unrest among many ladinos. Feelings of mutual distrust and fear between ladinos and indigenous groups in Joyabaj also resurfaced during the *Consulta Popular* in May 1999. During this popular referendum people had to vote on a package of 47 reforms to the Guatemalan constitution. The reforms covered important issues of the peace agreements, such as reform of the military, judicial reform and recognition of Guatemala as a multiracial, multilingual and multicultural state. A heated debated unfolded at the national level, as well as the local level, between 'yes' an 'no' voters. National opponents of the referendum (the 'no' voters) especially targeted recognition of indigenous languages and rights in different areas and denounced it as 'unnecessary, dividing, conflictive and racist, because it is based on race'.[140] Supporters of the referendum tried to counter the misinformation that was spread by the opposition, without success. Only 18 per cent of the eligible voters participated, of which a majority rejected the reforms with a little over 55 per cent of the vote.[141] A clear division in voting behaviour could be detected between the indigenous departments, where the majority voted 'yes', and the departments where ladinos were in the majority, which voted 'no'.[142]

In Joyabaj, discussions about the proposed reforms in the *Consulta Popular* were multiple and often heated. Especially the ladino minority felt personally attacked by some of the reforms, and many ladino prejudices against the indigenous majority resurfaced. During a Sunday family dinner, a prominent ladino

---

138 See Chapter 3 for a detailed analysis of local leadership in the rural areas of Joyabaj. Chorraxaj is used as a case study.
139 Interview 36-99 (19/8/99). EGP (*Ejército Guatemalteco de los Pobres*) was one of the guerrilla organizations active in the south of Quiché.
140 Prensa Libre, 15/5/99.
141 Prensa Libre, 17/5/99. Voting results for the Consulta Popular in Joyabaj were not available.
142 Arnson (1999: 9).

family discussed their reasons for voting against the referendum. Their criticism centred mainly on the recognition of indigenous languages. The head of the household thought it preposterous that all 24 indigenous languages should be recognized. According to him this would mean that everything had to be translated into 24 languages. 'How are they going to do that with street names? Put 24 translations below each other?', he laughed.[143] His son, a teacher, agreed with him, adding that he was afraid he would have to learn *K'iche'* and perhaps even all other indigenous languages just to be able to keep teaching. Many ladinos who teach in indigenous communities in the rural areas of Joyabaj do not speak *K'iche'*, and teach only in Spanish. The whole family was convinced that the indigenous people were not interested in learning their own language, but wanted only to learn Spanish, 'The only way to develop themselves'.[144] Another difficult issue was the reform recognizing indigenous spirituality and access to religious places, like mountains or caves. Ladinos thought they might lose land or even their church buildings. Another highly sensitive issue among *Joyabateco* ladinos was the proposed recognition and partial incorporation of *derecho consuetudinario*, or indigenous customary law, into the existing judicial system. According to local ladinos this meant that they, as ladinos, were going to be tried under indigenous law. This was of course totally unacceptable.

These misconceptions about what the reforms really entailed were widespread among ladinos in Joyabaj, and were reinforced by the propaganda machine of the opposition. To counter these 'unfounded fears', a large advertisement was placed in the newspapers two days before the referendum. In ten points, the groups in favour of the referendum (the 'yes' voters) tried to counter some of the most common misconceptions about the referendum, including those mentioned at the Sunday dinner table.[145] Such advertisements, however, reached only a tiny minority of the Guatemalan population, given that a large percentage cannot read. The ones who can read often do not read 'quality' newspapers like *Prensa Libre*, which is most often used to carry such advertisements. In Joyabaj, around 30 copies of this paper were distributed on a daily basis to a population of around 50,000.

Although most ladinos in Joyabaj were happy with the referendum results, a radio speech by former guerrilla leader Pablo Monsanto still caused some unrest a few days after the elections. Monsanto had supported the 'yes' vote and said that once again the indigenous people had been denied their rights. If it was impossible to get these rights by legal means, then illegal means were necessary.

---

143 Diary 12/5/99.
144 Diary 12/5/99.
145 Prensa Libre, 14/5/99.

Some ladinos interpreted his words as a 'threat to start another civil war'.[146] Of course not all ladinos were opposed to the referendum, and some Catholic Church activists and left-wing politicians supported the 'yes' vote. Supporters of the referendum, under whom many indigenous people who were actively involved in campaigning for left-wing political parties for the coming presidential elections in November 1999, perceived the outcome of the referendum as a political defeat. A Conavigua activist explained: 'We demanded that those things [violence] would not come back any more ... that is why we wanted "yes" to win. Because if "yes" would win, we could have asked for our rights ... but now it all stays the same.'[147] At the national level, the outcome of the referendum was perceived as a setback for the peace process and democratization in general. The changes to the constitution were not approved and thus part of the peace agreements could not be implemented. Supporters of the peace process tried to understand what had happened and suggested that the peace agreements were never conceived as something that concerned the people. Many Guatemalans never felt any connection with the peace agreements and did not see their own situation improve after the signing of the final Peace Accords in December 1996.

These feelings could be detected also among ladinos and indigenous people in Joyabaj. An indigenous member of Catholic Action explained that nobody really knew what the *Consulta* was about. 'The whole peace process is something of a small group of leaders, who decided one day to stop fighting and make peace. We knew nothing. And now, all of a sudden, they come to us to ask what we think.'[148] Not only were ladinos suspicious about the referendum and the peace process in general; indigenous people also had their doubts, yet for very different reasons. According to an indigenous politician and former guerrilla combatant, 'the peace accord is just a paper accord. Nothing much has changed ... there is no participation'.[149] As an afterthought he added that there was, however, more freedom now: freedom to come and go as you like, freedom to organize and freedom to vote in a referendum. In that respect things had changed somewhat.

A small ladino vendor of maize and beans explained the whole peace process in his own words. He compared it with two sugar sellers on the market. They both agreed to sell sugar for a 150 *Quetzales* per *quintal*. After a short while one of them dropped the price to 140 *Quetzales*. 'So what is the use of agreeing on a set price at the beginning, if people do not keep their end of the bargain. It is the same with the agreements; so many have been signed, but nobody is really wil-

---

146 Diary 20/5/99.
147 Interview 26-99 (21/8/99).
148 Diary 27/5/99.
149 Interview 17-99 (14/8/99).

ling to work for them. So why bother in the first place to sign the accords?'[150] This was also the general attitude in Joyabaj towards the *Consulta* and the 1999 presidential elections, and probably one of the main reasons for the growing abstentionism amongst the voters.

Changing economic power relations

Local politics were not the only way people could ascend the social ladder towards local power and prominence. Economic power relations were another aspect of local community life that had changed markedly as a result of the violence of the 1980s, and new paths towards the accumulation of wealth had opened up. First of all, several of the wealthier ladino families, especially those who owned the largest shops, had left town in the early 1980s after repeated intimidation by guerrilla groups. Most of them never returned and sold their belongings in Joyabaj. Their departure not only meant more space for other shop owners, but also signified the end of ladino monopoly over commercial activities.

Towards the end of the 1990s, economic activity in Joyabaj was booming and the number of shops and local bus companies had multiplied enormously. The transportation business stayed primarily in the hands of local ladino families, while the stores were owned both by ladinos and by *indígenas*. Many indigenous families from the rural areas, who had come to live in town during the violence, started their own businesses. Many of their stores, however, remained small and marginal compared with those of some of the more prosperous ladino traders. A notable exception was the enormous Sunday market in the town square, currently spilling over into the park because of a lack of space. Market days used to be confined to Thursday and Sunday, with people from the rural areas coming to sell a few apples or some corn on a piece of cloth. There were hardly any stalls, and they were definitely not of a permanent nature. Nowadays, the weekly market starts on Wednesday evening and takes permanent possession of the town square and park until Sunday evening. Stalls are semi-permanent and people sometimes live in makeshift tents to protect their wares and avoid long trips back to their communities. The market vendors are almost without exception indigenous, although some of them are large traders from other municipalities.

Increased economic activity was largely the result of the remittances send back by temporary migrants working in the capital, Mexico and the United States. Migration, especially to the United States, has become an important alternative avenue towards attaining local wealth and also status. Government data estimate total remittances at $500 million a year, close to 25 per cent of

---

150 Interview 3-98 (17/7/98).

Guatemala's total export earnings. Remittances are the second most important source of foreign currency after the export of coffee, followed by tourism and the export of textile and sugar.[151] Approximately 20 per cent of the *Joyabatecos* (ladino and *indígena*), according to estimates of local municipal and bank officials, live and work in the United States, sending money to their families.[152] Postal and telephone needs have changed dramatically and the number of private delivery enterprises and international telephone booths has risen sharply. On a Sunday morning the queue in front of King Express, the largest postal service in Joyabaj, is enormous and people have to wait hours before receiving their correspondence and money orders from family in the United States. The enormous influx of American dollars into Joyabaj is also apparent from the amount of construction going on. Two- and three-storey houses are no longer the exception in a village where all buildings, except the church and the town hall, used to be one-storey. Mud walls, wooden beams and tiled roofs have given way to concrete and cement.

Not everybody is happy with the town's changed appearance, and some returnees have a hard time adjusting. Others are critical of the prosperity of some of the indigenous communities, where a majority of the population has left for the United States. Some ladinos think it not proper that the *indígenas* are also building large houses and driving around in big four-wheel drives. They are afraid it will generate problems in the future, because 'when they [*indígenas*] get used to such a life, maybe they will make trouble later on'.[153] The fact that economic power relations have changed in Joyabaj since the civil war, whereby the indigenous majority has taken over a considerable part of the local economy, does not seem to sit well with the ladino minority, which has seen its economic power diminishing since the beginning of the 1980s. The *'classe media'*, consisting mainly of ladinos, feels itself pushed out of business by a young indigenous generation that has been earning money in the United States. It is still to early to tell whether these changes in economic relations will translate themselves into changes in local power relations.

Human rights: a tainted concept
It is instructive to take a closer look at the concept of human rights, because it also reveals some of the ethnic tensions that existed and still exist in Joyabaj between ladinos and *indígenas*. During the 1990s, not everybody felt confident enough to present their case at one of the human rights offices, and there was a

---
151 Prensa Libre, 14/9/00.
152 Diary 22/6/98.
153 Diary 8/5/99.

marked difference between ladino and *indígena* attitudes towards human rights organizations like MINUGUA and PDH. Between 1989 and 1999 most denunciations were made by indigenous people, partly because they are a majority in the area and partly because they suffered most of the consequences of civil patrol violence. Ladinos presented only a few cases, which mostly concerned disputes with the local municipality.

The majority of the ladinos in Joyabaj were not very positive about the work of organizations like PDH and MINUGUA. They felt and often still feel that human rights is an 'indigenous thing' (*cosa de indio*) that has little or nothing to do with the ladinos (*no es cosa de nosotros*). It was seen as an instrument of the indigenous people which they used against the ladinos to better themselves or get back at the ladinos. For example, an older ladino man from a distinguished family explained that he was forced to sell part of his land north of Joyabaj to some of his former rancheros. They had threatened to go to the PDH office to denounce him and make trouble for his family. Although they did not say which complaint they were going to file, the threat was enough to persuade the ladino to sell his land.[154] Another young ladino man, economically very well-off, patiently explained his philosophical view on human rights while standing in front of his large shop. 'The doctrine of human rights came from outside [Guatemala] and did a lot of bad things ... They taught them [the indigenous people] that they had human rights, and now they think that they are the only ones that have human rights.'[155] This black-and-white view of human rights organizations is widespread among *Joyabateco* ladinos, right up to the use of the word 'doctrine'. In the late 1970s and early 1980s this word was used by anti-communists when talking about 'the doctrine of communism', which also came from the 'outside' and was also 'bad'. A clear line was drawn between 'us' (ladinos) and 'them' (*indígenas*), although many of the denunciations mentioned indigenous civil patrol commanders as the perpetrators. The situation was not as straightforward as several ladinos like to present it.

Some ladinos have a more positive attitude towards the human rights organizations and see them as a necessary step towards democratizing Guatemala. They do not, however, easily take the step of presenting human rights abuses to these organizations. Ladinos in Joyabaj perceive themselves as being much too divided to act as a group. Although the idea of taking a trip to the PDH office is talked about, they hardly ever actually travel to Santa Cruz to present a case. In the eyes of a ladino woman, 'indigenous people are much better organized and they undertake action together if something is not of their liking'.[156]

---

154 Interview 2-98 (21/6/98).
155 Diary 4/10/99.
156 Diary 14/5/99.

Clearly, 'human rights' was a controversial term and put on the same level as words like 'guerrilla', 'subversive', or even 'communist'. Although nowadays this comparison does not have the same consequences as it would have had in the early 1980s, only a few years ago people in Joyabaj were afraid to even use the term 'human rights'. For example, a former NGO worker in Joyabaj explained that in 1994 he was actually accused of doing something 'with human rights'. At that time they were training mental health promoters, and during their training they had talked about the right to life, the right to a teacher and the right to have a roof over one's head. But they had, intentionally so, not once used the words 'human rights'. The NGO worker had to explain that they were doing nothing illegal. The problem grew when civil patrollers started spreading the rumour that the food which this same NGO was donating actually came from the guerrillas. A meeting was quickly organized by the NGO, to which all patrol leaders were invited, explaining exactly what kind of work they were doing and why. Furthermore, the NGO asked the patrols to actually support them in their work instead of 'putting fear into people by spreading these rumours'.[157] The situation calmed down, but this was probably due to the fact that some of the NGO workers were locals, and thus knew some of the patrol commanders concerned. Even today, in 2002, many ladinos do not like to mention the fact that they knew or know people working for human rights organizations, like the truth commissions. As one very old ladino woman said about a family member, 'It embarrasses me that she does this work ... and it is too dangerous'.[158] She told me only after she had known me for more than a year. The same happened with another ladino women, who walked to her closet one afternoon and pulled out a copy of the truth commission report from under a heap of clothes. A close relative had been working with the organization for about two years, but she had never mentioned it before.[159] 'Human rights' were still tainted words, which were not used too openly in Joyabaj.

Distrust: a legacy of the civil war

Topics such as local politics, elections, the *Consulta Popular*, corruption, migration and economic change were talked about without much reserve. People had strong views and opinions about these topics, and were willing to share them with me after a relationship of trust had been established. When, however, talking about recent violent incidents, the war in general, the Peace Accords, the dismantling of the patrols and human rights in general, people were less outspoken

---

157 Interview 10-98 (31/7/98).
158 Diary 9/6/98.
159 Diary 16/6/99.

and chose their words more carefully. People were also much more aware of the possible impact their stories and memories could have on local power relations, on their own situation or on that of others. Topics such as recent lynchings and human rights were considered more threatening than others, especially in a postwar situation, where former opponents and allies were still trying to establish a secure foothold in society. 'I do not want any problems' was a recurrent phrase during the interviews and used in relation to every subject imaginable. This attitude, because it seemed more than just a meaningless phrase that cropped up every now and then in conversations, can be considered an important legacy of civil war violence. As Handy noted in 1985, after the first democratic elections had been held, 'a significant number of highland residents have abandoned links with outside agencies and have attempted once again to "disengage" from the state and close the valves that admit the most disruptive outside influences'.[160] Although the situation in the mid-1990s had changed, a number of *Joyabatecos* still seemed to prefer to be left alone and not to get involved in anything: for example, people who did not want to hear or know anything about the water problems, the *Alcaldía Indígena* who did not confront the people living illegally on the communal land, and communities who did not trust food aid they are receiving, because it was brought in by foreign donors.

A fundamental lack of trust (*confianza*) appeared to exist: distrust of local politicians and elections in general, of the final peace agreements and whom it really benefited, and of the justice system. Were the guilty going to be punished, or would they bribe their way out of prison? Distrust was also apparent within and between different groups in society (along ethnic, religious and political lines, or a combination of these), and towards outsiders, outside organizations and strangers in general. Of course, this attitude does not hold for all *Joyabatecos*, as many were and still are involved in local politics, national and international migration and the growing NGO business. *Joyabateco* candidates for the URNG/DIA coalition were not afraid to voice their opinion during their campaigns in the rural areas, while other individuals came forward to tell their story to the REMHI or CEH investigators. Nevertheless, distrust and the related attitude of avoiding problems seem to be a clear legacy of the civil war period.

It also has to be taken into account that time played an important role in most of the accounts or memories presented in this chapter. Only a short time span elapsed between experiencing the events and narrating them. The events took place a few years or even only a few months before the interviews were conducted, which influenced the way people memorized events. Memories and opinions were still being formed and adjusted, and people did not have much time to go

---

160 Handy (1991: 60).

over them with others. There had been no time yet to recount the stories, which has the effect of fixing them in the memory. There was less reflection on recent events and their place in local history. In such surroundings, rumours, misinformation and sometimes wilful distortion of the facts led to quite divergent stories about events.

Conclusion

A number of developments can be traced throughout this chapter—first of all, the process of dismantling the civil patrols, and the changing role of former civil patrol commanders within the communities. Not only was their power base being dismantled, but also people's perceptions of the role of civil patrols in the civil war changed. Initially they were considered the saviours of the country, especially by those who feared losing their powerful positions in Joyabaj, such as the ladino economic and political elite. This attitude gradually changed towards viewing civil patrollers as the bad guys whose violent activities were denounced to human rights organizations.

Second, after the peace agreement, whereby patrols were dismantled, the military scaled down, and guerrillas reinserted into society, the security situation did not much improve. Although political crimes diminished, everyday violence and organized crimes were on the rise. Especially in the rural areas, people decided to take justice into their own hands, which resulted in numerous lynchings of presumed criminals. In a number of cases, former civil patrol commanders or military commanders were involved and identified as instigators of these lynchings. The militarization of society, by way of the installation of civil patrols, had altered the way in which problems were solved at the community level. Instead of communication, people resorted to violent means.

A third development, apart from the dismantling of the patrols and a worsening of the security situation since the signing of the Peace Accords, was the political change at the local level. More political space seemed available, to judge from the fact that former guerrillas could campaign for elections in Joyabaj and even came second, although distrust of politicians and abstentionism remained. There was also more space for indigenous participants and their specific demands in the political arena. Their role was no longer confined to harvesting the majority of the indigenous votes, as had been done during previous elections. Finally, apart from the changes in the political arena, economic activity in Joyabaj had also boomed, after having been hampered by the civil war years, as a result of the US dollars coming in as remittances from the United States. These temporary migrants, many of whom were indigenous, started constructing houses, buying cars, and transporting and trading goods. Ladino monopoly of the local economy, which had existed until the civil war started in the early 1980s, was broken down and the economic arena diversified.

These changes in local politics and economy not only affected local power relations in general, but in particular influenced ethnic relations in Joyabaj. Ethnic tensions between ladinos and *indígenas* became more visible as a result of these changes. First of all, *indígenas* were increasingly participating in local politics. They were actively campaigning for the DIA/URNG coalition, coming second during the last municipal elections. To make matters worse in the eyes of a ladino minority, they were campaigning for a former guerrilla organization whose local candidate was perceived to have been connected to the civil war violence. During the *Consulta Popular*, tensions between ladinos and *indígenas* in Joyabaj became even more pronounced. Although some *indígenas* had also voted 'no' during the *Consulta*, because of misinformation, because they had been told to do so, or because they considered the *Consulta* to be a product of left-wing politics, the majority was in favour of the proposed changes in the constitution. Ladinos were mostly scared of possible changes and found it difficult to assess what the changes would mean for everyday living. They were afraid of becoming second-class citizens in their villages. The ethnic dimension was apparent also in economic relations. Because of the large number of indigenous people who migrated to the United States, their families were able to build nice houses, send their children to school ... in other words, to live as ladinos did. This did not sit well with some ladinos, who saw their privileged position in town being threatened and openly talked in terms of 'us' and 'them'. A final issue in which differences between *indígenas* and ladinos became apparent was human rights. Ladinos considered human rights organizations to be an indigenous thing, and not something they could use or support. The same goes for lynchings, which were perceived by ladinos as an indigenous thing (such a savage and inhumane thing to do), although the first lynching in Joyabaj, in 1996, proved the opposite, because both perpetrators and victims turned out to be almost exclusively ladino. It has become clear that, already before the civil war, a process was set in motion that caused ladinos to lose control over part of local politics, to lose their economic monopoly and to lose control over the indigenous population.

The picture I have painted may seem rather one-sided, portraying fearful ladinos who look with suspicion upon the increasing economic and political activities of the *indígenas*, and perceive this development as a threat to their way of life. I want to stress yet again that such a clear-cut division between ladinos and *indígenas*, between 'us' and 'them', does not do justice to the enormous complexity of social relations at the local level: a complexity which I have tried to reveal throughout this chapter. People changed roles and groups depending on their political beliefs, religious affiliation and position during the civil war. As a ladino shop owner who was hardly getting by because of the influx of indigenous shops, financed with US dollars, a person could complain bitterly of *indígenas* ousting ladinos from their traditional role in the local economy. But this ladino man was also active in the Catholic Church, and regularly worked together with indigenous activists during celebrations or processions. In this role, the 'others' are not *indígenas* as an ethnic group, but people from other denominations, such as evangelicals. Group boundaries along ethnic lines can be strong, but also seem flexible enough to adjust to changing situations at the local level.

7

Dealing with the past

(1996–2001)

In the previous six chapters I have dealt with the topic of memory mainly in relation to civil defence patrols and the civil war in general. I used the concept of memory to explain the diversity, flexibility and constant reconstruction of people's discourses about past occurrences such as the death of Padre Villanueva, the massacre of Xeabaj, or more recently the activities of Leonel Ogáldez as civil patrol commander. In this chapter, memory itself is the object of investigation. I look at the current role memory plays in the reconstruction of the past and the present in Guatemala, more specifically in Joyabaj.[1]

Since the mid-1990s, there have been several initiatives in Guatemala by national and international organizations to deal with the legacy of the civil war. These include the investigations and subsequent publication of truth commission reports by the Catholic Church (REHMI), as well as by the official truth commission (CEH) that was set up as part of the Peace Accord. They were both organized and large-scale attempts to 'piece together, in their own words, the many complex and divergent experiences of the populations touched by the war'.[2] They were, however, not 'established to judge, because for that purpose the justice apparatus exists'.[3] Apart from these official initiatives 'to reconstruct the historical memory',[4] people also remembered civil war violence at the local level. Candles were lit in church to remember a disappeared brother and graves were visited during All Saints day. I present various initiatives relating to memory and commemoration in Joyabaj and place them in the national context of truth commissions, discussions on international tribunals and disclosure of parts of the Guatemalan military terror network. This national context forms the backdrop against which memories and stories of the *Joyabatecos* about the past, especially the violent past, have to be placed. Apart from other important factors, such as the current socio-political context and the violent heritage of the armed

---

1 As I explained in Chapter 1, much has been written on the topic of memory, truth and reconciliation in other countries emerging from violent conflict, such as South Africa (Hamber and Wilson, 1999; Buur, 2000), Argentina (Kaiser, 2000; Jelin and Kaufman, 2002; Valdez, 2000; Baud 2001), Chile (Aguilar and Hite, 2000) and Northern Ireland (Hamber 1998). In this chapter, however, I restrict myself to the Guatemalan case, with occasional references to other countries when relevant.
2 ODHAG (1999: xxxii).
3 CEH, Vol. I (1999: 15).
4 ODHAG (1999: xxxi).

conflict, which have been analysed in detail in the previous chapters, this setting of large-scale memory initiatives influenced people's memories of the past, what they wanted to tell and what the did not want to tell. It influenced what they wanted to remember and what they did not want to remember, the way things were said and stories that were told. In this chapter I am more clearly present than in the previous chapters, because the events described and analysed occurred while I was doing research in Joyabaj. This was not the case with much of the material presented in the previous chapters, most of which came from archival research, newspapers, reports, interviews and informal conversations. My presence in the municipality influenced people's attitudes and behaviour in relation to memory activities, more so than in the previous chapters.

I first discuss the national context in which the different national and local discussions dealing with Guatemala's past have to be situated. Several national incidents influenced the way people talked about the past. The focus then turns to the local level and analyses the work of the Catholic Church because of its enormous reach and continuous impact at the community level in Guatemala.[5] The crucial role of the priests at the local level is discussed, as is the impact of commemorative events and the implementation of the REMHI project in Joyabaj. I then turn to the topic of exhumations, which are also considered as a way of dealing with the past in Guatemala, and introduce the different forensic teams working in the Quiche department. The chapter ends with a case study of the uncovering and subsequent exhumation of a large massacre site in Joyabaj in 1999, which triggered different memories and perceptions of the past and how to deal with it in the present.

Discussing Guatemala's violent past

I have already touched upon the fact that the reports from REMHI and CEH shaped the way people dealt with the past, thereby emphasizing existing differences within Guatemalan society with regard to civil war violence. The Catholic Church's setting up of the REMHI project was a way to institutionalize its attitude towards uncovering the past. The project was started in 1995, and aimed to gather personal testimonies about what happened during the civil war. The results were published in 1998 in a truth commission report called '*Nunca Más*' (Never Again).[6] REMHI was established because the official truth commission

---

5   The progressive stance of the Catholic Church in Guatemala, which was one of the reasons it was targeted heavily by the military during the civil war, contrasts with countries like Argentina and Chile, where the Catholic Church was extremely conservative and in close alliance with government and military forces during the civil wars in these countries.

6   The truth commission report in Argentina, which was published in 1984, carried the same title. Jelin and Kaufman consider the launching of this report in Argentina 'a benchmark for most people. The book has become part of one's own personal life and recollection' (2002: 35). It is not very clear whether this is also the case with the REMHI report in Guatemala, especially because many people cannot read, or do not have access to the four volumes.

in Guatemala (CEH – *Comisión de Esclaricimiento Histórico*),[7] which had been the result of peace negotiations between the guerrillas and the Guatemalan government, was considered weak, or limited to say the least, by national and international organizations.[8] The CEH had only a very short period to carry out its research (six months to investigate a 36-year civil war), it did not have legal powers to search or subpoena and it was not permitted to 'individualize responsibility' (name names of violators).[9] Apart from that, the CEH report did not have any legal implications, meaning that information obtained by commission investigators could not be used in later prosecutions.[10] The REMHI report could strengthen the impact of the CEH, because it had the opportunity to investigate for a much longer period and it worked more closely with the local communities because of their extensive network of Catholic laymen and other Catholic activists. More than 600 pastoral workers and lay activists were trained as interviewers, collecting a total of 6,500 interviews. The REMHI project could also identify victims as well as perpetrators by their names.[11]

The nine-volume report of the CEH was published on 25 February 1999, after the period of investigations had been extended for nearly two years thanks to donations from foreign sources. Despite the limitations of its mandate, its language was harsh and condemnatory, especially towards the Guatemalan military. 'Especially important was the commission's conclusion that from 1981 to 1983, "agents of the state committed acts of genocide against groups of the Mayan people".'[12] Genocide was a crime that did not fall under the amnesty law, which forbade the prosecution of anyone who committed political offences in the war. The CEH report therefore provided unexpected opportunities to file criminal charges against alleged perpetrators on the grounds of genocide.[13] The commission had been more effective than was hoped for in human rights circles. However, most of the CEH's recommendations to the Guatemalan government

---

7   Commission of Historical Clarification. The CEH project presented a twelve-volume report on the civil war in Guatemala in 1999, which was called Guatemala: Memoria del silencio (Guatemala: Memory of Silence).
8   Wilson (1997: 19-22); Cabrera (1998: 1) (www.incore.ulst.ac.uk/home/publication/research/dwtp/cabrera.pdf) [29/11/01].
9   Byrne (http:// www.igc.apc.org/lawg/back.html) [25/2/00].
10 Wilson (1997: 20).
11 The REMHI project was not implemented in all departments because some of the bishops were not willing to participate in the project. In the department of Zacapa the bishop refused, while in Sololá a very conservative diocesan official blocked the REMHI project. The clergy in Escuintla and Jalapa decided that only they themselves could do the interviews, and would not leave any of the research to other local members of the Catholic Church. These attitudes severely limited the number and quality of interviews from those areas (Jeffrey, 1998: 55).
12 Rohter (1999).
13 CEH, Vol. III (1999: 314-423). Zacualpa (bordering on the municipality of Joyabaj) was one of the regions where, according to the CEH report, a genocide had taken place.

have yet to be implemented.[14] The Guatemalan government responded negatively to the report by way of a newspaper advertisement. It argued that nothing needed to be done because it considered most recommendations to have been carried out and failed to comment on others.[15] The military, as well as the conservative Committee of Agricultural, Commercial, Industrial and Financial Associations (CACIF) were also not happy with the report and considered it to be incomplete and partial.[16] Clearly, different views on dealing with the past were being presented.

It was, however, not only the reports from REMHI and CEH that shaped the way people dealt with the past. A number of national incidents, of which I discuss three, also set the tone for a national discussion on civil war violence. First of all, former army spokesman Colonel Otto Noack was arrested and subsequently degraded in July 1998 after he had declared in a radio interview that the army should acknowledge, and apologize to the Guatemalan people for, atrocities committed during the civil conflict. According to the army, Noack was not authorized to express such opinions, and he was sentenced to 30 days in jail. Human rights activists praised his behaviour and accused the military of violation of the right to freedom of speech.[17] When the director of the CEH declared his support for Colonel Noack's stand and visited him in detention, he was criticized by government officials for exceeding his mandate and interfering in Guatemala's internal affairs.[18] Noack's apology was somewhat premature because a year and a half later, on 29 December 1999, President Arzú himself apologized for 'the violence suffered by the population as a result of decisions made at that time [during the war] by political powers and the actions of the military and other security force'[19] during a ceremony in Santa Cruz de Quiché commemorating the second anniversary of the Peace Accords. President Clinton followed in July 1999, apologizing for the 'mistake made by the United States in supporting a repressive, right-wing government'.[20] His apology was probably prompted by the exposure of the role of the United States in the CEH report, which was presented a few months earlier. The former guerrilla organizations followed two days after Clinton's apology, issuing a statement asking for forgiveness 'from the memory of victims, their families and communities'.[21] Although

---

14 The New York Times, 25/2/00.
15 Tomuschat (2000: 15). Tomuschat was the former coordinator of the CEH project in Guatemala.
16 CEG, no. 99/4, 13/4/99.
17 Prensa Libre, 21/7/98.
18 Prensa Libre, 18/7/98; 19/7/98 & 21/7/98.
19 The Siglo News Weekly, 6/1/99.
20 Boston Globe, 14/3/99.
21 Boston Globe, 14/3/99.

human rights and other popular organizations considered the stream of apologies a small step forward, they were anxious to point out that apologies did not mean forgetting and did not replace justice and financial compensation.[22]

A second affair, which emphasized the tense situation in the country and which made headlines for weeks in the Guatemalan newspapers, was the discovery of a military logbook of the Guatemalan armed forces by the National Security Archive (NSA) in May 1999.[23] This so-called 'Death Squad Dossier' or 'military diary', as the document was quickly nicknamed in the newspapers, was a detailed record of death squad operations between August 1983 and March 1985, during the rule of former general Mejía Víctores. It gave details of the fate of 183 people, including photographs apparently cut from identity cards, the way in which they were taken prisoner by the military, and classifying each victim by presumed membership of communist organizations. About 100 people had been actually killed, which was detailed in the logbook by using codes such as '300' (meaning the person was executed) and Guatemalan slang like 'he is with Pancho' (meaning that a person died or was killed).[24] The NSA presented the logbook as a 'death squad equivalent of an annual productivity report, an account from inside the files of Guatemala's killing machine'.[25] The logbook provoked strong, although conflicting, reactions in the military as well as human rights organizations in Guatemala. The military reacted furiously, at first declaring the document to be a fake. After a week of investigating the document, they added that it could not possibly have been a military document, because the Guatemalan military used letterheads and other identification marks.[26]

A third and final cause for discussion on the civil war past was different suits presented against former Guatemalan presidents (Lucas García, Ríos Montt and Mejía Víctores), in which they were accused of genocide.[27] In December 1999 Nobel Prize Laureate Rigoberta Menchú presented a genocide suit against the three presidents before the Spanish Supreme Court, following the 1998 Pinochet case. After initial dismissal of the case, it was accepted in February 2000. An organization of indigenous people from ten communities across Guatemala[28] filed a similar genocide case in May 2000 as co-plaintiff, with the human rights

---

22 Boston Globe, 14/3/99.
23 The NSA, a research institution based in the United States, which specializes in opening up government archives containing confidential material on sensitive issues such as US interference in Cuba, Nicaragua and Guatemala.
24 Doyle (1999: 3) (http: lasa.international.pitt.edu/Doyle.htm) [17/11/99].
25 National Security Archive Electronic Briefing Book No. 15, 1999: 1 (www.gwu.edu/nsarchiv/NSAEBB/NSAEBB15/press.html) [17/9/01].
26 Prensa Libre, 26/5/99.
27 Amnesty International (2002: 64-68).
28 AJR (*Asociación Justicia y Reconciliación* - Association for Justice and Reconciliation).

organization CALDH as legal advisers.[29] In October 2001, another eleven communities added their case.[30] The suits are still being processed by the judicial system.

Dealing with the past in Joyabaj

Joyabaj is a municipality that has only just begun to experience the first effects of memory work. Although since 1993 local initiatives have been taken touching upon the violent past, like the training of mental health promoters by a local NGO[31] and the yearly commemorative mass for Padre Faustino Villanueva,[32] large-scale and highly visible initiatives to commemorate and remember have not been initiated until quite recently. An example of such a highly visible initiative, which was of course in the first instance not geared towards remembering but nonetheless stirred up local memories of the past, was the first large exhumation in the centre of Joyabaj, which was carried out in January 2000. Before that only a few, very small and low-profile exhumations had been carried out in the Joyabaj area, which had little effect on the local community and community relations. Although more than eight massacres have been officially documented for Joyabaj, communities and individuals had not yet started coming forward to ask for exhumations of these clandestine graveyards. This is very different from the situation in communities in the nearby municipality of Rabinal (Baja Verapaz) and in the Ixil region (north of Quiché), where exhumations and other memory initiatives had a much larger impact on the local communities. A large number of organizations had been working in these areas for quite some time, focusing on mental health care, commemorations and other activities related to 'dealing with the past'.[33]

The spaces in Joyabaj to talk about the past and actively engage in memory

---

29 Guatemala's judicial system is considered unique in that it allows private citizens to petition the government to open a criminal case. Once a case is open, they have the right to become what is called an 'adhering complainant' or co-plaintiff. In that capacity the co-plaintiff and its legal advisers have a right to participate in both the investigation and the trial process.
30 Central America/Mexico Report, October 2001
(www.rtfcam.org/report/volume_21/No_4/article_4htm) [10/7/02].
31 The NGO *Centro Xoj* started training mental health promoters in several villages in the northern part of the municipality, where the violence hit hard. For this purpose an American nun, who was also a psychotherapist, lived in Joyabaj for several years, setting up the mental health programme of *Centro Xoj*. When *Centro Xoj* stopped its activities, the project was taken over by the local NGO Cedinco (Interview 21-98 (15/7/98) and diary 12/5/98).
32 Villanueva was the local priest in Joyabaj who was killed by people connected to the military on 10 July 1980 in his parish house. He was buried as a martyr of the Catholic Church, together with two other murdered priests, in the nearby municipality of Chichicastenango. See Chapters 3 and 4 for more details of his activities and his death.
33 Already in 1993 several large exhumations had been carried out in the Rabinal area, culminating in the publication of a book by the EAFG titled *Las Masacres en Rabinal* (1997).

activities seemed, at the time this research was carried out, not yet as large as in other areas in Guatemala. People preferred not to stir up too much trouble by digging into the past, because many were convinced it could get them involved in old conflicts over land or new ones, like the threats of some former patrol commanders to reorganize the civil patrols. Some still feared individuals who had occupied important positions as civil patrol leaders or military commissioners. These perceptions clearly influence people's behaviour towards memory initiatives like exhumations and truth commission reports. They also provide the setting in which memories and stories about the past are constructed.

Creating space: the role of the local priest

An institution in Joyabaj that addressed the violent past in several ways was the Catholic Church. The Catholic Church in Guatemala has had quite progressive ideas since the 1960s, when Catholic Action was transformed from a conservative Catholic organization trying to salvage strict Catholicism into a more community-oriented organization dealing with mundane issues such as poverty, land problems and organization-building. This progressive stance caused the Catholic Church to become one of the targets of the military during the civil war. Many priests, nuns and laypersons were killed or forced to flee the country. Churches were closed or used as military compounds, as in Joyabaj. In some cases the church grounds were used as clandestine cemeteries by the military.

Joyabaj also lost its priest and numerous activists of the Catholic Church as a result of the civil war. After the worst of the violence had passed in the mid-1980s, the Catholic Church started to rebuild itself and the communities it worked in. The first priest to come and work in Joyabaj after the violence was Padre Juan Vasquez, who arrived in January 1988. Slowly Catholic Action groups were being reorganized and the priest started going out into the rural communities again to say mass. In 1992 Padre Juan organized the first large-scale commemorative procession in honour of Padre Villanueva, something many ladinos were not too happy with.[34]

His work and that of Padre Rudi, who started working as a priest in Joyabaj in 1994, opened up space for *Joyabatecos*, especially those belonging to the Catholic Church, to organize and to come together and talk with each other about Bible stories and other religious topics, but also about the violent past if necessary. Good examples of such a space were some of the masses held by Padre Rudi. During my stay in Joyabaj, I often accompanied Padre Rudi to the surrounding communities where he was to celebrate mass. At first it was merely

---

34 See Chapter 5 for an analysis of the work of Padre Juan Vasquez in Joyabaj and the problems he encountered.

a way for me to get acquainted with the countryside and its people. Padre Rudi would present me at the beginning of mass and explain what I was doing in the area. He always stressed that everybody should feel free to talk to me 'in all confidence' (*con toda confianza*).[35] After having heard several masses, however, I was struck by the fact that the topic of the violence played such a prominent role in his sermon in certain villages, while in others he never touched upon the subject. Padre Rudi explained that some communities were much more open to hearing and talking about the past, while others did not want to hear any reference to it in his sermons. Thus the diversity in the sermons of Padre Rudi became in itself enough reason to accompany him on several visits to the communities.[36] It gave insight into the different ways in which communities had lived through the violence and how they perceived the war at that moment.

In Patzulá, for example, an indigenous community in the northern part of the municipality which had suffered greatly during the civil war and which was known to have harboured refugees from neighbouring communities who had fled the military, Padre Rudi spoke openly about past atrocities. According to him, the people in Patzulá were very '*conciente*' (aware) of what had happened during the civil war.[37] The theme of one of his sermons in Patzulá was reconciliation and forgiveness. He openly mentioned the role of the military and the civil patrols in the atrocities committed and made a connection with the question of guilt. 'Who are the guilty ones?', he asked rhetorically, answering that '[T]hose who do not want to know or say the truth are also guilty'. This view coincides with that of Cohen, author of several books about denying atrocities, whose analysis of the 'internal bystander'[38] refers to knowing about atrocities within one's own society, but as a passive bystander without initiating activity to change the situation. Often bystander passivity results from fear, leaving people in a state of acquiescence because it is dangerous to ask and to know. Cohen makes a distinction between passive bystanders and indifferent bystanders. While passive bystanders may still feel some unease about what they have heard or know, indifference points in another direction. Horwitz, writing about people's reactions to Mauthausen, a Nazi concentration camp nearby their village, says that 'They never sought to inform themselves of what happened. One encounters not a flat denial of the existence of the camps, only an indifference to their presence so long ago. In some instances one may not talk of forgetfulness, for one cannot forget what one has never attempted to know'.[39] Padre Rudi blamed those

---

35 Diary 17/3/98.
36 Diary 17/3/98; 19/3/98; 25/3/98; 12/5/99; 24/7/99; 26/8/99.
37 Diary 17/3/98.
38 Cohen (2001: 142-155).
39 Horwitz, in: Cohen (2001: 2-3).

Joyabatecos who had chosen not to know and who had in a sense looked the other way.

During the sermon in Patzulá the priest also touched upon the fact that many ladinos had blamed the guerrilla for the war and had welcomed the army as their saviours. 'But that is not the case. That is not the truth. And we have to know the truth before we can reconcile.'[40] This is a recurrent topic in the debates between those who want to bring everything about the past out into the open, and those who just want to forgive and forget. The Catholic Church clearly connects truth with reconciliation, as does Padre Rudi. In their view reconciliation is possible only when one knows what has happened and thus what one has to forgive. There cannot be forgiveness and thus reconciliation without the truth. The words Padre Rudi spoke in Patzulá reflect some of these views. Only a few years ago, these words could not have been uttered without creating at least a feeling of unease or outright hostility among some people in the communities.

Padre Rudi was, however, not as open about the war in the other communities as he was in Patzulá. Sometimes local tensions ran high and a very outspoken sermon could very well damage the fragile peace that existed. Other communities had not experienced much violence during the civil war and were not very interested in hearing about it. They had been able to keep trouble at bay during the bad times, so why talk about it in the present? According to Padre Rudi, some communities currently experienced more pressing problems than dealing with the past, which required their and his immediate attention. In one village the internal divisions between different groups of Catholics caused serious problems, while in another village the powerful position of one family running all Catholic groups and organizations caused discontent. Clearly, communities had multiple ways of dealing with the past, whether open, veiled, not at all or a combination of these three.

Apart from the masses in the rural communities and the weekly services in the main church in Joyabaj, special masses were required to celebrate the days of patron saints belonging to the different ladino *comunidades*. This was a very different audience from those in the rural communities. The *comunidades* were weekly Bible study groups, organized mainly to get the ladinos actively involved in Church matters and consisting therefore mostly of ladino women in their forties or older. In some cases indigenous women who had been living in the village for quite some time also took part in these *comunidades*. Many of these ladinos women were not very anxious to hear or talk about the civil war, which they considered to be something in the past and something to forget. They appeared to prefer not to know and not to remember, and were a vivid example of what

---

40 Diary 17/3/98.

Cohen (2001) describes as the 'internal bystander'. The women would become quite uneasy when people or the priest started addressing the war. They preferred to smile a lot and stay silent instead of giving their opinion on the matter, especially when they were together. When I was alone with some of them, they were more open and talkative. During some of the sermons Padre Rudi gave in honour of the patron saints of these *comunidades*, he did touch upon the past and its violence, but in a more roundabout way. One of the *comunidades* had Santiago as its patron saint, who had died as a martyr in his time. This topic was used by Padre Rudi to talk about martyrs within the Catholic Church in the past and present, slowly proceeding towards martyrs who had died during the recent civil war in Guatemala.[41]

On the surface, Padre Rudi did not always appear to be very actively involved in the follow-up of the REMHI process or other human rights initiatives of the Catholic Church. He seemed to be much more concerned with pressing problems within the Catholic Church, for example with Charismatic Catholic groups or between Catholic Action groups of different communities. But in his own, often indirect, way he did touch upon the violent past during his sermons, weekly sessions with Catholic Action directives, and celebrations of patron saints.

Remembering through commemoration

The commemoration and celebration of martyrs is an important feature of Catholic religion. In 1992 Padre Vasquez started the yearly commemoration of the death of Padre Villanueva, which was celebrated together with the feast of the Sacred Heart.[42] The two days were conveniently close together and incorporating them into one commemorative event was considered possibly less of a threat by the military than openly commemorating Villanueva's death. An additional reason to combine the two days was the fact that Padre Villanueva had been a priest of the order of the Sacred Heart (*Misionero del Sagrado Corazón* – MSC), as were most of the priests who went to work in the Quiché department at that time.

The celebrations in 1992 and 1993 attracted and activated a large, mainly indigenous audience, and was one of the few moments during which the violent past in Joyabaj was remembered in a more structured way. The large number of people participating in those processions did not sit well with military commissioners and civil patrol leaders, who saw Padre Vasquez as just another Catholic priest who sympathized with the left. Participation in commemorative events

---

41 Diary 24/7/99.
42 The feast of the Sacred Heart, during which the Sacred Heart of Jesus is celebrated, changes every year, depending on the date of Easter. It is always celebrated on the tenth Friday after Easter Sunday.

photo 19. *A small shrine inside the Catholic Church of Joyabaj, remembering the death of Padre Villanueva (anonymous, 1993)*

such as processions and commemorative masses in those years was perceived by the military as a clear statement against the government and in favour of the left and was therefore not without danger. Even in recent years many people have hesitated to participate openly in such events.

In 1998 the commemoration was different from previous years. Until then the celebration had consisted mainly of a mass in honour of Padre Villanueva, followed by a procession during which the portrait of the priest was carried around town. In July 1998, however, several events came together. First of all, the REMHI report had been published in April 1998 and several hundred copies of its summary had been distributed to the different parishes. The second phase of the REMHI project,[43] which consisted of returning the report and its information to the people, was about to be initiated by the local Catholic churches. Padre Rudi wanted to use the yearly commemoration of the Sacred Heart and Padre Villanueva as the starting point of this phase, and held an early mass on 10 July

---

43 The first phase consisted of the gathering of testimonies and their presentation in a truth commission report.

photo 20. *The Catholic Church in Santa Cruz de Quiché: remembering the murder of Bishop Gerardi, 40 days earlier. The banner reads; we demand to be witnesses to the truth (author, 1998)*

in which the work of the project was explained. A second and related incident, which was also incorporated into the celebration of 10 July, was the murder of Monsignor Gerardi in Guatemala City in April 1998, presumably by the military.[44] Gerardi had been the coordinator of the REMHI project and was killed two days after the REMHI report was presented. The Catholic Church and many other Guatemalans perceived his death as a warning from the military not to step too far outside the parameters set by the military and their allies of what was acceptable and not acceptable in the way of remembering, telling the 'truth' and naming names. His death also caused unrest in Joyabaj, especially among the indigenous people who had been working with the REMHI project or who were otherwise connected to the Catholic Church. People felt that the murder of Gerardi set them 20 years back in time. They were afraid that the death of Gerardi would be the first in a fresh wave of violence.[45] Although this did not turn out to be the case, a general feeling of fear surfaced again. The peace had been signed two years before, but it had not yet been consolidated.

---

44 In June 2001, three members of the military and a priest were convicted for the murder of Monsignor Gerardi. The members of the military received jail sentences of 30 years and the priest 20 years.
45 Diary 28/4/98 and interview 3-98 (17/7/98).

As noted, the 1998 celebration of the death of Padre Villanueva also commemorated the death of Monsignor Gerardi. In order to connect the Monsignor's death with the death of the hundreds of *Joyabatecos* during the civil war, Padre Rudi had asked the people to make little crucifixes for the relatives and friends they had lost during the violence. They were to write the names and the date of their death or disappearance on it, and to bring the crucifixes to the commemoration mass. Padre Rudi's sermon focused on the importance of remembering. 'Some people do not think it is necessary to remember, because so much time has passed since. Things have happened, however, which are too bad not to remember. Besides, the Church still remembers the killing of the Christians by the Romans, and this happened almost 1,500 years ago.'[46] After mass, a few hundred *indígenas* lined up in front of the church with the small crucifixes in their hands. Some people carried only one or two, but I saw people carrying as many as nine or ten. For many people this was the first time they had openly shown that they had lost family members, naming them and commemorating them. Everybody was very silent during the short procession that was lit by only a few torches. Onlookers watched the procession with an inquiring look on their faces, not entirely understanding what it was about. Some of the ladinos muttered 'oh, it's an Indian thing', and walked on because they felt it did not concern them. After the procession the crucifixes were collected and placed on the walls on either side of a small altar that was erected inside the church. Pictures of Padre Villanueva and two other priests[47] who had been killed in Quiché during the 1980s hung next to a poster commemorating Monsignor Gerardi. More than 400 crucifixes flanked the portraits. The small altar would not become a permanent feature in the church, as was the case in other churches where similar commemorations had been held throughout the years. The crucifixes eventually returned to their communities, where they were displayed in the local churches, stored away or just forgotten.

Before Padre Rudi left Joyabaj to go on to his next parish in the spring of 2000, he organized one other large commemoration, which did leave a permanent presence in the Catholic church of Joyabaj. When Padre Villanueva was killed in July 1980, he was buried in the nearby municipality of Chichicastenango together with the two other priests who had died during the violence. The *Joyabatecos*, however, had preferred to bury Padre Villanueva in Joyabaj, where he had spend so many years of his life. Finally, on 10 July 2000, the 20th anniversary of his death, he was exhumed from his grave in

---

46 Diary 12/7/98.
47 The two other priests were José Maráa Gran and Juan Alonso Fernández, both belonging to the MSC congregation.

photo 21. *Altar inside the Catholic Church of Joyabaj, remembering Bishop Gerardi and the victims of the civil war in Joyabaj (author, 1998)*

Chichicastenango and brought back to Joyabaj to be buried in a small chapel inside the church in Joyabaj. Fittingly, he shared this space with the image of the Sacred Heart, with whom Padre Villanueva had always shared his commemoration day. The re-burial itself attracted hundreds of people from all over the municipality, aside from dignitaries from the Catholic Church and family members of Padre Villanueva.[48] Again, like other commemorative events, it was largely an indigenous affair. A former ladino teacher explained that the re-burial of Padre Villanueva was attended mainly by an indigenous audience. 'Here in Joyabaj processions are loaded with *gente natural*,[49] ladinos only look at them from the door of their house, when they come by.'[50] Ladinos viewed the whole procession and other activities largely from the sidelines, without actually participating. Although Padre Villanueva had also been their priest, which was apparent from the affectionate way some of the older ladinos talked about him,

---

48 Personal correspondence with Harald Dornhaus (18/2/01).
49 The term *gente natural* or *naturales* (people of nature) is a derogatory term used by some ladinos to refer to indigenous people.
50 Interview 4-01 (11/5/01).

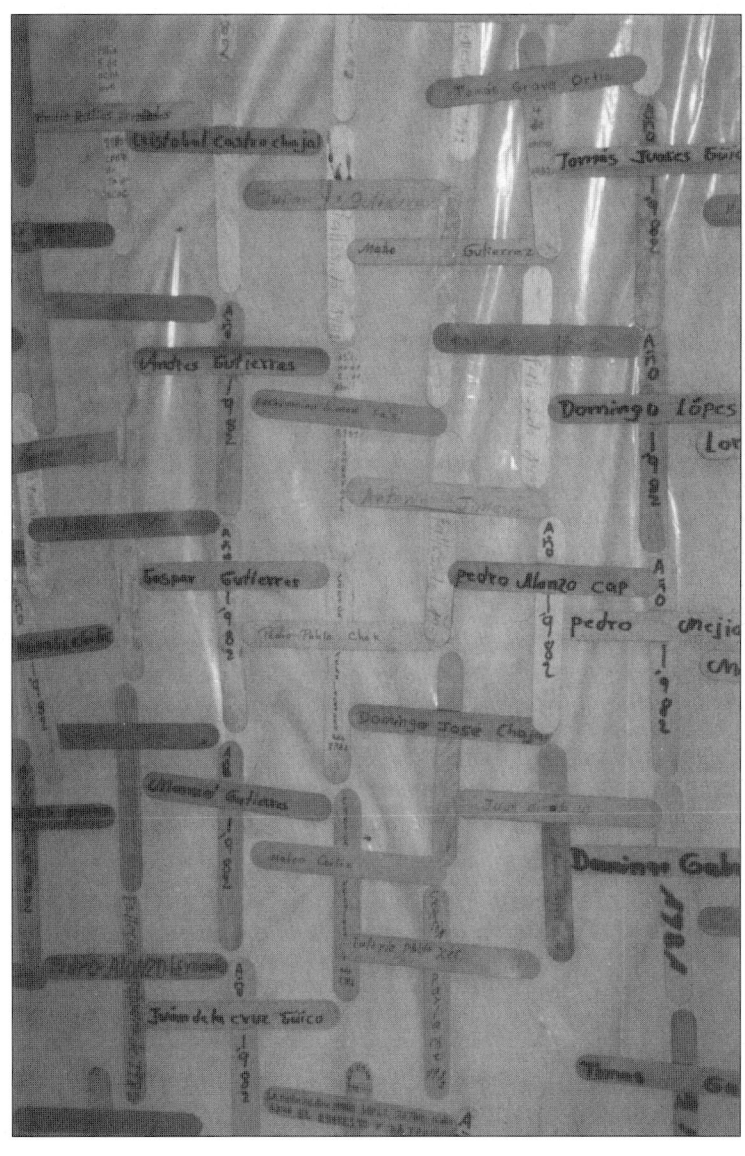

photo 22. *The small wooden crosses, which were carried during the commemorative procession for the civil war victims in Joyabaj (author, 1998)*

photo *23. Reburial of Padre Villanueva on 10 July 2000; largely an indigenous affair (anonymous, 1993)*

the whole business of commemorating his death and thereby also commemorating the violence of the 1980s did not appeal to them very much. A ladino woman said that 'they just should have left him in Chichicastenango. What good does it do to bring him here now, after 20 years?'[51] The re-burial clearly made people remember the civil war, something many tried very hard to forget.

REMHI in Joyabaj: implementation and results

Padre Villanueva's re-burial was not the first memory initiative of the Catholic Church in Joyabaj. The REMHI project in Joyabaj, as elsewhere in Guatemala, relied heavily on local clergy, such as the local priest Padre Rudi, and the elected leaders of Catholic Action. They played a prominent role in carrying out the REMHI project in Joyabaj. The attitude of the priest and other Catholic leaders towards the REMHI project had a significant impact on the willingness of local people to participate in the project. The priest was the one who had to find people who could be trusted to gather the testimonies and organize them into teams. Apart from Padre Rudi and another priest who was working in Joyabaj at that time, eight men and women were trained in interviewing techniques and handling a tape recorder: not many out of a total population of about 20,000. Most of the REMHI promoters (as they were called officially) were indigenous, literate and bilingual, although some of the women only spoke *K'iche'* and could not read or write.

In Joyabaj it was sometimes difficult to find people willing to work as interviewers, because the task was seen as dangerous. People who did accept often did not tell their families and friends, out of fear of the repercussions.[52] They hoped that their involvement in the REMHI project would remain unseen. One indigenous promoter explained that initially her parents were very much against her participating in the REMHI project; they thought it would be dangerous for her, and also for the family. She was, however, already very much involved in church activities and decided to go ahead anyway. When Padre Rudi announced her name and the names of the other promoters during Sunday mass, she got scared again. Although the names were mentioned only so that people would know whom to approach if they wanted to give their testimony, she thought that people with other purposes could do the same.[53] Fortunately nothing happened and she could do her work without any problems.

Padre Rudi was also the one who had to explain to people during mass and other meetings what REMHI was all about and why it would be a good idea for

---

51 Interview 5-01 (18/5/01).
52 Diary 6/5/98.
53 Interview 45-99 (29/7/99).

them to come forward and tell their stories. He was perceived, at least by the Catholic part of the population in Joyabaj, as their guide in such matters. The priest, however, was not the only Catholic authority in the communities. The *Junta Directiva* (elected board) of Catholic Action also played an important role in this respect, because it provided the direct link between the priest and the numerous communities he sometimes visited only once or twice a year. They were the ones passing on the messages given to them by Padre Rudi to the people in their communities who did not come to listen to the Sunday mass in town. In some communities the *Junta Directiva* discussed the REMHI project with the whole community, and decided not to participate at all. It urged the people not to give testimony, because in its view such actions could cause trouble for the community, such as threats and harassment from former patrol commanders or patrollers. A former member of one of the *Junta Directivas* said that many people did not see the point of giving testimony. When he explained the purpose of the REMHI project to people in the communities, they said to him that 'if my father wakes up from the dead, OK ... but if not ... why should I take the trouble to talk?' He himself was likewise not too happy with the whole REMHI project because 'who knows which problems might surface again ... new problems ... new vengeance'.[54]

A small number of people, 40 in all, did come forward to tell their stories on tape, mostly people from indigenous villages north of Joyabaj, like Chorraxaj, Patzulá and Xeabaj.[55] People from these villages had been actively involved in activities connected to the Catholic Church in the 1960s and 1970s, organizing and educating themselves. They were also among the villages that were hit hardest during the civil war, because their activities had been branded communist and subversive by the military. Almost two decades after the worst of the violence had passed, these were also the villages that were most open towards memory activities like the REMHI project. It was also in these villages that Padre Rudi could be much more open in his sermons about the civil war.

It was difficult to find witnesses to some of the massacres that had been committed, although everybody knew about them. In some cases, however, nobody was willing to tell their story in front of a tape recorder. Others send anonymous letters to Padre Rudi, writing down their life stories on paper. Unfortunately these did not meet the criteria of the REMHI project, and could not be used as testimonies. The promoters tracked down some of the letter writers, and tried to persuade them to tell their story in person and on tape. Most of them refused.[56]

---

54 Interview 30-99 (6/7/99).
55 Diary 6/5/98 & ODHAG, case files Joyabaj.
56 Diary 22/6/98.

When the REMHI report was published and a copy finally arrived at the parish house in Joyabaj, Padre Rudi started looking for the stories of Joyabaj. He could, however, find only tiny fragments of the 40 testimonies gathered in Joyabaj. He dryly remarked that 'my memory of Joyabaj seems to be much bigger than the memory REMHI has of Joyabaj',[57] thereby pointing out one of the problems of the REMHI project. Although an enormous amount of information and testimonies had been gathered during the course of the project, it could never provide the entire violent history of each village and community. The report was not the complete transcription of the testimonies gathered. This was of course not the object of the project, but it was something that people at the local level had sometimes hoped for. People who had told their stories wanted to find them in print in the REMHI report. Even some people who had not come forward to tell their stories had somehow expected them to appear in the REMHI report. One evening, when I was having dinner with friends, the husband told me that he had been to Zacualpa that day, where he had received a copy of the summary of the REMHI report from the local priest. Soon after, we pored over the summary, searching for the name of a small community where he had worked as a teacher in 1981. Although the community was mentioned in the long list of massacres, he was disappointed that he could find no trace in the report of the story behind the massacre. He thought that 'the report would tell it all'.[58] As well, at the national level the REMHI project was criticized, especially after the report had been published and follow-up activities in the communities were supposed to take place. After people had told their stories to the REMHI volunteers, they had hoped that the perpetrators would be caught, financial compensation would be paid, or that things would change from then onwards. But nothing changed, at least not in the experience of the people in the rural communities. Expectations had risen as a result of the REMHI project, but could not be met.[59]

Aside from some people who were disappointed with the information provided in the REMHI report, there was another group that was not at all happy with the publication of the report. A large number of civil patrol commanders, patrollers, military commissioners and the military preferred the past to stay buried. While REMHI was still gathering information and testimonies, civil patroller commanders and patrollers in several municipalities tried to dissuade people from giving testimony, by threatening to give their names to the local military base. It is very likely that this happened in Joyabaj, in view of the fact that only 40 people came forward to present their testimony. After the REMHI report

---

57 Diary 18/8/98.
58 Interview 3-98 (17/7/98).
59 Similar remarks were made by several human rights organizations during the *Congreso Internaciónal contra la Impunidad*, on 10 and 11 June 1999 in Guatemala City.

appeared, the military and other right-wing groups accused the Church of presenting a very one-sided view of the civil war in which there was no room for other groups and opinions. However, the testimonies of former military commissioners and civil patrol commanders were also present in the reports of both commissions.[60] A former patrol leader, when asked about his views on the REMHI report, replied that 'there is an inclination towards the guerilla, towards the left'. According to him, the two truth commission reports 'do not tell the true and complete story. This will only create resentment or rancour (*rencor*) between the people'.[61] This doom scenario was often ventilated to prevent people from becoming too actively involved in human rights work, memory activities or other organizations. Digging up the past would only create problems.

In general a majority, both inside and outside Guatemala, considered the REMHI project to be a success. Was it a success because it gathered a very large number of testimonies, or was it already a success because it provided people with a space to talk even though they refrained from giving official testimonies? Or was the media attention it received whenever new information was uncovered already a success in itself? A combination of these factors was responsible for the many positive reactions the REMHI project received from organizations inside and outside Guatemala. It created spaces to talk, to ask questions and to commemorate. It also gathered an enormous wealth of detailed information about what happened during the civil war, thereby creating an historical record of at least a part of its violent past.

Exhumations: a factual record of the past

Apart from the reports of REMHI and the CEH, a record of the violent past in Guatemala was also created through the exhumation of mass graves. More than 600 massacres were documented by the CEH, half of which were carried out in communities in the Quiché department.[62] Most of the people killed during these massacres were buried in clandestine graves near or in their own villages. These were sometimes mass graves, large pits into which 50 or more bodies had been thrown. In other cases two or three people were buried together in a grave, sometimes dug by themselves.

What exactly does an exhumation entail? In general the exhumation of a mass grave in Guatemala passes through several stages, starting with the interviewing of relatives of the deceased to reconstruct a biography of the victims

---

60 See CEH, Vol. I (1999: 53-54) and ODHAG, Vol. II (1998: 219-224) for a discussion of the testimonies of perpetrators of violence, such as former patrollers, patrol commanders and intelligence personnel.
61 Interview 12-01 (21/5/01).
62 CEH, Vol. III (1999: 257).

(which clothes they wore on the day they disappeared, dental information, known fractures and other birth marks). The second phase consists of the identification, mapping and actual excavation of the massacre site. Archaeological techniques are used to recover not only the bodies but also artifacts like personal belongings and bullet fragments, and to record, for example, the positions and exact locations in which the bodies are found. Technical drawings, photographs and videos are made throughout the whole process, to be used as scientific evidence in court cases. The third phase consists of laboratory analysis, establishing the cause of death and other specifics of the crime. After this examination has been brought to a close, the remains are returned to their communities and reburied according to the wishes of individual relatives and/or the community as a whole.

After the signing of the Peace Accords in 1996 and the publication of the truth commission reports of REMHI and the CEH, the number of exhumations increased significantly. Before 1996 only 23 exhumations were carried out in the whole of Guatemala, almost exclusively by the Guatemalan Forensic Anthropology Team (EAFG),[63] the first Guatemalan forensic team, set up in 1992. This number increased significantly after the signing of the Accords. Between January 1997 and June 2000, a total of 106 exhumations were carried out in Guatemala, the majority again by the EAFG. In 1997 most of the EAFG team formed a new organization, the Guatemalan Foundation of Forensic Anthropology (FAFG),[64] while the remaining part of the old team started the forensic team of Human Rights Office of the Catholic Church (ODHAG). A third forensic team was set up in 1997, forming part of the human rights organization CALDH,[65] while a fourth team, attached to the *Oficina de Paz y Reconciliación*, was set up in 1998. This office is part of the *Diocesis de Quiché* and works exclusively in the Quiché department. It exhumed ten mass graves between 1998 and 2000.[66] It also carried out the exhumation in Joyabaj in January 2000, discussed in detail below. The existence of several exhumation teams, which form parts of different human rights organizations and the Catholic Church, sometimes leads to problems between the groups. Only limited international funds are available to carry out the exhumations, while political and ideological differences and even mutual envy hamper cooperation between

---

63 EAFG - *Equipo de Antropología Forense de Guatemala.*
64 FAFG - *Fundación de Antropología Forense de Guatemala.*
65 CALDH – *Centro de Acción Legal para los Derechos Humanos*. Centre for Human Rights Legal Action. The forensic team of CALDH was dismantled in 1999, after having carried out nine exhumations. Some of its team members subsequently set up CAFCA (*Centro de Análisis Forense y Ciencias Aplicadas* – Center for Forensic Analysis and Applied Science), which completed five exhumations in 2000.
66 MINUGUA (2000: 13-14).

the groups.⁶⁷ This is not something new in Guatemala, where NGOs in general have to compete heavily for limited donor aid.

Exhumations are an important and highly visible part of the memory work that is being done in Guatemala. They often stir up an enormous number of memories and reactions, especially at the local level where the actual exhumations are carried out. Truth commission reports, tribunals and trials also elicit strong reactions, but more at the national and international levels than at the local level, where many people cannot read the commission reports or do not have access to copies. Tribunals and trials mostly prosecute people not known in local communities, and therefore are of less interest to them. Exhumations, however, take place at or near the scenes where the actual massacres occurred, and are therefore highly visible to the local population. Family members of the victims and other community members are often directly involved in the exhumation process. They are the ones who report the mass grave to the proper authorities so that an official exhumation can be conducted, often with the help of human rights organizations or other NGOs. They also help by providing information about the exact location of the site and identifying the remains, or actually participate in the digging.

Exhumations thus often have a very direct but also diverse impact on the local community.⁶⁸ They stir up memories about the war and the atrocities committed. While some consider this a positive effect of exhumations, others see it as a negative effect. Human rights organizations, international donors, and especially the Catholic Church in Guatemala stress the positive effects of exhumations. According to them, exhumations can create some sort of space for the local community to talk about what happened. They also give room for mourning, healing, and possibly even reconciliation.⁶⁹ Disappeared family members are found, identified and given a proper burial. The state of not knowing what happened to disappeared relatives is ended, which makes mourning possible.⁷⁰ By literally laying bare the remains of dead relatives, survivors can make sense of what hap-

---

67 The sensitive topic of competition for funds and non-cooperation between NGOs (more specifically those involved in carrying out exhumations) was raised during a conference on impunity (*Congreso Internacional contra la Impunidad*) on 10–11 June 1999 in Guatemala City. Several of the speakers, belonging to different human rights organizations like Famdegua and Fundación Myrna Mack, touched upon the subject.
68 See Zur (1998: 279-296) for a detailed account of an exhumation, initiated by widows from Conavigua, in the Quiché department.
69 ODHAG (1999: 317).
70 EPICA/CHRLA (1996: 15-20). Although many people were openly killed during the civil war, instead of disappearing as happened in for example Chile and Argentina, family members often did not know exactly where a person was buried or were afraid to mourn for him at his grave, because in many cases this was the massacre site itself, where many others had also lost their lives.

pened during the violent 1980s. Exhumations also serve a very practical purpose. They provide material evidence of what happened during the years of civil war. They are a vivid document of the atrocities committed and are a way for people to show the outside world what happened to them. The material evidence provides legal proof of death in court cases involving property rights, marriage or inheritance.[71]

Exhumations can, however, also have negative effects on a local community. In some cases they polarize community relations, because not everybody is equally pleased with the fact that the past is being dug up. People responsible for the atrocities committed are, in most instances, not happy with exhumations; but neither do the victims of the repression always feel comfortable when an exhumation is being planned and prepared. They are afraid because the perpetrators still walk around freely, or because they think exhumations will stir up trouble again. Community members believe that they can rekindle old animosities between different groups or individuals in the community. In a small community in the south of Quiché, people working with Caritas (an organization which forms part of the Catholic Church) were involved in an exhumation.[72] Before the exhumation took place, several meetings were organized with the local community, during which the exhumation was discussed and prepared. After the actual exhumation was concluded another round of meetings with family members of the victims was organized to discuss the exhumation and come to terms with the memories it had stirred up about the past. It soon became apparent that the people who had originally participated in the preparation and the actual exhumation had stopped attending these meetings. What had happened? It seems that, shortly after the exhumation was carried out, some community members had killed an important local leader who had initiated the petitioning for the exhumation to take place. Everybody agreed that he had been killed because of his active role in the exhumation process. Therefore many of the original activists refrained from any further connection with the exhumation process, including the discussions afterwards. In a way, the exhumation had polarized community relations, dividing the population between those in favour and those against an exhumation, and had only briefly opened a space to talk about the past. This space was (temporarily) closed with the murder of the local community leader.

---

71 See for example EPICA (1996), Jeffrey (1998), REMHI (1998) and CEH (1999) about the positive effects of exhumations.
72 Interview 6-98 (17/6/98). One of the people working with Caritas was Barbara Ford, a nun from the United States who had been living in the south of Quiché since the late 1980s. She was killed in Guatemala City on 5 May 2001. Although the killing looked like a car robbery that had got out of hand, many people were convinced she was killed because of her work with Caritas. The investigation into her death was not closed yet at the time of writing (November 2001).

It is clear that exhumations play an important role in the way local communities deal with the past. Information about the massacres is gathered, victims are found and if possible identified, and decently buried with the necessary rituals. People get a chance to talk about what happened during the civil war, sometimes for the first time since the atrocities took place. It must be taken into account, however, that exhumations can, in some instances, polarize relations within or between communities and add to feelings of mutual distrust and fear. Opinions that were never voiced come out into the open, and divisions within the community can resurface. The case that is described in the previous paragraph is in some ways an extreme example. In many of the communities where exhumations are contested and debated, polarization takes place when certain individuals involved in the exhumations process are threatened, are sent letters warning them not to participate, or have their lives made difficult in other ways. An actual killing is the exception and not the rule.

As is stressed in the REMHI report, it is important that the rhythm and demands of the community direct the actions of a forensic team.[73] An exhumation should not be initiated by an outside organization, but by the community. The community should also be involved in all facets of the exhumation process and the period afterwards.[74] This is difficult to put into practice. It is sometimes not easy to ascertain whether a request for exhumation is something that is supported by the majority of community members and even more difficult to predict what the local consequences of an exhumation will be. Forensic teams have their own time schedules and agendas and receive too many requests for exhumations. Some of the teams' work schedules are full for the coming two years. They also have to cooperate with local and national authorities in seeking permission to operate, and rely on foreign donors to fund their work. This means that they have no alternative but to carry out a small number of exhumations. It is clear that the exhumation process in practice does not always coincide with how it should ideally be carried out.

The first exhumations in Quiché and Joyabaj
In the south of the Quiché department, the area in which the municipality of

---

73 ODHAG (1998: 62).
74 An evaluation of the work of FAFG, carried out by the embassy of the Netherlands in Guatemala, was very positive about its actual exhumation work and the investigative work carried out by social anthropologists prior to the exhumations (reconstructing what happened by interviewing witnesses). They were, however, quite critical of the psycho-social or mental health component, asking whether the mental health activities 'really responded to the demands of the people, or if they based their work on their "interpretation" of what the people needed. If this last attitude is the case, it is easy for the social scientists to fall into a paternalistic attitude . . .' (Kruijt, Fondebrider and Alvarez Medrano, 2002: 29).

Joyabaj is situated, several exhumations took place from the late 1980s on. The first was carried out as early as 1988, in the municipality of Zacualpa. At that time there were no official exhumation teams and the exhumation itself was carried out by the volunteer fire brigade from Joyabaj. Five persons who had disappeared in 1984 were exhumed. Little attention was given to the exhumation, and only one tiny article appeared in a national newspaper. No information was given about possible perpetrators and no connection was made with the civil war.[75] This was not very surprising because 1988 was only a few years after some of the worst atrocities had taken place, and exhumations were not yet high on the agendas of national and international organizations. Professional forensic teams did not appear on the stage until 1992, when the first exhumations in the south of Quiché were carried out by the EAFG.[76] Its subsequent exhumations in Rabinal[77] attracted a lot of national and international attention, especially after the EAFG eventually published a book about its findings in the Rabinal area.[78] From 1996 on several exhumations were carried out in the south of Quiché, some of which attracted national attention because of the location where they were found[79] or because of the number of victims recovered.[80] Newspaper articles about the exhumations not only reported the numbers of victims found, but also started telling the story behind the exhumation, the story of the massacre committed. Mention was made of the possible involvement of the military, the military commissioners and the civil patrols.[81] This was very different from the earlier exhumations, which often did not make the newspapers or did so only as five-line articles.

In Joyabaj the first exhumation was carried out in 1994, with the purpose of recovering the body of Tomás Lares Ciprian, who was killed in 1993 and whose case is described in detail in Chapter 5. This was not an actual exhumation because the body could not be removed from its grave. It could be examined only at the scene by a forensic surgeon, due to pressures from nearby communities. The second exhumation was carried out in 1996 under the supervision of the *Juez de Paz* from Joyabaj and the forensic surgeon (*médico forense*) from the depart-

---

75 Prensa Libre, 8/6/88.
76 The EAFG carried out its first exhumation in 1992 in Lemoa, a village near Santa Cruz de Quiché, and the second exhumation in Tunajá (Zacualpa), also in 1992.
77 Municipality in the department of Baja Verapaz, which lies close to the municipality of Joyabaj.
78 EAFG (1997).
79 In 1998, during an exhumation inside the church in San Andrés Sajcabajá, the remains of 26 people were uncovered (El Periódico, 27/1/98).
80 During two exhumations in Zacualpa in 2000, the bodies of more than 100 people were recovered.
81 See for example newspaper articles about exhumations in: Prensa Libre, 28/5/97 (*Guerra interna deja legado de osamentos en varias regiones*); Siglo XXI, 9/5/98 (*Inhuman víctimas de masacres*); El Periódico, 21/5/99 (*Exhumación en Chiché, Quiché*).

mental hospital. The exhumation was initiated after an anonymous phone call had been made to the PDH[82] office reporting the whereabouts of a massacre site near the community of Caquil.[83] The remains of ten people were recovered, although no intact skeletons or other large bones were found. Presumably the skeletons had been removed before the exhumation took place, so that only small bone fragments were left. These fragments were, however, enough evidence to reconstruct a mass grave which had contained at least ten people. Evidence of burns, fractures, machete cuts and bullet fragments were found. The exhumation seems to have stirred up little local interest and was never mentioned to me during the research. I learned about it when going through the PDH archives in Santa Cruz de Quiché.

Exhumation behind the Joyabaj convent
The exhumation behind the convent, carried out in January 2000, was the first large-scale and highly visible exhumation in Joyabaj, carried out by a forensic team and involving a significant part of the local community.

It was a sunny Monday morning in August 1999, after it had rained for days. I was walking to the village of Chorraxaj together with my interpreter, a Mayan woman in her thirties. We were to conduct an interview with a group of Mayan women about their experiences during the civil war. My companion spoke fluent Spanish and *K'iche'*, and was herself involved in the Catholic Church. She had participated as a promoter in the REMHI project, helping gather testimonies from the people in Joyabaj. For most of the time we had been silently struggling uphill on a muddy slope, sometimes commenting on the corn, the weather, or a horse overtaking us at full gallop. All of a sudden my companion asked if I had heard about the toilets that had come down from the mountain. I really had no idea what she was talking about and asked her to elaborate. She then went into a detailed description of a mud-slide that had occurred behind the convent, which had destroyed the toilets of the *Casa Comunal*. The heavy rains had caused them to slide several hundred meters down the ravine behind the convent, together with large amounts of earth and dirt from the rubbish heap that littered the ravine. The mud-slide, however, also uncovered something else. Several human bones, rope, pieces of cloth and even a complete human skull had been exposed. The mass grave behind the convent, which the military had occupied from 1981 until 1986, had been uncovered by accident.

During my entire stay in Joyabaj many people had, openly or in a more indirect way, told me about the existence of this particular mass grave.[84] Nobody,

---

82 PDH – *Procuraderia de Derechos Humanos*/Human Rights Ombudsman.
83 PDH files Santa Cruz de Quiché.
84 Diary 8/4/98.

however, had ever reported it to the authorities or a human rights organization. People always said, 'why stir up trouble, let the past rest' and 'the dead will not come back if we dig them up', when referring to exhumations in general and the massacre behind the convent in particular. The rains, however, had literally opened up the massacre site and directly confronted people with a past some wanted desperately to forget. Some people clearly recognized the hand of God in the whole situation. 'Now we must do something with the dead, because God wants it', one person told me in a resigned voice.[85]

It turned out that the mud-slide had taken place the week before, but the news had been brushed aside because some days before the mud-slide several people in the communities Tunajá I (Zacualpa) and Tunajá II (Joyabaj) had been lynched by a large mob.[86] Everybody talked about the lynching, while nobody had yet mentioned the uncovering of the bones behind the convent. Soon after it became clear that a mass grave had indeed been exposed, the local priest had send word to the *Oficina de Paz y Reconciliación* (Office of Peace and Reconciliation) in Santa Cruz to come and investigate the situation. This office was part of the Catholic Church and carried out exhumations in several communities in the Quiché department. This had to be done quickly because new rains could cause a new mud-slide and damage the site and the remains.

In the first week of September, I was present at a meeting in Joyabaj between the people from the *Oficina de Paz y Reconciliación* and the *Junta Directiva* of Catholic Action in Joyabaj. The Catholic Church was the owner of the land behind the convent and was also the reporting party. The meeting started with an extensive introduction by the exhumation team about the work of their office, about what an exhumation actually entailed and how they would proceed with the exhumation process.[87] Subsequently the members of the *Junta* started asking many questions, several of which were quite critical of the whole exhumation process. Although the members of the *Junta* knew that they had to do something with the bones that were uncovered, most of them were not at all happy with the situation because an exhumation could stir up old trouble. The majority of the *Junta* was most anxious to avoid any problems and explained that, if there was any chance of trouble, they preferred not to continue with the exhumation at all. They also wanted to be sure that an exhumation would not automatically lead to pointing fingers at guilty persons or even trials. A third important issue for the *Junta* members was whether or not family members of the victims would receive the remains after investigation, and whether or not they could decide for them-

---

85 Diary 1/9/99.
86 See Chapter 6 for a detailed analysis of this lynching.
87 Diary 3/9/99.

selves where and how to bury them. An extensive and often heated discussion followed, during which the exhumation team tried to remove some of the doubts that had been voiced. Although it was impossible to guarantee a problem-free exhumation, the exhumation team stressed that it would never initiate any judicial action itself against the alleged perpetrators of the atrocity. Only family members of the victims themselves could initiate a criminal investigation as a result of an exhumation.

The Joyabaj exhumation was distinct from other exhumations for a number of reasons. First of all, many *Joyabatecos* were not very happy with the uncovering of the massacre site behind the convent, although it was common knowledge among them. Normally family members of victims would visit the *Oficina de Paz y Reconciliación* to report the existence of a mass grave and to officially petition for an exhumation. In this case the priest made the request because the site was found on church lands and no family members had yet come forward. After this request was made, family members normally had to wait many months before all the paperwork was completed and for the exhumation to actually start. Besides, in 1999 the Santa Cruz office could not consider all requests for exhumations because there were just too many of them. A waiting list had to be formed. Joyabaj, however, was also in this respect an exception because it could not wait. The bones and other material evidence lay outside in the open air while the rain poured down, destroying much of the evidence. Joyabaj was to be an emergency exhumation. Nevertheless, it took until January 2000 before the paperwork was in order and the exhumation could actually start.

A third and last issue that distinguished the Joyabaj exhumation from others surfaced during the discussion between the *Junta* and the *Oficina de Paz y Reconciliación*. The *Junta* had already started rebuilding the latrines behind the convent before the exhumation team had the chance to examine the site. Although the *Junta* had carefully removed some of the bones that had been uncovered by the mud-slide and the reconstruction work and put them in a corner under a plastic sheet, they explained that it was impossible to delay the reconstruction work until the exhumation was finished. They needed the toilets for people from the surrounding villages, who frequently stayed at the *Casa Comunal* during market days. A clear conflict of interests.[88]

After extensive discussion and a short visit to the site of the massacre, the *Oficina de Paz y Reconciliación* decided to go ahead with preparations for the exhumation, which was eventually carried out in January and February 2000. It turned out that most of the exhumation site was located down the ravine and the reconstruction of the toilets would probably not interfere with the exhumation

---

88 Diary 3/9/99.

photo 24. *The mudslide behind the convent in Joyabaj, uncovering a massacre site. Concrete foundations are already laid, while family members are looking fhuman or remains further down the slope (author, 1999)*

work. During the preparations it became clear that local enthusiasm for the exhumation was not very great. Only a few family members of possible victims came forward, although the priest had mentioned the forthcoming exhumation in his sermons and had asked family members to present themselves. He had also given the necessary information to all local leaders of Catholic Action, with the request to pass it on to the other people in their villages.

In the course of almost two months twelve graves were uncovered behind the convent, some of which contained the remains of several individuals.[89] The remains of a total of 32 people were exhumed.[90] Relatives could identify only one individual, because in his breast pocket he still carried his identification card of the Social Security Service (IGSS). The others were never identified. It was impossible to determine the cause of death of all individuals, because some of the remains were not complete while others were in a bad state. Many, however, were found with their hands tied behind their backs with ropes, which were also

---

89 The exhumation was carried out between 18 January and 24 February, 2000 (Oficina Paz y Reconciliación, 2001).
90 The remains consisted of the complete or almost complete skeletons of 28 persons, four separate skulls and several human bones scattered around the site. Thirty individuals could be identified as male, two could not be identified.

tied around their necks. In other cases metal bullet fragments were found or there was evidence of severe trauma to the head or around the throat. For the forensic team, the Joyabaj exhumation was interesting because many of the bodies were found in the positions in which they were originally buried, despite the landslide, showing clearly the way in which they were killed and buried. As well, the torture method of tying hands and neck together with a rope was very well preserved in the Joyabaj exhumation.[91]

One of the team members remembered the Joyabaj exhumation as a very difficult one, because there was little moral or practical support from the *Joyabatecos*.[92] It had been difficult to mobilize people to help in the actual exhumation and for family members to come forward. According to the team member this was partially because neither the *Junta Directiva* nor the local priest were very actively involved in the exhumation process. They seemed somehow not very happy with the exhumation and the subsequent feelings of fear and unease it stirred up in the community. Although they did facilitate the work of the exhumation team, their attitude towards the exhumation remained unclear. The result was that only a few *Joyabatecos* helped with the actual digging and nobody came forward to offer information to the team about the exact location of the graves.[93] After the exhumation had been carried out, some people told me that the team had failed to uncover the largest pit, in which many more bodies were supposedly buried. During the exhumation, however, they had refrained from pointing this out to the exhumation team. This was possibly because they distrusted the team or because they thought the whole ravine would be dug up anyway. This was not the case, because the team lacked time, resources and information regarding the exact massacre site. The exhumation team had to rely on its own method of systematically uncovering grids of five-by-five meters, which was very time-consuming.

Around July 2000 the exhumation team finished investigating the remains and wrote up their findings of the Joyabaj exhumation. In February 2001 the forensic report (*dictamen antropológico forense*) was sent to the office of the prosecution (*Ministerio Público*). It took until July 2001, almost a year after the exhumation had been carried out, for the remains to be reburied in Joyabaj.

Exhumation triggers reactions
The exhumation in Joyabaj stirred up many different reactions among *Joyabatecos*. They ranged from favouring the exhumation to not wanting trouble,

---

91 Oficina Paz y Reconciliación (2001) and diary 9/5/01.
92 Diary 9/5/01.
93 Diary 9/5/01.

not caring, not remembering, not wanting to remember, wanting to forget, fear of powerful individuals and fear of the consequences of remembering and getting involved. Many people voiced a complicated combination of two or more of these reactions.

Before we examine reactions to the January 2000 exhumation, it is interesting to look at the attitude of some *Joyabatecos* towards exhumations in general before it was known that one would be carried out in their own municipality. In 1999 I had asked a former member of Catholic Action why *Joyabatecos* were so much more hesitant to report massacre sites than neighbouring municipalities. He explained that '[H]ere the people do not want this [exhumation] ... the people are very humble. With it [exhumation] comes an investigation ... to see who did it ... and they do not want that ... they do not want the situation to get worse. They do not want more trouble and are also afraid.'[94] The uncovering of the massacre site in August 1999, however, forced the *Joyabatecos* to deal with an exhumation and the subsequent feelings it stirred up.

A small group of *Joyabatecos*, often connected to human rights organizations or left-wing political parties, actively supported the exhumation. 'That they [the military] remember', one indigenous woman said. According to her 'they [the military] do not want the truth. They do not want us to talk about them and about what they did in those days'.[95] Another group that supported the exhumation were those who had lost family members during the civil war, who could possibly be buried behind the convent. A few individuals came forward, telling their individual stories about an uncle who was asked to present himself to the military in the convent and who had never come back, or a nephew who had been dragged off his bike and taken into the convent, never to be seen again.[96]

But the fear of threats and the charged atmosphere surrounding the national and local elections, which were to take place in November 1999, also caused a reserved attitude among supporters of the exhumation. This feeling was enhanced by the fact that one indigenous man who did actively participate in the exhumation process and had put his signature to the papers denouncing the massacre site became the object of threats. He received an anonymous letter, warning him to stop collaborating with the exhumation or he would be in trouble. He silently dropped out of the project, without any explanation to the exhumation team. I heard about the anonymous letter he had received only when I returned to Joyabaj in the spring of 2001, almost a year after the exhumation had been carried out.[97] He stayed active, however, in political organizations at the

---

94 Interview 30-99 (6/7/99).
95 Diary 22/5/01.
96 Diary 30/9/99.
97 Diary 20/5/01.

national level. According to him, this was much less dangerous work because it was something that took place outside Joyabaj. The exhumation behind the convent, however, was a local activity and perceived by him to be much more dangerous. Local conflicts involving local players started to re-emerge.

Not wanting to remember?

The majority of the *Joyabatecos* were not very happy with the exhumation. Some were afraid of what could happen if one was to dig into the past, some were genuinely not interested and did not care, while others did not want to know about the exhumation or about the past for that matter. Others preferred not to remember or said that it was much better to forget. Most people used several of the above reasons to explain their negative attitude towards the exhumation.

The first group of people, those who had nothing to gain by remembering the past, were former civil patrol leaders, military commissioners and other individuals responsible for the atrocities committed. Investigations and trials against former patrol leaders were being conducted in nearby municipalities at the time of the research, using forensic evidence from exhumations and numerous eyewitness testimonies.[98] Although it was apparent that this group was not very enthusiastic about the exhumations and other memory activities, they rarely voiced their opposition out loud. Instead, they appeared to keep a low profile, and did not go around openly fulminating against exhumations or other activities. There were, however, veiled threats such as the anonymous letter sent to one of the villagers who was involved in the exhumation behind the convent. When I asked one of the most important former patrol leaders in Joyabaj what he thought of the exhumation behind the convent, he had a very clear reply, although it did not really answer my question. He refrained from giving his opinion on the exhumation, categorizing it as neither a good nor a bad thing, but he was very strong in his conviction that, if he had only had the slightest evidence that his disappeared brother (presumably kidnapped by the guerrilla in 1981) was buried there, he too would want the exhumation to proceed.[99] He had read in the newspaper about an exhumation in a nearby municipality, in which women and children were exhumed from a grave inside the church.[100] 'That [killing women

---

98 See for example the Candido Noriega case (Chiché), the Colotenango case (Huehuetenango) and the Río Negro case (Baja Verapaz. These were covered extensively in the media. The Noriega case was especially important to Joyabatecos, because Candido Noriega was a well-known ladino among the ladinos in Joyabaj, and was not perceived as someone guilty of the crimes for which he was sentenced. At his third trial (he was acquitted at the first two) Noriega was sentenced to 220 years in prison (Prensa Libre, 16/2/00).
99 Interview 12-01 (21/5/01).
100 He was probably referring to the exhumation in San Andrés Sajcabajá in 1997, during which the remains of 26 men, women and children were found (El Periódico, 27/1/98).

and children] is not of humans ... OK, people die in battle when fighting man to man ... but this way, no. . .', and his voice trailed off.[101] He appeared to answer as a brother and not as a former patrol commander, although he must also have been aware of the growing anti-patrol sentiment.

Apart from civil patrol commanders, the *Junta Directiva* of Catholic Action was, as I have shown in the previous paragraph, also afraid that the exhumation would provoke trouble. They just wanted to identify and re-bury the dead without pointing fingers at guilty parties and without starting criminal investigations into what exactly happened at the convent during the time the military had occupied it. They preferred to 'bury the past' (*echar arena*)[102] rather than open old wounds. Others explained that 'what happened, happened ... you should not look back to remember. That way the violence will not come back'.[103] A former municipal secretary was also very clear in his reactions to the exhumation. He said, 'I do not occupy myself any more with that period ... that is already forgotten. It is better to forget'.[104] Many other ladinos, but also indigenous people, shared this reaction and used the same words and phrases in many of the interviews.

A related reaction is to say *we do not care*, 'because it happened a long time ago and everything has changed now'. This notion of not caring, however, often seemed to be closely related with *fear*: fear of the past and fear of getting into trouble when thinking or talking about this past. A young indigenous woman, who had helped gather testimonies for the truth commission of the Catholic Church, explained why so many indigenous people in Joyabaj did not want to give their testimony to the REMHI project. At first she said, 'they don't care'. After a short silence she added, 'because they are still scared. That is why they say they don't care, because they do not want problems, they do not want to get involved in anything'.[105] The refrain 'I do not want any problems' is typical of the attitude of many *Joyabatecos*, both ladinos and *indígenas*, towards, for example, outside organizations, new initiatives and community relations in general, but also towards many of the memory initiatives that have been taking place in Joyabaj. Not wanting to get involved seemed to be a general attitude, born sometimes out of fear, sometimes out of a genuine lack of interest.

Many ladinos refrained from having an opinion on the matter and acted as if the exhumation was no concern of theirs. They talked about the mud-slide after it had happened, and about the toilets that had been washed away, but hardly

---

101 Interview 12-01 (21/5/01).
102 Interview 8-99 (20/6/99).
103 Interview 26-99 (21/8/99).
104 Interview 15-01 (15/5/01).
105 Interview 22-98 (15/7/98).

ever mentioned the bones that had been uncovered. They did not seem to be at all interested in the exhumation or anything connected with the war and just wanted to get on with their old lives. Others claimed that they had never known what happened in the convent and thus had never known about the massacre site, although some of them lived only a few houses away from the convent and had stayed in Joyabaj through the worst of the violence.[106] They had seen people enter the convent, but had never noticed they did not came out again. They remembered only that times were hard, and that maize and beans were expensive. They remembered the military checkpoints in front of their houses, and smiled at the thought of their maize being weighed before they were allowed to go to the mill to grind the corn: when they returned home, the dough was weighed again to make sure that none of it had secretly been given to the guerrilla.[107]

They had kept their ears and eyes closed during the civil war and had concentrated on their families and businesses. Not knowing, at that time, was used as a survival mechanism because ignorance about what happened gave you some protection. This meant that no questions were asked in the early 1980s, and when stories were told about, for example, what happened behind the convent, people did not listen or just walked away. They chose not to know. One ladino explained how other ladinos tried to live through those times. 'In the village they were like frozen people ... they did not want to hear anything, they did not want to get involved in anything.'[108] After the first acts of violence by the military 'people had learned to survive ... people had learned a lot, they had learned to shut their mouth and not to protest, they had learned not to talk and not to ask, they had learned to obey when you were called for patrol duty'. According to a ladino who had been openly hostile to the military in the early 1980s, people felt trapped and had no way out, while the ones who did stand up to the military 'are the ones that are now in the graves behind the convent'.[109] This seemed to be a clear example of 'the enquiring mind' that 'had been long since punished into obedience'.[110] People had learned not to know and not to ask, something that was still apparent at the time the research was carried out. Not getting involved in things, not taking part in community life was seen by some people as the best option for avoiding any problems. An older ladino woman who lived all her live almost adjacent to the convent explained that she had never known what happened behind the convent. She never wondered what happened, 'because if you would know, you would die of fear. It was better not to know'.[111]

---

106 Interview 5-01 (18/5/01).
107 Diary 19/5/01.
108 Interview 7-01 (23/5/01).
109 Interview 7-01 (23/5/01).
110 Cohen (2001: 124-132).
111 Diary 19/5/01.

According to Cohen, in many Latin American states fear of the violence 'generated a state of self-censorship—you avoided talking in public or even with your friends, you monitored your internal thoughts and dialogues'.[112] Foucault's explanation of the functioning of a panopticon is similar, in that it ensures a permanent feeling of being watched even if no actual surveillance is being carried out. Out of fear of the repercussions, people will discipline themselves. At that point, actual surveillance by way of civil patrols and military commissioners is no longer necessary, because the threat of surveillance appears to be enough to induce self-control. This situation continues, although in a less terrorized way than before, in present-day Guatemala. People secretly read the newspaper summary of the REMHI report at home, looking up places and events they had heard or knew about.[113] They denied doing so in the presence of other people. These were people who, in public, did not seem to be very interested in talking about the violent past, claiming that it no longer had any bearing on the present. Memories and narratives of the violent past were sometimes carefully monitored or censored. Some stories came out easily, while others stayed buried or were only partially revealed.

The attitude of 'internal bystanders' (Cohen 2001), who did not act and did not want to know in the past, appears to persist into the present. Some people still do not want to know what happened in the past and are not interested in the outcomes of the truth commission reports or a re-burial in their own community. It seems that the general attitude among *Joyabatecos*, especially but not exclusively among ladinos, towards the exhumation was negative because it stirred up so many memories of the past. They wanted the past to stay buried so that they could get on with their lives. They felt that the exhumation was forced upon them by the mud-slide. They had not requested the exhumation and probably would not have done so for some years. There was also a conflict of interest between the needs of the community and the wishes of the exhumation team. The majority of the people clearly did not approve of the exhumation and it was not the community rhythm which was followed. Therefore the possible benefits of the exhumation could be much smaller than in cases where the community itself is the initiator of the exhumation process.

A civil patrol memorial

In this final section of a chapter devoted to dealing with a violent past, I want to look at a very different reminder of the past. It took me more than eight months to discover, by accident, that there actually existed a memorial commemorating

---

112 Cohen (2001: 154).
113 Interview 3-98 (17/7/98).

civil patrollers who had died during the violence. It was situated in the town square. When I heard about it, I walked straight to the town square because I could not imagine having failed to see such a monument in such a prominent place. When I arrived at the *plaza*, I began to understand why I had never seen it. As usual, the *plaza* was packed with markets stalls, hiding trees and lamp posts. I finally discovered the monument half hidden behind one of the stalls, which had used it to secure the poles and plastic covering the stall. A broom was propped up against one of the sides. The owner did not understand why I was interested in the cement structure behind his stall, but obligingly held up the plastic coverings so that I could read the plaque at the front of the memorial and take some photographs of it. He had no idea what the memorial was for. The plaque consisted of a list with names of patrol members 'who had died in combat'. The text continued, 'Their memory lives on in our hearts, as an example of the duty and glory to our free and sovereign fatherland'. There was no date on it, the paint was fading and chips of cement had come off. It made a forlorn impression.

Thinking it might once have been an important memorial, I asked several people about it. Their answers were very vague regarding when it was built, by whom and for what. They were clear, however, on the fact that it was something of little significance. One ladino got rather angry when I showed him my pictures of the plaque and explained that not one civil patroller ever died in combat as the plaque said. 'Fallen in combat means that you die in combat ... combat between the military and the guerrilla ... but that never happened here.'[114] According to him, most patrollers on the list died in other ways, or were killed by the army itself. Others just laughed at my interest in the memorial, saying that one day the 'thing was just there'.[115] The only one whose memories were somewhat less vague on the subject was former patrol commander Leonel Ogáldez. According to him it was constructed in 1983 and 'the monument was an idea of the people from the rural communities'.[116] Apparently, more than 5,000 patrollers gathered for a kind of ceremony when the memorial was finished. Most people I talked to, however, could not remember much at all and did not consider it of much importance. Apparently, the civil patrol memorial does not function as a reminder of a heroic past.

Conclusion

The initial question concerning whether and how to deal with a violent past was answered positively in Guatemala, to judge from the various initiatives taken. Two truth commissions set out to reconstruct as much from the civil war past as

---

114 Interview 9-01 (15/5/01).
115 Interview 3-01 (7/5/01).
116 Interview 12-01 (21/5/01).

photo 25. Memorial for fallen civil defense patrollers, located on the central square of Joyabaj (author, 1999).

possible, using different avenues to do so. Stories were told, taped and written down. Exhumations were carried out and commemorations of murdered citizens, like for example the martyred priest Padre Villanueva, were held. Although considerable space was created at the national level to talk about the past, the topic was less out in the open at the local level. In most cases it took several months of intensive contact with the people before they were willing to give their opinion on such sensitive topics as truth commissions, trials against presumed war criminals and exhumations. People were also not very open about their own role in some of these institutions and activities geared towards dealing with the past. It was not something that was talked about while drinking coffee after mass on a Sunday morning. The large majority of *Joyabatecos*, whether ladino or indigenous, refrained from talking too much about the past. Better not to talk about it, better to forget, better to get on with your life. Getting involved could only mean trouble. Only a minority, mainly but not exclusively indigenous people, did get involved in these initiatives, and considered them as an opportunity to speak out and address the past as well as the present. As I have explained in the previous chapters, it is tempting but also incorrect to paint a picture of an indigenous population wanting to remember on the one side, against a ladino minority that does not want to deal with the past on the other side. Reality is not so nicely ordered, meaning that divisions between people and groups do not occur only along ethnic lines but also along religious, political and economic lines.

The attitudes of former civil patrol commanders, patrollers and military commissioners towards the different commemorative initiatives depended mostly on their involvement in violent incidents during the civil war. The ones who had been closely involved stood to lose much in the event that the past would be opened up, by way of exhumations or reports from truth commissions. Patrollers who had tried to stay out of most conflicts seemed somewhat more ambivalent towards such initiatives. On the one hand they wanted to continue keeping out of trouble, which meant not initiating any activities that would stir up the past. On the other hand, they also wanted to find lost family members and tell their stories about what they went through during the time they patrolled their communities.

On the whole, reconciliation in Guatemala, as in any other country emerging from violent conflict, is a difficult and lengthy process. Years of civil war, pitting different groups within society against each other, only added to the already existing polarization between different groups in Guatemalan society. What is even more important is that no political consensus seems to exist as to how to deal with the past. Although many initiatives have been taken, like the two reports of the truth commissions, the numerous exhumations by the various forensic teams, commemorative events at the national and the local levels and the increasing number of trials of alleged perpetrators of crimes during the armed conflict, it is unclear which road lies ahead. Expectations had risen after the publications of the reports, but were not met by actual changes. This uncertainty only increased after the elections in 1999, when the right-wing FRG won the elections with former President Ríos Montt as its leader.[117]

Reconciliation is also hindered by the fact that local memory of individual people and victims does not always follow the same track as the official memory of the state. Contesting memories and stories of past events exist and will multiply only when more people are willing to come out into the open. The idea of a coherent and complete story of the civil war violence, neatly summarized in four (REMHI) or nine (CEH) volumes, is of course a myth. The truth commissions themselves were very aware that they presented only part of the story and that their work should act only as a starting point for discussion of the past, and not as a final closure after which nothing is left to be said, done or investigated. While human rights groups continue to point out that most recommendations of the CEH after the publication of its report have not yet been implemented, the government appears to be hiding behind national problems such as security and economics. Apparently these, and not the implementation of the Peace Accords, are considered priorities by the government.

---

117 He was barred from becoming the official presidential candidate for the FRG because the Guatemalan constitution does not allow former dictators to assume such a position.

8

Concluding and reflecting

My first encounter with civil patrols in Guatemala, in 1995, was influenced by the fearful attitude of the returning refugees towards these organizations, of which I heard stories only of abuse and violence. Then, I could see only 'agents of the state', carrying rifles and being hostile towards anyone connected to returning refugees and human rights organizations, which clearly included myself. When I returned in 1998, the role of researcher was more prominent, and although my background as a human rights observer was always present, slowly a very different picture emerged in which patrollers became individuals who had their own stories to tell, their own memories and their own reasons for participating. My view of the patrols changed, although my memories of that first encounter with the patrols, together with other information, knowledge, opinions and memories I have gathered since then, clearly influenced that view.

In this book I have attempted to reconstruct the different local narratives on civil defence patrols and civil war violence which exist in the municipality of Joyabaj. Did I succeed in doing so? I am under no illusion that I have captured *all* the different local narratives in Joyabaj, but I have managed to capture some, which kept resurfacing during the research and were clearly considered important by the people themselves at the time of the research. In the course of talking to people about past events, on whatever subject, different and sometimes contrasting narratives on one and the same event kept coming up, and the people in Joyabaj were no exception. By openly putting different memories, narratives and opinions (the difference between them is not always clear) of the *Joyabatecos* side by side in this book, writing it was not always an easy task. Conflicting views, gaps in the information and even hostile villagers were all part of the process. I have tried to preserve these influences in this book, because I did not want to present a narrative of civil war violence in Joyabaj that was more smooth and flowing than reality seems to have been.

From open terror towards control and surveillance
Throughout the chapters I have touched upon the topics of violence and control in connection with the civil patrol system. Especially during the first years of their installation, civil patrols were foremost 'agents of the state', to cite Walter's (1969) words, receiving orders from higher up the military hierarchy, or the

'directorate' (citing Walter again), with little room to manoeuvre at the local level. Nevertheless, civil patrols were also local organizations, headed by local civil patrol commanders who were often trusted army allies, keeping the military informed about the community and its inhabitants. The intensity of the conflict, the presence of guerrilla groups in the area, and for example whether or not a political party such as the DCG had many followers were all influential factors in the way civil patrols functioned at the local level and whether or not patrols were kept under tight military surveillance. Villages such as Chorraxaj, with a long and considerable history of Catholic Action activism and a growing number of local indigenous leaders, were considered by the military to be safe havens for guerrilla groups and were therefore hit hard. After initial resistance, the men from Chorraxaj were eventually also forced into the civil patrols, which turned out to be quite violent, possibly the result of an overzealous patrol commander. The role of the patrol commander was also crucial to the functioning of the civil patrols. While some were active allies of the military, aiding them in their search for subversives, others were only trying to survive without doing too much harm to the civilian population, of which they themselves were, paradoxically, also part. They were a target of state terror as well as the state agents carrying out those same acts of terror. Schirmer (1998: 81) was correct to conclude that the 'army managed to mobilize and divide an indigenous population against itself', forcing victims to become accomplices and kill one another.

After the initial years of tight military control, during which the military consolidated its grip both on the rural communities and on the civil patrol structure, the space to manoeuvre for local patrol commanders seemed to become somewhat larger. In some communities, these changes resulted in a slackening of patrol discipline, while in other communities patrol duty intensified. Patrol commanders had created their own little kingdoms, and had grown quite independent of the military hierarchy. They were anxious not to lose this position, and therefore fervently opposed the anti-civil patrol lobby that was growing in the late 1980s and the early 1990s. While the patrols were actually dismantled in the town of Joyabaj in 1986, they continued to function in the surrounding rural areas until the Peace Accords were signed in 1996.

Patrols functioned remarkably like Foucault's (1977) panopticon system, as described in Chapter 1. Open surveillance during the early years of the conflict was followed by more veiled forms of control whereby people controlled their own behaviour. Even after the dismantling of the patrol structure, its surveillance function continued as people incorporated the possibility of being permanently watched into their daily lives. During the fieldwork many *Joyabatecos* did not want their stories taped, because they were afraid they could fall into the wrong hands or because they were convinced that military intelligence still compiled files on suspects and possible enemies of the state. They considered it a confirmation of this view when, in 1999, military archives of the civil war period, detailing the abduction and subsequent murder or in a few cases release of 183 Guatemalan citizens, were made public by the National Security Archives. Clearly, the control and surveillance functions of the civil patrol system worked not only during their most active years but even after they had been dismantled. Many preferred to keep quiet and only mind their own business to avoid getting into trouble with, for example, former patrol commanders. Others were afraid that the war could come back, especially after Ríos Montt's political party, the FRG, won the presidential elections in 1999. Fear of a possible revival of the patrols system or a possible resurge of the violence was fuelled by the actual organization of former patrollers in 1999 and again in July and August 2002 to pressure the government into paying financial compensation for services rendered. Although this reorganization does not mean an actual revival of the patrol structure, the perceived threat of the mere possibility is enough to instil fear into people: a clear legacy of civil war violence.

Conflicting memories and narratives

One of the aims mentioned in Chapter 1 was to reconstruct the different local narratives on civil war violence in Joyabaj, focusing on the impact of civil patrols. The diversity I encountered resulted partly from personal experiences during the war. People experienced the war as victim, perpetrator, bystander, or a combination of these roles. They experienced it as mothers, as wives of civil patrollers, as young people actively engaged in the revolutionary movement, or as older Catholic activists who were hunted down by military forces. Clearly, multiple stratification mechanisms operated in the community of Joyabaj, such as ethnicity (ladino-*indígena*), geography (town-rural areas), politics (conservative, right-wing, pro-military versus left-wing), religion (Catholics, evangelicals and Mayan religion), and socio-economic position (poor, middle class, wealthy elite). Changing combinations of these mechanisms constantly shaped and reshaped *Joyabateco* society and influenced people's memories and narratives. Memories were also influenced and distorted during the storing and subsequent retrieval of memories, through context, the tendency of people to harmonize and streamline memories, the issue of time, the influence of audience or the purpose for which the memory was recounted.

These different memories give insight into how different groups in society experienced and currently look back at the war. While, for example, one group presented the nun María de Boládo, whose case was presented in Chapter 3, as a guerrilla sympathizer, holding her partially responsible for the violence in Joyabaj, others remembered her as a very liberal and open person, far ahead of her time. The same goes for Alianza, the NGO working in Joyabaj in the 1970s and early 1980s. While people (ladinos as well as *indígenas*) to the right of the political spectrum remembered it with suspicion or even hatred because of its alleged connections with guerrilla groups, others (more to the political left or those working in other development organizations) regretted that Alianza had to leave Joyabaj and were certain that the municipality suffered as a result of it. The same holds for the military occupation of the church buildings in Joyabaj, and the installation of the civil patrols. While right-wing ladinos in particular were certain that, without the military intervention and the installation of the civil patrols, the guerrillas would have 'have flooded the municipality', another part of the *Joyabatecos* regarded the military as an enemy force trying to suppress local activism and development.

Apart from conflicting memories and opinions about central events or individuals, there also appeared to be gaps in local memory; events that were not talked about although they had been extensively covered by the media in the national and even the international arena—such as when the ladinos in Joyabaj petitioned the president for help in their fight against the guerrillas late 1981, or the visit by Benedícto Lucas García in November 1981 during which the creation of the first civil patrols was announced, or the killing of human rights activist Tomás Lares Ciprian, which was a well-known case in international human rights circles but hardly mentioned in Joyabaj. Local memory appeared to be different from national or official memory, but this was not so strange if we recall that former victims, perpetrators, and bystanders (or a combination of these) in many communities still live side by side and have to work and live which each other. In such a context, opening up old wounds because an exhumation is going to be carried out, or a former patrol commander is being tried for the atrocities committed, can be potentially threatening. Even the Guatemalan truth commission reports, REMHI as well as CEH, were unable to tell the complete story. When a summary of the REMHI report came out, some *Joyabatecos* were disappointed to find so little about what had happened in Joyabaj during the civil war. They felt as if their story had not yet been told. Memory clearly is contested, depending on whose version of events will be sanctioned as the 'official' memory of a country or a people. In Guatemala, the battle over this memory is still being waged with the current government as well as sections of the military only partly willing to admit the truthfulness of some of the information printed in the reports of the truth commissions. They consider the reports to be flawed, incomplete and focusing too much on the actions of state forces while neglecting guerrilla activity.

Clearly, the legacy of the civil war still shape day-to-day relations in various ways. Not only are the reminders of the war still apparent, but in a less obvious way social relations between people are marked by mutual suspicion and fear: fear of current violence in the form of lynching, or fear of a possible reorganization of the civil patrols. Former patrols in several departments have organized themselves to pressurize the government into paying them for services rendered during civil patrol duty. Although their demands may not seem so strange, because the patrollers were in fact forced into participating in the patrols without financial compensation, their position is fraught with difficulties.[1] Patrols, although a minority, have been involved in numerous human rights violations and only a few have ever been brought to justice. That these groups are now calling for their own justice is difficult for an outsider to understand, and apparently not only for an outsider, because according to a Guatemalan peasant leader 'they are rewarding violators of human rights'.[2]

I want to stress, however, that current social relations in Joyabaj are not marked only by suspicion and fear, because that would paint a rather one-sided picture. Although several *Joyabatecos* abstain from any involvement in, for example, the exhumations, commemorations or any other activity that has to do with the legacy of the civil war violence, because they do not want to get into trouble, many have become active again. They have started working for local NGOs, participate as volunteers in the Catholic Church or have worked for the REMHI project. Others are actively involved in new political parties, or take advantage of new economic opportunities such as migration to the United States.

Stigmatization and denial

In the first chapter I asked how people such as local patrol commanders or civil patrollers were forced into obedience to military strategy. Kelman and Hamilton (1989) made a distinction between three processes that can create conditions under which people may actually participate in carrying out violent acts, namely, authorization, routinization and dehumanization. The adherence to authority ('authorization') appears to have been an important process in Guatemala, with former patrol commanders stressing that they only followed orders, thereby

---

[1] Aside from the organization of former patrollers in the Petén department, former patrollers in Nebaj (Ixil region in the north of the Quiché department) and the department of Alta Verapaz, have asked for financial compensation (Prensa Libre, 10/7/02). It is strange to see men holding their patrol identification cards in front of the camera to prove that they actually formed part of the patrol system, while people were not very open in providing such information (both those who did and those who did not belong to the patrols) while I was doing fieldwork in Joyabaj.

[2] Prensa Libre 10/7/02.

trying to diminish their own responsibility in the process. Former patrollers and their family members always stressed that they had been forced to participate, that they had been forced to carry out orders, that they had been forced to carry arms. Because patrollers had little choice at the time, since disobeying the orders of the patrol commander or the military could get a person thrown into jail or even killed, only a few refer to their own responsibility for what happened. However, one must not make the mistake of grouping all patrollers together as obedient individuals carrying out orders from higher up the military hierarchy. Significant differences could be found between different civil patrols, depending on, for example, the local commander and military control of the area. A small number of patrollers participated eagerly, because they supported the military strategy and/or they were motivated by personal gain. Another small group did not want to participate, and initially tried to oppose patrol duty, getting into trouble as a result. The large majority, however, seem to have participated because they were ordered to do so. Some patrols, like the teacher patrol discussed in Chapter 4, preferred not to encounter the enemy when patrolling, sometimes deliberately looking the other way or, for example, hiding in an abandoned shed with food and drink for the duration of patrol duty.

The issue of obedience is also closely connected to what Cohen (2001) calls 'not-knowing', meaning that people deny any responsibility (as some patrol commanders did), or deny any knowledge, or do not have an enquiring mind. This last form of 'not-knowing' was especially apparent in many of the interviews conducted with for example ladino women in Joyabaj who had not been actually involved in the civil war violence, because they did not have to participate in the civil patrols. They did, however, live in town when many of the atrocities were committed, were married to men who were forced to participate or did so out of their own free will. It must have been very hard not to see, hear and thus know what was going on in town. Some of these 'internal bystanders', as Cohen labels them, maintained that they had no idea what was going on and that they did not want to know either. They chose not to know and not to listen to what others were telling them. In one of his sermons, Padre Rudi accused such people of being as guilty as the actual perpetrators of acts of violence.

The second process, that of routinization, is particularly prevalent in bureaucratic settings, and seems therefore less applicable to the activities of the civil patrols in Guatemala. Although the duties of the patrols were routinized, especially in the early 1980s, by making daily rounds, doing weekly sweeps of the areas, and having weekly meetings at the military base, it is unclear whether violent actions were also routinized at the local level. The process of dehumanization, whereby a large part of the indigenous community was stigmatized as subversive, communist or guerrilla, was the third important process and a known military tactic during the early years of the civil war.[3] This process, whereby several groups within *Joyabateco* society (or *Guatemalteco* society for that matter) were being cast out and branded as different, did not stop when the Peace Accords were signed and the patrols dismantled at the end of 1996. *Joyabatecos*, notably but not exclusively the ladino minority, continue to stigmatize former guerrilla combatants, people who used to work for Alianza, returning refugees, or human rights organizations such as MINUGUA as belonging to the 'other side', contrasting them with their own position as a ladino minority.

In Guatemala, the indigenous population had always been set apart or had been 'dehumanized' by a ladino minority which feared losing its privileged position to the indigenous majority. Fear of 'the other' was exacerbated by military propaganda during the civil war, labelling the indigenous population as subversive and communist. Such mutual tensions and feelings of fear do not change easily, even now, when *indígenas* in Joyabaj are becoming increasingly active in local, regional or even national politics or occupying important niches in the local economy. Tensions resurfaced, for example during the *Consulta Popular* in 1999, when people had to vote on fundamental changes to the constitution. Ladinos were afraid to lose their positions of influence to the indigenous majority. It is also in this situation of mutual prejudice and misunderstanding that the issue of lynchings is discussed. Many ladinos considered lynching to be an indigenous, and implicitly savage, way of dealing with community problems. They do not appear to connect the increasing number of lynchings with the militarization of society during the civil war, when problems were almost exclusively solved by force. Ladinos seem to have forgotten, however, that the first lynching in Joyabaj in 1996 involved mainly ladino victims and perpetrators.

Joyabaj: a changing society
A final aim of this book has been to map the process of changing power relations at the local level as a result of the violence, especially the impact of the civil defence patrols. When one examines the current political and economic situation in Joyabaj, it is clear that significant changes have occurred since the 1940s. After decades of ladino monopoly, a progressive period in the 1960s and 1970s, and a devastating war in the 1980s when political, economic and social life came to a virtual standstill, there now appears to be more space for civil society, especially for the indigenous part of civil society.

Before the violence of the 1980s, the local ladino establishment in Joyabaj had close ties with the state and the military and occupied most of the important

---
3   Kelman and Hamilton (1989: 19-20).

economic and political positions in town. Most of them voted for right-wing political parties, such as the MLN and were opposed to major changes that would create a space for the indigenous majority. The indigenous majority was excluded, socially, economically and politically. However, from the 1960s on, several groups in society were trying to change this, notably the Catholic Church through its Catholic Action programme. Many indigenous activists laboured to build schools and medical posts in their communities, aided by NGOs such as Alianza. A small but growing indigenous leadership was emerging in the indigenous communities in the 1960s and 1970s, apart from the traditional hierarchy of the *cofradias*. While a large part of the indigenous population supported these developments, traditional indigenous authority was not too happy about them. Despite their connections with the ladino elites and the MLN, they rapidly lost some of their influence in the communities.

During the violence of the 1980s, many ladinos left town because of the violence, thereby ending the ladino monopoly over economic resources. Some of the ladinos who stayed in Joyabaj during the war were military commissioners or otherwise committed to military intervention and were convinced that harsh measures were necessary to prevent *indígenas*, who were considered to be subversives and guerrillas, from taking over power. They became civil patrol leaders or closely collaborated with the military in other ways. The majority of the ladinos, however, tried not to get involved in anything. Often used phrases during interviews like 'when violence came to Joyabaj' are a clear indication of the way in which this group, consisting mainly of ladinos, looks at the past. To them the war just happened to them, and was clearly not something of their making. Most do not claim any responsibility or a direct involvement, and present themselves as pawns in the hands of bigger entities, like the military or civil patrol commanders. The indigenous population was one of the main targets of military repression. Local leaders, whether members of Catholic Action or of an Improvement Committee, were considered guerrillas or at least sympathetic towards them, and were an important military target. Clashes within the indigenous communities between activists and those with ties to right-wing political parties like the MLN and with the ladino elite only added to the violent situation in the rural areas.

After the war, political and economic power was no longer in the hands solely of a few wealthy ladino families. Participation by the indigenous population in the political as well as the economic arena grew rapidly. Economic opportunities in the United States also helped *indígenas* to take over part of the economic activity in Joyabaj. They opened up stores, not only at the outskirts of town but around the central square, a space which used to be reserved exclusively for ladino families. *Indígenas* also became legitimate actors in politics again. They had already been so in the 1970s, when the DCG won in several municipalities with indigenous candidates for mayor, but had not been given the chance to continue. Thus, both economic and political opportunities for the indigenous *Joyabatecos* have expanded markedly, while the ladinos have lost their monopolistic position in the municipality.

Dealing with the past
The slow and difficult process of transition to democracy in Guatemala entailed an elaborate reconstruction of state institutions with the aim of demilitarizing the country. The size of the army was to be reduced by a third, military intelligence was to be purged and reorganized, a new police force was to be set up to replace the existing corrupt one, guerrillas were reinserted into society, civil patrollers had to hand over their weapons and their organizations were dismantled. While the new police force received human rights training and schooling in the peace process, and former guerrillas could participate in development projects set up especially for them, hardly any attention was paid to the civil patrols and the people behind them. The patrols' influence on the local communities had been enormous for years and their legacy of violence and human rights abuses not easily erased. The Peace Accords stipulated only their dismantling, which was clearly not enough. Dismantling an organization such as the civil patrols does not end years of military indoctrination and militarization of a society. People were still afraid to trust outsiders or to speak out, for fear of getting into trouble. Most people were forced to participate for years in these abusive institutions, and were thoroughly indoctrinated by the military. Many violent incidents had occurred, causing rifts between communities and families. Former opponents of the patrol system can see that those involved in the massacres or other violations still walk around freely. In their eyes, the rule of law does not function properly, and they have little faith in the democratic process. The government and the legal system are considered weak, poorly equipped and understaffed. Only a few patrol commanders have been tried (like Noriega and Santos Chich Us); many more have never been called to account, or there has been insufficient evidence to pursue the case.

It is even more difficult to change the attitudes of those who supported the patrol system, gained positions of influence in the community as a result of it, and lost control over the local population when the patrols were dismantled. They had to hand over their weapons, were told that was the end of it, and had to get on with their lives as usual. They were hardly debriefed, receiving little if any information on the peace process, which caused many to feel that peace was forced upon them. Others felt that they were wronged because they did their duty in the patrols, and were now tossed aside as human rights violators. In their opinion, the enemy (guerrilla) has won the war because they have converted into an official political party, they participated in the elections (coming in second in Joyabaj), and none of the former guerrilla leaders has been sent to prison. According to some patrol commanders, the reports of the truth commissions unevenly blame the military, military commissioners and civil patrollers for the human rights violations that were committed during the war.

According to Jelin (1996: 102), citizens must learn to be ordinary citizens again, to embrace beliefs and practices suitable to a democracy and abandon taking the law into their own hands. A culture of citizenship has to emerge. But how does one go about this when people at the local level have very different ideas about what caused the war, what actually happened, who is to blame, and who are the victims? Although forensic evidence appears to deliver hard facts on who was murdered how, when and where, testimonies of eyewitnesses regarding those responsible for such acts are often discredited by the defence as being inaccurate memories and narratives. Whose truth will become the main narrative on civil war violence in Guatemala in the years to come?

Supporters of the patrols system are trying to limit the damage caused by their violent behaviour during the civil war, while some survivors do not want to look back because doing so will not bring back their dead relatives and they are too busy surviving on a day-to-day basis. Others are still afraid to look back, while activists and those who actively opposed the patrols system want those responsible for the violence to appear in court. It will probably take several generations before these different and often contrasting attitudes towards the past become less prominent and divisive. Even in our own society the past is not untroubled, with the older Dutch generation still having a difficult relationship with our German neighbours, while the activities of Dutch soldiers in Indonesia during the Politionele Acties remain a black hole in Dutch history books.

Principal abbreviations and acronyms

AC	*Acción Católica*	
	Catholic Action	
AJR	*Asociación Justicia y Reconciliación*	
	Association for Justice and Reconciliation	
AMJ	*Archivo del Municipio de Joyabaj*	
	Municipal Archives of Joyabaj	
ANN	*Alianza Nueva Nación*	
	Alliance of the New Nation	
AGCA	*Archivo General de Centro América*	
	General Archive of Central America	
AGST	*Archivo General: Sección Tierras*	
	General Archive: Land Section	
AJPDQ	*Archivos de la Jefatura Política del Departamento del Quiché*	
	Archives of de *Jefatura Política* of the Quiché department	
ASC	*Asamblea de la Sociedad Civil*	
	Assembly of Civil Society	
AVANCSO	*Asociación para el Avance de las Ciencias Sociales en Guatemala*	
	Association for the Advancement of Social Sciences in Guatemala.	
CAFCA	*Centro de Análisis Forense y Ciencias Aplicadas*	
	Center for Forensic Analysis and Applied Science	
CACIF	*Comité Coordinador de Asociaciones Agrícolas, Comerciales, Industriales y Financieras*	
	Coordinating Committee of Farming, Commercial, Industrial and Financial Associations	
CAL	*Comité Agrario Local*	
	Local Agrarian Committee	
CALDH	*Centro de Acción Legal para los Derechos Humanos*	
	Centre for Human Rights Legal Action	
CAN	*Central Auténtica Nacionalista*	
	National Authentic Central	
CAPS	*Centro de Adiestramiento de Promotores Sociales*	
	Training Centre for Social Promotors	
CEG	*Conferencia Episcopal de Guatemala*	
	Guatemalan Bishops' Conference	

CEH	*Comisión de Esclarecimiento Histórico*
	Comisión of Historical Clarification
CERJ	*Consejo de Comunidades Étnicas Runujel Junam*
	Council of ethnic communities Runujel Junam
CNR	*Comisión Nacional de Reconciliación*
	National Reconciliation Comisión
CVDC	*Comité Voluntario de Defensa Civil*
	Voluntary Civil Defense Committee
Conavigua	*Coordinadora Nacional de Viudas de Guatemala*
	National Coordination of Guatemalan Widows
COPAZ	*Comisión Presidencial de la Paz*
	Presidential Peace Commission
CUC	*Comité de Unidad Campesino*
	Committee of Campesino Unity
CVDC	*Comité Voluntario de Defensa Civil*
	Voluntary Committee for Civil Defense
DCG	*Democracia Cristiana Guatemalteca*
	Guatemalan Christian Democratic Party
DIA	*Desarrollo Integral Auténtico*
	Integral Authentic Develpment
D-5	*Directivo de Asuntos Civiles*
	Army Civil Affairs Directorate
EAFG	*Equipo de Antropología Forense de Guatemala*
	Guatemalan Forensic Team
EGP	*Ejército Guerrillero de los Pobres*
	Guerrilla Army of the Poor
EMDN	*Estado Mayor de la Defensa Nacional*
	National Defense Staff
ESA	*Ejército Secreto Anticomunista*
	Secret Anticommunist Army
FACS	*Frente Agusto Cesar Sandino*
	Front of Agusto Cesar Sandino
FAFG	*Fundación de Antropología Forense de Guatemala.*
	Guatemalan Foundation of Forensic Antropology
FAR	*Fuerzas Armadas Rebeldes*
	Rebel Armed Forces
FRG	*Frente Republicano Guatemalteco*
	Guatemalan Republican Front

FDNG	*Frente Democrático Nueva Guatemala*
	New Guatemala Democratic Front
FUNCEDE	*Fundación Centroamerica de Desarrollo*
	Central American Foundation for Development
GAM	*Grupo de Apoyo Mutuo por el Aparecimiento con Vida de Nuestros Familiares*
	Mutual Support Group for the Appearance of our Relatives Alive
GNIB	Guatemalan News and Information Bureau
GRICAR	*Grupo Internacional de Consulta y Apoyo al Retorno*
	International Consultancy Group to Help the Return
INC	*Instancia Nacional de Consenso*
	National Consensus Body
MAS	*Movimiento Acción Solidaria*
	Solidarity Action Movement
MINUGUA	*Misión de las Naciones Unidas para la Verificación de los Derechos Humanos en Guatemala*
	UN Human Rights Verification Mission in Guatemala
MLN	*Movimiento de Liberación Nacional*
	Movement of National Liberation
MSC	*Misionarios del Sagrado Corazón*
	Missionaries of the Sacred Heart
NDG	*Noticias de Guatemala*
	News from Guatemala
NSA	National Security Archive
ODHAG	*Oficina de Derechos Humanos del Arzobispado de Guatemala*
	Human Rights Office of the Archbishop of Guatemala
ORPA	*Organización Revolucionario de los Pueblos en Armas*
	Revolutionary Organisation of the People in Arms
PAC	*Patrullas de Autodefensa Civil*
	Civil Defense Patrols
PAN	*Partido de Avanzada Nacional*
	Party of National Advancement
PCG	*Partido Comunista de Guatemala*
	Communist Party of Guatemala
PDH	*Procuraderia de los Derechos Humanos*
	Human Rights Ombudsman
PGT	*Partido Guatemalteco de Trabajo*
	Guatemalan Workers' Party

PID	*Partido Institucional Democrático*
	Institutional Democratic Party
PMA	*Policía Militar Ambulante*
	Mobile Military Police
PNC	*Policía Nacional Civil*
	National Civil Police
PR	*Partido Revolucionario*
	Revolutionary Party
PRG	*Partido de la Revolución Guatemalteca*
	Party of the Guatemalan Revolution
PUA	*Partido de la Unificación Anticomunista*
	Party of the Anti-communist Unification
Redención	*Partido Democrático de Reconciliación Nacional*
	Democratic Party of National Reconciliation
REMHI	*Recuperación de la Memoria Histórica*
	Recuperation of the Historical Memory
TSE	*Tribunal Supremo Electoral*
	Supreme Electoral Tribunal
UCN	*Unión Centro Nacional*
	National Centrist Union
UNAGRO	*Unión Nacional Agropecuario*
	National Farming and Ranching Union
UNID	*Unidad de Izquierda Democrática*
	Unity of the Democratic Left
URNG	*Unidad Revolucionaria Nacional Guatemalteca*
	Guatemalan National Revolutionary Unity
WCC	World Council of Churches

Glossary

alcaldía indígena: indigenous municipality
arma blanca: gun
autogolpe: self-coup
azote: whip
barrio: neighbourhood
caballería: approximately 112 acres, or 66 *manzanas*
cantón: district of a municipality
cofradía: indigenous brotherhood
comandante general: general commander (of the civil patrols)
comité de amas de casa: committee of housewives
comité cívico: civic committee, a municipal alternative to the established political parties
comité de emergencia: emergency committee
comité de Pro-mejoramiento: improvement or betterment committee
comité (or *junta*) *de seguridad:* security committee
composiciones: regularization of land possession with the state
común indígena: indigenous community/indigenous communal corporate identity
comunidades: communities; or religious study groups, mainly consisting of ladino women
confianza: trust
consulta popular: public referendum
costumbre / costumbrista: traditional religious authority
cuadro político: political cadre (EGP unit)
cuadra: (town) block (part of a *barrio*)
cusha: alcohol made from sugarcane
derecho consuetudinario: indigenous customary law
derechos humanos: human rights
diputado: member of the departmental council
ejido: communal village grounds
empadronado: registered and thus eligible to vote
escopeta: shotgun
esquadron de muerte: death squads
finca: large landholding / plantation
finca de mozos: labour plantations

guerrillero: guerilla fighter
guardian / celador: guardian / keeper
impunidad: impunity
indígenas: indigenous population
indio: indian (derogatory term)
intendente: appointed representatives of central liberal government at municipal level, replacing chosen mayor
Joyabatecos: inhabitants of Joyabaj
jefatura política: departmental office associated with liberal administration
jefe: leader / boss / commander
judicial: informers
juez de paz: justice of the peace
junta local: neighborhood watch
junta directiva: elected board (in this case of Catholic Action groups at the municipal as well as at the community level)
junta parroquial: parish board, at the municipal level
kaibil: elite unit of the Guatemalan army
libro de acta: book of minutes from the municipality
libro de acuerdo: book of decrees, which replaced the book of minutes from March 1982 until elections in 1985
mano dura: firm hand / harsh treatment
manzana: 1.7 acres. 66 *manzanas* is 1 *caballeria*
médico forense: forensic surgeon
ministerio público: office of the prosecution
ministro de gobernación: minister of the interior
misionero del sagrado corazón (MSC): priest of the sacred heart
monte: forest area / mountain
moral: knitted bag, used mainly by indigenous people
municipio: municipality (town)
municipalidad: town hall
natural: derogatory term for *indígena*
nunca más: never again / title of the REMHI report
oreja: literally ears, or local people providing information to military intelligence
palo volador: flying pole (indigenous dance)
paz: peace
Patrullas de Autodefensa Civil: Civil Defense Patrols
plaza: central town square
pozo: pit; hole in the ground

principales: indigenous elders at town or municipal level
pueblo de indio: corporate indian town / forcibly settled indigenous communities, in which no non-Indian was allowed to reside
rancheros: people living and working on the land of someone els, in exchange for part of the crop
reconciliación: reconciliation
rencor: rancour
ronda: patrol
sajorin: Mayan priest
subversivos: subversives or guerrillas
teniente: army lieutenant
tierra baldía: uncultivated lands
vigilar: to watch over
viuda: widow

Bibliography

Adams, R. *Encuesta Sobre la Cultura de los Ladinos en Guatemala.* Guatemala: Centro Editorial 'José de Pineda Ibarra', 1964.

Aguilar, P. and K. Hite. Historical memory and authoritarian legacies in processes of political change: Spain and Chile in comparative perspective. Paper presented at the Conference Cultures of Political Transition: Memory, Identity and Voice. Organized by the Institute of Common Wealth Studies, the Institute of Latin American Studies and the Institute of Romance Studies, LSE, London, 14-16 September 2000.

Alba, J. and L. Hasher. Is Memory Schematic? *Psychological Bulletin*, Vol. 93, No.2, 1983, pp. 203-231.

Americas Watch Committee. *Guatemala: A Nation of Prisoners.* New York: Americas Watch Committee, 1984.

Americas Watch Committee. *Civil Patrols in Guatemala.* New York and Washington: Americas Watch Committee, 1986.

Americas Watch. *Closing the Space. Human Rights in Guatemala, May 1987 – October 1988.* New York: Americas Watch, 1988.

Amnesty International. Guatemala. *Human Rights Violations under the Civilian Government.* London: Amnesty International, 1989 (AMR 34/07/89).

Amnesty International. *Guatemala. Lack of Investigations into Past Human Rights Abuses: Clandestine Cemeteries.* London: Amnesty International, 1991 (AMR 34/10/91).

Amnesty International. *(Guatemala?) Human Rights Defenders on the Front Line.* London: Amnesty International, 1996 (AMR 02/01/96).

Amnesty International. *Guatemala's Lethal Legacy: Past Impunity and Renewed Human Rights Violations.* London: Amnesty International, 2002 (AMR 34/001/2002).

Anderson, K. and J. Simon. Permanent Counterinsurgency in Guatemala. *Telos*, No.73, 1987, pp. 9-46.

Antze, P. and M. Lambek. *Tense Past. Cultural Essays in Trauma and Memory.* New York, Routledge, 1996.

Arenas, C., C. Hale and G. Palma Murga (eds.) *¿Racismo en Guatemala? Abriendo el Debate Sobre un Tema Tabú.* Guatemala: AVANCSO, 1999.

Arendt, H. *Eichmann in Jerusalem. A Report on the Banality of Evil.* New York, Viking Press, 1965.

Arias, A. Changing Indian Identity: Guatemala's Violent Transition to Modernity. In: C. Smith. *Guatemalan Indians and the State: 1540-1988*. Austin: University of Texas Press, 1990, pp. 231-257.

Armon, J., R. Sieder and R. Wilson. *Negotiating Rights: The Guatemalan Peace Process*. London: Conciliation Resources, 1997.

Arnson, C. (ed.) *La Consulta Popular y el Futuro del Proceso de Paz en Guatemala*. Documento de Trabajo No 243. Washington: Woodrow Wilson International Center of Scholars, 1999.

Aronson, E., T. Wilson and R. Akert. Social Cognition: How We Think About the Social World. In: E. Aronson, T. Wilson and R. Akert. *Social Psychology: The Heart and the Mind*. New York: Harper Collins College Publishers, 1994.

Bartlett, F.C. *Remembering. A Study in Experimental and Social Psychology*. Cambridge: Cambridge University Press, 1932.

Bastos, S. and M. Camus. *Quebrando el Silencio: Organizaciones del Pueblo Maya y sus Demandas (1986-1992)*. Guatemala: FLACSO, 1993.

Baud, M., K. Koonings, G. Oostindie, A. Ouweneel and P. Silva. *Etniciteit als Strategie in Latijns-Amerika en de Caraïben*. Amsterdam: Amsterdam University Press, 1994.

Baud, M. *Militair Geweld, Burgerlijke Verantwoordelijkheid. Argentijnse en Nederlandse Perspectieven op het Militaire Bewind in Argentinië (1976-1983)*. The Hague: SDU, 2001.

Bauman, Z. *Modernity and the Holocaust*. Cambridge: Polity Press, 1989.

Boyarin, J. (ed.) *Remapping Memory. The Politics of TimeSpace*. Minneapolis: University of Minnesota Press, 1994.

Bornschein, D. *Las Izquierdas en Guatemala. Reflejos de un futura incierto*. Guatemala: Fundación Friedrich Ebert, 2000.

Brow, J. Notes on Community, Hegemony, and the Uses of the Past. *Anthropological Quarterly*, Vol. 63, No. 1, 1990, pp. 1-5.

Burgos-Debray, E. (ed.) *I, Rigoberta Menchú. An Indian Woman in Guatemala*. London: Verso, 1984.

Burke, P. History as Social Memory. In: T. Butler. *Memory, History, Culture and the Mind*. Oxford: Basil Blackwell, 1989.

Buur, L. In the name of the victims. The politics of representivity in the work of the South African Truth and Reconciliation Commission. Paper presented at the Conference Cultures of Political Transition: Memory, Identity and Voice. Organized by the institute of Common Wealth Studies, the Institute of Latin American Studies and the Institute of Romance Studies, LSE, London, 14-16 September 2000.

Cabezas Carcache, H. La Tierra. In: Asociacion de Amigos del Pais. *Historia General de Guatemala*, Vol. III. Siglo XVIII hasta la Independencia. Guatemala: Asociación de Amigos del Pais, 1995, pp. 279-290.

Cabrera, R. Should We Remember? Recovering Historical Memory in Guatemala. In: Hamber, B. (ed.). *Past Imperfect: Dealing with the Past in Northern Ireland and Societies in Transition.* Ulster: Incore/University of Ulster, 1998. (www.incore.ulst.ac.uk/home/publication/research/dwtp)

Carmack, R. *Harvest of Violence.* Norman: University of Oklahoma Press, 1988.

Carmack, R. M. The Story of Santa Cruz Quiché. In: R. M. Carmack. *Harvest of Violence.* Norman: University of Oklahoma Press, 1988, pp. 39-69.

Casaús Arzú, M. *La Metamorfosis del Racismo en Guatemala.* Guatemala: Editorial Cholsamaj, 1998.

CEG (Conferencia Episcopal de Guatemala). *Monseñor Juan Gerardi: Testigo fiel de Dios.* Guatemala: CEG, 1999.

CEG (Centro de Estudios de Guatemala). *Guatemala: Un Paiz Militarizado.* Mexico: CEG, 1993.

CEH (Comisión para el Esclarecimiento Histórico). *Guatemala. Memoria del Silencio.* Vols. I – XII. Guatemala: UNOPS, 1999.

Chance, J. Mesoamerica's Ethnographic Past. *Ethnohistory*, Vol. 43, No. 3, 1996, pp. 379-403.

Claridge, D. Know Thine Enemy. Understanding State Terrorism. *Pioom Newsletter and Progress Report*, Vol. 9, No. 1, 1999/2000, pp. 12-17.

Claridge, D. The Dynamics of the Terrorist State: a Comparative Analysis of the Effect of Policy Decisions and Structural Factors upon the Shape of State Terrorism. Unpublished doctoral dissertation, University of St. Andrews, 2000.

Cohen, H. The Unmaking of Rigoberta Menchú. In: D. Lorey and W. Beezley (eds.). *Genocide, Collective Violence, Popular Memory.* Wilmington: Scholarly Resources, 2002.

Cohen, S. *States of Denial. Knowing about Atrocities and Suffering.* Cambridge: Polity Press, 2001.

Davis, S. Introduction: Sowing the Seeds of Violence. In: R. M. Carmack. *Harvest of Violence.* Norman: University of Oklahoma Press, 1988, pp. 3-36.

DeCormier, C. *Report on Joyabaj.* Guatemala: Alianza, 1976.

Deli Sante, A. *Nightmare or Reality? Guatemala in the 1980s.* Amsterdam: Thela, 1996.

Diócesis del Quiché. *El Quiché: El Pueblo y su Iglesia.* Santa Cruz del Quiché: Diócesis del Quiché, 1994.

Diócesis del Quiché. *Plan Diocesano de pastoral 1999-2003.* Santa Cruz del Quiché, 1998.

Diócesis del Quiché. *Y Dieron la Vida por el Quiché.* Santa Cruz del Quiché: Diócisis del Quiché, 2000.

Doyle, K. *Guatemala's Ghosts.* Washington: National Security Archive, 1999. (http://lasa.international.pitt.edu/Doyle.htm) [17/11/99].

EAFG (Equipo de Antropología Forense de Guatemala). *Las Masacres de Rabinal. Estudio Histórico Antropológico de las Masacres de Plan de Sánchez, Chichupac y Río Negro.* Guatemala: EAFG, 1997.

Eidson, J. Which Past for Whom? Local Memory in a German Community during the Era of Nation Building. *Ethos. Journal for Psychological Anthropology,* Vol. 28, No. 4, 2000, pp. 575-607.

Engel, S. *Context is Everything. The Nature of Memory.* New York: W.H. Freeman and Company, 1999.

EPICA (Ecumenical Program on Central America) / CHRLA (Center for Human Rights Legal Action). *Unearthing the Truth. Exhuming a Decade of Terror in Guatemala.* Washington: EPICA, 1996.

Fentress, J. and C. Wickham. *Social Memory. New Perspectives on the Past.* London: Blackwell, 1992.

Festinger, L. *A Theory of Cognitive Dissonance.* Evanston: Row, Peterson, 1957

Flores Alvarado, H. *Gobierno Locales y sus Conflictos, Guatemala.* Guatemala: PROECODI, 1996.

Foucault, M. *Discipline and Punish.* London: Penguin Books, 1977.

Frente Guatemala. Testimonio de la iglesia perseguida. November 1980.

Fumerton, M. *From Victims to Heroes: Peasant Counter-rebellion and Civil War in Ayacucho, Peru, 1980-2000.* Amsterdam: Rozenberg, 2002.

FUNCEDE (Fundación Centroamerica de Desarrollo). *Diagnostico y Plan de Desarrollo del Municipio de Joyabaj.* Departamento de Quiché. Guatemala: FUNCEDE, Fundación Konrad Adenauer (KAS) and Asociación Nacional de Municipalidades (ANAM), 1995.

FUNCEDE (Fundación Centroamerica de Desarrollo). *Los Conflictos Municipales en el Período Post Acuerdos de Paz.* Guatemala: FUNCEDE, Fundación Konrad Adenauer (KAS) and Asociación Nacional de Municipalidades (ANAM), 1997.

Fundación Rigoberta Menchú Tum. Querella de Rigoberta Menchú Tum. Guatemala: Fundación Rigoberta Menchú Tum, 1999. (www.pangea.org/impunitat/querella.html) [February 2001].

Fundación Rigoberta Menchú Tum. *Jurisdicción Universal. Para el Juzgamiento del Genocidio en Guatemala.* Casos y Adhesiones. Guatemala: Fundación Rigoberta Menchú Tum, 2000.

García Escobar, C. El Palo Volador. *Tradiciones de Guatemala.* Revista del Centro de Estudios Folklóricos de Guatemala. No. 32, 1989, pp. 127-137.

Gillis, J. Memory and Identity: the History of a Relationship. In: J. Gillis (ed.). *Commemorations. The Politics of National Identity.* Princeton: Princeton University Press, 1994, pp. 3-24.

Glebbeek, M. *In the Crossfire of Democracy. Police Reform and Police Practice in Post Civil War Guatemala.* Amsterdam: Rozenberg, 2003 (forthcoming).

Gleijesis, P. *Shattered Hope: The Guatemalan Revolution and the United States, 1944-1954.* New Jersey: Princeton University Press, 1991.

González, M. *Se Cambió el Tiempo. Conflicto Y Poder en Territorio K'iche'.* Guatemala: Avancso, 2002.

Green, L. *Fear as a Way of Life. Mayan Widows in Rural Guatemala.* New York: Columbia University Press, 1999.

Hamber, B. (ed.) *Past Imperfect: Dealing with the Past in Northern Ireland and Societies in Transition.* Ulster: Incore/University of Ulster, 1998. (www.incore.ulst.ac.uk/home/publication/research/dwtp)

Hamber, B. and R. Wilson. *Symbolic Closure throught Memory, Reparation and Revenge in Post-conflict Societies.* Paper presented at the Traumatic Stress in South Africa Conference, CSVR, South Africa, January 1999.

Handy, J. Resurgent Democracy and the Guatemalan Military. *Journal of Latin American Studies,* Vol. 18, 1986, pp. 383-408.

Handy, J. Insurgency and Counterinsurgency in Guatemala. In: J. Flora and E. Torres-Rivas. *Sociology of 'Developing Countries'. Central America.* New York: Monthly Review Press, 1989: 112-139.

Handy, J. Anxiety and Dread: States and Community in Modern Guatemala. *Canadian Journal of History,* Vol. 26, No. 1, 1991, pp. 43-66.

Handy, J. *Revolution in the Countryside. Rural Conflict and Agrarian Reform in Guatemala, 1944-1954.* Chapel Hill and London: The University of North Carolina Press, 1994.

Hayner, P. *Unspeakable Truths: Confronting State Terror and Atrocities.* New York and London: Routledge, 2001.

Henry, Y. Reconciling Reconciliation: a personal and public journey of testifying before the south african truth and reconciliation commission. Paper presented at the Conference Cultures of Political Transition: Memory, Identity and Voice. Organized by the institute of Common Wealth Studies, the Institute of Latin American Studies and the Institute of Romance Studies, LSE, London, 14-16 September 2000.

Human Rights Watch. *Los Derechos Humanos en Guatemala Durante el Primer Año del Presidente de Leon Carpio.* New York, Washington, Los Angeles, London:

Human Rights Watch, 1994.
Huttenbach, H. The Psychology and Politics of Genocide Denial: A Comparison of Four Case Studies. In: L. Chorbajian and G. Shirinian. *Studies in Comparative Genocide*. London/New York: Macmillan Press/St. Martin's Press, 1999, pp. 216-229.
IGN (Instituto Geográfico Nacional). *Diccionario Geográfico de Guatemala. Tomo II*. Guatemala: IGN, 1978.
INE (Instituto Nacional de Estadísticas). *Características Generales de Población y Habitación. X Censo Nacional de Población de 1994*. Guatemala: INE, 1994.
Jay, A. *Persecution by Proxy. The Civil Patrols in Guatemala*. Washington: The Robert F. Kennedy Memorial Center for Human Rights, 1993.
Jeffrey, P. *Recovering Memory. Guatemalan Churches and the Challenge of Peacemaking*. Uppsala: Life and Peace Institute, 1998.
Jelin, E. and E. Hershberg (eds.) *Constructing Democracy: Human Rights, Citizenship, and Society in Latin America*. Boulder: Westview Press, 1996.
Jelin, E. and S. Kaufman. Layers of Memories: Twenty Years After in Argentina. In: D. Lorey and W. Beezley (eds.). *Genocide, Collective Violence, and Popular Memory. The Politics of Remembrance in the Twentieth Century*. Wilmington: Scholarly Resources, 2002, pp. 31-52.
Jonas, S. *Of Centaurs and Doves. Guatemala's Peace Process*. Boulder: Westview, 2000.
Kaiser, S. Fear and Silences in Young Argentineans' Memories of Terror. Paper presented at the 2000 meeting of the Latin American Studies Association (LASA), Miami, 16-18 March 2000.
Kelman, H. and V. Hamilton. *Crimes of Obedience. Towards a Social Psychology of Authority and Responsibility*. New Haven and London: Yale University Press, 1989.
Kobrak, P. Village Troubles: The Civil Patrols in Aguacatán, Guatemala. Unpublished doctoral dissertation, University of Michigan, 1997.
Koonings, K. and D. Kruijt. *Societies of Fear. The Legacy of Civil War, Violence and Terror in Latin America*. London: Zed Books, 1999.
Koonings, K. and D. Kruijt. Military Politics and the Mission of Nation Building. In: K. Koonings and D. Kruijt. *Political Armies. The Military and Nation Building in the Age of Democracy*. London: Zed Books, 2002, pp. 9-34.
Krog, A. *Country of My Skull*. London: Jonathan Cape, 1999.
Kruijt, D. Exercises in State Terrorism: the Counter-insurgency Campaigns in Guatemala and Peru. In: Koonings, K. and D. Kruijt. *Societies of Fear. The Legacy of Civil War, Violence and Terror in Latin America*. London: Zed Books, 1999, pp. 33-62.

Kruijt, D., L. Fondebrider and F. Alvarez Medrano. *Informe de Evaluación de los Proyectos Ejecutados por la Fundación de Antropología Forense de Guatemala (FAFG).* Versión definitiva. Guatemala and Lima: Embajado Real de los Países Bajos, 2002.

Kruijt, D. and K. Koonings. Introduction: Violence and Fear in Latin America. In: Koonings, K. and D. Kruijt. *Societies of Fear. The Legacy of Civil War, Violence and Terror in Latin America.* London: Zed Books, 1999, pp. 1-30.

Lansdale, S. and K. Santora (eds.) *Un Paso Adelante. Una revista de desarollo para Joyabaj.* Vol. 1, No. 1, 1998.

Le Bot, Y. El Palimpsesto Maya. Violencia, Comunidad y Territorio en el Conflicto Guatemalteco. In: A. Breton. *Representantes del Espacio Político en las Tierras Altas de Guatemala.* Mexico: Cemca, 1993, pp. 17-28.

Le Bot, Y. *La Guerra en Tierras Mayas. Comunidad, Violencia y Modernidad en Guatemala (1970-1992).* Mexico: Fondo de Cultura Económica, 1995.

Lent, T. The Search for Peace and Justice in Guatemala: NGOs, Early Warning, and Preventive Diplomacy. In: R. Rotberg. *Vigilance and Vengeance. NGOs Preventing Ethnic Conflict in Divided Societies.* Cambridge: The World Peace Foundation, 1996, pp. 73-92.

Lent, T. *Blessed are the Spacemakers. Constructing Peace and Peace Processes in Conflictual Situations.* Cambridge: The Collaborative for Development Action, 1998.

Linenthal, E. The Boundaries of Memory: The United States Holocaust Museum. *American Quarterly,* 1994, Vol. 46, No. 3, pp. 406-433.

Loftus, E. and K. Ketcham. *The Myth of Repressed Memory: False Memories and Allegations of Sexual Abuse.* New York: St. Martin's Press, 1994.

Loftus, E. and J. Palmer. Reconstruction of Automobile Destruction: An Example of the Interaction Between Language and Memory. *Journal of Verbal Learning and Verbal Behavior,* 1974, Vol. 13, pp. 585-589.

Macleod, M. *Poder Local. Reflexiones Sobre Guatemala.* Guatemala: Oxfam, 1997.

McClintock, M. *The American Connection. (Volume II). State Terror and Resistance in Guatemala.* London: Zed Books, 1985.

McCreery, D. *Rural Guatemala, 1760-1940.* Stanford: Stanford University Press, 1994.

Milgram, S. *Obedience to Authority: An Experimental View.* New York: Harper and Row, 1974.

Minow, M. *Between Vengeance and Forgiveness.* Boston: Beacon Press, 1998.

MINUGUA. *Primer Informe del Director de la Misión de las Naciones Unidas de Verificación de Derechos Humanos en Guatemala y del Cumplimiento de los Compromisos Asumidos en el Acuerdo Global Sobre Derechos Humanos.* Guatemala: MINUGUA, March 1995.

MINUGUA. *Suplemento al Quinto Informe Sobre Derechos Humanos.* Guatemala: MINUGUA, September 1996.

MINUGUA. *Suplemento al Octavo Informe Sobre Derechos Humanos.* Guatemala: MINUGUA, June 1998.

MINUGUA. *Décimo Informe Sobre Derechos Humanos.* Guatemala: MINUGUA, January 2000.

MINUGUA. *Suplemento al Undécimo Informe Sobre Derechos Humanos.* Guatemala: MINUGUA, September 2000.

MINUGUA. *Informe de Verificación. Los Linchamientos: un Flagelo Contra la Dignidad Humana.* Guatemala: MINUGUA, 2000a.

MINUGUA. *Informe de verificación. Procedimientos de Exhumación en Guatemala (1997 – 2000).* Guatemala: MINUGUA, 2000b.

MINUGUA. *Los Conflictos en Guatemala: Un Reto Para la Sociedad y el Estado.* Guatemala: MINUGUA, 2001

Morin, E. *Las Voces de Patzulá.* Joyabaj: SCDRYS, 1996.

Muj Micalux, R. and D. Schramm. Earthquake Housing Reconstruction and Rural Development. Joyabaj, Quiché, Guatemala. In: M. B. Anderson and P.J. Woodrow. *Rising from the Ashes. Development Strategies in Times of Disaster.* Boulder: Westview Press, 1989, pp. 225-240.

Nagengast, C. Violence, Terror, and the Crisis of the State. *Annual Review of Anthropology*, Vol. 23, 1994, pp. 109-136.

Nairn, A. The Guns of Guatemala. The Merciless Mission of Ríos Montt's Army. *The New Republic*, April 11, 1983.

Neisser, U. *Cognitive Psychology.* New York: Appleton-Century-Crofts, 1967.

Nordstrom, C. and J. Martin (eds.) *The Paths to Domination, Resistance, and Terror.* Berkeley: University of California Press, 1992.

Ochoa García, C., R. Sánchez and A. Pacay Cú. *Los Comités Cívicos. Gestión Local de la Acción Política.* Guatemala: Fundación Friedrich Ebert and Organización de Estados Americanos.

ODHAG (Oficina de Derechos Humanos del Arzobispado de Guatemala). *Informe Annual 1993.* Guatemala: ODHAG, 1993

ODHAG (Oficina de Derechos Humanos del Arzobispado de Guatemala). *Guatemala: Nunca Más.* Vols. I – IV. Guatemala: ODHAG, 1998.

ODHAG (Oficina de Derechos Humanos del Arzobispado de Guatemala). *Guatemala. Never Again!* New York: Orbis Books, 1999.

Oficina Paz y Reconciliación. *Dictamen Antropológico Forense del Cementerio Clandestino Ubicado en el Convento del Municipio de Joyabaj, Departamento del Quiché.* Santa Cruz de Quiché: Oficina Paz y Reconciliación, 2001.

Oglesby, E. Labor Technology, and Social Control on Guatemalan Sugar Estates. Forthcoming doctoral disseration, University of Berkeley, 2002.

Organización del Pueblo en Armas. Las Patrullas Civiles. *Siembra*, December 1982.

Osiel, M. *Mass Atrocity, Collective Memory, and the Law.* New Brunswick: Transaction Publishers, 1997.

Ouweneel, A. 'Welcome to the Nightmare': Thoughts on the Faceless Warriors of the Lacandona Revolt of 1994 (Chiapas, Mexico). In: Koonings, K. and D. Kruijt. *Societies of Fear. The Legacy of Civil War, Violence and Terror in Latin America.* London: Zed Books, 1999, pp. 88-101.

Palencia Prado, T. *Towards a New Role for Civil Society in the Democratization of Guatemala.* Montreal: International Centre for Human Rights and Democratic Development, 1996a.

Palencia Prado, T. *Peace in the Making. Civil Groups in Guatemala.* London: Catholic Institute for International Relations, 1996b.

Pasupathi, M. The Social Reconstruction of the Personal Past and its Implications for Adult Development. *Psychological Bulletin*, Vol. 127, No. 5, 2001, pp. 651-672.

Paul, B. and W. Demarest. The Operation of a Death Squad in San Pedro La Laguna. In: R. Carmack (ed.). Harvest of Violence: The Mayan Indians and the Guatemalan Crisis. Norman: University of Oklahoma Press, 1988, pp. 119-154.

PDH (Procurador de los Derechos Humanos). *Los Comités de Defensa Civil en Guatemala.* Guatemala: PDH/AECI/ASADI, 1994.

Pendergrast, M. *Victims of Memory: Incest Accusations and Shattered Lives.* Hinesburg: Upper Access Books, 1995.

Piel, J. *Sajcabaja. Muerte y Resurreccion de un Pueblo de Guatemala (1500-1970).* Mexico and Guatemala: Centre d'Etudes Mexicaines et Centraméricaines and Seminario de Integración Social, 1989.

Piel, J. *El Departamento del Quiché Bajo la Dictadura Liberal (1880-1920).* Guatemala: FLACSO/CEMCA, 1995.

Pinto, M. *Report by the Independent Expert, Mrs. Monica Pinto, on the situation of human rights in Guatemala.* Commission on Human Rights, Economic and Social Council, United Nations document number E/CN.4/1995/15, 20 December 1994.

PNUD (Programa de las Naciones Unidas para el Desarrollo). *Informe del Diagnóstico de las Juntas Locales de Seguridad Ciudadana.* Guatemala: PNUD, 1999.

Political Database of the Americas. *Guatemala: 1995-1996 Elecciones Presidenciales.* Georgetown University and the Organization of Amcrican States.

(www/georgetown.edu/pdba/Elecdata/Guate/95elec.html) [2 February 2000].

Popkin, M. *Civil Patrols and Their Legacy. Overcoming Militarization and Polarization in the Guatemalan Countryside*. Washington: The Robert F. Kennedy Memorial Center for Human Rights, 1996.

Remijnse, S. Remembering Civil Patrols in Joyabaj, Guatemala. *Bulletin of Latin American Research*, Vol. 20, No. 4, 2001, pp. 454-469.

Rey Rosa, R. *Si me maten si ...* Barcelona: Seix Barral, 1997.

Reyes Illescas, M. Conflicto Social en San Martín Jilotepeque. *Polémica*, No. 6, 1982, pp. 6-10.

Robben, A. The Assault on Basic Trust: Disappearance, Protest, and Reburial in Argentina. In: A. Robben and M. Suárez-Orozco (eds.) *Cultures under Siege. Collective Violence and Trauma*. Cambridge: Cambridge University Press, 2000, pp. 70-101.

Rohter, L. Guatemalan Commission's Report is Searching Indictment on Military. *The New York Times*, 27/2/99.

Rosada-Granados, H. *Soldados en el Poder. Proyecto Militar en Guatemala 1944-1990*. Amsterdam: Thela, 1999.

Ross, M. and R. Buehler. Creative Remembering. In: U. Neisser (ed.). *The Remembering Self. Construction and Accuracy in the Self-narrative*. Cambridge: Cambridge University Press, 1994, pp. 205-235.

Russel Tribunal. [no title] 1984.

Sanford, V. Buried Secrets: Truth and Human Rights in Guatemala. Unpublished doctoral dissertation, Stanford University, 2000.

Schacter, D. Memory Distortion: History and Current Status. In: D. Schacter. *Memory Distortion. How Minds, Brains, and Societies Reconstruct the Past*. Cambridge: Harvard University Press, 1995, pp. 1-43.

Schacter, D. *Searching for Memory: The Brain, the Mind, and the Past*. New York: Basic Books, 1996.

Schacter, D. The Seven Sins of Memory. *American Psychologist*, Vol. 54, No.3, 1999, pp. 182-203.

Schirmer, J. *The Guatemalan Military Project. A Violence Called Democracy*. Philadelphia: University of Pennsylvania Press, 1998.

Schirmer, J. The Guatemalan Politico-Military Project. Whose Ship of State? In: K. Koonings and D. Kruijt. *Political Armies. The Military and Nation Building in the Age of Democracy*. London: Zed Books, 2002, pp. 64-89.

Schudson, M. Dynamics of Distortion in Collective Memory. In: D. Schacter. *Memory Distortion. How Minds, Brains, and Societies Reconstruct the Past*. Cambridge: Harvard University Press, 1995, pp. 346-364.

Sichar Moreno, G. ¿Guatemala: Contrainsurgencia o Contra el Pueblo? Madrid: H+H, 1997.

Sichar Moreno, G. Historia de los Partidos Politicos Guatemaltecos. Quetzaltenango: Editorial Los Altos, 1999.

Sieder, R. 'Paz, Progreso, Justicia y Honradez': Law and Citizenship in Alta Verapaz during the regime of Jorge Ubico. Paper presented at the 2000 meeting of the Latin American Studies Association (LASA), Miami, 16-18 March 2000.

Sluka, J. Death Squad, the Anthropology of State Terror. Philadelphia: University of Pennsylvania Press, 2000.

Snodgrass, A. Justicia a Mano Propia: The Privatization of Justice in Postwar Guatemala. Paper presented at the 2000 meeting of the Latin American Studies Association (LASA), Miami, 16-18 March 2000.

Solomon, J.A. Institutional Violence. Civil Patrols in Guatemala. Washington: The Robert F. Kennedy Memorial Center for Human Rights, 1994.

Starn, O. Nightwatch. The Politics of Protest in the Andes. Durham and London: Duke University Press, 1999.

Stoll, D. Rigoberta Menchú and the Story of All Poor Guatemalans. Boulder: Westview Press, 1999.

Teitel, R. Transitional Justice. Oxford: Oxford University Press, 2000.

Tomuschat, C. Lessons Learned From the Historical Clarification Commission in Guatemala. Paper presented at the 2000 meeting of the Latin American Studies Association (LASA), Miami, 16-18 March 2000.

Valdez, P. La Construcción de la Memoria Sobre el Pasado Autoritario en Argentina. Paper presented at the 2000 meeting of the Latin American Studies Association (LASA), Miami, 16-18 March 2000.

Wagenaar, W. and J. Groeneweg. The Memory of Concentration Camp Survivors. In: Applied Cognitive Psychology, Vol. 4, 1988, pp. 77-87.

Walter, E. Terror and Resistance. A Study of Political Violence. New York: Oxford University Press, 1969.

Warren, K. Interpreting La Violencia in Guatemala: Shapes of Mayan Silence and Resistance. In: K. Warren. The Violence within; Cultural and Political Opposition in Divided Nations. Boulder: Westview Press, 1993, pp. 25-56.

Warren, K. Death squads and Wider Complicities. In: J. Sluka, Death Squad, the Anthropology of State Terror. Philadelphia: University of Pennsylvania Press, 2000, pp. 227-247.

WCC/GRICAR (World Council of Churches/Grupo Internacional de Consulta y Apoyo al Retorno). Situation Report, #42, 27 September 1996.

Wilson, R. Violent Truths: The Politics of Memory in Guatemala. In: J. Armon, R. Sieder and R. Wilson. *Negotiating Rights: The Guatemalan Peace Process.* London: Conciliation Resources, 1997a, pp. 18-27.

Wilson, R. Representing Human Rights Violations: Social Contexts and Subjectivities. In: R. Wilson. *Human Rights, Culture and Context. Anthropological Perspectives.* London: Pluto Press, 1997b, pp. 134-160.

White, G. Histories and Subjectivities. *Ethos. Journal for Psychological Anthropology*, Vol. 28, No. 4, 2000, pp. 493-510.

Wouters, M. Ethnic Rights under Threat: The Black Peasant Movement Against Armed Groups' Pressure in the Chocó, Colombia. *Bulletin of Latin American Research*, Vol. 20, No. 4, 2001, pp. 498-519.

Yamauchi, P. Guatemalan Violence Information System (GVIS). Nagata-Yamauchi Education Fund (NYEF), 1998.

Zur, J. *Violent Memories. Mayan War Widows in Guatemala.* Boulder: Westview Press, 1998.

Other Information Sources

Archivo General de Centro América (AGCA)
Archivo General: Sección Tierras (AGST) (1798 – 1923)
Archivos de la Jefatura Política del Departamento del Quiché (AJPDQ)
Archivos del Municipio de Joyabaj (6 packages: 1880-1946) (AMJ)

Parroquial archives of Joyabaj
Libros de Confirmaciones (1786; 1901; 1912; 1916)
Libros de Bautizos (1791-1805; 1967 – 1996)
Libros de Indices de Bautizos (1902 – 1947)
Libros de Casamiento (1777-1800; 1848-1855)
Libros de Matrimonios (1865-1876; 1901-1952; 1977 – 1995)

Municipal archives of Joyabaj
Libros de Difuntos (1978 – 1988)
Libros de Actas de Joyabaj (1928 – 1996)

Archives of the Alcaldía Indígena (indigenous municipality)
Mapa de las tierras que pertenecen al pueblo de Joyabaj (1750)
Plano de la medido del ejido de Joyabaj (1912)

Procuraderia de los Derechos Humanos (PDH)
Auxiliatura de Santa Cruz de Quiché: case files on Joyabaj (1989 – 1998)

Oficina de Derechos Humanos de Guatemala (ODHAG)
REMHI: case files on Joyabaj (1996)
Area legal: case file Tomás Lares Ciprian

Newspapers and magazines
El Día (México)
Diário El Gráfico (Guatemala)
El Imparcial (Guatemala)
El Mundo Libre (Guatemala)
Espíritu Xoj (Joyabaj, Guatemala)
La Nación (México)
New York Times (United States)
Noticias de Guatemala (NDG) (Guatemala)
Nuestro Diario (Guatemala)
El Periódico (Guatemala)
Prensa Libre (Guatemala)
Siglo Veintiuno (Guatemala)
Unomásuno (Mexico)

(Electronic) information services
CEG (Centro de Estudios de Guatemala)
GNIB (Guatemalan News and Information Buro) (United States)
Inforpress Centroamericana (Guatemala)
Latin American Regional Report (United Kingdom)
Latin American Weekly Report (United Kingdom)
NSA (National Security Archives) (www.gwu.edu/~nsarchiv/)

Bulletins and documents
CUC (Guatemala)
CERJ (Guatemala)
Conavigua (Guatemala)
GAM (Guatemala)
EGP (Guatemala)
ORPA (Guatemala)

Index

agrarian reform 69, 71, 72, 313
Agrarian Reform Law (1952) 68
Alcaldía Indígena 48, 62, 89, 133, 134, 192, 232, 246, 305, 320
Alianza 6, 9, 85-90, 92, 97, 103-6, 109, 111, 114, 117, 122, 123, 124, 149, 151, 152, 160, 175, 177, 239, 294, 297, 298, 311
Alonso, Padre Juan 98 (n33), 263 (n47)
Amnesty International 11, 52, 53 (n104), 182 (n61 and 62), 255 (n27), 309
ANN 236, 237, 301
Arbenz Guzmán, Col. Jacobo 57, 58, 68, 69, 71-3, 76, 79, 90, 102 (n102)
Arévalo, Juan José 57, 58, 66, 67, 68, 70, 71, 76, 90, 102 (n51)
Argentina 20, 22 (n20), 40, 251 (n1), 252 (n5), 272 (n70), 314, 318, 319
authorization 29, 30, 295
avoid, to
    problems 28, 151, 193, 246, 277, 284
    trouble 12, 148, 156, 166, 293
    conflicts 192
    contacts with guerrillas 166
    killing 154
    mentioning names 28
    talking 17, 285

Balconi, Defense Minister Julio 142, 145, 179, 216, 226
Barrios, Justo Runfino 57, 59, 63

blacklist 27, 57, 73, 90, 96, 98, 102, 107, 114, 122, 161, 174, 228, 239
Boqueron 15, 159
bystander 26, 30, 37, 38, 39, 40, 153, 156, 157, 167, 293, 294
    internal bystander 258, 260, 285, 296

CAL 5, 71, 72, 301
CALDH 228, 256, 271, 301
CAN 174 (n25), 301
CAPS 80, 301
Caquil 15, 155, 156, 158, 276
Carbonell, Padre Fernando 78, 79
Caritas 86, 273 (n72)
Castillo Armas, Col. Carlos 57, 69, 73, 74, 75
Catholic Action
    activist 76, 90, 191, 197, 180
    and the indigenous communities 6, 76-8
    and local politics 74, 81, 82
    catechist 41, 57, 81, 95, 138, 149, 187
    in Chorraxaj 79-81, 86, 106, 107, 153, 194, 238-9, 292
    in Xeabaj 86, 117, 238-9
    in Xecnup 149, 150
    leaders (*directivo/junta directiva*) 49 (n99), 97, 98, 190, 229, 267, 268, 277, 279, 283, 298, 306
    revitalizing (reorganizing) 187, 188, 204, 257
CEH 23, 31, 41, 42, 116, 142, 151 (n85), 180 (n49), 246, 251-4, 270,

271, 289, 294, 302, 311
cemetery (or grave), clandestine 164, 165, 185, 209, 219, 256, 257, 270, 309
Cerezo Arévalo, Vinício 169, 171, 172, 178, 181, 185
CERJ 7, 170, 171, 181-6, 197, 198, 204, 205, 212, 213, 302, 321
Chiché 14, 88, 165, 182, 183, 275 (n81), 282 (n98)
Chichicastenango 14, 79, 97, 116, 256 (n32), 263, 264, 267
Chicotón 15, 117, 150, 158
Chinique 14, 218
Chorraxaj 6, 77, 79-81, 82, 93, 106-8, 117, 137, 147, 149, 150-2, 153, 156, 159, 166, 184, 194, 195, 197-9, 200, 238, 268, 276, 292
Nuevo Chorraxaj 81, 117
Civic Committee *Palo Volador* 231, 232, 234, 236, 305
CNR 172, 302
cofrades 72, 133, 134, 190, 232
cofradía 44, 45, 54, 63, 74, 76, 133, 134, 305
Colotenango 202, 282
Comité de Emergencia 84, 305
Comité de Pro-mejoramiento (see also Improvement Committee) 80, 176, 177, 178, 230, 305
communism 65, 69 (n56), 197, 244
anti-communist 5, 54, 57, 58, 66, 68-70, 73-4, 76, 78, 119, 128, 136, 144, 145, 149, 183, 197, 244, 304
Communist Party 66, 108 (n75), 303
común indígena 59, 62, 72, 92, 305
Conavigua 48, 152, 170, 171, 181, 183-6, 190, 197, 203, 204, 205,
212, 237, 241, 272 (n68), 302, 321
confianza (see also trust) 132, 137, 208, 237, 246, 258
Consulta Popular 8, 239-42, 245, 248, 297, 305
contratista (see also labour contractor) 62
control
state control during the Liberal era 63, 65, 66
ladino control over municipal affairs 57, 61, 62, 63, 66, 90, 144, 159, 162, 248
cooperative(s) 78, 79, 80, 81, 82, 95, 102, 107, 122
costumbre 74, 75, 77, 90, 149, 150, 305
costumbrista 74, 76, 77, 78, 86, 88, 305
counter-insurgency 18, 91, 118, 125-7, 136, 139, 143, 171, 212, 309, 313, 314
Cruz Chich 15, 114, 137, 144, 151, 185, 198
CUC 138, 171, 181, 196, 197, 198, 210, 302, 321
CVDC (see also PAC) 171, 211 (n24), 220, 302

D-5 (directorate of civil affairs) 140
DCG 9, 58, 76, 78, 79, 81, 82, 88, 89, 90, 91, 98, 101-3, 104, 107, 173, 174, 182, 204, 231, 236, 292, 299, 302
dealing with the past 5, 8, 21-3, 55, 251-89, 299, 300
death squad (*esquadron de muerte*) 19, 55, 74, 96, 99, 102, 108, 109, 110, 114, 123, 126, 255, 305, 317, 319

dehumanization 5, 28-30, 157, 166, 295
  and the 1985 municipal elections 191, 192, 194, 195
denial 5, 8, 37-9, 163, 207, 221, 224, 258, 295, 311, 314
  and the enquiring mind 38, 221, 284, 296
dissapearances 24, 102, 142, 168 (n76), 208 (n6), 228, 263, 318
distrust 8, 20, 21, 25, 27, 28, 70, 88, 123, 178, 239, 245-7, 274, 280

EAFG 256 (n33), 271, 275, 302, 312
earthquake (1976) 6, 9, 58, 61, 82-5, 86, 94, 103, 177, 316
EGP 92, 93, 102, 108, 126 (n4), 201, 239, 302, 305, 321
El Imparcial 69, 174, 119 (n124), 321
EMDN (National Defense Staff) 140 (n57), 302
ESA 99, 102, 105, 302
Espíritu Xoj 176, 178, 204, 321
ethnic tension (racism) 5, 43, 43 (n91), 44, 243, 248
evangelical 42, 44, 45, 48, 85, 88, 127, 189, 219, 238 (n132), 249, 293
exhumation 8, 12, 23, 41, 42, 50, 164, 199, 219, 231, 252, 256, 257, 270-85, 288, 289, 294, 295

FACS 109, 302
FAR 108 (n74), 126 (n4), 302
FDNG 236 (n122 and n123), 303
fear
  fearing memory 7, 163-4
  of being branded subversive 28
  of getting involved 27
  of repercussions 28, 93, 215, 267, 285
forgetting 5, 35, 37-9, 163, 188, 255
  forget (preferring to/it is better to) 40, 259, 267, 277, 281, 282, 283, 288
forgiveness 23, 258, 259, 315
FRG 10, 12, 226-9, 238, 289, 293, 302
Fuerza de Tarea Iximché 116

GAM 197, 213, 303, 321
genocide 11, 38 (n72), 253, 255, 311, 314
gente buena, la 60, 61, 67
Gerardi, Bishop Juan 10, 23, 96, 262, 263, 311
guerrilla organization (see also EGP, FAR, ORPA, URNG) 91, 97, 108 (n74), 126, 145, 236, 248, 254

Hermana María de Jesús Boládo 6, 93-5, 97, 101, 110,
Herrera family 62, 84, 85, 86
home guard 6, 92, 118-22, 123
Huehuetenango 14, 20, 41, 91, 140, 145, 226, 282 (n98)

intendente 66, 306
Improvement Committee (see also *Comité de Pro-mejoramiento*) 107, 204, 298
impunity 194, 202, 205, 209, 272, 306, 309
indoctrination 25, 163, 199, 299
injustice 181, 224
Ixil 99, 256, 295 (n1)

Jefatura Política 65, 66, 301, 306, 320

325

judicial 116, 130, 306
Juez de Paz 199, 201, 202, 224, 230, 275, 306
Juntas Locales 228, 230, 306, 317
justice 202, 215-6, 246-8, 255, 259, 301, 306, 315, 319
    justice system, 7, 22, 40 (n82), 162, 199, 201, 202, 223, 225, 251
    obstruction of 201

labour contractor (see also *contratista*) 67, 114
Lares Ciprian, Tomás 7, 170, 195, 197-202, 203, 205, 210, 214, 215, 220 (n54), 275, 294
Las Lomas 15, 128, 144, 145, 159
León Carpio, Ramiro de 173, 208, 210, 213, 217, 313
Libro de Actas 73, 102, 103, 193, 194, 195 (n104, 106, 108 and 109), 231 (n107), 306, 320
Liga Campesina 79, 80, 88
Lucas García, Col. Benedicto 115, 118, 119, 124, 139, 294
Lucas García, Gen. Romeo 91, 94, 108, 111, 122, 125, 126, 127, 138, 139, 255
lynching 7, 24, 53, 54, 162, 190, 207, 222-4, 230, 246, 247, 248, 295, 297
    lynching in Tunajá 224-6, 229, 277

María Gran, Padre José 96, 97, 98 (n33)
MAS 172, 191, 195, 303
massacre(s)
    definition of 116 (n110 and 111)
    forced participation in 156
    in Boqueron 159
    in Chicotón 117, 158
    in Xeabaj 6, 153-8
    number of 116-7
    site 10, 186, 252, 271, 272 (n70), 276-81, 284
Mejía Víctores, Gen. Oscar Humberto 111, 127, 170, 255
memory
    constructed (constructing) 5, 31, 32-4, 251, 257, 315, 317, 318
    and coherence 5, 34-5
    and context 5, 7, 21, 32, 36-7, 39, 153, 162, 164-5, 252, 293, 294, 312
    and audience 5, 36-7, 293
    not wanting to remember 8, 281, 282-5
    collective 5, 20, 39-40, 157, 317, 318
    conflicting memories 7, 8, 30, 153, 219-22, 293-5
Menchú, Rigoberta 40 (n81), 110-2, 255, 310, 311, 312, 319
militarization 46, 63, 123, 168, 247, 297, 299, 318
military control 6, 19, 118, 119, 122, 125, 128-32, 136, 139, 165, 179, 186, 187, 292, 296
Military Zone 20 (ZM 20) 97, 100, 187, 201, 202, 214, 216
Ministerio Público 216, 280, 306
MINUGUA 23 (n21), 53, 208 (n6), 209, 212, 214, 215-6, 218, 223, 224, 244, 297, 303, 315, 316
MLN 57, 172, 303
    in Joyabaj 6, 44, 58, 74-6, 78, 81, 82, 88, 89, 90, 92, 97, 102,

108, 109, 110, 114, 123, 132, 144, 149, 152, 160, 166, 174, 191, 223, 227, 231, 236, 298
MSC 77, 78, 81, 96, 260, 263 (n47), 303, 306
municipal politics 6, 61, 74, 128, 132-4, 173

National Security Archive (NSA) 31 (n41), 255, 293, 303, 321
NGO 11, 45, 48, 50, 55, 58, 85-6, 88, 90, 103, 105, 122, 124, 175, 209 (n7), 217, 236 (n122), 245-6, 256, 272, 294, 295, 298, 315
Noack, Otto 254
Northern Ireland 20, 22, 251, 311, 313

obedience 28-30, 157, 229, 284, 295, 296, 314, 315
   obedient 30, 296
   disobedience (disobedient) 28, 157, 158
Oficina de Paz y Reconciliación 41, 44, 271, 277-9 (n89)
order 27, 65, 166
   order and security 67, 153, 161, 162
oreja (ears) 96 (n18), 108, 119, 130, 306
ORPA 108, 126 (n4), 145 (n68), 146, 303, 321
'the other' 128, 162, 166
   fear of 'the other' 29, 123, 162, 297

Pachalum 14, 218
Patrulla de Autodefensa Civil (PAC)
   and abolition (dismantling) in Joyabaj 7, 169, 170, 180, 207 (n2), 218-9, 220, 230, 247, 292, 293
   and abuse of power 7, 153, 158-61, 149, 166, 171, 180 (49), 182, 183 (n65), 197, 202, 208, 211, 212, 216, 217, 219, 220, 231, 291, 299
   and chain of command 140, 157
   and demands for financial compensation 201 (n133), 227, 228, 255, 293, 295 (n1)
   and hierarchy 26, 30, 126, 145, 204, 291, 292, 296
   and local diversity 6, 21, 125, 126, 143-7, 152, 153, 166
   and national abolition (dismantling) 7, 8, 21, 27, 52, 55, 171, 180, 181, 186, 207, 208-10, 214, 216-8, 226, 247, 297, 299
   as keeper of order and security 161-2
   general commander of 151, 160, 198, 200, 201, 211, 220, 305
   in Xecnup 6, 148-50
   in Chorraxaj 6, 150-2
   memorial of 8, 10, 285, 286
   negative memory of 153, 153-9, 166
   positive memory of 153, 161-3
   protest against 7, 119, 166, 170, 178, 179-83, 196, 204
   ronda 120, 125 (n1), 307
   tasks 6, 19, 27, 38, 118, 142-3, 145, 147-8, 162, 185, 221
   teacher patrol 6, 147-8, 154, 166, 296
   reorganizing (reorganize) 7, 55, 226, 227, 228-30, 257

Paíz Balcárcel, Ramiro (the pharmacist) 6, 75, 82, 92, 105, 107, 109-14, 119, 120, 122, 123, 147, 149, 154
Palo Volador 10, 232, 233, 306, 313
PAN 238, 303
panopticon 27, 142, 285, 292
Patzulá 15, 117, 149, 238, 258, 259, 268, 316
Paxtup 117
PDH 47, 140 (n54 and 55), 158 (n109), 164, 170, 173, 180, 181, 183, 186 (n76), 196, 198, 200, 201, 208, 209, 211, 212-4
Peace Accord 18, 23, 172, 207, 216, 235, 241, 245, 247, 251, 254, 271, 289, 292, 297, 299, 317
peace process 55, 169, 170-3, 212, 241, 299, 310, 314, 315, 320
Pericón Chuacorral 15, 117
perpetrator 22, 23, 26, 28, 30, 33 (n49), 36-9, 153, 163, 216, 244, 248, 253, 269, 270 (n60), 273, 275, 279, 289, 293-7
PGT 108 (n75), 126, 303
PID 102 (n51), 126 (n2), 304
PNC 210 (n15)
PR 102 (51), 304
PRG 69, 304

Rabinal 14, 119, 256 (n33), 275, 312
reconciliation 20, 22, 23, 172, 255 (n28), 258, 259, 272, 277, 288, 289, 301, 302, 304, 307, 310, 313
Redención 75, 304
REMHI 12, 22 (n17), 23, 31, 41, 47, 97, 116 (n110), 180 (n49), 252, 253 (n11), 254, 261, 262, 274, 289, 304, 306, 321

in Joyabaj 8, 42, 116, 136, 148, 151 (n85), 229, 246, 252, 260, 267-70, 276, 283, 285, 294, 295
remittances 208, 242, 243, 247
Ríos Montt, Gen. Efraín 10, 12, 55, 111, 119, 125-7, 132 (n22), 139, 146, 162, 165, 224, 228, 229, 255, 289, 293, 316
routinization 29, 30, 295, 296,

Saljij 15, 117
San Andrés Sajcabajá 14, 122 (n129), 186, 218, 275 (n79), 282 (n100)
scorched earth 6, 18, 115-8, 123
self-censorship 27, 190, 202, 203, 285
sermon 60, 190, 226, 258-60, 263, 268, 279, 296
Serrano Elías, Jorge 169, 170, 172, 208, 210
stigmatization 8, 183, 204, 295-7
stigmatized 30, 199
South Africa 11, 20, 21, 22, 26, 33 (n49), 40, 53, 207 (n3), 251 (n1), 310, 313
subversive 28, 50, 95, 96, 120, 128, 138, 142, 158, 166, 172, 184, 197, 201, 204, 226, 245, 268
  subversives 24, 27, 88, 123, 128, 130, 145, 155, 157, 161, 179, 180, 185, 232, 292
  language 155, 199
surveillance 5, 8, 19, 24, 27-8, 65, 115, 125, 142, 143, 145, 165, 169, 203, 285, 291-2

Talaxcoc 15, 117, 196 (n113)
teniente 132, 146, 151, 155-6, 307
terror 5, 8, 23-8, 82, 96, 99, 100, 115,

122, 126, 127, 173, 179, 190, 199, 203, 291, 312, 313, 314, 315, 316, 317, 319
  agents of the state 30, 92
  agents of terror 26, 37, 143, 159
  military terror 91, 137, 251
  state terror 25, 30, 53, 137, 199, 203, 208, 292
  terror apparatus 143
  terror directorate 37, 159
  terror staff 25, 26
  terrorizing effects of massacres 117
torture 128, 130, 142, 180, 208, 228
  torture chamber 9, 122, 130, 131
  tortured 105, 130, 155, 212, 225
  torturer 35
Tribunal Supremo Electoral (TSE) 171, 174, 175, 195, 204
trust (see also *confianza*) 41, 42, 49, 51, 71, 88, 132, 185, 189, 194, 245, 246, 267, 292, 299
Tunajá 15, 183 (n65), 224-6, 230, 275 (n76), 277

Ubico 57, 65-8, 70, 136, 137, 223, 319
UCN 191 (n88), 304
UNID 236 (n122)
URNG 48, 126, 171, 172, 197, 226, 235, 236 (n122), 238, 304
URNG/DIA coaltion 236-9, 246, 248

Villanueva, Padre Faustino 9, 10, 96-9, 101, 102, 105, 106 (n64), 107, 110, 111, 122, 123, 134, 186, 189, 251, 256 (n32)
  commemorating 189, 190, 202, 204, 256, 257, 260, 261, 263, 264, 288
  reburial of 263-7
Violencia, La 24, 25, 27, 32, 48, 187, 237, 315, 319
Virgen de Tránsito 9, 63 (n30), 64, 72, 76 (n91), 85

Xeabaj 6, 9, 15, 82, 86, 93, 117, 137, 149, 150, 153-8, 166, 184, 196 (n113), 238, 251, 268
Xebalamguac 15, 117
Xecnup 6, 15, 114, 117, 137, 144, 147, 148-52, 156, 166, 212, 216, 218

Zacualpa 14, 15, 88, 93, 96, 100, 108, 115, 116, 130, 131, 182, 183, 224, 225, 253 (n13), 269, 275

Samenvatting

Dit boek bevat een reconstructie van de verschillende lokale herinneringen en verhalen over de activiteiten van burgermilities (*Patrullas de Autodefensa Civil*) tijdens het 36 jaar durende gewapende conflict in Guatemala. In december 1996 is dit conflict tot een einde gekomen, met de ondertekening van een vredesakkoord door de strijdende partijen; de guerrilla en de Guatemalteekse overheid. Het onderzoek naar de invloed van burgermilities op lokale gemeenschappen binnen de context van een gewapend conflict past binnen wetenschappelijke discussies over de verschillende manieren waarop landen en regeringen omgaan met een gewelddadig verleden. Er is veel gepubliceerd over thema's als verzoening en wraak, en de functies en het nut van waarheidscommissies, waarheidsrapporten en tribunalen in landen als Rwanda, Zuid Afrika, Chili, El Salvador, voormalig Joegoslavië en Guatemala. Veel van dit werk concentreert zich op het nationale niveau, en kijkt naar de manier waarop een land als geheel met een gewelddadig verleden omgaat. Dit boek is echter een studie naar lokale effecten van een gewapend conflict en de manieren waarop mensen op dorpsniveau met dit geweldadige verleden omgaan. Op welke manieren worden dagelijkse relaties tussen mensen nog steeds beinvloed door de erfenis van het verleden en hoe worden herinneringen hierover geconstrueerd?

Het onderzoek is uitgevoerd in Joyabaj, een gemeente (*municipality*) bestaande uit een stadje dat dezelfde naam draagt en een zestigtal omringende dorpjes. Mijn analyse start in de periode vóór het uitbreken van het gewapende conflict, en concentreert zich vervolgens op de installatie van de burgermilities, hun activiteiten, hun opheffing in 1996 en de recentelijke pogingen tot reorganisatie.

De burgermilities waren één van de belangrijkste mechanismen van militaire controle op het Guatemalteekse platteland. Het Guatemalteekse leger zette de milities tegen het einde van 1981 op, met als expliciet doel het beschermen van dorpsgemeenschappen tegen guerrillaaanvallen. Alle mannen (zowel ladinos als *indígenas*) tussen de 18 en de 60 jaar waren verplicht deel te nemen aan deze milities, die voornamelijk opereerden binnen het eigen dorp en de omringende gemeenten. Degene die weigerden hieraan deel te nemen, werden zwaar gestraft. Naast het beschermen van de lokale bevolking, fungeerden de milities ook als een inlichtingendienst voor de militairen, en werden ze verplicht mee te doen aan massamoorden en andere mensenrechtenschendingen. Militie leden waren dus zowel dader als slachtoffer, omdat zij enerzijds gedwongen waren te participeren in geweldsdelicten (hoewel een klein deel vrijwillig deel nam uit ideologische of andere motieven), en anderzijds het doelwit waren van de terreur acties (als zijnde inheemse bevolking). De milities werden in eerste instantie werden opgezet om het leger bij te staan in hun strijd tegen de guerrillas, maar de relatie tussen het leger en de milities werd gaandeweg losser. De milities werden meer en meer een onafhankelijke machtsfactor in de lokale gemeenschappen, waarbij vooral de lokale commandant van de militie een belangrijke rol speelde. In feite fungeerden de burgermilities als een *panopticon* (zie Foucault, 1977), waarbij open terreur op den duur plaats maakt voor meer verborgen manieren van controle en er ten slotte zelfs toe leidt dat mensen hun eigen gedrag (vrijwillig) controleren.

Eind 1996, vlak voordat de Guatemalteekse overheid en de guerrilla het vredesakkoord tekenden, werden de burgermilities officieel ontmanteld en hun wapens ingenomen. De controlerende (*surveillance*) functie van de burgermilities duurde echter voort, omdat mensen het besef van de voortdurende controle hadden geïncorporeerd in hun dagelijkse bestaan. Gedurende het veldwerk wilden de meeste *Joyabatecos* (inwoners van Joyabaj) niet dat ik de interviews op band zou opnemen, omdat ze bang waren dat deze in de verkeerde handen konden vallen, of omdat ze ervan overtuigd waren dat de militaire inlichtingendiensten nog steeds dossiers bijhielden van zogenaamde 'staatsvijanden', ofwel guerrillasympathisanten.

Wat vaak ook bleef voortbestaan, was de macht van individuen die binnen de milities een belangrijke rol hadden gespeeld, zoals de militiecommandanten. Veel *Joyabatecos* hadden weinig behoefte om over het verleden te praten, veelal uit angst voor repercussies van deze voormalige commandanten, die uit hetzelfde dorp afkomstig waren. Anderen waren ervan overtuigd dat de oorlog nog niet voorbij was, met name na de verkiezingsoverwinning in 1999 van de rechtse FRG,[1] de partij van voormalig dictator Ríos Montt. Angst voor een mogelijke opleving van de burgermilities werd gevoed door de daadwerkelijke reorganisatie van verschillende voormalige burgermilities in 1999 en recentelijk in 2002, met als doel het verkrijgen van financiële compensatie van de Guatemalteekse overheid voor geleverde 'diensten' tijdens het gewapend conflict.

Hoewel deze reorganisatie niet betekent dat men dezelfde functies uitoefent als tijdens het gewapende conflict, is de mogelijkheid hiertoe voldoende aanleiding voor een toenemende angst onder de lokale bevolking. Al met al hebben de burgermilities enorme invloed gehad op de politieke, sociale en economische relaties binnen en tussen lokale gemeenschappen.

Eén van de doelen van dit boek is om de verschillende lokale verhalen en herinneringen over het geweldadige oorlogsverleden in Joyabaj te reconstrueren, waarbij de nadruk heeft gelegen op de burgermilities. Er blijkt een enorme diver-

---

[1] *Frente Republicano Guatemalteco* – Republikeins Guatemalteeks Front.

siteit aan herinneringen en verhalen te bestaan, welke afhangt van het feit of de *Joyabatecos* de oorlog hebben meegemaakt als slachtoffer, dader, toekijker (*bystander*), of een combinatie van deze rollen. Men herinnert zich de oorlog als moeder die een kind heeft verloren, als lid van de burgermilitie, als jongere die actief is geweest in de linkse boerenbeweging, of als guerrillastrijder. Verschillende stratificatiemechanismen hebben een rol gespeeld, zoals etniciteit (ladino-*indígena*), geografie (stad-platteland), politiek (conservatief, rechts en links van het midden), religie (katholiek, evangelisch, Maya geloof) en sociaal-economische positie (arm, middenklasse, rijke elite).

Dit scala aan, soms tegenstrijdige, herinneringen en verhalen geeft inzicht in de manieren waarop verschillende groepen en individuen binnen een samenleving het oorlogsverleden ervaren hebben en hoe zij momenteel terugkijken op dit verleden. Een deel van deze verhalen en herinneringen is opgetekend in één van van de twee waarheidsrapporten die zijn gepubliceerd door ODHAG[2] (1998) en CEH[3] (1999). ODHAG maakt deel uit van de Katholieke kerk in Guatemala die een progressieve rol heeft gespeeld tijdens het gewapende conflict, terwijl CEH is opgericht in het kader van de vredesonderhandelingen tussen overheid en guerrilla. Er zijn echter maar weinig *Joyabatecos* naar voren gekomen om hun verhaal te vertellen aan één van beide organisaties, omdat zij zich hier niet erg betrokken bij voelen. Ze beschouwen de waarheidsrapporten niet echt als hun verhaal, en het is niet het verhaal van Joyabaj zoals zij zich dat herinneren.

Hoe nu verder? De ontmanteling van de burgermilities maakt geen einde aan jaren van militaire indoctrinatie en militarisering van een samenleving. Mensen kijken nog steeds uit met wat ze zeggen, wie ze vertrouwen en ze zorgen ervoor om niet in de problemen te komen. 'Ik wil geen problemen', is een uitspraak die tijdens de interviews met *Joyabatecos* telkens weer terugkomt. Mensen zijn jarenlang gedwongen tot participatie in de milities, en hun gewelddadige optreden heeft ernstige problemen veroorzaakt binnen en tussen gemeenschappen en families. Voormalige tegenstanders van het militie systeem zien dat degenen die (vrijwillig) hebben geparticipeerd in de massamoorden niet worden berecht en nog steeds vrij rondlopen. In hun ogen functioneert de wet niet zoals het hoort en hun vertrouwen in het democratiseringsproces is dan ook gering. De burgers beschouwen de overheid en het justitiële apparaat als zwak, slecht toegerust en onderbezet. Slechts enkele militiecommandanten zijn berecht; de meesten zijn nooit vervolgd vanwege gebrek aan bewijs materiaal, getuigen en politieke wil.

Het is nóg moeilijker om de houding te veranderen van degenen die het mili-

---

2 *Oficina de Derechos Humanos del Arzobispado de Guatemala*. Zij publiceerden het REMHI rapport: *Recuperación de la Memoria Histórica* – Herstel van het Historisch Geheugen.
3 *Commission del Esclarecimiento Histórico* – Commissie van de Historische Opheldering.

tie systeem hebben ondersteund of er zelf beter van zijn geworden. Van de één op de andere dag is hen verteld dat de organisatie is opgeheven, dat ze hun wapens moeten inleveren en dat ze weer gewoon verder moeten met het leven van alledag. Ze zijn niet of slecht ingelicht over het verloop van het vredesproces en de gesloten akkoorden en hebben het gevoel dat de vredesakkoorden aan hen zijn opgedrongen. Anderen voelen zich verraden omdat ze nu worden afgeschilderd als schenders van mensenrechten, terwijl ze slechts hun plicht hebben gedaan door in de milities mee te vechten. In hun ogen heeft de vijand (de guerrilla) de oorlog gewonnen, omdat geen van de guerrillaleiders is berecht en omdat de URNG[4] zich heeft omgevormd tot een officiële politieke partij. Deze werd tijdens de burgemeestersverkiezing in 1999 in Joyabaj tweede, nog vóór de rechtse FRG. Verschillende militiecommandanten beschouwen de twee rapporten van de waarheidscommissies als partijdig, waarbij volgens hen onevenredig de nadruk is gelegd op de mensenrechten schendingen door militairen, *comisionados militares* en burgermilities.

Volgens Jelin (1996) moeten de Guatemalteken weer leren om gewone burgers te zijn, en moet er een cultuur van burgerschap ontstaan. Maar hoe zoiets tot stand te brengen in een situatie waarin mensen op lokaal niveau heel verschillende ideeën hebben over de oorzaken van het gewapend conflict, wie de schuld heeft en wie de slachtoffers zijn? Hoewel forensisch bewijsmateriaal harde feiten lijkt te leveren met betrekking tot de vraag wie, wanneer, en onder welke omstandigheden is vermoord tijdens het conflict, worden ooggetuigenverslagen vaak niet ontvankelijk verklaard door de rechtbanken omdat ze inaccuraat, onvolledig en partijdig zouden zijn. Het zal moeten blijken wiens waarheid de komende jaren het officiële verhaal zal worden over het gewapend conflict in Guatemala.

---

4 *Unidad Revolucionaria Nacional Guatemalteca* – Guatemalteekse Nationale Revolutionaire Eenheid. Hierin werken de vier strijdende guerrilla organisaties sinds 1982 samen.

Curriculum Vitae

Simone Remijnse was born on November 4, 1966, in Arkel, the Netherlands. She completed her secondary school education (VWO) at the Oude Hoven in Gorinchem in 1986. She studied cultural anthropology at the University of Amsterdam, specializing in informal credit relations in Bolivia. She obtained a Master's degree in cultural anthropology in 1993. Since 1997, she has been employed as a Ph.D. candidate at the capgroup Cultural Anthropology, Utrecht University, where she is currently teaching.

Thela Latin America Series is published jointly with the Facultad Latinoamericana de Ciencias Sociales (FLACSO), Programa de Costa Rica and the Center for Latin American and Caribbean Studies (CLACS) of Utrecht University, the Netherlands.

Thela Latin America Series es una edición con la Facultad Latinoamericana de Ciencias Sociales (FLACSO), Programa de Costa Rica y el Center for Latin American and Caribbean Studies (CLACS) de la Universidad de Utrecht, Holanda.

Carlos Alba Vega & Dirk Kruijt *The convenience of the minuscule - Informality and microenterprise in Latin America* ISBN 90 5538 006 7

Willem Assies *Going nuts for the rainforest - Non-timber forest products, forest conservation and sustainibility in Amazonia* ISBN 90 5538 027 X

Mario Fumerton *From Victims to Heroes. Peasant counter-rebellion and Civil War in Ayacucho, Peru, 1980-2000.* ISBN 90 5170 658 8

Henri Gooren *Rich among the poor. Church, Firm, and Household among small-scale Entrepreneurs in Guatemala City.* ISBN 90 5538 034 2

Gemma van der Haar *Gaining ground - Land reform and the constitution of community in the Tojolabal highlands of Chiapas, Mexico* ISBN 90 5170 559 X

Kees Jansen *Political ecology, mountain agriculture, and knowledge in Honduras* ISBN 90 5538 030 X

Jeanette Kloosterman *Identidad indígena: 'Entre romanticismo y realidad' - El derecho a la autodeterminación y la tierra en el aeresguardo' Muellamués, en el sur-oeste de Colombia* ISBN 90 5538 021 0

Kees Koonings *Industrialization, industrialists, and regional development in Brazil - Rio Grande do Sul in comparative perspective* ISBN 90 5538 008 3

Dirk Kruijt *Revolution by decree* ISBN 90 5538 004 0

Dirk Kruijt, Carlos Sojo, Rebeca Grynspan *Informal citizens - Poverty, informality and social exclusion in Latin America* ISBN 90 5170 581 6

Sonja Leferink *Wij armen kunnen niet sterven. Doodscultuur en marginalisering in Argentinië* ISBN 90 5170 634 0

Paul van Lindert & Otto Verkoren *Small towns and beyond - Rural transformation and small urban centres in Latin America* ISBN 90 5538 011 3

Wil G. Pansters *Citizens of the pyramid - Essays on Mexican political culture* ISBN 90 5538 017 2

Simone Remijnse *Memories of Violence – Civil Patrols and the Legacy of Conflict in Joyabaj, Guatemala* ISBN 90 5170 674 X

Marieke Riethof *Responses of the Brazilian Labour Movement to Economic and Political Reforms* ISBN 90 5170 634 0

Esther Roquas *Stacked law – Land, propery and conflict in Honduras* ISBN 905170 582 4

Héctor Rosada-Granados *soldados en el Poder – Prjoecto Militar en Guatemala, 1944-1990.* ISBN 90 5538 037 7

Ton Salman *The diffident movement - Disintegration, ingenuity and resistance of the Chilean Pobladores, 1973-1990* ISBN 90 5538 022 9

Rob van Vuurde *Los Países Bajos - El petróleo y la Revolución Mexicana, 1900-1950* ISBN 90 5538 022 9

Klaas S. Wellinga *Entre la poesía y la pared -from Política cultural Sandinista 1979-1990* ISBN 90 5538 018 0